THE
FURNITURE
MAKER'S
HANDBOOK

THE FURNITURE MAKER'S HANDBOOK

By the editors of
The Family Handyman Magazine

CHARLES SCRIBNER'S SONS · NEW YORK

On the cover: Craftsman Walter Winkler at
work in the Riverton, Connecticut, factory of The
Hitchcock Chair Company. Photo courtesy
Stanley Tools Division, The Stanley
Works, New Britain, Connecticut.

Copyright © 1977, 1973, 1972, 1971, 1970, 1969, 1968, 1967,
1966, 1965, 1964, 1963, 1962, 1961, 1960, 1959, 1958 Universal
Publishing and Distributing Corporation.

Library of Congress Cataloging in Publication Data
Main entry under title:
The Furniture maker's handbook.

Includes index.
1. Furniture making—Amateurs' manuals.   I. Family
handyman.
TT195.F86   684.1'04   75-38972
ISBN 0-684-14499-9

This book published simultaneously in the
United States of America and in Canada -
Copyright under the Berne Convention

1 3 5 7 9 11 13 15 17 19 MD/C 20 18 16 14 12 10 8 6 4 2

Printed in the United States of America

Contents

Chapter 1
FURNITURE-MAKING MATERIALS

Wood is the material of the home furniture-maker. Of course, handsome wood furnishings have always been hallmarks of prestige. Even in this age of synthetic and metallurgical miracles, fine woods still enhance and serve innumerable needs of modern living as no other furniture material can. Wood combines the possibilities of great beauty with strength. The strength is not overly rigid and can absorb such shock as being moved and sat on. Wood is generally not unduly heavy for its size. It is relatively easy to work and embellish—as in turning and carving—and has a wide range of prices depending, as with most other materials, on rarity. There is an enormous variation in colors, grains, figures, and textures. These possibilities are expanded by the different qualities a wood grown in one locale has from the same wood grown in another soil and climate, much like a fine wine.

FURNITURE WOODS

There are well over two hundred varieties of wood in commercial use in the United States today. Only about two dozen, however, can be considered popular in furniture-making. The two main so-called classifications of wood are hardwood and softwood. Hardwoods are the deciduous trees like oak, maple, and hickory, which lose their leaves in the fall. The softwoods are the evergreens or the conifers like pine and spruce. These terms are slightly misleading in that you will run across hardwoods that are relatively soft and softwoods that are hard.

In general, though, hardwoods are more difficult to work with but are somewhat more durable than softwoods. They also have more attractive grains and take finishes better. They should be used where appearance and sturdiness are important factors. The common hardwoods used in home workshops are, in descending order of working ease, walnut, mahogany, cherry, oak, birch, and maple.

The softwoods most frequently used are pine, cedar, fir, and redwood. For general utility indoors, use white pine and sugar pine. Sugar pine is softer and more expensive than white pine. Poplar (frequently called whitewood) and gumwood, though considered hardwoods, will work almost as easily as white pine. Other softwoods often cause difficulties in painting and staining because of their large, riotous grains.

All wood contains hundreds of small cells called pores. In some hardwoods these pores are quite pronounced. Mahogany and oak, for example, have very noticeable pores and are called open-grain woods. Birch and maple, on the other hand, have small pores and are referred to as close-grained woods. (See pages 8-9 for wood-grain characteristics.)

Wood can be cut in three distinct planes with respect to the annual rings. A piece of wood cut at

Fig. 1-1.   Cross section of a log showing annual growth rings. Light rings are springwood; darker rings are summerwood.

1

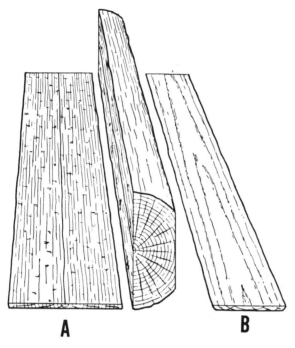

Fig. 1-2.   Grain depends on how lumber is cut from log. Board A is quarter-sawed, or edge-grained. Board B is plain-sawed, or flat-grained.

the end shows a cross section of the annual layers, or rings, of growth. This end, or transverse surface, shows the size and arrangement of the cells better than any other surface or plane. When wood is cut lengthwise through the center, or pith, of the tree, the exposed surfaces are called radial or quartered surfaces. A longitudinal surface that does not pass through the center is called a tangential surface. Lumber classified as plain-sawed is tangentially cut.

Plain-sawed lumber is cut with less waste and generally costs less than that which is quarter-sawed. In some types of wood—ash, chestnut, or elm—and in all the coniferous species, plain-sawed lumber has a figure or grain superior to that of quarter-sawed.

Despite its usually higher cost, quarter-sawed lumber has certain advantages that must be considered. It shrinks less in width and is less subject to twisting or checking. In many hard-

Fig. 1-3.   Most softwood used in furniture construction is of Select classification. Shown here (*left to right*) are Ponderosa Pine Grade B & Better, Grade C, and Grade D.

woods, such as oak, walnut, and mahogany, quarter-sawed lumber has a much more attractive grain. Quarter-sawed lumber also is known as edge-grain, rift-grain, and comb-grain.

Grades and Sizes of Lumber

Lumber is sold according to grade and size. For commercial purposes it is standardized under two codes, one for softwoods, the other for hardwoods.

Softwood Grades. Yard lumber is classified as Select and Common. Each of these, in turn, is graded according to quality—that is, freedom from knots, blemishes, or defects.

Select lumber is generally clear or contains only minor defects, which can be covered by paint or other finishes. It is graded A, B, C, and D.

Common lumber contains numerous defects and blemishes, which prevent its being used for finishing purposes, but it is suitable for general utility or construction. It is graded as Construction Grade (No. 1 Common), Standard Grade (No. 2 Common), Utility Grade (No. 3 Common), and Economy Grade (No. 4 Common). Construction Grade is about the only common-grade softwood that you'll generally use in furniture-making.

Hardwood Grades. Hardwood grades are based on the percentage of clear cuttings that can be obtained from a piece of lumber. The system is

---

Table 1-1

CHART OF GRADE REFERENCE FOR BUYING SOFTWOODS

Select: Lumber of good appearance and finishing qualities.
Suitable for natural finishes:
    Grade A. Practically free from defects
    Grade B. Allows a few small defects and blemishes
Suitable for paint finishes:
    Grade C. Allows a limited number of small defects or blemishes, which can be covered with paint
    Grade D. Allows any number of defects or blemishes, which does not detract from a finish appearance, especially when painted
Common: Lumber containing defects or blemishes that detract from a finish appearance, but suitable for general utility and constructional purposes
Lumber suitable for use without waste:
    Construction Grade (No. 1 Common). A sound and tight-knotted stock. Size of defects and blemishes limited. May be considered graintight lumber
    Standard Grade (No. 2 Common). Allows large and coarser defects. May be considered graintight lumber
Lumber permitting waste:
    Utility Grade (No. 3 Common). Allows larger and coarser defects, such as decay and holes
    Economy Grade (No. 4 Common). Low-quality lumber admitting the coarsest defects, such as decay and holes

Table 1-2

HARDWOOD GRADES

General grading—Indicates decrease in quality

Hardwoods	1st and 2nd grades	3rd grade	4th grade	5th grade	6th grade
Alder, ash, beech, birch maple, oak, sycamore	Firsts and seconds	Selects	No. 1 Common	No. 2 Common	Sound Wormy
Cherry	Firsts and seconds	Selects	No. 1 Common	No. 2 Common	No. 3A Common
Chestnut	Firsts and seconds	Selects	No. 1 Common	Sound Wormy	No. 2 Common
Elm, hickory	Firsts and seconds	No. 1 Common	No. 2 Common	No. 3A Common	No. 3B Common
Mahogany, walnut	Firsts and seconds	Selects	No. 1 Common	No. 2 Common	No. 3 Common
Poplar	Firsts and seconds	Saps	Selects	Stained saps	No. 1 Common

First: $91\frac{2}{3}$ percent clear both sides
Seconds: $83\frac{1}{3}$ percent clear both sides
First and seconds: Not less than 20 percent first (best commercial grade)
Selects: 90 percent clear one side
No. 1 Common: $66\frac{2}{3}$ percent clear face
No. 2 Common: 50 percent clear face
No. 3A Common: $33\frac{1}{3}$ percent clear face
No. 3B Common: 25 percent clear face
Sound Wormy: No. 1 Common with wormholes

much more difficult to understand than that of softwood. Numbered gradings are not comparable between different woods. For example, the fourth grade of mahogany is much better wood than the fourth grade of hickory. The essential grading information is given in Table 1-2; this chart is not complete or absolutely accurate, but it can be taken as a general guide for the purchase of hardwoods.

To save money, always buy the lowest grade of lumber that will fill your needs. If, for example, you are buying 1x2 strips for furring, shelf cleats, or drawer rails, it is foolish to buy B or better lumber.

Sizes of Lumber. Manufactured lumber as shipped from the mill to the lumberyard is classified as (1) rough, (2) surfaced, and (3) worked. *Rough lumber* is furry and splintery. It is generally sold to factories or large woodworking shops that can dress their own lumber. *Surfaced lumber* is dressed by running it through a planer machine that leaves the wood smooth. It may be surfaced on one side (S1S), two sides (S2S), one edge (S1E), two edges (S2E), or a combination of sides and edges (S1S1E or S1S2E). The lumber you will normally use will be dressed on four sides (S4S). *Worked lumber* has been cut into moldings. Many kinds, shapes, and sizes are stocked by the average lumberyard.

Lumber comes from the saw in nominal sizes such as 2x4, 1x6, and so forth. In this form it is classified as "rough" or nominal size. When run through the planer, the surface dwindles in size by the amount of wood removed. A nominal 2x4 surfaced on four sides (S4S) thus shrinks to $1\frac{5}{8}$ by $3\frac{5}{8}$ inches in cross section, a 1x6 board to $\frac{25}{32}$ by $5\frac{5}{8}$ inches (actual size). A "five-quarter" board, nominally $1\frac{1}{4}$ inches thick, actually comes to $1\frac{1}{16}$ inches when dressed. Refer to Table 1-3 for nominal and average actual sizes of stock lumber. In some areas of the country the actual size may be slightly larger.

Moisture and Shrinkage

Freshly cut lumber contains a good deal of moisture. As the moisture disappears, the board shrinks somewhat. When the moisture content of a board drops to about 20 percent, the lumber is considered seasoned. For furniture and cabinet use, only stock with 6 to 12 percent moisture content should be used. This seasoning is generally

Table 1-3

NOMINAL AND ACTUAL SIZES OF LUMBER (INCHES)

NOMINAL THICKNESS	AVERAGE ACTUAL THICKNESS SOFTWOOD	HARDWOOD	NOMINAL WIDTH	AVERAGE ACTUAL WIDTH SOFTWOOD	HARDWOOD
$\frac{1}{2}$	$\frac{7}{16}$	$\frac{1}{2}$	1	$\frac{25}{32}$	$\frac{7}{8}$
1	$\frac{25}{32}$	$\frac{7}{8}$	2	$1\frac{5}{8}$	Usually
$1\frac{1}{4}$	$1\frac{1}{16}$	$1\frac{1}{8}$	3	$2\frac{5}{8}$	sold to nearest
$1\frac{1}{2}$	$1\frac{5}{16}$	$1\frac{3}{8}$	4	$3\frac{5}{8}$	nominal
$1\frac{3}{4}$	$1\frac{1}{2}$	$1\frac{5}{8}$	6	$5\frac{5}{8}$	size at random
2	$1\frac{5}{8}$	$1\frac{3}{4}$	8	$7\frac{1}{2}$	widths
3	$2\frac{5}{8}$	$2\frac{3}{4}$	10	$9\frac{1}{2}$	with edges left rough
			12	$11\frac{1}{2}$	

accelerated by placing the wood in an oven, a process called kiln drying. Lumber with a high moisture content is difficult to work with, and when the project is finished and the lumber begins to dry out, it will shrink, and may open up glued joints and seams or even crack. For this reason, store lumber in a warm, dry place. Do not let the lumber sag, or it will warp and twist out of shape.

If you want to test wood for moisture content and shrinkage, saw off a piece 1 inch long and exactly 6 inches across the grain. Weigh it carefully. Bake in the oven at 212°F. for at least four hours. Then measure it or compare it to an undried piece of the same stock. To determine the moisture content, find the difference between the wet and dry weight and divide the difference by the dry weight. Example: A piece that weighed 16 ounces weighs 12 ounces after drying (a difference of 4 ounces); dividing 4 by 12 gives $\frac{1}{3}$, or a moisture content of 33⅓ percent.

Lumber Defects

Several defects must be avoided in the selection of lumber:

1. Knots are places at which the branch of a tree has caused a fibrous, woody mass to form. Sometimes, when knots are solid, this wood is in demand for such things as knotty-pine paneling, but most often knots are a defect that must be removed from furniture lumber.

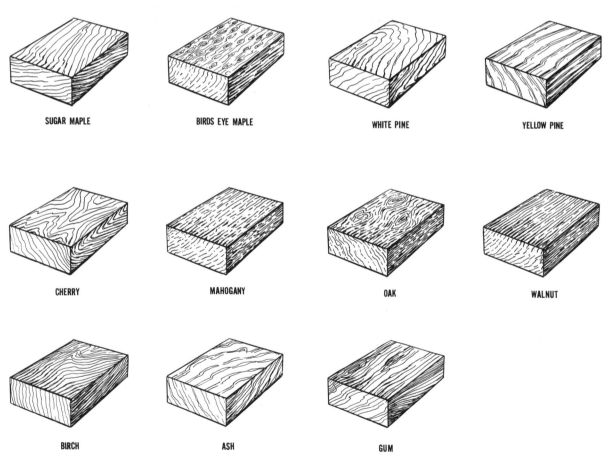

SUGAR MAPLE   BIRDS EYE MAPLE   WHITE PINE   YELLOW PINE

CHERRY   MAHOGANY   OAK   WALNUT

BIRCH   ASH   GUM

Fig. 1-4.   Grain identification of the common furniture woods.

2. A split is a large break in a board.

3. A check is a slight lengthwise separation in a board. This is often found at the end of the board and must be trimmed off before cutting stock to length.

4. Warp is a curve across the grain that occurs during the drying process.

5. Wind is a longitudinal twist in a board.

6. Decay is rotted area in the wood that causes a soft spot.

7. A shake is a separation of wood along the annual ring.

8. Insect damage causes small holes in the wood surface.

9. Molds and stains cause discoloration of the wood surface.

Home Furniture-Maker's Woods

Most furniture is made from hardwood. Softwood is primarily used in making reproductions of certain Early American pieces and in making inexpensive, unpainted furniture. Furniture woods vary in popularity, just as furniture styles do. When we think of Chippendale, we think of dark mahogany. When people talk of Biedermeier, light fruitwoods come to mind. In the last few years teak and some of the other exotic woods have become great favorites. There are so many species of hardwood that you have an almost unlimited range of textures and natural colors from which to choose. Let us take a look at some of the more popular furniture woods.

Ash is grayish brown in color, with fairly conspicuous grain markings. It is heavy, hard, strong, stiff, and highly resistant to shock.

Mahogany, a longtime favorite of furniture-makers, is reddish tan to pale reddish brown. It has a straight, close, and delicately beautiful grain, is hard and durable, and has relatively low shrinkage.

Oak—both red and white oak—is heavy, hard, tough, and durable. Red oak is brown with a reddish tinge; white oak is yellow to grayish brown. The attractively prominent grain is straight and dense.

Cherry, also called black cherry or chokecherry, varies from light to dark reddish brown, with a distinctive luster. It has a fairly uniform texture, and the grain consists of delicate lines.

Sugar maple, also known as hard maple or rock maple, is generally a light reddish brown in color. It is heavy, strong, and stiff, with a fine uniform texture and a straight, fairly coarse grain. It has large shrinkage and should be thoroughly dried. A variety is bird's-eye maple, which has small swirls in the grain.

Gum, or sweetgum, is reddish brown, with a form of cross grain that results in a beautifully figured ribbon stripe and thus makes this wood highly desirable for furniture. It is moderately hard and strong.

Walnut, usually called black walnut, varies in color from light to a warm, dark brown. The grain is normally straight, fine, and fairly distinct. Walnut is heavy, hard, and strong, yet it is easily worked.

Birch varies from light brown to dark reddish brown in color. The wood is fine and uniform in texture, with a close, distinct, but not conspicuous grain pattern. Birch shrinks greatly in drying.

White pine is a soft and easily worked wood with a fairly straight, strong, and clear grain. It ranges from cream to light reddish brown in color and is moderately light in weight, with fairly large shrinkage.

Yellow pine has a grain similar to, but more conspicuous than, that of white pine. It is orange to reddish brown in color and is harder, heavier, stronger, stiffer, and more durable than white pine.

Within the space of this book, it would be impossible to list in detail the qualities of all woods used in the home workshop. But in choosing a wood for a particular project, you should be guided by several qualities of the wood: ease of working, the grain and the finish the wood will take, its susceptibility to warpage, its hardness and resistance to the wear and tear of normal usage, its availability, and finally, its price.

Table 1-4 lists some of the properties of the more common woods available for home and furniture purposes. Most of these woods can be purchased either in solid or plywood form.

Table 1-4

CHARACTERISTICS OF WOODS

E=excellent/G=good/F=fair/P=poor

NAME OF WOOD	Hardness	Strength	Stability	Weight	Rot-resistance	Split-resistance	Working quality for hand tools	Shaping	Turning	Mortising	Planing and jointing	Nailing	Gluing	Sanding	Remarks
Alder	Med.	Weak	G	Light	F	F	G	F	F	F	G	G	G	F	A Pacific Coast favorite
Ash	Med.	Med.	E	Med. heavy	F	G	P	E	F	F	G	G	F	E	Interior trim, tool handles; wears well
Basswood	Soft	Weak	G	Light	P	E	E	P	P	F	G	E	E	P	Used as core stock
Beech	Hard	Med.	P	Heavy	P	G	F	F	F	G	F	P	G	G	Not durable outside; hard on hand tools
Birch	Hard	Strong	G	Heavy	F	G	P	E	G	E	G	P	F	F	Fine furniture, trim, and veneers
Butternut	Soft	Weak	E	Light	F	F	G	F	G	F	G	F	G	F	Furniture, sometimes called "white walnut"
Cedar	Soft	Weak	G	Med.	E	P	G	P	P	F	F	P	G	P	Trim, chest lining, outside use
Cherry	Med.	Med.	G	Heavy	F	P	G	E	E	E	E	F	E	E	Furniture, joiner work, novelties
Chestnut	Soft	Weak	E	Light	E	P	G	G	E	G	G	G	E	E	Scarce; fine for turning
Cypress	Soft	Med.	G	Med.	E	F	F	P	P	P	G	F	F	F	Excellent for outdoor use
Elm	Med.	Med.	P	Med. heavy	F	G	F	P	P	G	P	E	F	G	Blends well; very durable under paint
Fir (Douglas)	Med.	Med. strong	F	Med. heavy	G	F	F	P	P	G	G	G	G	F	Common plywood veneer
Gum (Red)	Med.	Med.	P	Med	F	G	G	F	E	F	F	G	E	F	Furniture; substitute for mahogany and walnut
Hickory	Hard	Strong	G	Heavy	P	F	P	F	G	E	G	P	G	E	Blends easily; furniture
Magnolia	Soft	Weak	F	Med.	F	G	G	G	F	P	G	E	E	G	Bends easily
Mahogany	Med.	Med.	E	Med. heavy	F	P	G	E	E	E	G	G	E	G	Excellent furniture wood
Mahogany, Philippine	Med.	Med.	E	Med.	G	P	G	F	G	F	G	G	E	P	Furniture
Maple, hard	Hard	Strong	G	Heavy	P	P	F	E	E	E	F	P	F	G	Excellent furniture wood, trim, fine for turning
Maple, soft	Med.	Med.	F	Med.	F	G	G	F	F	P	P	F	G	G	Difficult to machine-smooth

NAME OF WOOD	Hardness	Strength	Stability	Weight	Rot-resistance	Split-resistance	Working quality for hand tools	Shaping	Turning	Mortising	Planing and jointing	Nailing	Gluing	Sanding	Remarks
Oak, red	Hard	Strong	E	Heavy	P	F	P	F	G	E	E	G	G	E	Substitute for white oak in less expensive work
Oak, white	Hard	Strong	E	Heavy	F	F	P	G	G	E	E	G	G	E	Excellent furniture wood
Pine, white	Soft	Weak	G	Light	F	P	E	G	G	F	G	E	E	G	Best all-around soft wood
Pine, yellow	Hard	Strong	F	Heavy	G	P	F	G	P	G	G	F	F	F	Carpentry work
Poplar	Soft	Weak	G	Med.	P	G	E	P	G	F	G	E	E	P	Good for toys and carving
Redwood	Soft	Med.	E	Med.	E	G	G	F	P	G	G	E	E	P	Excellent for outdoor furniture
Sycamore	Med.	Med.	P	Heavy	F	G	G	P	G	E	P	E	G	P	Furniture and trim
Walnut	Med.	Strong	E	Heavy	G	F	G	G	E	E	G	F	E	E	Excellent for furniture, cabinetwork, trim

PLYWOOD

Today, as in the past, most of the beautiful and most expensive furniture is made of veneer, which is a thin sheet of wood glued to a piece of solid wood. This is important because a plywood panel, from which 90 percent of today's fine commercial furniture is made, is actually a wood "sandwich" consisting of an odd number of layers, usually five or seven. It is much stronger than wood of comparable thickness, and the large-size sheets eliminate the need for many joints and seams that would be necessary if regular boards were used. There is practically no shrinkage, expansion, or contraction, and the panels possess rigidity and strength in all directions. If well secured, they won't warp.

Posts, bases, pilasters, legs, stretchers, and other supporting or bracing parts of furniture should generally be made of solid wood unless the design makes plywood practical. Remember that bonding is not a cheap process. Actually good plywood is frequently more costly than solid wood.

Plywood Construction

Every plywood panel consists of two faces. Under each face is a cross-band layer. Then comes the panel core, which consists of more plies or solid lumber, particleboard, chipboard, or flakeboard.

A problem with standard plywood is that screws don't hold well in edge grain. Another is that the multiple plies are sometimes considered unattractive. Lumber-core plywood overcomes these objections and has a number of other advantages. If the panel is a tough wood, such as oak or birch, its workability is much improved because the solid boards making up the plywood core are of such relatively soft woods as poplar, gum, or basswood. Solid-core plywood can be edge-glued as easily as solid lumber. It saws like solid lumber, and you can cut relatively thin slices without its disintegrating.

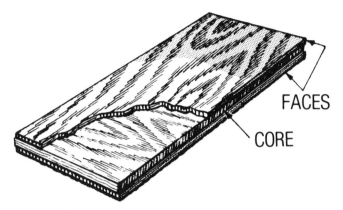

Fig. 1-5.   The veneer type of plywood core.

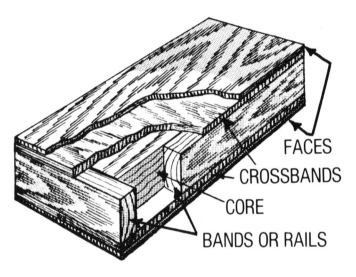

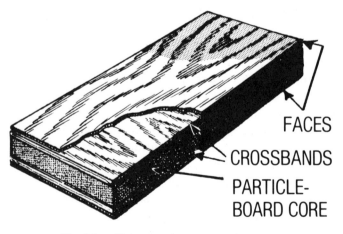

Fig. 1-6.   The two most common types of core construction used in furniture-making, lumber core (*top*) and particleboard (*bottom*).

A particleboard (flake or chip) core has an additional advantage in that it is the most dimensionally stable of any plywood. Because it is less likely to bow, twist, or warp than any other material, it is especially preferred for doors. But it does have limitations. Because particleboards are soft, the only screws that will hold are those that are bigger and longer. Particleboards are difficult to edge-glue. You have to fill the edge first, either with adhesive or with special filler. Because of the softness of the core, this kind of plywood dents more easily.

Plywood Sizes

The standard panel size for most plywood is 4x8 feet, but usually you'll have no difficulty in getting 2x4-, 3x4-, 4x4-, 3x6-, and 2x8-foot panels. If it's the kind of plywood used in boatmaking, you may also find it available in 4x12, 4x14, and 4x16 sizes.

Thicknesses commonly available are $\frac{1}{4}$, $\frac{3}{8}$, $\frac{1}{2}$, $\frac{5}{8}$, and $\frac{3}{4}$ inch. In the case of fir plywood, veneer thickness usually varies with the panel thickness. For example on $\frac{1}{4}$ inch it may be $\frac{1}{16}$; on $\frac{3}{8}$ inch, $\frac{1}{12}$; on $\frac{3}{4}$ inch, $\frac{1}{10}$. On very expensive and rare woods the veneer thickness may be $\frac{1}{32}$ or less; walnut may be $\frac{1}{35}$. Such panels must be handled with care, for they can't be sanded down and refinished like ordinary plywood.

Though cabinet-grade plywood is nominally $\frac{3}{4}$ inch thick, you may find that it varies $\frac{1}{32}$ inch or more, plus or minus. These small differences add up, so watch them.

In all plywoods the $\frac{1}{4}$- and $\frac{3}{4}$-inch thicknesses are most commonly available. A special $\frac{1}{8}$-inch plywood is made for covering flush doors. You can use it for covering less-expensive grades of plywood. If you need a thickness other than these, you can laminate it yourself. Use contact-bond cement.

You can get flakeboard-core panels in $\frac{3}{4}$-inch thickness with such wood facings as birch, cherry, oak, pine, lauan, and walnut. You can also get panels with a phenolic (plastic) face, which is an exceptionally good surface for paint. The stores will know it as medium-density overlaid plywood. Some

Table 1-5

CORES FOR HARDWOOD PLYWOOD PANELS

Core type	Panel thickness	Advantages	Disadvantages
Veneer (all inner plies of wood veneers)	¼″ (3-ply) or less	Inexpensive	Difficult to machine. Exposed edge shows core voids and imperfections. Most susceptible to warpage (doors).
	⁵⁄₁₆″ - ½″ (5-ply)	Inexpensive	
	Over ½″ (7-ply)	Best screw-holding power	
Particleboard (also called flakeboard)	¼″ (infrequent) through 2″ (usually 3 plies)	Most stable; least expensive (generally)	Poor edge screw holding; heaviest core.
Lumber core (consists of strips of lumber 1½″ to 4″ wide)	⅝″ thru 2″ (usually 5 plies)	Easiest to machine; exposed edges are solid; stable construction.	

economy panels, instead of being faced with real wood, are faced with print grains of walnut, cherry, or teak.

Plywood Grades and Cuts
Hardwood plywood and softwood plywood are each graded by separate systems.

Hardwood Plywood. The Hardwood Plywood Manufacturers Association (HPMA) designates five grades of plywood for the backs and faces of hardwood panels. The grade-marking may be stamped on the backs of the panels.

In describing hardwood plywood, the word "type" is used to indicate glue-bond durability, the ability of the plies to stay together under different exposure conditions. Plywoods having Type I glue bond are made using one of the following adhesives: phenol, resorcinol, phenol-resorcinol, melamine, or melamine-urea. Plywoods having Type I glue bonds can be used in outdoor work. Almost all of the Type II hardwood plywood is made using urea-resin adhesives. The Type II glue bond is water-resistant but not waterproof; it is an interior glue bond not suitable for outdoor use. Type III plywood, not commonly made, is used for containers and occasionally for other purposes. This type of plywood is made using urea-resin adhesives, but with higher proportions of water and/or extenders than are normally used in a type II urea glue mix.

The grade of hardwood plywood denotes the appearance of the face and face plies. The grades of the inner plies are important, but the face-ply grade in hardwood plywood is exposed, and thus more important. The following are the basic HPMA grade standards. (These standards are the result of consultations between HPMA and major producers and distributors.)

Premium Grade (A). The face veneer may be made from more than one piece. With most species multipiece faces must be book-matched, or slip-matched. The quality of veneer is high—only a few small burls, occasional pin knots, slight color streaks, and inconspicuous small patches are allowed.

Good Grade (1). The faces are similar to that of Premium Grade faces except that matching is not required. However, sharp contrasts in color and great dissimilarity in grain and figure of two adjacent pieces of veneer in multipiece faces are not allowed. This grade of veneer allows only a few small burls, occasional pin knots, slight color streaks, and inconspicuous small patches.

Sound Grade (2). This grade provides a smooth surface. The veneer need not be matched for grain or color but must be free of open defects.

Utility Grade (3). Open defects are allowed—knotholes up to 1 inch in diameter, wormholes and splits not exceeding 3/16 of an inch wide and not extending half the length of the panel are permitted.

Backing Grade (4). This grade is similar to Utility Grade except that larger-sized open defects are permitted—knotholes not greater than 3 inches and splits up to 1 inch wide, depending on the length of the split.

A grade designation of A-3 means a panel is Premium Grade on one side, Utility Grade on the other.

Softwood Plywood. Over 90 percent of all softwood plywood and two-thirds of all plywood manufactured in this country today is Douglas fir plywood. Since 1933 manufacturers of Douglas fir plywood have adhered to a set of standardized grading rules, which are set forth in a periodically revised United States Commercial Standard. The American Plywood Association (APA), a nonprofit association of most American fir-plywood manufacturers, administers a rigid inspection and quality-control program to keep production up to these standards. The symbol of quality control is the APA grade-trademark, which can be used only by those manufacturers who continue to meet the association's requirements.

The grade-trademark includes information on both type and grade of plywood. As with hardwood plywood "type" refers to the glue, "grade" to the appearance quality of veneer on face and back panels.

In the APA grade-trademark exterior and interior types are indicated by "EXT" and "INT,"

respectively. Fir plywood for exteriors is made with a hot-pressed synthetic-resin adhesive that is permanent and insoluble under practically any condition, including boiling. It is designed for permanent exterior exposure. Fir plywood for interiors is made with soybean-base protein glues in either a hot or a cold press or with extended phenolic resins in a hot press—most commonly by the latter method. Such plywood is designed for permanent interior service, but it will also withstand temporary weather exposure or, when used for subfloors, sheathing, and similar purposes, wetting during construction. In general this type is suitable where the moisture content of wood or plywood will not reach more than 20 percent; in other words wherever there is no danger from mold, fungus growth, or decay.

Grades are indicated by letters. Briefly here is what the grade-mark means:

A. High-quality veneer with highest standard veneer appearance. No open defects. Smooth and paintable. Suitable for light stain-glaze finishes. Can be made of more than one piece, well joined and reasonably matched. Neat repair patches are permitted, as are shims, streaks, and sapwood. All patches and repairs must run parallel to the grain. Also admits approved plastic filler in splits and other minor defects up to 1/32 inch in width.

B. Similar to A veneer but permits circular plugs, edges of which may be slightly rough. Also permits sound, tight knots (up to 1 inch); the veneer surface must be free from open defects except splits not wider than 1/32 inch; slightly rough grain is allowed.

C (repaired). Surface-improved C veneer used by the manufacturer for underlayment. Tight knots up to 1½ inches in greatest dimension and worm and borer holes or other open defects not to exceed ¼ and ½ inch are allowed. Solid, tight-pitch pockets, ruptured and torn grain, minor sanding defects, and sander skips up to 5 percent of the panel area are also admitted.

D. This quality of veneer is used only in interior-type plywood panels. Permits knots to 2½ inches, pitch pockets, limited splits, worm or borer holes, minor sanding defects, and repair patches.

N. Special-order "natural-finish" veneer. Very select, all heartwood, free from knots, splits, pitch pockets, and other open defects. If joined, not more than three pieces of veneer are used; joints must be well matched as to color and grain; all joints must be parallel to the edges of the panel. May contain a few specific small repairs if well matched, but neither overlapping of repairs nor plastic filler is permitted.

Thus a panel marked A-A has the highest standard quality veneer on both face and back panels; A-B indicates A appearance on the face panel, B on the back. The latter would be used where appearance is highly important for one side, slightly less so for the other. Where only one side will be seen, use A-C or A-D panel.

Most plywood manufacturers produce panels of other softwoods (hemlock, cedar, larch, noble fir, spruce, redwood, knotty pine, white firs, and white pines) in types and grades comparable to Douglas fir plywood. Many of these plywoods are APA-tested and grade-marked except that they are indicated by a prefix symbol, WSP.

You will find considerable variation in grain. Sometimes it is due to the natural variation in the wood. At other times it is due to the method of cutting. Actually veneer for plywood can be cut in four ways:

1. Rotary lathe. The log is chucked in the center of each end and is rotated against a knife, producing veneer like unwinding a roll of paper. A bold, variegated-grain pattern is generally evident in rotary cutting; 80 to 90 percent of all veneer is cut by this method.

2. Slicing. Most slicers consist of a stationary knife. The flitch to be cut is attached to a log bed that moves up and down; on each downward stroke a slice of veneer is cut by the knife. Slicers are used primarily for cutting decorative face veneers from woods such as walnut, mahogany, cherry, and oak.

3. Stay log cutting. This method makes veneers in a manner between rotary cut and sliced veneer. A rotary lathe is used; a flitch is attached to a stay log or metal beam, mounted off-center in the lathe. The stay log method produces half-round veneers, which is generally used for faces.

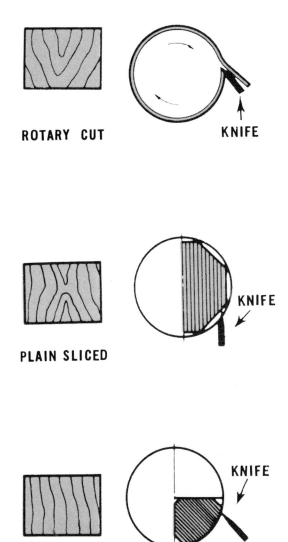

QUARTER SLICING

Fig. 1-7. Most veneers are either rotary cut (*top*) or plain sliced (*center*). Another method of slicing frequently used is quarter slicing (*bottom*).

4. Sawn veneer. A very small quantity of veneer is cut in this manner. A circular-type saw called a segment saw with a thin, segmented blade turns on an arbor. The thin blade reduces saw kerf. This method generally is used only for certain species and to achieve special effects. Oak, red cedar, and Spanish cedar are often cut by this process.

Douglas fir and Philippine mahogany may be rotary-cut; the grain is accentuated, erratic, and wild. Most cabinet-grade hardwood is plain-cut, flat-cut, or quartered. In all these cuts the veneers are shaved off the flat surfaces of the sawn logs in the same direction as the grain. The grain is pleasingly subdued, straight, and coherent.

There is still great variation in individual panels, however. If you can visit your lumberyard and personally select the panels, you are better off. You can pick the kind of graining that pleases you most.

How to Buy Plywood

There is a kind of plywood for every use, and the right selection will be both satisfactory and most economical. Unfortunately too many plywood users buy grades that are more expensive than they need be for ordinary uses. For instance plywood with both sides of top quality is sometimes put into cupboard walls and shelves where only one side could possibly show. Familiarity with grade-marks and what they mean will help you to select the right plywood. Sometimes it is possible, with a little extra work, to upgrade plywood. In other words by purchasing a low-grade plywood and filling defects and sanding, you may raise the grade to meet your requirements.

The species and grade, and consequently the price, will be governed by the nature of the project and the type of finish desired. For a paint finish Sound, or B-grade, plywood is adequate, but for a natural-wood effect Good, or A-grade, will give better results. It is more economical to use Utility grade for backs and concealed construction.

Economy comes into the picture again in laying out the work. By careful planning, you can often fit all of the pieces of your project into one good-size rectangle, say 4x6 feet. This means you need only a single panel of that size, and there will be little waste. While some dealers will make no cuts and will sell nothing less than the standard 4x8-foot panel, others will cut to whatever size you request and will even make mitered and rabbeted edges. (Many dealers sell scraps at reduced prices and encourage the customer to browse at the remnant racks.) For all these extra services there will probably be a nominal charge, so if economy is your object, it is always best to do your own cutting. In the case of hardwood plywoods most dealers will

order the size to meet your exact specifications if it is in stock. Plywood is ordered and priced in square-foot measurements. A piece of plywood 4x8 feet is 32 square feet.

When the plywood panels come from the lumberyard, store them indoors or under cover where they will stay dry. They should be stacked on a solid bed rather than stored on end. Remember that the faces may darken if exposed to direct sunlight for any length of time, so cover the top panel.

HARDBOARD

Hardboard, basically, is a wood product. It is made from logs that have been converted to chips, then to wood fibers, and permanently bonded together under heat and pressure into panels up to 5 feet wide and 16 feet long, with the lignin within the wood acting as the natural binder. Thus as an "engineered" wood product, hardboard is more dense, has more strength, and is more durable than a comparable panel of wood. Hardboard has no grain or knots, a factor that gives uniformity in strength and appearance and permits superior painting or other finishing treatment. Factory-finished hardboards are highly resistant to moisture, scuffing, and denting, and won't crack, chip, split, or check. Hardboard can be worked with ordinary woodworking tools: sawed, planed, sanded, drilled, and punched.

While there are many types and classifications of hardboard, only the following four are generally used by the home furniture-maker.

Standard Hardboard. Dark or blond in color, this is most commonly used for case, drawer bottoms, vertical dividers, and cabinet facing that will be painted. It is available smooth on one side and screen-textured on the back, or smooth on both sides. Thickness varies from ⅛ to ⅜ inch, and lengths run up to 16 feet. The most common width is 4 feet, although 5-foot-wide panels are available.

Tempered Hardboard. This classification is similar to Standard, except that it is generally employed for exterior applications and those interior uses where higher strength, moisture resistance, and abrasion resistance are required.

Prefinished Hardboard. This hardboard material is specifically treated for resistance to stains and moisture; it is highly resistant to dents, mars, and scuffs. In most cases the material is prefinished in wood grains—such as walnut, oak, teak, cherry, pecan, and in a variety of shades—exceptional marble reproductions, plain and speckled colors, and filigree designs. Vinyl-clad panels are also available in decorative and wood-grain finishes. The thickness is usually ¼ inch, and the most common size is 4 feet wide and up to 10 feet long.

Perforated Hardboard. This versatile panel product has been punched to receive hooks and hanging hardware. When fitted with these metal or plastic accessories, perforated hardboard panels are a handy way to create "working walls" that provide extra storage space for tools, kitchen utensils, toys, sports equipment, clothing, and hundreds of other items. It is also popular for sliding cabinet doors. Perforated hardboards are available in natural color, prepainted, preprimed, V-grooved, and also prefinished and wood-grained, tempered or standard, in ⅛- to ¼-inch thickness.

PARTICLEBOARD

Particleboard or flake-type boards combine the plywood principle of lamination with use of resin. It is a three-ply panel consisting of a ¹⁄₁₆-inch surface of wood veneer flakes, a core of medium-size chips, and another ¹⁄₁₆-inch layer of wood flakes (the chips and flakes are impregnated with resin). The plies are simultaneously formed and fused together under extreme heat and pressure. The result is a panel of unusual flatness with a gleaming, mosaic-textured surface that requires no painting or staining. These panels are attractive on both sides, with no patches or plugs and no danger of grain raise; they are practically warp-free, will not change dimensions, are medium in weight, and are

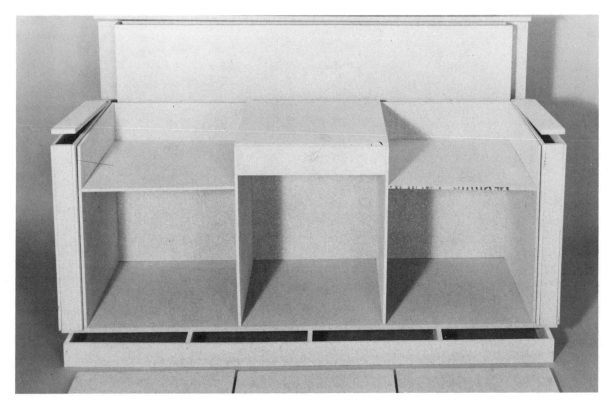

Fig. 1-8.   Stereo cabinet being assembled is made completely of particleboard.

easy to work. Particleboard can be fabricated with ordinary tools or high-speed power machines, and it holds nails and screws firmly without splitting. Because of its beauty and flatness it is ideal for furniture, cabinets, and built-ins of all kinds. This material may be readily finished by using standard plywood-finishing procedures. Particleboard is made from a number of different wood species, including cedar, redwood, maple, fir, pine, and a combination of fir and pine.

OTHER MATERIALS

Glass, marble, leather, and tile are used by the home furniture-maker for decorative purposes and for special surfaces such as tabletops. The use of

these materials is covered in later chapters of this book.

Because of the difficulty of fabricating, plastics and metal have never been popular materials with the home furniture-maker. The exception is laminated plastic sheets, which are widely used as veneers over plywood for tabletops, countertops, and bartops. The standard grade is not affected by boiling water, alcohol, fruit juices, or diluted acids. It will also withstand heat up to 250°F. The cigarette-proof grade is guaranteed to withstand the heat of lighted cigarettes and cigars. Made of paper layers impregnated with synthetic resins, the hard surface is easy to clean and nearly impervious to scratches and moisture. Available in a wide range of colors, patterns, and wood finishes,

Table 1-6

LUMBER CALCULATOR—BOARD FEET FOR VARIOUS LENGTHS

Size in inches	8-feet	10-feet	12-feet	14-feet	16-feet
1x2	$1\frac{1}{3}$	$1\frac{2}{3}$	2	$2\frac{1}{3}$	$2\frac{2}{3}$
1x3	2	$2\frac{1}{2}$	3	$3\frac{1}{2}$	4
1x4	$2\frac{2}{3}$	$3\frac{1}{3}$	4	$4\frac{2}{3}$	$5\frac{1}{3}$
1x5	$3\frac{1}{3}$	$4\frac{1}{6}$	5	$5\frac{5}{6}$	$6\frac{2}{3}$
1x6	4	5	6	7	8
1x8	$5\frac{1}{3}$	$6\frac{2}{3}$	8	$9\frac{1}{3}$	$10\frac{2}{3}$
1x10	$6\frac{2}{3}$	$8\frac{1}{2}$	10	$11\frac{2}{3}$	$13\frac{1}{3}$
1x12	8	10	12	14	16
$1\frac{1}{4}$ *x 4	$3\frac{1}{3}$	$4\frac{1}{6}$	5	$5\frac{5}{6}$	$6\frac{2}{3}$
$1\frac{1}{4}$ *x 6	5	$6\frac{1}{4}$	$7\frac{1}{2}$	$8\frac{3}{4}$	10
$1\frac{1}{4}$ *x 8	$6\frac{2}{3}$	$8\frac{1}{3}$	10	$11\frac{2}{3}$	$13\frac{1}{3}$
$1\frac{1}{4}$ *x10	$8\frac{1}{3}$	$10\frac{5}{12}$	$12\frac{1}{2}$	$14\frac{7}{12}$	$16\frac{2}{3}$
$1\frac{1}{4}$ *x12	10	$12\frac{1}{2}$	15	$17\frac{1}{2}$	20
2x4	$5\frac{1}{3}$	$6\frac{2}{3}$	8	$9\frac{1}{3}$	$10\frac{2}{3}$
2x6	8	10	12	14	16

*Sometimes referred to as five-quarter boards.

Table 1-7

SAMPLE LIST OF LUMBER REQUIREMENTS

Item	Name	No. pcs.	Size in inches	Wood
A	Sides	2	¾x18¾x96	plywood
B	Back	1	¼x35¼x96	hardboard
C	Shelves	4	¾x18¾x35¼	pine
D	Top	1	¾x18¾x35¼	plywood
E	Bottom	1	¾x20¼x35¼	plywood
F	Dividers	10	¾x2⅝x5½	pine
G	Base	2	2x4x35¼	pine
H	Base	1	2x4x18¾	pine
I	Trim	9 linear feet	¼″ quarter round	pine

standard-size sheets are 2, 2½, 3, and 4 feet wide, 5, 6, 7, and 8 feet long, and 5/32 inch thick.

ESTIMATING MATERIAL AND COSTS

Lumber is measured in various ways, depending upon the type of wood and its width and thickness. Lumber more than 4 inches wide and ½ to 2 inches thick is measured in board feet. A board foot is a square foot of lumber 1 inch thick. To figure the total board footage, multiply the thickness (nominal) of the board in inches by its width (nominal) and length in feet, or

B F = thickness in inches x width in inches x length in feet.

Thus a piece of lumber 1 by 6 inches by 10 feet would measure 5 board feet—(1x6)÷12x10 = 5. The number of board feet in lumber of various sizes and lengths is shown opposite in Table 1-6.

Lumber less than 4 inches wide and of any thickness is ordered by the linear foot. Thus an order for a board 10 feet long would specify 10 linear feet. Plywood and hardboard are ordered in square-foot measurements. A piece of plywood 4x8 feet equals 32 square feet.

When you order lumber, make a list of the number of boards you need, their sizes, types, and ultimate uses, similar to the sample list in Table 1-7. From this list add all lengths of lumber of similar wood, width, and thickness to get the total footage needed for each type.

You can then estimate costs by multiplying the price per board foot, linear foot, or square foot by the total footage needed. Because yard lumber is usually sold only in standard lengths, 15 percent should be added to the estimated cost for the additional footage you may have to buy.

Chapter 2
FURNITURE-MAKING TOOLS AND HOW TO USE THEM

Some tools are absolutely essential to all types of furniture-making. Some are not as vital but are very convenient to have available. Others are necessary for specific operations that you may or may not want to do. In this chapter we will take a look at the various categories of furniture-making tools—both hand and power—so that you can decide on what your shop should contain. Some equipment important to furniture-making, such as clamps, screwdrivers, and sanders, is discussed in upcoming chapters, and a complete rundown on tools is given in Appendix B.

HAND SAWS OR POWER SAWS

There are very few, if any, furniture projects that do not begin by requiring that pieces of material first be cut to a specific size or shape. And chances are that the tool you will need for doing the necessary cutting is a saw of some kind. Some saws are special-purpose tools that you will only have occasional need for in your furniture-making, while others are so frequently used that they should be part of every home handyman's tool kit. Before you can decide on just which ones you actually need, you have to know something about the various types available and the kind of work that each can do.

Hand Saws
Regardless of how complete a workshop you now have (or plan to have), regardless of how many power tools you now own (or plan to buy), your shop will not be complete without an assortment of hand saws. They not only cost considerably less than power saws, but are also sometimes more convenient to use on small jobs where only one or two cuts will be required. In addition, a hand saw is

essential for those jobs where it may be awkward or even impossible to use a power saw.

The most commonly used saws for cutting wood are the crosscut saw and the ripsaw. The crosscut saw is designed for cutting across, or at an angle to, the grain, while the ripsaw is made for cutting parallel to the grain. Both come in various lengths, from small 16-inchers for carrying in a tool box to the "standard" 26-inch length that is the most popular and most practical for all-around use. As with most other saws, the teeth on both a crosscut saw and a ripsaw have a "set" to them—every other tooth is bent out on opposite sides—so that the blade cuts a kerf that is slightly wider than the thickness of the saw. This is an important aid on all saws to keep the blade from binding, especially when making long cuts in soft or green wood.

Better-quality saws also have their blades ground to a taper so that they are slightly thinner along the back edge than they are along the cutting edge. This provides added clearance for the blade to prevent binding in long cuts and minimizes the amount of set required on the teeth. It also makes sawing a lot easier when working with green or gummy wood.

Although ripsaws and crosscut saws look very much alike, the shape of their teeth and their cutting principles are entirely different from one another's. On crosscut saws the teeth are filed to a bevel across the front and back edges so that each tooth slices through the grain just as a sharp knife would. The set of the teeth lets the two parallel rows make cuts on each side of the kerf so that the wood in between is crumbled out as the teeth move back and forth. The crosscut saw actually cuts slightly on the back stroke as well as on the forward stroke.

The teeth on a ripsaw are filed straight across on

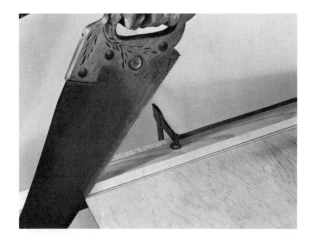

Fig. 2-1.   The crosscut saw can be used to cut light metals such as aluminum (*left*), if necessary. For precision in cutting any material, clamp a straightedge to the work and follow it instead of a pencil mark.

the front, and the front cutting edge is almost perpendicular to the length of the blade (unlike the crosscut saw, whose front edge slants back at about a 15-degree angle from the blade). As a result its teeth act like a gang of tiny sharp chisels arranged in an almost straight line. Thus instead of slicing the wood out the way a crosscut saw does, a ripsaw chips out small pieces from alternate sides and then pushes them out through the kerf.

In addition to varying as to length hand saws also vary as to the number of teeth per inch. As a rule crosscut saws will have anywhere from eight to twelve points (teeth) to the inch, with the eight-point saw being the most popular for general use. The finer blades—those with ten or twelve points— cut slower but give a smoother cut. You will want one if you plan to do a lot of cabinetwork or if you are building with hardwood and plywood and are willing to sacrifice speed for quality.

Ripsaws are coarser and generally have either five and one half or six points to the inch. This helps them give the faster cutting action that most people want, since ripping cuts are generally longer than crosscuts.

When cutting lumber with a crosscut saw, try to keep the cutting edge at approximately a 45-degree angle to the work surface. This is the angle at which the saw will cut most rapidly and with the least effort. For ripsaws the best angle is about 60 degrees—in other words, with the saw more nearly

vertical to the work (assuming you are cutting a horizontal board).

When starting a cut, always place the blade on the waste side of the line near the handle end. Then, while using the tip or the knuckle of your thumb as a guide, make a short draw stroke by pulling the handle toward you with a minimum

Fig. 2-2.   While the all-purpose eight-point saw can be used to rip lumber along the grain, the four-and-one-half-to-five-and-one-half-point ripsaw does it better and faster. The saw is held at an angle of about 60 degrees.

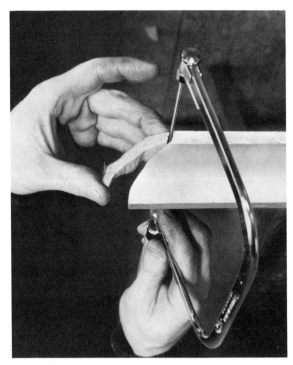

Fig. 2-3. A coping saw's spring-steel blade is held in a rectangular frame. It can be held at any angle, can work its way along a straight line, and can turn a right-angle corner or cut circles.

amount of downward pressure. Repeat this once or twice until you have enough of a groove to cover the teeth, then start conventional forward stroking to begin actual cutting.

Both the ripsaw and the crosscut saw are primarily designed for making straight cuts. You will need other hand saws for making curved cuts. For tight curves and intricate scrollwork in thin lumber, plywood, hardboard, plastic, or sheet metal, a coping saw is the tool to use. It has a U-shaped frame with a handle projecting straight out from one end of the U. A very narrow blade fits across the open end of the frame; tension is applied to the blade by tightening the threaded handle to which one of the blade supports is attached.

Most coping saws are designed so that the blade can be turned at any angle—up, down, or sideways—to permit cutting in tight corners where the frame might get in the way. As a rule, the blade should be mounted so that the teeth point toward the handle rather than away from it as on most saws. In other words, you do your maximum cutting on the "pull" stroke rather than on the

Fig. 2-4. These close relatives, the compass and keyhole saws, have a specialized job. The blades are tapered so that they can enter a drilled hole and move about in all directions from that point. Their purpose is to make cutouts in the center of a piece of wood without cutting the edges. The compass saw (*left*), a rugged eight-pointer, tapers to a point, while big brother keyhole (*right*), finer-toothed at twenty-four points, is longer and not always sharply pointed at the end. Many manufacturers include an assortment of interchangeable blades to fit a single handle. In some cases the handle also rotates, making circle-cutting easier from a given position. Use the big-toothed shorty for plywood cutouts, the finer-toothed styles for cutting plastics.

"push" stroke. Although suitable for fine scroll-work and thin materials, the coping saw is limited by the depth of the throat (the U-shaped frame). To reach into the center of larger panels, special deep-throated models often listed as scroll saws are also available.

When faced with the job of making curved cuts in thicker lumber or in the center of panels where a coping saw could not possibly reach, you need either a keyhole saw or a compass saw. These are actually two different versions of the same tool. Both have tapered blades with teeth that will either crosscut or rip, and both can be used for making straight cuts as well as curved cuts. The tapered blade and the lack of a frame enables it to reach into places where no other type of saw would fit.

Compass saws are usually 12 to 14 inches long, while keyhole saws vary from 8 to 12 inches in length. In addition to being smaller, keyhole saws also have narrower blades that come to a sharper point and they have finer teeth—twenty to twenty-four points to the inch as compared with about eight or ten points on a compass saw. The narrow blade and fine point enable the keyhole saw to cut small openings where the compass saw would not fit. The compass saw can twist around sharp curves with comparative ease.

Nests of saws, which consist of one handle with an assortment of interchangeable blades, are also available. They will perform the functions of the compass saw, the keyhole saw, and a small hacksaw. Nests are usually supplied with three or four blades, one of which is a metal-cutting blade tapered to a blunt point like the blade of the keyhole and the compass saw. As a rule these sets include one large woodcutting blade with coarse teeth that can be used for pruning, one medium blade for general woodcutting, and one metal-cutting blade.

For really accurate work when cutting wood furniture joints or doing cabinetwork, a backsaw is the tool to use. Designed primarily for crosscutting, this saw has a stiff blade that will not bend because it is reinforced along the back edge with a steel brace. These saws have exceptionally fine teeth—twelve to sixteen points to the inch—so they cut cleanly without splintering. Sometimes called miter box saws, they are widely used with miter boxes for accurate cutting and mitering of moldings and trim.

Backsaws vary from 6 to 28 inches in length, although the most widely used model, and the one you will most likely want for use with a miter box, measures about 12 inches in length. The handle on the backsaw is set at an angle for comfortable working with a miter box, but you will find many

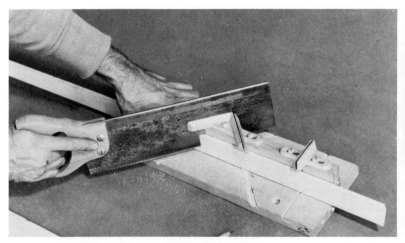
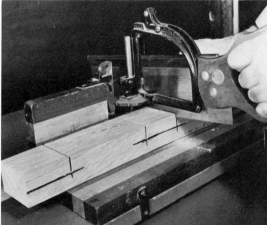

Fig. 2-5. *Left:* The backsaw has anywhere from eighteen to thirty-two teeth per inch, not sharply set. The edge it cuts is almost smooth, always straight. *Right:* The big brother of the backsaw is known as a miter box saw. It is longer and is usually used with a miter box of some sort.

Fig. 2-6.   The veneer saw.

other jobs where the backsaw is handy—for instance, when you have to trim off a molding that is nailed flush against an existing surface.

The dovetail saw is actually a smaller version of the hacksaw. It has a round handle (like a file or chisel) instead of the usual pistol grip, and the blade is only 10 inches in length and about 1½ inches wide. As its name implies, it was principally designed for cutting dovetails (and tenon joints), but you will also find it handy for fine cutting when working with small moldings as well as for trimming woodwork in tight corners where most other saws would not fit.

A specialized saw that you may want is the veneer type, which is primarily designed for trimming thin sheets of wood veneer. This saw has very fine teeth on both sides of the blade and a projecting handle attached to the flat of the blade. Thus the veneer saw can be used to cut off veneer flush with a surface or for any other delicate work requiring a saw that can cut in a corner.

In addition to a selection of saws for cutting wood and other comparatively soft materials you will also need at least one good metal-cutting saw— a hacksaw—in your furniture-making workshop. Unlike wood saws, hacksaws all have replaceable blades that are comparatively inexpensive, so all you are buying is a frame to hold the hacksaw blade. In its most common form the frame is adjustable to accept blades either 10 or 12 inches in length. The hacksaw has a pistol-grip handle with a

wing nut for applying needed tension to the blade.

To increase their versatility, many hacksaws are designed so the blade can be installed in any one of four positions—with teeth facing downward, to either side, or upward. This handy feature permits you to reach into places where clearance for the frame otherwise would not be enough.

Hacksaw blades come with either fourteen, eighteen, twenty-four, or thirty-two teeth to the inch. Broadly speaking, the coarser blades are for soft and thicker metals than the finer ones. In addition the coarser teeth are better for soft metals such as copper or aluminum, while the finer-toothed blades are best for hard steel, hard bronze, and similar tough materials. You should always try to select a blade with teeth fine enough so that at least three teeth are always in contact with the work. As an example, when cutting thin angle iron, position the metal in the vise so that you can cut on one of the flat sides rather than on one of the edges. It's a good thing hacksaw blades are inexpensive, since it is a good idea to keep at least one of each grade on hand so that you will always be able to select the right one.

As a rule it is best to grip the saw with both hands, one on the handle and one at the front end of the frame. Bear down with moderate pressure on the forward stroke, but lift up slightly on the back stroke. All of the cutting action takes place on the

Fig. 2-7.   The main purpose of the hacksaw is cutting metal. The blade should be inserted in the hacksaw with the teeth pointing away from the handle.

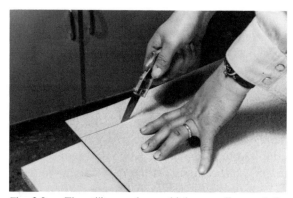

Fig. 2-8. The utility saw has multiple uses all around the house and shop. Small, resembling the keyhole saw and the hacksaw, it cuts metals as easily as a hacksaw. Fine teeth make it ideal for cutting plastic. It does passably well cutting curves and will do as well as the coping saw on some intricate cuts.

forward stroke; bearing down on the back stroke only helps to dull the blade.

Another inexpensive little metal-cutting hand saw that you will find useful is a utility, or all-purpose, saw. This miniature version of the compass or keyhole saw has a metal-cutting blade 6 to 8 inches in length. These handy little tools are ideal for reaching into tight corners or between boards when necessary to cut off hidden nails, bolts, or screws.

The Circular Saw

There is no doubt that hand saws are basic to any workshop—convenient to use and certainly less expensive than power saws—but, if you do any quantity of work at all, sooner or later you're certain to want one or more of the many handy portable power saws that are now available. You'll save hours of time and arm-tiring effort.

A circular, or table, saw is the basic power tool for any furniture shop. In choosing a circular saw, it is best to get a tilting-arbor saw. With this type of saw you always have the convenience and safety of a level surface to work on—the blade tilts for angular ripping or crosscutting. You will find better workmanship and quality in the tilting-arbor saws than in the tilting-table or stationary-blade saw. Remember that it is a good idea to get the best first.

There is no limit to the operations you can do on a tilting-arbor saw with expert results. You can

crosscut and rip wood and other materials. You can make rabbet and mortise cuts as well, and rough lumber can be cut to the size and shape desired.

Saws are designed to operate most efficiently at a predetermined arbor speed depending on the size of the saw blade. If you buy your saw complete with a matched motor and pulleys, the speed is probably correct; otherwise make sure that the blade is being driven at the proper speed:

Blade diameter	Arbor speed
6 inch	6300 rpm
7	5400
8	4700
10	3800
12	3200

To check your saw speed, take the operating rpm from the serial plate on the motor, measure the diameters of the two pulleys, and apply this formula:

$$\frac{arbor\ speed}{motor\ speed} = \frac{diameter\ of\ motor\ pulley}{diameter\ of\ arbor\ pulley}$$

If the speed doesn't figure out properly, purchase a new set of pulleys that will convert the motor speed to the proper speed for your saw (your hardware store should have charts giving the correct size).

The Blade. There are blades manufactured for every kind of work, so make sure that you have the right type for the job you are doing. The all-purpose combination blade is standard equipment for most jobs; for work with soft wood, a hollow-ground combination blade gives very satisfactory results. Crosscut blades and ripsaw blades are designed strictly for those cuts and should be used for maximum efficiency when doing production work in large quantities.

The hollow-ground blade is designed for specialized sawing. The teeth are not bent outward to form a set. The body of the blade is ground in on both sides to obtain clearance and permit free running without binding. Since the teeth are not bent outward, they don't scratch the sides of the kerf, hence the cut edge of the board looks as if it had been planed. The hollow-ground-type blades

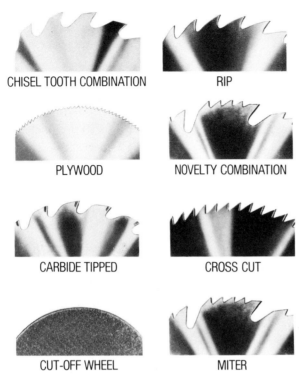

CHISEL TOOTH COMBINATION   RIP

PLYWOOD   NOVELTY COMBINATION

CARBIDE TIPPED   CROSS CUT

CUT-OFF WHEEL   MITER

Fig. 2-9.   The various blades that may be used in a home furniture-making shop.

will get plenty of use in your furniture-making workshop.

To install the blade on the arbor, first crank the arbor up to maximum elevation. Slip the blade onto the arbor, making sure that the teeth are pointing in the right direction. Place the washer on the arbor, and run the nut so that the wrench handle is resting against the front edge of the well. Grab the top edge of the blade and pull it firmly toward you, securely seating the retaining nut.

To remove a blade, reverse the procedure, wedging the front teeth of the blade with a wood block and pulling the wrench handle toward you.

Your saw will cut just as well with the blade raised all the way as it will with the blade barely clearing the top of the workpiece, but it won't cut as safely. Ideal adjustment of the blade is with the upper edge clearing the workpiece by about ¼ inch. The long cutting angle of the blade in this position will require a little more power to drive the saw, but by keeping the blade's angle of entry into the wood more nearly parallel to the direction of feed, you will reduce the danger of binding. The blade guard should always be used. (The photo-

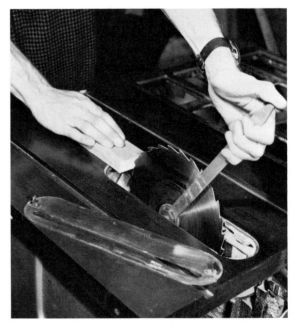

Fig. 2-10.   *Left:* To install the blade, hold the nut with the wrench and pull the blade toward you to tighten. *Right:* To remove the blade, wedge the teeth with a block of wood and pull the wrench toward you.

graphs in this book do not show the blade guard because the operations described can be seen more clearly without it.) The guard provides valuable protection to the operator and will also prevent the kerf from closing behind the blade and binding.

When you use the miter gauge, hook your thumb over the back edge of the gauge face; when cutting a mitered angle, use both hands. This double grip keeps the fingers out of harm's way and helps keep the workpiece from sliding on the gauge face and giving an inaccurate cut.

Don't stand directly in front of the blade. If you

Fig. 2-11.   The safest cutting position for the blade is ¼ inch above the top of the workpiece.

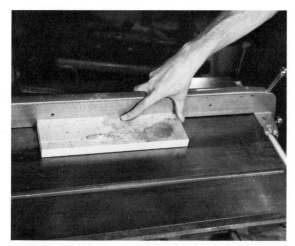

Fig. 2-12.   *Left:* When cutting, hook last three fingers over the fence and push work with the thumb. *Right:* For narrow rips use a push stick and hold work with other hand.

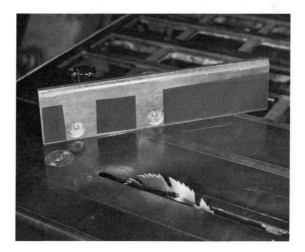

Fig. 2-13.   *Left:* Use both hands to cut mitered angle, holding work to gauge. *Right:* Miter gauge extension helps keep long boards under control.

use the gauge in the left slot, stand to the left of the blade; if you use it in the right, stand to the right. And never pick a free piece of wood off the table while the blade is running. It takes only a few seconds for the blade to stop after the switch has been turned off, and it's well worth the wait.

If you intend to do much angle-cutting with the miter gauge, make an extension for the face of the gauge and surface it with sandpaper. The extra length of the extension will make it much easier to keep long boards under control (for straight as well as for angle cuts), and the sandpaper on the face will keep the work from creeping sideways when you make acute-angle cuts.

Crosscutting. Since most of your lumber will have its greatest dimension in the direction of the grain, crosscutting is almost always done with the miter gauge, necessitating the placement of the wood crosswise on the saw table. If you intend to cut several short pieces from a long plank, lay out your cuts, allowing for saw kerf, and make the one nearest the middle first. If the plank is long enough so that it overhangs the edges of the table more than three-quarters of the table's width, or if it is so heavy that you have trouble holding it flat, make your first (center) cut with a hand saw and trim the edge on the table saw later. If the board is too wide to use the hand grip suggested previously, it can be held firmly in place by gripping its forward edge

Fig. 2-14.   To prevent binding, it sometimes is wise to keep the work "open" by using a screwdriver.

directly in front of the miter gauge with one hand while you push it through with the other hand on the gauge. If it is so wide that it completely covers the table in front of the blade, try reversing the miter gauge in its slot and pushing the work through behind the gauge. It may be necessary to stop the cut part of the way through to remove the gauge and refit it in the other end of the slot. If so, stop the saw before reversing the gauge!

When cutting warped pieces of wood with the miter gauge, use the same rule as with the rip fence: Keep the concave side down. If it is up, the workpiece can rock and will be likely to bind.

Binding and Kickback. Kickbacks occur when the blade binds in, or against, the workpiece and throws it back at the operator. Here are some common causes of kickback and how to avoid them:

1. Twisting the workpiece. This happens most often when you are trying to freehand-feed a large piece of lumber, such as a 4x8-foot plywood panel. When the wood is shifted laterally, it throws the kerf out of parallel with the blade and binds the saw. The possibility of the saw throwing a piece of wood this size is remote; all it will generally do is stall and perhaps blow a fuse from the overload on the motor. One way to cut a full-size sheet of plywood accurately is to clamp a straightedged board to the bottom of the sheet for use as a guide, letting it ride against the edge of the saw table as the wood is fed into the saw. The only other way to guard against binding when working with a large piece is to pencil-mark the cut before you start, feed slowly, and follow the line as closely as possible.

2. Binding between rip fence and blade. This will happen if the rip fence is out of parallel with the blade either because the alignment bar on the fence hasn't been adjusted properly or because the alignment bar wasn't tight against the front of the table when the fence was locked. To avoid the latter, always push firmly on the front edge of the fence before locking it in position. You also run the risk of binding when you feed a warped board with the convex side down, since this will permit rocking or twisting of the workpiece. When you rip a warped board, always feed with the concave side of the board against the surface of the table. The same holds true when ripping a board with a rabbeted edge; feed with the rabbet up. When ripping a board with a bowed or irregular edge, eliminate the possibility of binding (and ensure a true cut) by tacking a straight strip of wood to the edge of your workpiece so that you have a true edge to ride against the fence.

3. Stopping and restarting. Stopping the saw in the middle of a cut should be avoided whenever possible, but when this is absolutely necessary, the workpiece must be firmly held until the blade is completely stopped. Before restarting the saw, back the workpiece off the blade slightly and make sure that you have a firm grip to guard against binding and kickback. When possible, back the workpiece completely off the blade and refeed it.

4. Other causes. A dull or rusty blade will often bind, so keep the blade clean and sharp. Don't try to feed the work too fast; if you jam it into the blade, one of the teeth may hook into the wood instead of cutting through it. Use special caution with gummy or damp wood; feed it slowly and keep it tight against the table.

Keep your fingers away from the blade at all times! When you rip a small board or push through the end of a long one, hook your last three fingers over the top of the fence and use it for a guide. Use the forefinger to hold the work tight against the table and the thumb to push it along carefully. If the distance between the fence and the saw blade is less than the width of your hand, use a push stick. Once the front end of the work is past the blade, hold it down with one hand and work the push stick with the other. Never push a board through and leave the piece between the blade and the fence free—it may come flying back at you.

Cutting Duplicate Pieces. If you need to cut a quantity of duplicate pieces, you will get more precision and production by using either a miter gauge stop rod or a stop block. A stop rod can be purchased from your saw dealer; all you need for a stop block are a piece of wood and a clamp.

The stop block is made by clamping a small block of wood to the inside of the rip fence near the front of the saw. The fence is then positioned on one side of the saw blade and the miter gauge fitted in its slot on the other side. Adjust the rip fence so that the edge of the block is the same distance from the saw blade as the length of the pieces you want to cut. The work stock is then placed against the miter gauge with the end of the stock butted against the stop block on the fence. Slide the miter gauge up and make the cut, repeating the process for as many pieces as you need. Make sure that the stop block is set far enough back on the fence so that the end of the workpiece will clear the end of the block before it is cut free; if it does not, it may bind and kick back.

 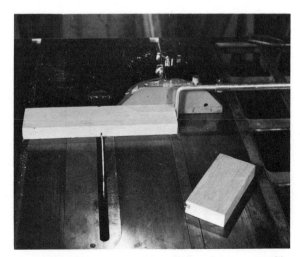

Fig. 2-15.   *Left:* A stop block clamped to the rip fence facilitates duplicate cutting. *Right:* A stop rod is set in the miter gauge on side away from the saw blade.

To set up a stop rod, fasten the rod in its hole in the miter gauge on the side opposite the saw blade. Adjust the rod so that the right-angle end is the same distance from the blade as you want your finished work and just clears the surface of the table. Cuts are made in the same way as with the stop block. Two points of caution should be observed when using a stop rod: Never set it so that the stop is closer to the saw blade than the center of the miter gauge, and never set up the stop rod with the stop on the opposite side of the saw blade from the miter gauge—it will bind every time. Both of these setups can be used for slotting, grooving, or dadoing operations on a series of duplicate pieces (see page 43).

Bevels, Miters, and Compound Cuts. Bevels are cuts made at an angle to the surface of the workpiece; miters are cuts made at an angle to the edge of the workpiece. Most saws are adjustable for cutting bevels of from 1 to 45 degrees by either tilting the saw blade or the saw table. Miter settings from 1 to 45 degrees can be made on the miter gauge. A compound cut is a bevel cut at an angle to the edge of the workpiece and is made by making the necessary adjustments on both the blade and the gauge.

Resawing. Resawing is the operation of standing a wide board on one edge and ripping it to produce two narrower ones. Because of the limitations as to how high you can elevate your saw blade, you will be restricted on the width of boards you can resaw. Maximum board width will be about 4¾ inches for an 8-inch saw and 6 ¼ inches on a 10-inch model. If the board is narrow enough, you can resaw it with a single pass, but most work will take two cuts. When two cuts are needed, adjust the saw blade to an elevation about ¼ inch higher than the center of the board to be cut. If your first cut goes much farther past the center, the kerf will close and bind the blade as you make the second pass; even if the blade does not bind, the closed kerf will throw the two sides out of parallel and the blade will cut into the outside board and ruin its surface. Adjust the fence and make your first cut, keeping the board tight against the fence and gripping it securely to guard against kickback. Now turn the board end

for end, keeping the same side against the fence, and make the second cut. Watch your fingers (you can't see the blade) and finish the cut by pushing the board through with a push stick. If the board is too wide, make a maximum-depth cut on each edge and finish the job with a hand saw; if there is a ridge remaining, it can be removed with a plane.

End-Cutting. Whether slotting, grooving, dadoing, or making the first cut for an edge rabbet, end-cutting requires special support if you are going to have a good, safe job. In end-cutting a large board, you will need a high support to prevent its rocking from side to side. Your rip fence probably already has holes in the side that can be used to attach a support panel; if it does not, it is a simple matter to drill some. Countersink holes in the panel and bolt it to the fence. Adjust the blade for depth and the fence for position, and make the cut in the normal manner. If you are working with a thin piece of wood, its front corner may drop into the blade slot in the table insert and snag when it gets to the rear of the slot; if this happens, just lift up slightly and finish the cut.

When you end-cut a small or narrow piece, the problem is rocking forward and backward rather than from side to side, and you will need a different support arrangement. Stand the workpiece on end and clamp it to another piece of wood about a foot long. The support piece should be lying on its side, and the clamp should be positioned so that it clears the top of the rip fence. With the support block riding against the edge of the rip fence, feed the work through the saw blade. Be sure that the clamp is tight enough so that the workpiece can't be upset and kicked back.

Cutting Stopped Grooves and Gains. A stopped groove is a groove in the edge of a board that stops before it reaches the end. A gain is the same thing closed at both ends instead of just one. Both are used primarily in making joints. Since you can't see the saw blade when cutting these, it is difficult to know when the groove is up to the end of the board and to make sure you don't go too far and run it all the way out. A stop block (for gains you need two) clamped to the side of the rip fence is the solution if your fence is long enough to get the blocks where

Fig. 2-16. *Left:* Adjust blade carefully when making a bevel cut. *Above:* To make a compound cut, adjust both the blade and the miter gauge.

Fig. 2-17. *Left:* Attach a support to the rip fence when edge-cutting a large board. *Right:* To end-cut a small board, clamp it to a larger piece of wood.

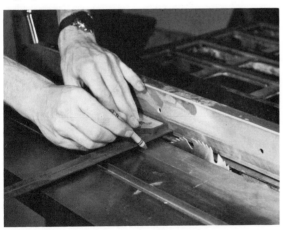

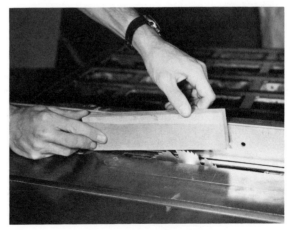

Fig. 2-18. *Left:* To cut an end groove, mark the location of the blade edges on the saw table. *Right:* Then carefully lower the work-piece onto the blade where the lines indicate.

you need them for the length of the piece you are grooving. Otherwise simply raise your blade to the required height, line up a square with the edge of the blade and the side of the rip fence, and make a mark on the table with a crayon to show the location of the blade edges in relation to the ends of the workpiece. Adjust the fence, turn on the saw, line up one end of the work with the mark, and lower it down on the blade. Advance the workpiece until the other end of the desired groove lines up with the other mark, and you will have a perfect cut every time.

Accessories. There are several so-called accessories available that make a circular saw even more valuable as furniture-making tool. Possibly the most valuable of these is the dado head, which may be used to cut dadoes, grooves, and rabbets. (A dado is a slot that runs across the grain; a groove is one that runs with the grain; a rabbet is a steplike cut made on the end or edge of a board.) The dado head is composed of two outside saw blades and a set of chippers. If two or more chippers are used, they should be spaced as equally as possible around the circumference of the assembled head to avoid vibration. First mount one of the saw blades, which are the combination type, on the saw arbor. Then mount one or more chipper blades. The cutting edges of the chipper blades are swaged, or spread.

Fig. 2-19.   *Left:* A dado set consists of two outside blades and several chippers. The number of chippers between the blades adjusts the dado width. *Right:* The four metal disks of the dado sawing washer set can be adjusted so the blade "wobbles" as it rotates, cutting a dado slot.

 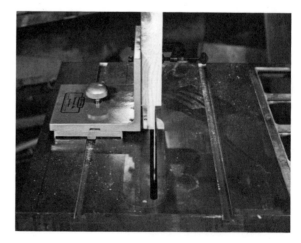

Fig. 2-20.   *Left:* The tenoning jig is valuable for making precision joints. *Right:* A clamp holds the workpiece firmly and in the correct position. The tenoning jig slides freely in the miter gauge slot, while keeping the operator's hands safely clear of the rotating blade.

The chipper cutting edges should coincide with the gullets (the space between tips of adjacent saw teeth) of both saw blades. If the saw blades have both crosscut and raker teeth, the chipper cutting edges should coincide with the raker teeth gullets. After the assembled dado head is placed in position, replace the outer washer and the arbor nut. Be sure to tighten the arbor nut securely. If the dado set is too wide, the outside washer can be left off. The guard and splitter assembly should be removed when the dado head is used. Whenever the dado head is used, the dado insert plate should be placed in the saw table.

A tenoning jig is a valuable gadget that makes easy work of precision joints. The jig was used in making most of the joints that are described later in this chapter.

Neat dovetail joints can be easily cut with a dovetail blade, a ¼-inch-thick, 6-inch-long blade that has the faces of all its teeth beveled in the same direction at 15 degrees. To cut a dovetail, mount the blade, set the elevation, and crank the tilt over to a 15-degree angle to the surface of the saw table, thus setting the face of the blade teeth parallel to it. The female cut is made in two passes using the miter gauge; the workpiece is reversed between the first and second passes. The male cut is made with the tenoning jig in the same manner, again reversing

Fig. 2-21.   *Top left:* Molding cutter head with knives for cutting molding and trim with a table saw. *Top right:* Close-up of molding cutter and its fence. *Bottom left and right:* Actual cutting of the head.

the workpiece between cuts, but from the end rather than from the surface.

The molding cutter is another frequently used attachment. The cutter head replaces the regular blade and converts the saw to a shaper. By using the various blades that are available, you can make your own moldings and trim. A typical molding head assembly is composed of the molding head, an Allen-type wrench, a spacer bushing, and ½- and ⅜- inch arbor bushing. The head should be assembled as follows:

1. Insert each cutter blade into the head with the cutting (high) edge toward the front, and secure with the lock screws.

2. Install the molding head in place of the regular saw blade, with the cutting edges facing the saw. As the regular saw insert plate can't be used in the table, it will be necessary to use a molding cutter insert plate.

It is easy to adapt your rip fence to a molding cutter fence as follows:

1. Make two ¾- inch auxiliary fence boards the exact height and length of the rip fence.

2. From a ¾-inch-thick piece of scrap lumber, make a shim board the exact height and length of the rip fence.

3. Place the rip fence in operating position on the saw table.

4. Place the shim board against the rip fence and one auxiliary board against the shim board so that they will match the height and length of the rip fence.

5. All three parts should be securely clamped together and the rip fence clamped into position so the auxiliary board will be over the cutter head.

6. Use a set of planer and jointer cutter blades in the head to cut a semicircular notch in the bottom edge of the auxiliary board for cutter clearance.

7. The cutter blades should be below the top of the table when the work is placed in position.

8. Start the saw and gradually raise the height of the molding head, taking as many shallow cuts as necessary to cut the notch 1 inch deep. Feed work slowly.

9. Prepare the other auxiliary fence board in like manner and mount the two boards on opposite sides of the rip fence with countersunk bolts and nuts.

Other joint-cutting techniques and uses of the circular saw can be found in Chapter 4.

The Saber Saw
The portable circular saw is seldom found in a well-equipped furniture-making shop; the table type is much more popular. However, there is a useful portable power saw, the saber saw. A compact and inexpensive tool that can do the work of almost any other type of hand or power saw, the saber saw cuts

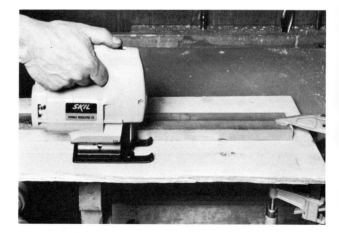

Fig. 2-22.   *Left:* Edge guides are available for most saber saws, enabling you to cut a parallel line to any straight edge. Note left hand holding the guide snug and parallel to the edge of the lumber. *Right:* Straight cuts can also be made by C-clamping a straightedge and running the edge of the saber saw against a straightedge.

with a reciprocating action. Its blades usually measure from 3 to 4 inches in length. This is adequate for cutting through a conventional 2x4, but a few models also have extra-length blades that can cut lumber up to 5 inches thick.

Blades are available for both wood or metal in various styles and grades of coarseness. Some have six to seven teeth per inch for rough woodcutting, while others, for smoother results, come with ten teeth to the inch. In addition blades vary as to set

Fig. 2-23.   The double-edge blade enables you to push the saw forward or to pull it backward. It is very handy for working in tight corners.

and in the way they are ground. Those with wide-set teeth are for rapid and rough cutting, while hollow-ground models are for a finished cut in plywood and veneer.

Metal-cutting saber saw blades usually have either fourteen or thirty-two teeth to the inch; thus you can select the blade that is best for the thickness and hardness of the metal being cut. To permit cutting flush up against a wall or into a corner, some companies also make special offset blades, which project forward so that the teeth are in line with the front of the baseplate.

The two features that first made the saber saw popular are undoubtedly its ability to cut all kinds of curves with ease and its ability to make a starting hole in the middle of a board or panel, thus eliminating the necessity of first drilling a starting hole. It can cut curves because the blades are comparatively narrow and only a short turning radius is required. Plunge cuts, which enable you to make cutouts in the center of a panel or board, are possible because of the unique cutting action of the blade, which tapers to a semipoint at the tip. Tip the saw forward so that it rests on the front edge of the baseplate; then, with the motor running, gradually rock it back into its normal cutting position while allowing the blade to chip its way through the panel. When the saw breaks through

Fig. 2-24.   *Above:* Plunge-cutting is best accomplished with saws having orbital action. The thumb of your hand is used to steady the saw as the plunge is made. *Right:* Plunge-cutting permits you to use the saber saw to cut such intricate work as this chair back.

 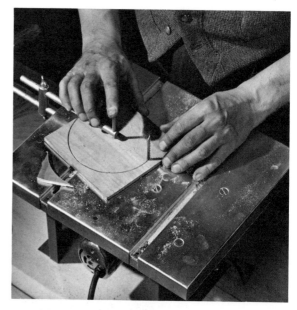

Fig. 2-25.   *Above:* With an edge guide mounted upside-down and a nail through a hole in the edge guide, precise circles can easily be cut. *Right:* A table for the saber saw also allows you to cut circles.

and comes back to its normal position with the base flat against the surface, you can finish the cut in the usual manner. Since the teeth on a saber saw blade point upward, the blade does all its cutting on the upstroke. Therefore, for a smooth edge on the finished, or face, side, panel cuts should be made from the back. If any splintering takes place, it will be on the back where it can't be seen.

Although helpful in ripping, the accessory guide has its limitations, most important of which is the width of the rip it lets you make. When the guide's capacity is insufficient to rip a long board, tack or clamp a straightedge to the workpiece. For shorter cuts a steel square provides a handy and accurate line.

Many saber saws have provision for cutting arcs and circles of various sizes. Most craftsmen use the rip guide here, too. You'll find a small hole at each end of the part of the guide that is parallel to the direction of cutting. A small nail driven through one of these holes into the workpiece will provide a pivot point around which the saw will swing as it cuts. The radius of the arc or circle is equal to the distance from the center of the pivot point to

the cutting edge of the blade. Set the guide accordingly.

Because the speeds that are best for cutting wood are higher than those that are ideal for metal, many of the newer models of saber saws are available with variable speed controls. Some have a choice of two or three speeds, while others have infinitely variable speed controls. Table 2-1 gives the preferred speed for cutting various materials.

Most of the better-quality saber saws have bases that can be tilted 45 degrees to permit accurate miter-cutting and beveling. Some will tilt either left or right, while others will tilt to one side only. In addition, a few of the newest models also have rotating or scroller blades, which can be turned in any direction while sawing without turning the body of the saw. In other words, while you're guiding the body of the saw with one hand, your other hand can turn a knob at the top to rotate the blade in any direction for intricate curved cutting and for maximum control of scrollwork.

Most new saber saws offer double-insulated, shockproof models, with plastic housings and special internal insulation which eliminate the need

Table 2-1

CUTTING SPECIFICATIONS

Class of material	Material to be cut	Type of cut	Speed of blade	Blade teeth per inch
WOOD	Soft woods ¾ ″ or thicker	Rough	Fastest	7
	Soft woods under ¾ ″ thick	Fine	Medium	10
	Soft woods up to 2 ″ thick	Smooth	Medium	6
	Hard & wet woods under ¾ ″	Smooth	Medium	7
	Plywoods ½ ″ to ¾ ″	Smooth	Medium	10
	Hard & wet woods ¾ ″ & thicker	Smooth	Medium	6
	Plywood up to 1 ″	Fine	Medium	10
	Plywood ¾ ″ & under	Medium Fine	Medium Fast	7
	Plywood ¾ ″ to 1 ″ thick	Coarse	Fast	5
METALS	Iron and steel ³⁄₁₆ ″ to ⅜ ″ & brass, bronze copper aluminum to ⅛ ″	Fine	Slow	14
	Hard steel, iron ¹⁄₆₄ ″ to ³⁄₃₂ ″	Fine	Slow	32
	Iron and steel ⅛ ″ to ¼ ″	Smooth	Medium	18
	Iron and steel ¹⁄₁₆ ″ to ³⁄₁₆ ″	Fine	Medium	24
	Aluminum, brass, bronze, copper, ¼ ″ to ½ ″ thick	Smooth	Medium	10
PLASTICS	Plastic tile, lucite, nylon, linoleum, fiber, plastic laminates, plexiglass, rubber ¼ ″ to 1 ″ thick	Fine	Medium	10
	Same as above	Smooth	Fast	5

for the third ground wire. The tool has an ordinary two-prong plug that eliminates the need for adaptors in older outlets.

The Bandsaw

In woodworking the bandsaw is able to cut all kinds of curves, curves in combination with straight cuts, and dimensional compound cuts. If this isn't enough, it will perform these tasks with stock up to 6 inches thick!

Most home-workshop bandsaws are designed with continuous one-piece blades that track around two large, rubber-faced wheels. The average model has a working "throat" capacity (distance from the working edge of blade to the rear blade guard)

of about 14 inches. The secret of the saw's tremendous cutting ability (unlike the reciprocating blade action of the scroll saw) is the band principle: the blade's teeth speed steadily through the work. This action delivers double the cutting action at the same blade speed—and discharges the sawdust.

One limitation does exist: the blade cannot be threaded through an auger hole for inside cuts. To do so, it would have to be cut and then rewelded. To stabilize the cutting edge of the blade and keep it from wandering, there are two guide assemblies. The upper guide is fitted to a sliding arm that can be raised or lowered, depending on the thickness of the work. The bottom guide is mounted on the saw

Fig. 2-26. *Right:* To cut a tenon in a narrow piece of wood, clamp it between two scrap strips to provide adequate surface for baseplate of saw to ride on. Cut part with narrow edge up first. *Far right:* Make second part of tenon cut with wide surface of part up; then make short cuts inward to remove sections.

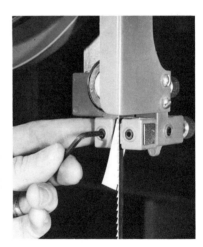

Fig. 2-27.   The bandsaw. *Left:* The back edge of the blade should barely clear the back roller, and bear against it only when cutting. *Center:* A view of the second back roller, under the table. *Right:* To adjust the side guides properly, set a blade clearance equal to the thickness of a piece of paper. If the guides are too loose when cutting stock, the blade will always twist to the side.

frame below the tilting table. Each of the guide assemblies consists of a pair of adjustable side guide blocks that keep the blade from twisting. A back roller prevents the blade from being pushed off the wheels.

Proper blade adjustment is indicated when there is just enough clearance for a slip of paper to be inserted between the blade and one of the blocks. The rear roller should be set to not quite touch the back edge of the blade (except when force is exerted on the leading edge of the blade, as in cutting).

Blade tension is adjusted when light finger pressure on the side deflects it about ⅛ inch (with the upper blade guide set at its highest position).

Tracking is controlled by the tilt adjustment on the upper wheel. Correct setting is achieved when the blade tracks close to the center of the idler wheels' rubber rims.

Another important adjustment is that blade alignment must run at exactly 90 degrees to the table surface. Check with a small square. Once set, it rarely requires further attention. If a minor adjustment is necessary from time to time, turn the tilt-stop screw underneath the table.

Choosing the Right Blade. Woodcutting blades for the bandsaw are available in a variety of widths, each serving a particular use. A good rule of thumb to keep in mind is that the narrower the blade, the more capable it is of cutting the tighter curves.

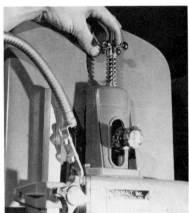

Fig. 2-28. *Far left:* The blade should track in the center of the wheel's rubber facing. *Left:* Adjust by tilting the idler wheel with the double knobs.

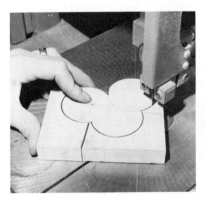

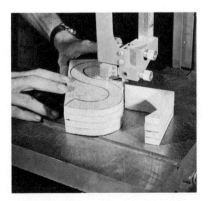

Fig. 2-29. *Left:* Radial relief cuts help ease the technique of turning inside corners, allowing scrap stock to fall away as the cut progresses. *Center:* Bandsaw demonstrates its great depth-of-cut capacity on 6x6 stock. *Right:* Multiple, or "pad," sawing permits the operator to make duplicate pieces in one operation; the stacked stock is nailed together in scrap areas.

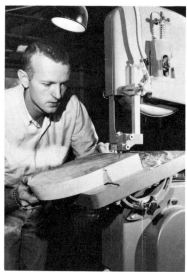

Fig. 2-30.   *Right:* The bandsaw equipped with an all-purpose blade can cut nonferrous metals as well as plastics and wood. Commonly used blades vary in width from ⅛ inch to ¾ inch and are called narrow bandsaws. A popular width is ¼ inch, which is used for all curve cutting and for most straight cuts. *Far right:* By tilting the table to any desired angle, a round can be cut with a beveled edge, eliminating most of the roughing work usually required on a lathe-shaping project.

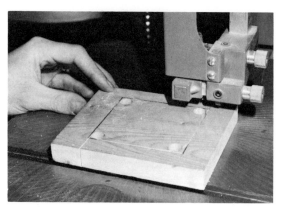

Fig. 2-31.   *Above:* Relief holes help to cut inside corners when making cutouts. *Right:* Make center-finding end crosscut by tilting table 45 degrees and setting fence just clear of blade.

Under normal conditions, a ¾-inch blade will cut 1¾-inch radii; a ½-inch blade will cut 1¼-inch radii; a ⅜-inch blade will cut 1-inch radii; a ¼-inch blade will cut ¾-inch radii; a 3/16-inch blade will cut ½-inch radii; and a ⅛-inch blade will cut ¼-inch radii.

When cutting a tight curve, it helps to make radial or tangent relief cuts from the work edge to the pattern edge. This technique allows scrap stock to fall away as the cut progresses, providing more maneuverability for blade action in tight spots. Sharp curves often may be cut easily by first drilling a hole near the turn. Square corners are cut out by first cutting a radius, then returning to saw out the corner from each side. Get the feel of the blade with a few practice cuts. Don't force work against the blade in excess of the cutting capacity.

When making a straight cut, as in resawing, maintain a straight-cut line parallel to the sides of the saw table. Occasionally the blade may develop a tendency to veer right or left—a condition called "lead." This may be the result of unusual wood grain (corrected by temporarily increasing blade tension) or worn and twisted blade guides. But it is

Fig. 2-32. A setup for producing identical-length crosscuts when a stop rod is not available. Clamp a block of scrap stock to the saw table as shown and use it as a measuring stop. Set the stop back from the blade so that the workpiece will not bind.

most often the result of an imbalanced set to the teeth (more bite on one side of the blade). New blades of cheaper quality may have "lead." However, the condition may also result from normal wear or from cutting through a nail, dulling one side of the blade.

Leads can be corrected by lightly touching the sides of the blade with a fine oilstone while the machine is in operation. Overuse of this remedy can dull the blade.

One big advantage of the bandsaw, as noted, is its depth of cut. Several identical pieces can be cut at the same time. The operation is called "pad" sawing because boards are stacked in a pad, nailed together (through the scrap area), and cut as a single block. When making this type cut, be sure that the nailed scrap portion is part of the last cut.

It is a simple matter to fold bandsaw blades into small spiral of thirds, if you follow instructions carefully. Avoid kinking the blade. Always hold it firmly and don't let it twist in your hand while folding. Teeth are toward you. Twist with arrows as in Fig. 2-33 and keep following through, gradually moving hands closer together, until the blade flops into a spiral. If you fail on the first try, keep at it—it will suddenly come to you. Do not kink the blade.

Compound Cuts. Cuts that are made on all four

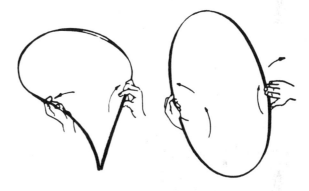

Fig. 2-33. To fold or coil a bandsaw blade, grasp it as shown above and twist slowly.

sides of the work are known as compound cuts. One example is in the profiling of a design. There are two approaches.

1. If the first cut can be made to produce a single piece of scrap, the scrap can be tacked or taped back on the work. In this manner you will have a firm, flat surface to work with when making the second, right-angled cut. When all cuts are completed, the scrap is finally removed.

2. Intricate designs, producing a number of small scrap pieces, prohibit taping or tacking. Instead, drive a nail into the work. This provides a

"leg" that will support the work in the upright position required for the second cut.

Almost all bandsaws have tilting tables that permit bevel resawing. This operation is used as a handy way to produce strips of lumber with a tapered cross section. These strips make exceptionally fine blanks for cutting running molding. Most of the waste is eliminated, and the profile of the stock allows a very shallow cut during the shaping operation. Practice with a few test cuts. One pass on the bandsaw will produce two identical strips.

By setting the table tilt at 45 degrees, the bandsaw will cut your stock for glue blocks. The setting also makes center-finding crosscuts in the ends of turning squares (when turning wood on the lathe). When making these or other bevel cuts in a straight line, always use either a rip fence or a piece of scrap stock clamped to the table. Work is thus positioned at the center, securely supported.

The rip fence can also be used for cutting curved sections of uniform width. First the outside curve is cut freehand. Then the fence is set at a distance from the blade that equals the finished work. For the second inside cut keep the crown of the curve (the outside cut) against the fence as the work is fed through the saw.

Crosscuts of Equal Length. The bandsaw will do a good job of crosscutting boards, depending on the saw's throat capacity. Use the miter gauge to hold crosscuts square or at a predetermined angle.

If there is need to cut a series of equal-length pieces, use a piece of scrap stock clamped to the table (to serve as a stop block). For a small investment you may also purchase a set of miter gauge stop rods designed for this purpose.

Wood is not the only material the bandsaw can handle. With special or multipurpose blades you can cut brass, aluminum, and most other nonferrous metals. Plastics are easily cut and patterned. With the addition of a speed-reducing unit and another special blade, the bandsaw can even slice through steel.

The Jigsaw

The jigsaw, or scroll saw as it is sometimes called, is an ancient device. It probably got its name from

Fig. 2-34. *Left:* To make a compound cut, put the scrap from the first cut back in place; this affords a flat surface for making the second cut at right angles. *Right:* At times it is not practical or possible to replace scrap from compound cuts for the purpose of temporarily restoring the straight-line guides. An alternate technique makes use of nail supports driven into the workpiece at an angle and depth that produce the same effect. Nail holes can be filled with putty after second cut.

the early use made of such a saw—sawing out scrolls and fretwork. In today's home furniture-making shop the power jigsaw is slowly being replaced by the saber saw. The latter is more versatile and performs the same tasks as does the jig type, like cutting on the inside of an enclosure or cutting around an exterior outline. Its principal use is for cutting out enclosures. A jigsaw may be used for sawing metals as well as wood and fiber. For cutting metal a special blade should be used.

The essential parts of a jigsaw are a supporting frame, table, top and bottom chucks, a top guide, a motor, and blower arrangement to keep the sawdust away from the cutting blade. Some machines have a lower guide, too. Frequently the top guide functions as a hold-down as well as a guide. The capacity of a jigsaw is limited by the distance from the saw to the column and the thickness of stock it will cut. Few jigsaws will cut stock thicker than 2 inches.

The speed of jigsaws varies from about 500 to 1,800 rpm or more. Some machines are equipped with a speed control that enables you to increase or decrease the rpm. Ordinarily it's desirable to decrease the speed when cutting curves, especially sharp curves. The actual cutting procedure is the same as for cutting on the bandsaw. Never attempt to follow a line continuously from one end to the other. Pick out the most prominent parts of the curve or pattern. First cut these out and then return to the smaller and more intricate sections. An inside cut must be started from a hole that has previously been bored. Insert the blade in the hole, mount it on the saw, and make the inside cut.

The Radial Arm Saw

Radial arm saws are, after circular saws, easily the second most popular stationary electric tool available to the home furniture-maker. The key to the rising popularity of this type of saw is its immense versatility. There is almost no woodcutting operation that you cannot do on a radial arm saw.

Pioneered by the DeWalt Co. in the 1920s when it was an experimental oddity, it is now made by several major manufacturers for home use in 8-, 9-, and 10-inch sizes of blade diameter. A radial arm saw has a movable arm that can swing around in a complete horizontal circle. The arm is the radius of such a circle, hence the term *radial*. The arm is a three-sided steel channel mounted at the rear on a steel post. Riding a set of tracks on the lower edges of the arm is a carriage that can move back and forth along the length of the arm—about 24 inches.

The motor is carried between the arms of a yoke, or fork, attached to the carriage and is pivoted at the sides so that it can turn in a full circle vertically inside the yoke. The motor can also be turned horizontally along with its yoke in a full circle. Some models have a double arm—a fixed upper arm pivoted to a lower arm that can move in a full circle.

The table of a radial saw has three sections, all of equal length but different widths. The outermost and widest section is fixed, while the other sections are narrower and movable. Most tables are made of chipboard, plywood, or some other material that resists warping. The guide rail, or fence, which protrudes an inch above the level of the table, can be inserted between any of the sections and thus vary the usable width of the table. The fence has slots in it that permit the saw blade to pass through it for straight, miter, and bevel cuts.

In the surface of the fixed section of the table there are shallow grooves leading from the slots to the outer edge. These grooves permit the teeth of the blade to go slightly below the surface of the table in order to cut entirely through the piece of wood. When the saw is being used, the movable sections of the table and the fence are pressed tightly together against the fixed section and held firmly in place by a pair of clamps or screws operated from the front or back of the machine.

Crosscutting. Suppose you want to cut through a piece of 1x4. Put the blade in the crosscut position behind the fence at the back end of the overhead arm. Place the 1x4 on the table against the front of the fence. If you have drawn a line on the 1x4 to mark the place where the cut is to be made, the line must be in front of the slot in the fence through which the saw must pass. Hold the 1x4 firmly against the fence with one hand and with the other hand draw the saw blade forward along its overhead track until it passes through the 1x4. Then push the saw back to the rear end of the track behind the fence. Although you'll find yourself holding the work tight against the fence with your free hand, it isn't actually necessary. Since crosscutting with the radial arm saw is done with what is known as a climbing cut, the force of the cutting action alone is sufficient to hold the work in place against the fence. In fact, when cutting thick or hard stock, it may be necessary actually to hold back the carriage and keep the blade from jamming from too rapid a feed.

Stock wider than 12 inches may be handled in several ways. By loosening the lock screws at the rear of the table and positioning the fence behind the spacer block, you can extend the length of crosscut by a couple of inches. If this won't do the trick, make a first cut, then reverse the stock and finish the cut from the other side. A special accessory can be purchased for most saws which will extend the arm length by 6 inches. Very wide pieces can be handled by making the first cut, moving the fence all the way to the back of the table, and extending the cut. When the carriage is against the front stop, lift the front of the workpiece up so that the cut is extended to the full forward edge of the blade.

Ripping. To perform this operation, the blade is brought forward in front of the fence and raised a little above the surface of the table. Raising the arm (and with it the motor and blade) is accomplished by turning a crank, which in some models is at the front and in others is at the top of the post that supports the arm. After loosening a locking lever, the motor is turned around until the blade is parallel with the fence. The locking lever is closed again, and the arm is cranked down until the bottom teeth of the blade almost touch the curved bottom of a very shallow trench in the surface of the table. Extending from the fence to the front edge, the trench, like the grooves mentioned before, allows the teeth of the blade to go slightly below the table surface.

If you want to cut a 3-inch strip from a board,

Fig. 2-35. The plow-cutting operation being done with a dado head in the rip position.

move the blade until it is exactly 3 inches from the fence. A scale on the side of the arm tells you how far the blade is from the fence, or you can measure this space with a ruler. The carriage that rides the arm is locked by turning a lever or knob to keep the blade fixed in its position. Adjust the antikickboard device at the back of the blade guard to the thickness of the board. (All this takes longer to tell than to do. Actually it takes only about one or two minutes to set the saw for ripping.)

Now place the board on the table against the fence and push it into the saw with steady, even pressure until the end of the board is cut through.

To cut a 4x8-foot sheet of plywood down the middle or to do some other wide ripping job, move the fence to the farthest position in the rear. Instead of facing the fence, the blade would be turned around 180 degrees and moved to the front edge of the table. Then place the panel face up on the table and push it along the fence until it is cut.

Mitering. To make the cuts for miter joints, first raise the arm so the blade will clear the fence. Then turn the locking lever to free the arm for movement. Next swing the arm to the right or left to a 45-degree position, where an indexing pin (on most models) may stop it automatically. There is also a scale that you can use for angles other than 45 degrees. Lower the arm until the blade is in its cutting position behind the fence. Place the molding or other piece against the fence, and pull

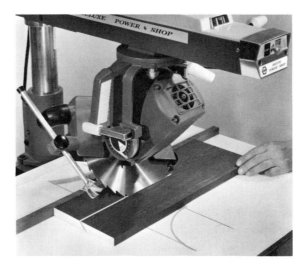

Fig. 2-36.   Two bevel cuts.

the blade forward through the mitering slot in the fence until it cuts through the wood at exactly 45 degrees. The resulting cut is so accurate that the pieces fit together for perfect miter joints.

Beveling. Bevels can be cut in the crosscutting or ripping positions by tilting the blade to a 45-degree or any other angle. To tilt the blade, you just pull out a plunger or indexing pin and open a locking lever and turn the blade down to the desired angle. On most saws the blade will automatically be stopped at 45 degrees by a pin or spring-loaded plunger. For any other angle you read the bevel scale and lock the blade in position desired.

Bevel-Mitering. A bevel miter (sometimes referred to as a double, combination, or compound miter) is nothing more than a miter cut with the saw blade set in a bevel position. Adjust the motor and blade for the desired angle of bevel, set the arm for the required miter angle, and proceed just as you would when cutting a regular miter.

End-Cutting. Sometimes, as in the case of mortise and tenon joints, it is necessary to make cuts across the end of a long or narrow piece of stock. The easiest way to do this is to tip the motor on end in the yoke, then lower the blade to the required height. The depth of the cut is set by moving the carriage on the arm and locking it in position. The stock may now be end-cut by butting the end against the fence and pushing it through with a piece of square scrap. Cuts may be made in

this manner using either the regular or dado blades. The same setup, without the push block, is used for making edge cuts.

Cutting Duplicate Pieces. Cutting a number of pieces of stock to the same length is a simple matter if you use a stop block clamped to the fence or table. However, you will have to be careful that sawdust doesn't accumulate in the corner formed

Fig. 2-37.   The compound miter cut, frequently used in making picture frames, is easy to accomplish with a radial arm saw.

by the block and the fence and keep the work from butting up tight against your guide.

Accessories. There is a tremendous variety of gadgets that add to the usefulness of a radial arm saw. Most of them permit you to do things that cannot be done with a saw blade. Others do what a saw blade can do but do it faster and more conveniently. Some accessories such as dado heads, sanding disks, and molding cutter heads used in shaping can be put on the front arbor where saw blades are placed. Others can be attached to a rear shaft with a threaded adapter or by means of a standard-geared chuck screwed onto the shaft.

Dado Head Operations. The dado head for the radial arm saw is exactly the same as for conventional saws, consisting of a pair of outside cutting blades and an assortment of chipper blades. Place the ¼-inch arbor collar on the shaft. Next mount one of the outside cutter blades and then the chippers to achieve the needed width. Finish by mounting the other cutter blade and securing the assembly with the brass arbor nut.

Operation of the dado head is almost identical to that of the regular saw blade. The main difference

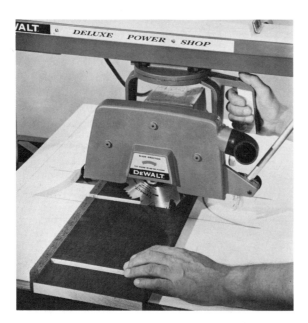

Fig. 2-38.   To make a dado cut, replace saw blade with dado head. Use it for across- or angle-dado cuts as you would use a saw blade.

is that dado cuts do not go completely through the work. There are two simple ways to adjust the saw accurately for the depth you want your cut. One is to use a rule and mark on the side of the stock where the bottom of the dado should be; then you lower the column until the bottom of the dado head lines up with the mark. The other method is to lower the column until the bottom of the dado head just touches the surface of the work. Depth is then set by further lowering the column, keeping in mind that each full turn of the elevating crank moves the column up or down exactly ⅛ inch. The work must be removed from below the dado head before turning the crank.

To avoid mistakes and minor inaccuracies in cutting dados, it is a good idea to mark both sides of the cut. If you're cutting a plain dado (across the grain), it sometimes helps to use a piece of scrap stock for a new fence and make your first cut in the fence. In this way the cut in the fence gives you an exact reference for lining up your workpiece.

Blind dados, or gains, can be cut by raising the saw so the work will slide under it without contacting the blades. After positioning the work, lower the saw and make the cut. When the cut is completed, stop the saw, raise it, and remove the work. Square the ends with a chisel. Making a series of these cuts, or repeating the operation on a quantity of workpieces, can often be simplified by clamping stop blocks to the table or fence.

Disk and Drum Sanding. Flat sanding can be done in any position by pasting a sandpaper disk to the face of a metal disk that screws onto the arbor. Tilt the motor upright so that the disk is horizontal and pass rough boards between the disk and the table to smooth them and get them down to precise dimensions. The disk can be tilted 45 degrees to sand bevels smooth, or you can do edge-sanding by putting the disk in a fixed position in the middle of a special fence and making repeated passes with the edge against the face of the whirling disk. And, of course, you can do freehand sanding against the disk of small objects, especially with outside curves.

There are also cylindrical, or drum, sanders that fit on the arbor with an adapter supplied by the manufacturer. Small drum sanders in diameters

Fig. 2-39.   To sand with radial arm saw, place disk sander directly on motor spindle.

such as 1, 1¾ inches, and 3 inches are especially useful in smoothing curved inside edges.

Drilling and Routing. Drilling with a radial arm saw is always done horizontally. To set the saw up for drilling, a geared chuck of ¼- or ⅜-inch capacity is screwed to the rear shaft of the motor, and a drill bit is inserted in the chuck. The position in which the motor is placed depends on the kind of drilling to be done. If, for example, you want to drill holes in the end of a 2x4, place the motor and

chuck parallel to the fence. Place the 2x4 on a jig (a raised platform about 2 inches high with a fence of its own) so that its end lines up with the point of the drill. Then push the wood forward on the jig into the drill to the desired depth. If the saw is the double-arm type, the lower arm and its track are positioned parallel to the fence and the drill is pushed along the track.

If you want to drill holes into a board, place the arm in the crosscut position, and swing the motor about so that the drill is directly under the arm, pointing to the post at the back of the table. Then clamp the board in position in front of the post, and push the drill along the track and into the board. Drills over ¾ inch should not be used because they require slower speed than that of the saw.

Routing on the radial arm saw is similar to drilling. The routing bit is inserted in the same geared chuck on the rear shaft, but the motor—instead of being horizontal—is tilted to a vertical position so that the chuck and its bit point down toward the table.

In routing either feed the wood into the bit or move the bit through the wood. To make a groove down the length of a board, bring the routing bit out along the arm to the point where it would be in the path of the board as it was being pushed along the fence—in other words the wood would be fed

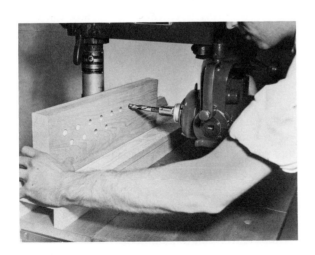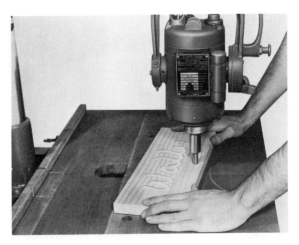

Fig. 2-40.   Both drilling (*left*) and routing (*right*) operations can be performed with radial arm saw if proper accessories are used.

into the bit. In freehand routing you also move the material instead of the bit. Thus when you recess a design or shape, say $\frac{1}{16}$ inch below the surface, you bring the bit down $\frac{1}{16}$ inch in the middle of the design and lock it in that position. Then you move the wood around under the bit until all the stock is removed in the design.

To make straight grooves across the grain, pull the bit along the overhead arm through the wood. Routers work best at high speeds, about 18,000 to 20,000 rpm. However, since most radial saw motors do not develop more than 3,400 rpm, the resulting fineness of cut can only be classed as pretty good, compared to the really fine smoothness achieved at higher speeds.

Shaping. You can make your own moldings and shape the edges of cabinet doors and furniture parts with the accessories offered by most radial saw manufacturers. The type of accessory usually used on this saw is a molding cutter head, a metal disk with three identical cutters fastened to the rim. Also available is a three-lipped single cutter. Any of these accessories is mounted on the front shaft, or arbor, of the motor in place of the blade. The motor is placed in a vertical position with its arbor pointing down so that the molding cutter head operates horizontally. A special fence or an auxiliary table with its own fence is necessary when using the shaper. These are very simple devices (jigs) that you can make yourself. Diagrams and

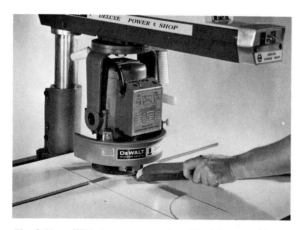

Fig. 2-41. With the proper guard and jig, it is no problem to do circular shaping with a radial arm machine.

drawings showing how to make them are usually included in the owner's manuals that are packed with the saw along with instructions on how to use the various cutters. A special guard must be used with these shaper cutters to protect your fingers.

OTHER HAND CUTTING TOOLS

Two of the most important group of tools in home furniture-maker's workshop are chisels and rasps. Both are excellent cutting tools.

Wood Chisels

Wood chisels are basically knives. The blades, which range from $\frac{1}{4}$ inch to 2 inches wide, should be kept razor-sharp and square. It's not a bad idea to give them a honing stroke or two on a hard, fine-grit oilstone before each use to ensure top performance.

If there is a nick in the blade, grind the end of it square enough to remove the nick. Then regrind the bevel, dipping the blade in water frequently to keep it from getting too hot and losing its temper. (For all-around work the best bevel angle is between 25 and 30 degrees. If you're doing most of your work on hardwood, make the angle a bit steeper—between 30 and 35 degrees.) Now carefully hone the blade, bevel down, first on a coarse grit, then on a very fine oilstone. Use plenty of oil as you hone, and finish by giving the flat side a few very light strokes to remove the fine wire edge that builds up during sharpening. After any sharpening, touchup, or complete regrinding, a good way to check sharpness is to see if the edge can cleanly slice a sheet of newspaper. If it tears or cuts raggedly, more honing is required.

Although many wood chisels have steel button inserts in the top of the handle so that you can use a metal hammer with them, you'll get better results and longer wear with a wood mallet or soft-face hammer. On wood-handle chisels a soft-face hammer is a must, or you'll soon find the end of the handle looking like a misplaced mushroom. For delicate work we find that the heel of a hand gives better control than a hammer.

As with most tools, there are proper techniques

to get best results. The grain of most milled lumber does not exactly follow the length of the board; it usually angles slightly. In such cases if you cut with the grain, the blade will tend to follow it, digging into and even splitting the work. Cut against this angular grain. The scrap will break free as you cut, and you will maintain complete control of the chisel. The cleanest cuts of all are made by moving the chisel blade sideways in a slicing motion, as you push it forward. For these cuts the bevel is kept against the work; the depth is controlled by raising or lowering the handle.

For a flat, recessed cut keep the bevel up and the blade flat with the plane of the bottom of the cut. If there isn't room to position the chisel this way, however, a pretty fair job can be done by cutting with the bevel down, holding it parallel to the bottom of the cut. Slightly rocking the handle from side to side will assist the cutting action. Never gouge with the blade when making this type of cut. If you want to split out a piece of scrap, rotate the blade as you move forward so that one side of it lifts the scrap and breaks it out.

When cutting across the grain, such as in squaring a tenon, hold the flat side of the blade against the shoulder of the work and start the cut with a corner of the blade. Apply pressure and rock the blade until it is level with the bottom of the cut.

Shallow, precise mortises, such as for sinking hinges, are made following four steps: (1) Carefully lay out the mortise on the work; (2) cut on the perimeter of the mortise with a wide-bladed chisel, keeping the bevel to the scrap side; (3) make a series of crosscuts, each to the exact width and depth of the finished mortise; (4) carefully slice away the scrap until you are flush with the bottom of the crosscuts.

Deep mortises are handled similarly, except that instead of using chisel crosscuts to ease cutting and to gauge the depth, drill a series of holes. Finish the mortise by cleaning out the scrap with your chisel, keeping the bevel to the scrap side.

For fine work get a set of carving chisels. While these are made particularly for wood-carving, they are also very handy for many other jobs where you need a very small, irregularly shaped blade. It is

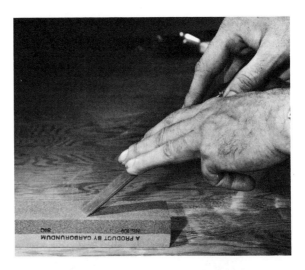

Fig. 2-42. It is important to keep a chisel sharp.

important to keep a chisel—as well as any cutting tool—sharp. When sharpening, use enough oil to keep the surface of the whetstone moist. Place the bevel of the cutter on the stone with the back edge of the bevel slightly raised, then move it back and forth parallel to the length of the stone. The wire edge or burr can be removed by taking a few strokes with the cutter held absolutely flat on the stone, beveled side up. Finish with a few strokes on a leather strap for a keener edge.

Wood Rasps

The wood rasp is able to do what no other hand or power tool can: it shaves down wood rapidly yet with a high degree of control over the cut. You can trim flat surfaces and cut notches, curves, and other irregular shapes quickly but with lathe precision. That is, while coping, keyhole, jig, and bandsaws may be used with skill to the point where near perfection is possible, a neat, smooth curve or circle requires hand retouching. Here's where the rasp comes to work. A few light strokes remove saw marks, imperfections, and errors. When cutting notches, rounding edges in simulation of Colonial effects, and shaping irregular curves, the entire job can be quickly and accurately finished by use of the rasp; no other tools are needed. The roughing out is done with the heavy-toothed end, then the rasp is

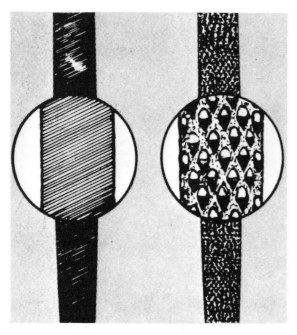

Fig. 2-43.   Here you can clearly see the difference between the fine teeth of a file (*left*) and the coarse ones of a rasp (*right*).

reversed and the job finished up with the finer teeth. When the rasp is properly used, virtually no sanding is needed on such work.

There is often confusion between a rasp and a file, and using one where the other is called for can only lead to trouble. The teeth of a rasp are individual raised surfaces more or less triangular in shape, arranged in rows. Single-cut files have parallel rows of shallow grooves; double-cut files have two sets of rows of grooves that crisscross to form a grid. A rasp cuts rapidly, so it is the tool to use for removing a lot of wood rapidly; a file cuts slowly and is used on highly critical work where you want to make sure you don't shave off too much. So you'd use a rasp to remove most of the wood from a workpiece and a file to remove the material next to the stop line.

Conventional Rasps. Selecting the right rasp for the job is tantamount to doing a good job, because its actual use is very simple. For furniture-making you'll want the three types: flat, half-round or round, and bastard- (coarse) or smooth-cut teeth. As its name implies, the flat wood rasp is for use on flat surfaces, such as the edge of a board. It's available only with bastard-cut teeth and is designed for maximum removal of wood in the shortest time. You can get it in 8-, 10-, 12-, and 14-inch lengths. As with any rasp, the length to select is the one you find most comfortable.

Half-round wood rasps have one flat side, one round; the flat side is used as just mentioned, the

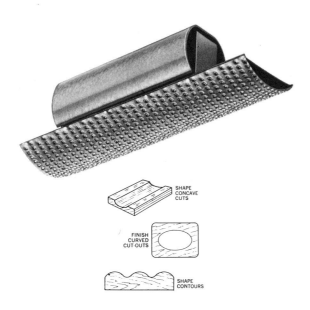

Fig. 2-44.   A new style of conventional rasp (*left*) and a new type of wood rasp (*right*).

round side for making curved and irregular cuts. It also comes in various lengths and in smooth and bastard cuts.

The round wood rasp is for enlarging holes. It's especially useful on very small holes, where a half-round rasp won't fit. It's available in various lengths, but only with bastard-cut teeth.

The shoe rasp, also known as the four-in-hand, is another type worth considering. It is really half-rasp, half-file, with one side half-round, the other flat. It's available in bastard, smooth, or second-cut teeth (between bastard and smooth in coarseness). While it is convenient to have a two-in-one tool, the shoe rasp also has disadvantages. It doesn't have a tang for a handle, which some craftsmen say reduces control, and it's slower than other rasps because you can't take long strokes with its shorter working surfaces. The shoe rasp is available in 8-, 9-, and 10-inch lengths.

The New Rasps. Today you may have not only what might be called a conventional rasp for your shop, but a new type whose main virtue is jet-speed cutting—you can take a 1x8 down to a virtual toothpick in amazingly little time. Sawdust tends to clog the teeth in conventional rasps, impairing cutting efficiency. You have to stop frequently and wirebrush the rasp clean. To overcome this and to provide even greater cutting speed, several companies have produced the new rasp. Available in a number of forms and tooth cuts, the heart of the tool's personality is its razor-sharp teeth. They are different from the teeth of a conventional rasp because they are open instead of solid metal. The openings allow shavings and sawdust to pass through freely, preventing clogging.

When using this new rasp on critical work, you have to be careful. Even though the tool has so-called fine-cut teeth, each stroke cuts very deeply, unless carefully controlled. As mentioned, the new rasps come in various forms, the standard one looking very much like a conventional flat rasp. Another resembles a plane, with front and rear handles. It has a cutting surface 5 or 10 inches long and can be used for planing, beveling, trimming, and rounding corners.

Another one of this new type is the round plane

rasp. It is 5 inches long and has a convex shape, good for making concave cuts, shaping contours, and finishing curved cuts. The three-way plane rasp is an interesting innovation. It's like the plane rasp except that its handle can be positioned and locked at different angles for more comfortable handling: at a 90-degree angle like a plane, flat like a conventional rasp, or at a 45-degree angle.

The new rasp has also been adapted for use with power tools. You can get one in the form of a drum for use with a drill, drill press, or lathe for power-shaping of irregular and round surfaces. There is also a disk rasp for power-shaving flat surfaces.

How to Use the Rasp. As we mentioned, rasp use is simple. Keep in mind that if the tool has a tang, you should first fit it with a handle. Otherwise, if the rasp slips, the tang could take a bite from your hand. Purchase a handle that fits the tang exactly. Just insert the tang into the hole in the handle, then rap the back end of the handle to seat it. Make sure that the handle is straight.

When using a rasp, first firmly clamp the work in a vise. Since the tool cuts only on the forward stroke, that's when you apply pressure—but just enough to keep it cutting. Work with smooth and even strokes. There should be no pressure on the back stroke.

DRILLS—HAND OR ELECTRIC

We have come a long way since the days when primitive man first learned to bore a hole through a log by twirling a pointed stick fast enough to make it smoke and long enough for it to burn its way through the log. Nowadays we have all kinds of easy-working, portable drilling tools available, some hand-powered and some electrically driven. No home furniture-making workshop is really complete unless it includes at least one or more hand drills as well as at least one portable electric drill.

Hand Drills

Hand drills are, of course, considerably cheaper than electric drills, but this is not the only reason you will want one. On some jobs a hand drill or brace and bit will fit into corners where no electric drill will, while on others you may find that the depth or size of the hole you need is beyond the capacity of some electric drills. With a large-diameter hole-cutter, for example, slow speed is essential and a bitbrace or hand drill will enable you to get the proper speed more easily than you could with a high-speed ¼-inch electric drill (unless you get one of the newer, variable-speed models described later on).

The most widely used tool for hand-boring of holes in wood is the bitbrace, or hand brace. A basic tool in every carpenter's kit, the brace is most often used with auger bits that are about 8 inches in length and that vary from ¼ inch to 1 inch in diameter. Most have built-in ratchet mechanisms that can be set for right- or left-hand operation to solve the problem of swinging the handle when you have to work in cramped quarters.

The chuck has notched, alligator-type jaws that are designed to hold the square-tapered shanks of the various bits used with this tool. The round knob at the top usually has ball bearings to permit free and easy swinging of the U-shaped handle. The handle's sweep, or diameter of swing, is usually 10 inches, although there are larger and smaller models with sweeps that vary from 8 to 14 inches.

Auger bits are the type of drill bits most frequently used with the hand brace. They vary from ¼ inch to 1 inch in size and are usually stamped

Fig. 2-45.   Brace and complete assortment of augers plus special-purpose bits, all properly stored in a 2x3-inch block, bored partway through.

with single numbers such as 4, 5, 6, etc. The number indicates the bit's size in sixteenths—thus a #4 bit would be ⁴⁄₁₆, a #8 bit would be ⁸⁄₁₆, etc. You can buy them individually or in sets that come in convenient plastic or leatherette rolls with a separate pocket for each bit. All have a threaded screw point that draws the bit into the work so that you need only apply a moderate amount of pressure on the handle. Two sharp spurs cut through the fibers on each side of the hole to control its diameter accurately, while cutters shave away the wood in between and feed the chips up through the spiral flutes.

The most widely used type of auger bit is the solid-center, single-twist bit. However, there is also a type known as a double-twist auger. It drills slower but cuts a smoother and more accurate hole, and is mainly used by cabinetmakers and others involved in very precise woodworking projects.

In addition to auger bits you can also get twist drill bits designed for use in a brace. These have a square-tapered shank similar to the one on an auger bit, and they vary from ¹⁄₁₆ to ⅜ of an inch in size (in ¹⁄₃₂-inch increments). They come in two types, one for wood only and the other for either wood or metal.

One of the big advantages of a bitbrace over most other drilling tools is its ability to bore large holes in wood. For holes over 1 inch in diameter you use an expansive bit. This has a threaded lead screw just like the auger bit, but it also has one or two interchangeable cutters that lock across the working end of the bit just above the screw point. The cutters fit in a slot, or groove, which has a locking screw that permits you to preset accurately the distance it projects out from the center—and thus the diameter of the hole it will cut.

Most expansive bits include two cutters, one to bore holes from ½ inch to 1½ inches in diameter, the other from ⅞ inch to 3 inches in diameter. Some of these bits are designed with an adjusting screw that permits you to regulate the size of the hole to be bored by simply turning it until you've achieved the proper diameter. On others you merely slide the cutter in and out to preset it according to markings indicated on the face of the

Fig. 2-46.   *Left:* In boring a hole, back up the work with a piece of scrap board and drill into it to avoid tearing the back of the stock with the emerging tip. *Right:* Always center the screw tip accurately on the point where the center of the hole should be.

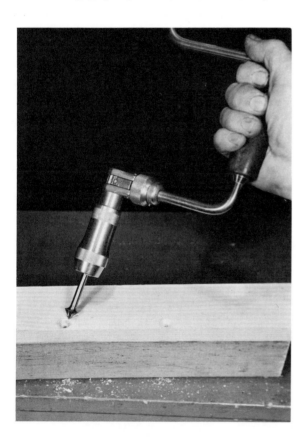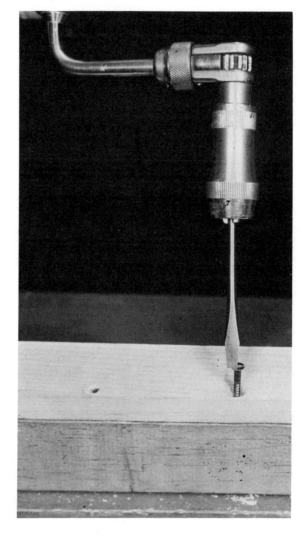

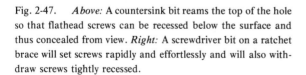

Fig. 2-47.   *Above:* A countersink bit reams the top of the hole so that flathead screws can be recessed below the surface and thus concealed from view. *Right:* A screwdriver bit on a ratchet brace will set screws rapidly and effortlessly and will also withdraw screws tightly recessed.

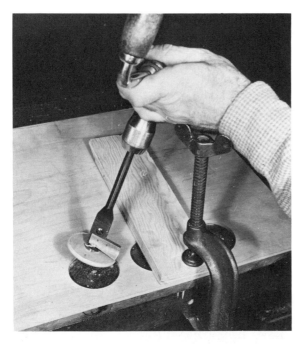

Fig. 2-48.   An adjustable circle-cutter has a screw tip for pilot hole and a cutting spur on the outer end. This operation should proceed halfway from one side, then be completed from the other side.

Fig. 2-49.   A brace chuck holds round- or square-shanked bits and drills. In this case the drill is centered with doweling jig for accurate bore.

cutter. Where accurate size is important, in either case it's a good idea to make a test bore first in a piece of scrap material to double-check the actual diameter of the hole that will be made.

The "eggbeater" type of hand drill is the tool you will want for drilling small holes in metal as well as in wood, plastic, and other materials. Usually equipped with a 3-jaw chuck of ¼-inch capacity, these hand drills were a mainstay of every tool kit in the days before portable electric drills became popular. They are still useful for jobs where no power is available as well as for "quickie" drilling chores where only one or two small holes are required and you don't feel like going to the bother of plugging in an electric drill.

Hand drills have a large gear wheel on one side that drives a pinion gear mounted on the shaft of the drill. This large wheel is turned by means of a knob attached to the outer rim. Press hard on the handle of the drill with one hand while spinning the large gear with your other hand. Some drills have controls that permit you to vary the gear ratio—and thus the speed at which the bit turns—while others also have ratchet mechanisms that are handy for cramped quarters where it may be awkward to make a full revolution of the large gear. When you are drilling horizontally and need extra pressure, you may find it easier on some jobs to butt the handle end against your stomach so that you can press harder while cranking.

Although you'll seldom find them in hardware stores nowadays, there is one type of hand drill that is specifically designed for this kind of heavy-duty hand drilling. Called a breast drill, it differs from the ordinary hand drill not only in that it is bigger and sturdier, but it also has a half-moon-shaped plate on the handle end against which you can lean your chest or stomach. Breast drills usually also have slightly larger chucks (⁵⁄₁₆- or ⅜-inch capacity).

For really rapid drilling of small pilot holes in wood or soft metals there is another tool that you will find useful—an automatic push drill. Resembling spiral ratchet screwdrivers in operation and appearance, push drills differ from ordinary hand drills in that there is nothing to turn or rotate. You merely push down on the handle with rapid strokes to spin the bit. A built-in spring mechanism returns the handle to its original length after each stroke. Because they are easily operated with one hand and they are narrow with no handle or ratchet to swing, they are ideal for awkward jobs where you can't use both hands or for jobs where no other type of drill might reach.

Push drills use special bits that have sharp points and straight flutes along their length. The bits vary from $\frac{1}{16}$ inch to $\frac{11}{64}$ inch in diameter, and they usually come with the drill in either a full set of eight or in a more limited set of four of the most popular sizes. Most models have magazines built into the handle for storing the bits. Drill points for push drills can also be purchased separately—in sets or individually—so that you can use them with a push-pull-type spiral ratchet screwdriver. They fit the same chuck as the screwdriver bits, so that all you have to do is insert one of these bits instead of the usual screwdriving blade.

Portable Electric Drills

Undoubtedly the first power tool most home mechanics acquire, the electric drill owes at least part of its popularity to the fact that it can—by means of suitable accessories and attachments—be used for many other operations besides drilling holes. However, for the home furniture-maker they are most often used to perform their primary function—drilling and boring holes in all kinds of material, including wood, metal, plastic, and glass.

Electric drills generally come in three sizes—$\frac{1}{4}$-, $\frac{3}{8}$-, and $\frac{1}{2}$-inch—according to the maximum-size shank that can be gripped in the chuck jaws. This is generally considered its maximum capacity for drilling in steel; that is, a $\frac{1}{4}$-inch drill will handle up to a $\frac{1}{4}$-inch hole when drilling in steel. In wood it can handle larger bits as long as they have a $\frac{1}{4}$-inch shank that will fit in the chuck.

The smaller-size drills will generally have a higher maximum speed with less power than the larger models. A $\frac{1}{4}$-inch drill, for example, will have a maximum speed of approximately 2,000 rpm, while a $\frac{3}{8}$-inch drill is generally rated at about 1,000 rpm. A heavy-duty $\frac{1}{2}$-inch drill may turn at

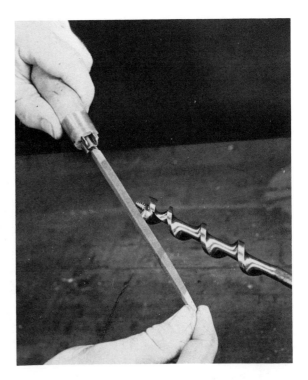

Fig. 2-50. An auger bit held in a vise can be sharpened, and burrs can be removed, with a fine file. This is an exacting job, but it keeps bits in shape.

only 400 to 600 rpm. The lower speed in the larger-capacity drills is usually derived from internal gears so that increased torque and power is provided at the same time. This enables them to handle larger bits more efficiently and with greater safety.

Most furniture-making work can be performed with a $\frac{1}{4}$-inch model. Of course, if you are planning to use the drill for other household duties, the $\frac{3}{8}$-inch drill size should be considered. It has more power and less speed than a $\frac{1}{4}$-inch drill, but it is generally not as bulky or as slow as a $\frac{1}{2}$-inch drill.

Most well-stocked hardware stores carry all kinds of drill bits and hole-cutting attachments that will enable you to bore holes up to 2 or 3 inches in diameter. They usually come with a $\frac{1}{4}$-inch shank that will fit the chuck of an ordinary $\frac{1}{4}$-inch drill. However, the high speed of the typical single-speed $\frac{1}{4}$-inch drill makes it difficult, and sometimes downright dangerous, to use some of the larger hole cutters in one of these drills—unless you

Fig. 2-51. When using an electric drill, always mark the center point for a hole with a punch or a nail to prevent the drill bit from "traveling" and to assure accuracy.

have one of the newer, variable-speed models now on the market.

Available in all three sizes—¼-, ⅜-, and ½-inch—variable-speed drills come in two basic forms. One type gives a choice of from two to four speeds by flicking a multiple-position switch or by flicking a lever that shifts gears on the inside (some use a combination of both). The other, and by far most popular, type offers an infinitely variable choice of speeds. A silicon-rectifier speed-control circuit is wired into the trigger switch so that the harder you press the trigger, the faster the drill goes. As a result you have full control from zero to maximum revolutions per minute (when the switch is fully depressed). This enables you to select whatever speed you need to suit the job at hand. You can go slower when working with large-diameter wood-boring bits or hole-cutters and faster when using small bits. In addition, when starting on smooth surfaces or when working without a center-punch mark, you can start at a very slow speed until the bit is accurately positioned, then speed up and finish the job. The electronic

circuit that controls this speed is so designed that there is little or no power loss at even the slowest speeds.

To permit even more accurate control of a variable-speed drill, some of the newer models can be preset to the maximum speed desired. By adjusting a small knob or switch, you can arrange to pull the trigger all the way back without going any faster than the predetermined speed, thus eliminating the problem of trying to keep a constant pressure on the trigger when only a certain speed is desired.

A further refinement available on many of the newer variable-speed drills is a reversing switch. This not only permits you to reverse the direction of rotation, it also gives you a choice of variable speed in either direction—a valuable feature when the drill is used for driving or removing screws as well as for extricating large bits that sometimes get jammed into the work or clogged with chips.

In addition to giving you a choice of sizes and speed ranges many companies also make shock-proof or double-insulated drills in both single-

Fig. 2-52. *Top left:* Auger bits are used primarily with an electric drill for making holes in wood up to 1½ inches in diameter. The lips on the auger score the circumference of the hole and then cut out the shavings as they revolve. *Bottom left:* Hole saws are made of tough, hardened steel, and will cut round holes in larger diameters than twist-drill bits. You can cut up to 1¼-inch-diameter holes using a ¼-inch electric drill. *Above:* You can cut out a circle as large as 4 inches in diameter using a circle cutter and a ¼-inch electric drill. The size of the hole is controlled by loosening a set screw and then sliding the cutter blade in or out.

speed and variable-speed models. Designed virtually to eliminate the possibility of accidental shock should a short circuit occur inside the housing, double-insulated power tools usually have a rugged plastic housing that makes them lighter in weight and practically shatterproof, even if dropped onto a concrete surface from a considerable height. Ideally suited for those who do a lot of work around the outside of the house or in locations where dampness may be a problem (thus increasing the shock hazard), double-insulated drills also eliminate the nuisance of worrying about grounding. They come with standard two-wire cords and plugs so that they can be plugged into an ordinary two-hole outlet with complete safety and without need for adapters.

All of these electric drills can be used with many different kinds of bits, depending on the size hole you need and the type of material you are working on. Twist-drill bits are probably the most widely used; they come in a wide range of fractional, decimal, and numbered sizes up to about ½ inch in

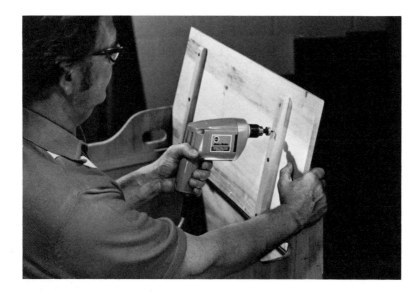

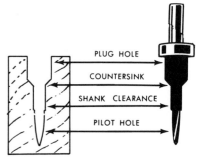

Fig. 2-53. Combination drill and countersink bits will save a great deal of time when you are countersinking wood screws in softwood or hardwood. The bits come in various sizes to fit all wood screws and they perform three cutting operations in one drilling.

diameter. Bits made of carbon steel (often labeled *tool steel*) are adequate for wood, soft metal, plastic, and similar materials. However, for drilling holes in hard steel or iron, you'll need bits made of high-speed steel; these are usually stamped H.S. on the shank.

Carbon-steel twist-drill bits designed for use in wood are available with turned-down shanks so that you can buy larger sizes to fit in a ¼-inch chuck. For drilling holes deeper than the bit will ordinarily reach or for reaching into places where the drill might not otherwise fit, you can also buy extensions that will fit into a ¼- inch chuck. Usually 12 inches in length, the extensions have a hollow socket at the working end with a setscrew that will lock onto any power bit with a ¼- inch shank.

Your electric drill can also be used to bore holes much larger than those that can be made with ordinary twist-drill bits. Flat, spade-type power bits are available with ¼-inch shanks in sizes that vary from ⅜-inch to 1 inch in ⅛-inch increments. These have a pointed spur tip with a flat cutter on each side and generally measure slightly more than 6 inches in length. Designed for drilling in wood, plastic, and other comparatively soft materials, most are made of tool steel, but you can also buy them of high-speed steel for cutting through hidden nails, screws, or wire. You can buy spade bits indi-

vidually as you need them, but if you buy a set of six in a plastic roll kit, you'll have all sizes on hand when needed.

For still bigger holes—up to about 2½ or 3 inches—you can use one of two types of circular hole saws. One is a continuous circle of steel with saw teeth along the cutting edge; the other is an adjustable model with three separate blades that project from a circular disk and cut out a circle when brought into contact with the work.

Continuous-circle hole saws are designed for wood only and are usually used with an arbor that mounts a pilot hole drill in the center. They come in sizes up to 2 ½ inches in diameter, and they are limited as to the depth of cut since you cannot cut after the arbor comes in contact with the surface. A different size is required for every different hole diameter.

Adjustable hole saws do not cut as fast as continuous hole saws, but they are infinitely adjustable for holes from 1⅛ to 2½ inches in diameter. An adjusting nut or disk is turned to move the three individual cutters at a uniform rate in or out from the pilot drill in the center. Once the correct diameter has been achieved, the setting is locked and the tool is ready for drilling. Like the continuous-circle hole saw, its depth of cut is also limited. However, some models can be equipped with metal-cutting blades for drilling large-diameter

Fig. 2-54.   *Top:* Cuts are started with a so-called electric chisel held at about a 45-degree angle to the workpiece. As cut deepens, tool is brought to a vertical position. *Bottom:* As cutting edges revolve, they slice through wood in much the same way as a hand chisel does.

Fig. 2-55.   The electric chisel cuts a mortise (*top*) in furniture leg to fit tenon cut in side rail (*bottom*). Adjustable ring on the tool sits on the guide strip when desired depth of cut is reached.

holes in sheet metal as well as in wood. As a rule both types of hole saw will cut more smoothly and be easier to handle if used at lower speeds in one of the larger slow-speed drills, or in a variable-speed model that can be slowed as necessary.

Drill Press

With modern techniques of woodworking and the multitude of cutting tools, fixtures, and attachments available, the drill press has become a basic tool of the home furniture-making workshop. The drill press consists of a vertical shaft (spindle) that is tapered or threaded on one end to hold a drill chuck, a tubular housing (quill) in which the spindle is mounted, a feed lever that moves the quill up or down, a power source, and a movable table upon which the work is placed. There is often a means of locking the quill, and on larger presses the table can be tilted.

The size of the press is usually expressed in terms of chuck capacity (the maximum-diameter tool shank it will hold) or distance between the spindle center and the column. A press with an 11-inch capacity lets you drill to the center of a 22-inch board or circle. A new radial drill press with a 16-inch capacity has a tilting head that allows drilling at any angle. The head is mounted on a horizontal arm that swivels on the supporting column to position the drill bit instead of the work.

Feeds and Speeds. Drill speeds are important if you want to do a good job. Each cutting tool will operate best at a given speed, depending on the material worked. On most drill presses it is impossible to get the exact speed, but you can come close by adjusting the drive belt on the step-cone pulleys. You will find a chart giving the various speed ratios available with your particular drill press somewhere in the instruction booklet that came with the tool. See Table 2-2 for exact recommended speeds. Generally, the larger the tool and the harder the material, the slower the speed.

Feed pressure is also of major importance. Too much pressure will force the tool beyond its cutting capacity and result in rough cuts and jammed or broken tools. Too light a feed, particularly with metal or other hard material, causes overheating of

Table 2-2

DRILL PRESS OPERATING SPEEDS

Material	Operation	Speed (rpm)
Wood	Drilling to ¼″	3,800
Wood	Drilling ¼″–½″	3,100
Wood	Drilling ½″–¾″	2,300
Wood	Drilling ¾″–1″	2,000
Wood	Drilling over 1″	600
Wood	Using expansion bit	600
Wood	Routing	5,000
Wood	Cutting plugs	3,000
Wood	Carving	5,000
Wood	Using fly cutter	600
Wood	Using dowel cutter	1,800
Hardwood	Mortising	1,500
Softwood	Mortising	2,200
Metal	Wire brushing—fine	3,300
Metal	Wire brushing—coarse	1,200
Soft metal	Buffing	3,800
Hard metal	Buffing	4,700
Plastics	Buffing	2,300
Metal	Using fly cutter	600
Metal	Grinding	3,000
Glass	Drilling with tube	600

the tool and burning of the cutting edge. The best results will be obtained by matching the correct speed with a steady feed pressure that lets the tool cut easily at an even rate.

Common Drilling Tools. There are numerous types and styles of tools to drill holes. The most common are the twist drill, the solid-center-shaft drill with interchangeable cutting blades, the double-spur-bit drill, and the power-wood-bit drill. All will do a good job if sharp, but the twist drills don't cut quite as smoothly as the others, since they do not have the outlining spurs that sever the fibers before actual boring starts.

The adjustable fly-cutter is very useful for cutting large-diameter holes and can be used to cut exact-size disks by reversing the cutter blade. Since fly-cutters are one-sided and not balanced, they should be used at the slowest speed available and fed very slowly to avoid binding. Fly-cutters can fool you into putting your hand too close to the tool; avoid nicked fingers by keeping your hands well out of the way.

When drilling all the way through a workpiece, always place a piece of scrap wood underneath. This will not only protect the worktable but will also assure a clean breakthrough. Another method of assuring a clean hole is first to drill a small pilot hole all the way through, then drill halfway with the dimensional bit, turn the piece over, and finish from the other side. In soft woods with pronounced grain there is sometimes a tendency for the hole to wander because of the varying hardness of the wood. In this case drilling a small pilot hole or clamping the work will do much to improve accuracy.

When a hole is to be bored to a predetermined depth, mark the depth on the side of the stock, then run the bit down so that it is even with the mark. The depth-gauge rod can now be set and any number of holes bored to exact and identical depth.

Round work can be held easily with either a commercial or homemade V block. Exact center holes can be located by placing the block so that the drill point centers in the bottom of the V when the quill is run down.

A series of holes with a common center line can be drilled faster and more accurately by using a fence. The positioning of the fence will determine

Fig. 2-56. *Left:* An adjustable fly-cutter is very good to use in cutting large-diameter holes. *Right:* Round work can be held easily with either a commercial or a homemade V block.

Fig. 2-57. *Top left:* When drilling a hole deeper than the length of your drill bit, clamp a flat scrap of wood to the table and bore a hole through it. *Top right:* Then drill as deep in the work as your bit permits. *Bottom left:* Remove the workpiece and use a straight length of dowel to align hole in the scrap with the bit. *Bottom right:* Replace this dowel with a short dowel and fit the workpiece over it. Drill the rest of the way through.

Fig. 2-58. *Left:* A straight piece of wood clamped to the drill press table serves as a fence. *Right:* A commercial fence has a hold-down to prevent work from lifting off table.

the distance from the center of the hole to the edge of the work. You can make your own fence by clamping a straight strip of wood to the table, or you can use one of the accessory fences made specifically for the drill press. Commercial fences have the added feature of an adjustable shoe-shaped hold-down clamp that rides lightly on the top of the workpiece and prevents it from lifting off the worktable when the drill is withdrawn.

When you need to drill a series of holes in sequence, such as for dowel pins in the corners of frame members, a stop block and spacer blocks can be used in conjunction with the fence. The fence is adjusted for the end-to-center distance, and the stop block is clamped in place to locate the hole farthest from the end of the workpiece. Spacer blocks are then cut to the same size as the distance between the hole centers. The blocks are fitted between the end of the workpiece and the stop block, then removed, one at a time, as the holes are drilled. If the spacing is to be irregular, cut and position the blocks accordingly.

When a series of several holes with equal distances between centers is to be drilled, a simple jig may be substituted for the spacer blocks. In this method a locating block with a removable pin is fixed to the fence so that when the pin is inserted in the first hole in the work, the bit is lined up to drill the next hole.

Another useful holding device, particularly when working with metal, is the drill press vise. This is a big, rugged screw vise that is adjustable for tilt and machined to be precisely square with the base on which it is used. Most of these units are supplied with several pairs of accessory jaws to facilitate holding round or irregular work, again at precise angles to the table.

Screw Holes. Wood screws go in easier and hold better if proper-size holes are drilled for them. Usually there is a lead hole, which allows the screw point to penetrate easily and lets the threads get a good grip without splitting the wood; a body hole, which provides clearance for the unthreaded screw shank; and a countersink, which either sets the

 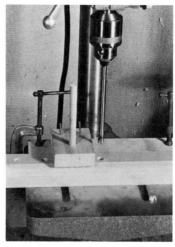

Fig. 2-59.   *Left:* A stop block, spacer blocks, and a fence are used when drilling a series of holes. *Right:* A jig with a removable pin may be used for drilling a series of equidistant holes.

screwhead flush with the work surface or recesses it so that the hole can be plugged with a short dowel.

Sets of profile bits especially made for drilling screw holes are available at moderate cost, but you can also drill a proper screw hole by matching the screw size to the specified drill sizes. Drill the lead hole first—this gives you a pilot hole to serve as a guide when you enlarge the body hole in the top piece. If the hole is to be plugged with dowel, you can now counterbore for the plug. For flush seating of flathead screws, use a countersink cutter and bore to appropriate depth.

Occasionally the need arises to drill deeper than the maximum feed of the quill. In this case drill as far as you can and then shut off the press. Raise the workpiece, with the bit inside it, and place pieces of scrap stock underneath to block it in place. You can now drill the hole the rest of the way.

If the hole depth is greater than the length of your drill bit, there's still a solution. Clamp a flat scrap of wood to the drill press table and bore a hole through it the same size as you want in your work. Lower the table and drill as deep as your bit permits in the work. Remove the workpiece. Run a length of rod or straight dowel (the same size as the hole) up through the hole you bored in the scrap

clamped to the table, and align the top of the rod with the drill bit by moving the table. When the table is centered, fit a short section of dowel (again the same size as the hole) in place of the longer dowel in the scrap. Invert the workpiece, placing the first hole over the pin in the scrap, and drill the rest of the way through.

Drilling metal is much the same as drilling in wood, with certain differences. Since the material is much tougher and harder, speeds and feeds are more critical to the quality of the work and the life of the cutting tool. When drilling metal, there is also a greater tendency for the work to twist, particularly when the point of the drill breaks through. For this reason care must be taken to see that the work is held securely to the table. The drill vise is best for small or round work, while large, flat work can be secured with clamps. Chip-clearing is also important, particularly when drilling a deep hole, so raise the drill often and don't let the flutes get clogged with chips.

Drill Press Accessories. Unless you operate a production furniture workshop, you probably bought your drill press with the intention of using it for more than just drilling holes. Make no mistake, your drill press, with the proper attachments, *will* do more than just drill holes. But think before you

Fig. 2-60 *Left:* Countersink bits are used to flare the top of a hole so that a flathead screw may be driven into a hole flush with the surface. *Center:* Profile bits are specially designed to drill proper-size holes for wood screws. *Right:* Depth gauge used with the profile screw-cutter lets you bore to exact depth to install a plug.

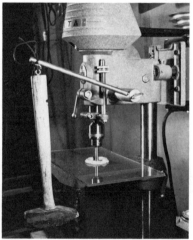

Fig. 2-61. *Right:* Use a brass rod for drilling in glass. Make a putty dam and fill with silicon carbide and turpentine. *Far right:* Weight on the feed lever will maintain required pressure.

buy—consider your needs, the price, and your budget. Remember, the drill press is like any other power tool. If you choose your accessories judiciously, you'll have equipment that you wouldn't trade for anything. If you rush out and buy every accessory in sight, you'll have a lot of hard-earned cash tied up in rarely used tools that clutter your workshop and collect dust.

Want to drill some square holes or to cut a clean mortise without using a hammer and chisel? If so, a mortise-chisel setup is what you need. Matched sets of hollow chisel and special bit are available in

¼-, ⅜-, and ½-inch sizes. You'll also need a mortising housing (one size fits all the chisels) and, unless you clamp the work each time you make a cut, a fence with hold-down. A fence is also a must.

To set up, remove the geared chuck by loosening its retaining collar with the handle of the chuck key and replacing the stop-rod collar with the mortising housing. The bit is inserted through the bottom of the chisel and locked in the chuck. Be sure to allow at least $\frac{1}{64}$ inch clearance between the bit and the bottom of the chisel. Watch your speeds, and don't force the feed. Mortise chisels will burn up when run too fast or too slow. Operate the ¼-inch chisel at 3,600 rpm, and the ⅜- and ½-inch at about 2,800 rpm.

When cutting a mortise, make the two end cuts first, then work toward the center. Overlap the preceding cut by about one-third the width of the chisel. If you're cutting a side mortise, clamp a piece of scrap to the side of the workpiece to ensure a clean cut.

The variable-speed attachment is a collection of pulleys, linkages, and belts that lets you set your spindle speed anywhere from 300 to 3,700 rpm merely by moving a speed-selector lever. It not only saves untold hours of juggling the belt on the pulleys, but gives you exact speed settings anywhere within the aforementioned range. By moving the drive belt to the second step on the motor pulley, you change your speed range to 480-6,000 rpm.

If you want to make drawers or boxes and like

Fig. 2-62.   A special collet chuck replaces the geared chuck on the spindle for dovetail-routing operation. Both workpieces are clamped in a dovetailing jig, and the router shank follows the guide comb of the jig.

the professional touch of neat, sturdy, dovetailed corners, you'll want a dovetailing jig. You will need a special collet chuck to hold the ½-inch dovetail router. It attaches to the tapered spindle just like the standard chuck, but is especially designed for side-thrust operations. Both workpieces are clamped in the jig, with the edge of one flush with the side of the other. The dovetail router is set for a ⅜-inch-deep cut, and the guide comb of the jig is followed with the router shank to make the cut. Release the clamps, fit the boards together, and you've got a perfect dovetail job.

The same collet and router bit can be used with a fence to cut straight dovetail slots, or "keys," such as are used to join stretchers to furniture legs. The best speeds for smooth cuts with any router kit (dovetail, carving, or straight) are between 6,000 and 9,000 rpm. Slower speeds will result in ragged edges and burned cutting bits.

The rotary planer is an inexpensive and valuable accessory. It does a fine job of reducing stock thickness and resurfacing old or warped lumber. The single cutting blade can also be adjusted for cutting rabbets, and the planer head replaces the geared chuck. At operating speeds of 3,000 to 4,000 rpm the chips fly high enough to make safety glasses a must.

A drum version of the new type of wood rasp (see page 49), run at minimum speed, makes quick work of edge trimming and contouring. Sanding drums are available in a variety of diameters and lengths and produce remarkably smooth edges when run at spindle speeds of 1,300 to 2,400 rpm. Like the rotary file, they should be used with a simple auxiliary table that supports the edge of the work above the lower edge of the drum.

A matched set of profile screw countersink and plug-cutters is a boon in any furniture-making workshop. When used in a drill press, they do a superb job. By using the special depth gauge with the countersink, you bore to exactly the right depth for either flush or countersunk screw-mounting. The unique design of this depth gauge—it's free-floating and actually rides on ball bearings—keeps it from marring the surface of the workpiece by revolving against it. With the matching plug

Fig. 2-63.   A shaper head and fence ready to cut molding or to trim work.

cutters it is simple to make perfect-fitting plugs for the countersunk screw holes. Cutting your own plugs means that you can match the wood and that the grain is always vertical if the plugs are purchased or cut from a dowel rod—and can be matched to the grain of the workpiece.

A trick that will save time when you're bolting a hold-down to the press table is to grind off two opposite sides of the clamp bolt heads. Thus instead of having to remove and replace the nut each time you mount or dismount a fixture, you have a sort of toggle that can be turned sideways and slipped up through the slots in the table and fixtures, then turned crosswise and tightened with a few turns of the nut. By replacing the geared chuck with a work arbor and cutter and fitting a shaper fence and auxiliary table to the press table, you can have a shaper. For curved-edge work a set of bearing collars takes the place of the fence to control the depth of cut. While most shaping can be done with the drill press head in the normal position, it is sometimes preferable to invert the head and mount it below the table so that the spindle and cutter project through the hole in the center of the press table. Spindle speeds for this should never be less than 4,000 rpm, and 6,000 to

8,000 rpm is considered best for high-quality results. You'll need at least a ½-horsepower motor to keep from stalling on any but the lightest cuts. As in all operations developing substantial side thrust, the spindle must be in the fully retracted position.

SHAPERS AND ROUTERS

Woodworking shapers and routers belong in the home furniture-maker's workshop. There are, conservatively, dozens of exacting jobs that can be cut, shaped, or finished in short order—from cutting decorative edging to trimming plastic laminate to simple rabbeting. If you can have only one of these tools in your shop, we recommend the portable router.

The Portable Router

With only one basic moving part—the armature or rotating part of the motor—the portable router is a simple tool. The armature rotates at speeds from 18,000 rpm to as high as 30,000 rpm, depending upon the make and model. The armature itself rides on only two ball bearings, making the tool very easy to service. Most manufacturers make routers from ½ hp to 2½ hp. For the average home furniture-maker the ⅞ to 1½ hp will be sufficient for almost any job. The smaller routers (½ hp or less) are good for light-duty work (setting in hinges, trimming plastic laminates, light dadoing, shaping in soft woods).

While routers are available in many models and weights, their specifications all include three basic parts: motor, base, and subbase. The motor is equipped with a chuck on one end of its shaft and fits upright (shaft down) in the base. Releasing a clamp screw allows the motor to rotate in the spiral-channeled base, the action raising or lowering the motor with respect to the base and therefore adjusting the depth of cut. The subbase, which provides a flat, low-friction surface for the tool to ride on, is interchangeable with other special-purpose subbases.

Actually, with the router as with almost any electric tool you can do nothing until you put in a

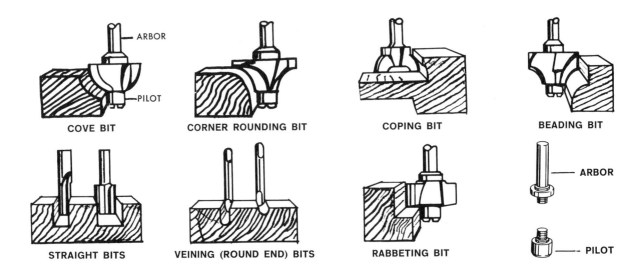

COVE BIT   CORNER ROUNDING BIT   COPING BIT   BEADING BIT

STRAIGHT BITS   VEINING (ROUND END) BITS   RABBETING BIT

Fig. 2-64.   Typical router bits and cutters and the work they can do.

Fig. 2-65.   *Left:* When using a bit with a pilot, the fastest and most convenient way to set the depth of the cut is to mark the workpiece with a pencil, then adjust the router so that the edge of the bit aligns with the mark. *Right:* When making the cut, the pilot rides along the edge of the work.

cutting bit. It is the blade on the saw that does the cutting, the drill bit in the drill that makes the hole, etc. The router has so many different bits that can be inserted into its collet chuck that the variety of its operations is tremendous. If we consider the different bits that go into the router, instead of the router itself, we can get a good idea of what the tool can do.

Typical Working Example. A rabbeting operation is a typical example. First release the motor clamp screw and remove the motor from the base. Place the cutter in the chuck and tighten it with the two wrenches provided. Replace the motor in its base. All router bits are available in three types—with pilots, without pilots, and with removable pilots. The pilot is a blunt, cylindrical tip below the cutter's edge that controls the horizontal depth of cut by riding along the edge of the work.

There are two ways to set the vertical depth of the cut, depending on whether the bit used is equipped with a pilot.

With no pilot, set the router on a flat board and rotate the motor until the end of the bit just touches the wood surface. Tighten the clamp screw. This releases the depth-scale ring, which can be aligned with the register mark on the motor. Then release the clamp screw, locking the depth ring. Turn the motor until the mark lines up with the mark for the depth of cut wanted. Lock the motor in position again, and the router is set.

With a pilot on the bit, measure and mark the edge of the board. With the machine standing on the edge of the board, lower the cutter until it lines up with the mark. Using a pilotless bit, mount the edge guide on the router and adjust it for the horizontal depth. Next start the router, slide it over until the cutter engages the work, and make the cut. For best results maintain a slow rate of feed, a pressure that doesn't slow the motor less than two-thirds of its free-running speed. However, don't proceed too slowly or the cutter will burn.

When cutting a cross-grain rabbet, feed from left to right. Clamp a piece of scrap stock against the right edge of the work to prevent splintering when the cut is finished.

Fig. 2-66.   Rabbets may be cut after the work is assembled; square corners are made with a chisel.

Another routine router operation is dado-cutting. A pilotless bit is used, and because these are available from ¼ inch to 1⅜ inches, a dado can be cut in a single pass. A T square is usually used as a guide. Measure from the edge of the bit to the edge of the router subbase, then clamp the T square to the work at an equal distance from the working edge. In operation the subbase rides along the edge of the T square to carve out a perfect cut. The depth of the cut is, of course, set by raising or lowering the motor within the base.

For a series of parallel dados or grooves a guide bar is fitted to the edge guide. It rides in the first dado, guiding the router for the second cut.

Decorative Edge Cuts. There is no end to the variety of decorative edge cuts that can be made with the router and its small corps of molding bits. It can cut or shape anything from a clean corner round to a combination cove-and-bead. Normally a cutter with pilot is used. The edge guide has an attachment that makes possible its use on curved or straight edges.

When edge-cutting all four sides of a piece, watch for edge splintering when a cross-grain cut is completed. Avoid this by making the first cut across the grain. If there is any chipping at the edge, it is trimmed away by the next cut.

The guide is an extremely valuable accessory,

Fig. 2-67.   *Left:* Cut a dado with a straight bit, using a shop-made T square as edge guide. *Right:* Cut a series of dadoes with an accessory edge guide; for all subsequent parallel cuts the first groove acts as channel guide. Guide is extended for each new cut, or each previous cut is used as new guide.

Fig. 2-68.   *Left:* Shelf edges can be made to look better and last longer if a decorative shape is put on them with a form bit in the router. Form bits come in three basic shapes: cove, bead, and ogee. *Right:* The ogee bit is used to decorate the edge of a furniture piece.

Fig. 2-69. *Left:* To make enclosed grooves at a set measure around the perimeter of a workpiece, use accessory edge guide. *Right:* By using a V-block attachment on the edge guide, the same type of cut can be made on a radius. Rods on edge guides slip into sockets on the router base; guide can then be moved in or out along the length of rods for any cut.

being a precise control for making inside cuts on the edges of straight or curved work, and easing the task of parallel slotting. It is also used to convert the router for use as an edge plane by fitting a tiny pivot pin to the base of the guide. With this conversion you can cut intricate circular designs and base-cut for inlay work.

Freehand routing requires practice, as no guide or cutter pilot guides the machine. Two examples are background routing and incised routing. Suppose you want to carve the lettering on a coffee table top. First draw the pattern on the workpiece. If the lettering is to be carved into the wood, the technique is incised routing; if you choose to rout out the background, producing figures in relief, the procedure is called background routing. (Woodcarvers background-rout first when modeling a workpiece, then apply finishing touches with chisels.) For either style use a small veining bit and a ⅛-inch depth of cut; this is easy to control while following the pattern.

For making joints the router is a regular workhorse. For half-laps set the depth of cut at slightly less than half the stock's thickness. Clamp the workpieces side by side, using a T square as a guide. For an end joint allow an extra inch of length as a rest or level for the router base. When the cut is finished, this can be trimmed away.

Making a Dovetail Joint. The strongest of the most widely used joints in professional furniture making is the dovetail. With the router and an accessory template you can make dovetails as precisely as those made by pros.

The template is secured to the front of the workbench. It has two bar clamps, one at the top and one in front. To cut the dovetail for a drawer, clamp one sidepiece vertically in front of the template. Then place the frontpiece underneath the plastic fingers on the top of the template. Make sure that: (1) both pieces are butted tightly against the stops on the left side of the template; (2) the front edge of the drawer front butts against the drawer side; and (3) the top edge of the drawer side is flush with the top of the front.

Secure the bar clamps. Then screw the guide (a small aluminum disk) into the hole of the router subbase and secure the dovetail bit in the chuck. Adjust the router carefully for depth of cut; it will vary, depending on the size of the bit.

Begin at the left edge of the template and make a cut to the right, removing stock in front of the template fingers. This must be done before working into the finger indentations, to avoid chipping the work edge. Then working from right to left, cut in and out around the template fingers.

That's all there is to it. Remove the two pieces

Fig. 2-70. *Right:* To cut a dovetail groove, provide a flat surface to support the router by clamping extra stock alongside; the edge guide will control positioning for the cut. *Far right:* Dovetail tongue is made by cutting two dovetail grooves, overlapping each edge of primary workpiece (center board in photo), and discarding waste; the match is perfect.

Fig. 2-71. *Left:* To cut perfect dovetail corner joints, the ends of both workpieces are butted together and held in clamp-template fixture. *Center:* At the same time the guide is fitted into the center hole of the router's subbase to follow finger guides to the template (same guide may be used for any duplicate pattern work whenever any template is used). *Right:* Mated workpieces of another dovetail pattern.

and they'll fit together to make a perfect dovetail corner joint. If the fit is loose, the cut wasn't deep enough; if it's tight, it was too deep. The template will handle either flush or rabbeted dovetails in various stock thicknesses.

The same cutter without template and guide will cut dovetail tongue-and-groove (used to join a cleat to the end of a table or drawing board).

To cut the slot, clamp the work and three or four pieces of scrap (equal in length to the proposed cut) securely in a vise with all edges flush. The extra thickness of scrap provides a wide, flat surface for the router to ride. Next, using the edge guide, make the cut down the center of the work.

To cut the matching dovetail tongue (tenon), use the same scrap and edge guide procedure to make two cuts, working partly into the supporting stock. The portion left between the two grooves is the mating tongue. If you place the work in the center,

you can make both cuts without resetting the edge guide; simply make one cut with the edge guide against each side of the clamped blocks.

Finishing Laminate Edges. With an inexpensive laminate-trimming cutter and subbase, tabletop plastic laminates can be professionally trimmed and finished. This special accessory, which replaces the regular subbase, has a small nylon roller that guides the router and prevents the bit from cutting too deeply.

Adjusting the roller for depth of cut is simple: the bit has a small stud on the bottom, and there's a matching hole on top of the roller. When the stud drops into the hole, the roller is correctly set and is locked in place. The cutter is designed to produce an upper bevel cut, while the lower portion cuts flush with the edge of the finished work.

If the tabletop is to be faced with laminate rather than wood trim, bond the facing so the laminate overlaps the top edge slightly. It can then be trimmed flush in preparation for the bonding of the top laminate. See page 138 for more information on how to install plastic laminates.

The Shaper Operation. By turning the portable router upside-down and securing it to a table, it serves as a first-rate shaper. Special cast-metal accessory tables (complete with guide fence) are available from most router manufacturers. Or you can make your own with a 2-foot-square piece of ¾-inch plywood, routing out a ½-inch-deep circle to accommodate the router's base. You will also have to rig a pair of hold-downs from scrap hardwood.

Next drill a hole for the bit to protrude through and add legs. A pair of C clamps and a length of hardwood (with a cutout in the center) act as a fence. This setup will permit use of all your shaper cutters and make it easier to handle small pieces.

The secret of achieving professional results with your router is in keeping bits razor-sharp. Here, once again, the router comes through. By chucking an abrasive wheel in the machine and using an accessory bit-holding fixture, you can sharpen cutters at regular intervals without trouble.

The Stationary Shaper. Table, or stationary, shapers are designed primarily for cutting mold-ings and grooves of various forms on straight or curved work. They are also used for cutting forms of different kinds—for example, arms for wheels, gear teeth, etc. Many of these operations require the use of a jig or form to hold the stock while it is being worked.

The common features of all shapers are a supporting frame, an adjustable vertical spindle, an adjustable fence, a table with a removable throat through which the spindle projects, an assortment of collars and cutters, and a motor. In addition most shapers are equipped with an adjustable guard. Most shapers except the portable type have indirect motor drive. The horsepower rating of the motors ranges from ½ to 5 or more. The speed of the spindle on heavy and medium machines varies from 5,000 to 10,000 rpm. Portable shapers have spindle speeds as high as 18,000 rpm.

The cutters used on shapers are of two types. The three-lip type is used on light-duty and portable shapers. The flat type is used on both heavy- and light-duty machines. Flat or blank knives, as they are commonly called, are made of high-grade, self-hardening tool steel with beveled edges. These often have a sandblasted surface that makes easy drawing of the cutter design directly on the face of

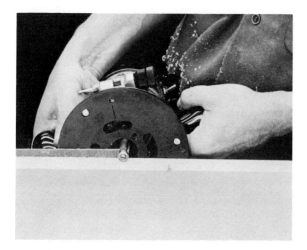 

Fig. 2-72. *Left:* Carbide flush-trim bit with pilot wheel as guide is used to trim overlapping laminated countertop flush with counter edge. *Right:* Laminated-edge piece is glued into place. Carbide bevel-trim bit is used to bevel edges of surface and edge pieces.

the blank. When a smooth blank is used some workmen paste a piece of paper on the surface, then draw the design of the cutter on the paper. The blank is then ground to shape and afterwards to a keen cutting edge. On heavy-duty machines, flat knives usually are held between accurately machine grooved collars. A modern development for holding flat knives is an accurately machined cutter head. With this device a setup may be preserved indefinitely as the whole head is removable without changing the position of the knives. When a machine is provided with several extra cutter heads, the operator can change from one operation to another, for which he has a setup, without going through the customary somewhat tedious routine of setting and adjusting each knife.

Operation of a Shaper. When preparing the shaper for use, use a cloth soaked in kerosene to remove any pitch buildup on the edge of the knife. Fasten the fence and lock in position. The shaper, if possible, should be set up in a central location in the workshop, as the length of the work that it can handle is limited by the distance from the spindle to the walls or other machines. Note that the spindle turns in a counter clockwise direction when viewed from the spindle end. The cutter must be put on to the spindle so the cutting edge faces in the direction of rotation. When putting the cutter on, be sure the keyed washer is between the bottom nut and the cutter. When a depth collar is used, the washer goes between the bottom nut and the collar.

Straight shaping is the process of cutting a profile or contour on the straight edges of table tops and bench tops, and cutting moldings on straight lumber. To align the fence for straight shaping, place a straight edge against the left one and move the right one up to the straight edge and fasten.

Irregular shaping is the process of shaping the irregular edges of oval-shaped tables, curved legs, table stretchers, and decorative moldings. For irregular shaping remove the fence and replace with a collar of the proper depth for the cut to be made. A ring guard should always be used when shaping curved work directly against collars. Besides offering protection, the guard provides a hold-

down by pressing the work down on the table surface.

Matched shaping is used in the construction of cabinets, furniture trim, and similar work. A pair of matched cutters is used: one to cut the female portion of the molding forming the joint, the other to cut the male portion. Best-known examples are tongue-and-groove or drop-leaf cuts.

All shaper cutters must be kept as sharp as possible. A flat oilstone, about 2 by 6 inches, and a slipstone of the same material are recommended. To renew the edge, no great amount of metal need ever be removed at any one time, and the cutting angle of the edge should be changed as little as possible.

PLANES

Professional and amateur furniture-makers alike have found that no other woodworking tool can match the accuracy and the smoothness of finish that can be achieved with a correctly sharpened and properly adjusted plane. We all owe a debt to the unknown medieval craftsman who first came up with the idea of mounting a sharp chisel in a block of wood so that it would be held firmly and at a constant angle while he was using the blade to trim lumber to a specific size or shape (and thus invented the first wood plane). However, there have been a great many changes since those early days. Many refinements and improvements have been made, and there are now many different sizes and styles available, both hand and motor-driven. Some planes are primarily designed to fill special needs, while others are for general all-round trimming, shaping, and smoothing. Before you can select the model, or models, that will best meet your particular requirements for various jobs, you will have to know something about the different types that are available. You should also be familiar with the most important characteristics of each type of plane used in furniture-making.

Hand Planes

The hand planes most commonly used around the home furniture-making workshop are of two gen-

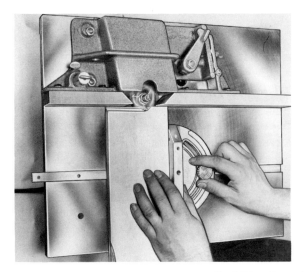

Fig. 2-73.   Examples of straight shaping.

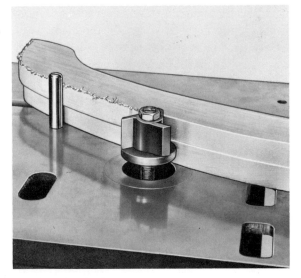

Fig. 2-74.   Examples of round and irregular shaping.

eral types: bench planes and block planes. Bench planes are bigger and come in various styles that measure from 8 to 22 inches in length; block planes are smaller, usually measuring 6 or 7 inches in length. Bench planes are held with one hand on the large handle at the back and one hand on the knob at the front end. Block planes are used with only one hand: you butt the palm of your hand against a contoured rest at the back end and place

your forefinger on the small knob at the front end. The other fingers are wrapped around the body of the tool to hold it firmly.

In both bench and block planes there is a chisel-like blade (called the plane iron) that is held in place so that it projects down through the base, or sole, of the tool at a sharp angle. A second piece of metal (called the plane iron cap) is clamped on top of this blade to reinforce it and to curl the shavings away without splintering the wood and in a continuous ribbon no thicker than the clearance provided between the bottom of the tool and the projecting edge of the blade.

All modern planes have some means for controlling the depth of cut by adjusting the amount that the plane iron blade projects down through the base of the tool.

Bench Planes. These are the most widely used and most versatile of all hand planes. The plane iron cap assembly is held in place by a heavy cast piece called the lever cap. It locks the plane iron and cap against an angled metal casting (called the frog), which supports the entire blade assembly and which has an adjusting screw at the back to permit raising or lowering the blade for regulating the depth of cut. In addition a lever at the top provides for a slight lateral adjustment—if you move the lever to one side, the whole assembly pivots slightly so that you can tilt the blade when necessary to line up its cutting edge exactly parallel across the base of the plane. The easiest way to do this is to turn the plane upside-down and sight along the base while you move the adjusting lever to one side or the other, as necessary, until you can see that the blade projection is equal across the entire width of the tool. This will ensure a shaving of uniform thickness across the width of the blade and will minimize the possibility of gouging.

Depending on their length, bench planes generally fall into three different categories. The smallest and most popular group are the *smoothing planes*, which may be either 8 or 9 inches in length. Next are the *jack planes*, which vary from 11 to 15 inches in length. The longest ones of all are the *fore planes* and *jointer planes*, which may be anywhere from 18 to 24 inches in length. Actually there is only a slight difference between fore planes and jointer planes (the latter are longer—22 to 24 inches in length), so the names are often used interchangeably. Both are used for essentially the same kind of work—for trimming and truing up the edges of doors and long boards. The long base on these tools makes it much easier to trim to a straight line; shorter planes, like the smoothing planes that are only 8 or 9 inches in length, will

tend to follow dips and curves without leveling them out. Longer planes will slide over the low spots and knock off the high spots until a level surface—or a straight edge—is attained.

The smoothing planes are most popular with home carpenters because their shorter length makes them easier to use on most projects and because they are generally easier to handle and carry around (they also cost less than the longer models). Jack planes are in between the two. Of the various size jack planes the 14-inch size is most popular. Jack planes are excellent for rough work where you have to dress lumber to size, as well as for trimming doors and taking waves out of warped lumber. They are available with either a smooth or corrugated bottom. The smooth bottom is the most popular for general work, although the corrugated bottom is preferred by some because it offers less friction. On green or sappy wood the corrugated bottom minimizes the likelihood of sticking or gumming up.

The plane iron (blade) on all bench planes, regardless of length, has a cutting edge that is beveled on one side only, like a chisel. It is ground to an angle of about 25 or 30 degrees and sits in place with its beveled side down. The plane iron cap is clamped on top so that there is approximately $\frac{1}{16}$ of an inch clearance between the cutting edge of the blade and the lower edge of the cap. The curved edge of this cap must fit snugly against the top face of the blade so that shavings cannot get wedged between the two. The assembled unit should be held firmly by the cam-action lever cap so that there is no chance of the blade wobbling or slipping while in use.

Block Planes. These little brothers of the hand plane family are, as previously mentioned, designed to be held with only one hand. There are tiny models that are only about 3 inches in length, which are used for light trimming and model-making, but the most popular versions are either 6 or 7 inches length. In addition to its more compact size, the block plane's principal difference from the bench plane is that its blade is mounted at a lower angle. This makes it more suitable for trimming end grain and for taking off very thin shavings.

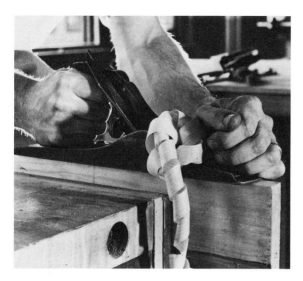

Fig. 2-75.   Bench plane (*left*) and block plane (*right*) in use.

Like bench planes, block planes have a plane iron cap to keep the blade from digging in and to curl shavings off in a uniform thickness. Block planes also have controls for adjusting the depth of cut by raising or lowering the blade to vary the amount it projects through the base. On the simplest and cheapest models the blade is held in place by a wedge, while in the better-quality models there are regular adjusting screws and lateral adjusting levers similar to those on the larger bench planes. Unlike bench planes, however, block planes are almost always designed so that the beveled edge on the blade faces upward, instead of downward, because it cuts at a much lower angle. In addition the beveled edge of the block plane's blade is usually ground to an angle of about 20 degrees, as compared with the 25- or 30-degree angle on a bench plane's blade.

Since block planes are used primarily on end grain and other trimming jobs where thin shavings are desired, they should be adjusted so that the blade barely projects beyond the base of the tool. Most people allow the blade to project too far and then find that it tends to dig in or gouge the surface, particularly on end grain. A small projection will actually cut faster because it will enable you to use the block plane properly—with a series of light, rapid strokes rather than with the heavy, long strokes more appropriate for a bench plane.

When trimming end grain, however, regardless of the type of plane you are using, remember always to work from each edge in toward the center. Running your plane all the way across the end grain of a board will invariably split it at the far end. However, if the piece is too small or located in such a way that it is impractical to work from both sides toward the middle, then a backup block of scrap wood can be clamped on the far end. If this is clamped tightly against the edge of the board, it should help prevent splitting, but play it safe and cut with light strokes only.

Special Furniture-Making Hand Planes. There are several specialized hand planes that you will probably find useful in furniture-building, particularly if your shop is not equipped with power tools such as a router or a table saw with a dado cutter.

Rabbets, dadoes, and grooves can be cut with a number of different types of rabbet planes. The most popular and versatile is an 8-inch-long model that has a large handle at the back end and two positions for the cutter blade, one in the middle for regular work and the other at the front end for

Fig. 2-76.   *Left:* A combination plane has a variety of interchangeable cutter blades that enable you to form practically any shape along edges and surfaces in a single operation. It can be used for producing fancy decorative effects on wood or for shaping a variety of moldings. *Right:* The edge-trimming block plane is a particularly useful plane that makes it easy to square up a board. The plane is machined to a perfect 90-degree angle, and the cutter blade is set at an angle to make cutting easier.

bullnose work (for working close into tight corners and up against right-angle corners). The 1½-inch cutter blade goes across the full width of the frame so that you can cut flush up against either side. The tool also has an adjustable fence that can be used on either side and a removable depth gauge that enables you to control the depth of cut precisely. A special spur cutter is supplied for cutting across the grain (not parallel to the grain), and with the blade in the bullnose position you can cut stopped or blind rabbets that do not go all the way across the work.

In addition to this type of combination rabbet plane, which can be used for either regular or bullnose work, there are also smaller specialty versions available. One is a 5½-inch-long side rabbet plane with cutters only ½ inch wide, which is handy for side rabbeting jobs when trimming dadoes, moldings, and grooves. It fits easily into your pocket, so you can carry it to any job without difficulty, and is handy for such jobs as widening the grooves in a tongue-and-groove joint or taking off thin shavings from the side of a stopped groove or blind dado.

A small, 5½-inch-long regular rabbet plane is also available with a cutter only 1 inch wide, as is a tiny bullnose rabbet plane that measures only 4 inches in length. Both have adjustable blades and have sides and bottoms ground square to one another for use on either side.

If you're up against a curve, you'll appreciate the value of these planes that will smooth a circular edge, either concave or convex. Built with flexible steel bottoms, they can be adjusted to form a curve to fit the work (20-inch minimum radius). Separate planes are used for convex and concave work.

The spokeshave plane is a tool that is designed for curved work and is always pushed rather than pulled. Most have adjusting nuts that set the depth of the blade or cut.

Portable Power Planes
Although most home craftsmen are familiar with the labor-saving advantages of portable electric

drills, power saws, and motor-driven sanders, many are not yet aware that they can also buy motor-driven electric planes that will do trimming and smoothing jobs in a fraction of the time required for hand planing and with no more effort than that required to move the tool along the surface. Professional craftsmen have been using these for a number of years to speed the work of trimming and hanging doors or installing cabinets, but it is only in the past five or ten years that home-size models have been introduced by several prominent manufacturers.

The cutting action of an electric plane is derived from a high-speed rotating cutter head similar to that on a stationary jointer-planer or wood-shaper. The cutter head is usually equipped with two spiral blades and is mounted in the middle of a sole plate, or base, so that the cutting edges project slightly below the surface. Although they are relatively compact and light in weight, electric planers must have powerful motors since a very high speed is essential for a smooth and rapid cut. As is true with shapers, routers, and other tools that cut with rotating knives, the higher the speed the smoother the cut.

The principal manufacturers of electric hand planes currently produce them in three basic styles. The most popular, especially with professionals, is actually a planing attachment that uses a router motor as the source of power. Consisting of a 16-inch-long base with a pistol-grip handle at the back end, these tools are used with the appropriate router motor by taking off the router's base, then slipping the motor sideways into the plane attachment. A special spiral cutter blade fits on the arbor of the router motor and projects down under the plane's base so that it contacts the wood when the tool is resting on the surface.

The depth of cut is regulated by a threaded micrometer adjustment that regulates how deep the cutters project below the base of the tool. Since router motors operate at speeds of 20,000 rpm or more, and since those adaptable for use as planes are generally rated at approximately 1 horsepower, they are ideal power sources for an electric plane. Actually planing attachments that are available for

routers will plane stock slightly wider than 2 inches and will cut as deep as $3/32$ of an inch in one pass. Since the base, or sole, plate of the tool is about 16 inches long, it is ideal for rapid planing and trimming of doors and long boards as well as for edge-trimming of long panels. All come equipped with a right-angle adjustable fence to help guide the tool accurately along the face of the work, and almost all have bevel adjustments for planing at an angle.

As with the hand planes, electric planes also come in a smaller version known as a power block plane. Although its width of cut is almost the same as the larger 16-inch planes (it will dress lumber up to $1\frac{3}{4}$ inches wide), its maximum depth of cut is only $1/64$ of an inch in one pass. However, it is much smaller and lighter and it is designed to be operated with only one hand. Because of these advantages, most home furniture-makers will actually find it easier and more convenient to use on many jobs, including trimming doors, fitting furniture parts, or shaving off end grain on lumber. Its high speed (21,000 rpm) gives an extremely smooth cut even on end grains and plastics, and it is designed so that the cutter fits flush on one side to permit cutting into corners. You can also use this handy little electric tool for cutting rabbets and tenons as well as for planing flat surfaces and edges.

THE JOINTER-PLANER-MOLDER

By a change of its cutting knife or head this power tool can perform an unlimited number of woodworking tricks. Where a saw cuts to length and a drill makes holes, the jointer-planer reduces wood to exact thickness and shape. Since it can perform so many varied functions, the tool itself is known by a great many different names. You may know it as a molding cutter, a thickness planer, a jointer, or a jointer-planer—and a good many more names as well. But basically it's the same tool with different "heads" on the business end.

Among its many accomplishments are jointing (making edges interlock or preparing them for gluing); surface planing (smoothing wood or reducing its thickness); rabbeting, bevel-cutting, and taper cutting; shaping moldings; and edging cutouts.

The Jointer

One part of the tool under discussion, the jointer, eliminates hours of hand planing on jobs that are always better done by machine. It does in minutes what would take hours by hand, and more accurately besides. In effect the tool becomes a motorized plane. It planes smooth the surfaces and edges of pieces of wood for joining with glue and prepares lumber for a final sanding on exposed surfaces.

In many jointers the wood is pushed along a divided table and over rapidly whirling cutters that protrude a measured distance above the tables. The front table, on which the wood starts its trip, is separated from the rear table (which is elevated above the front table) by the whirling knives. The cutter head is usually somewhat cylindrical, and the knives are inserted into it. As the blades wear down, the rear table can be adjusted to compensate.

All jointers have a fence, or guide, that can be set at any desired angle. Auxiliary fences can be added, which helps when jointing wide boards on the edges. A spring-tensioned guard protects the operator from the knives. *Don't remove the guard.* A muzzled dog can't bite you, and a jointer with a guard over the cutting knives is equally harmless.

In making use of the machine, never cut deeper than $\frac{1}{8}$ inch with each pass of the wood past the blades. In fact cuts as thin as $\frac{1}{32}$ inch make for a better job, even as hand planing is better done with fine rather than deep strokes.

Edge-Planing or Jointing. The most common function of this power tool is edging for jointing. The fence is set square to the table at 90 degrees. The depth of cut is set— $\frac{1}{16}$ to $\frac{1}{8}$ inch—and the best face of the wood to be cut is set against the fence. Place the wood lightly upon the front table and press it against the fence. Hold the wood with both hands and move it forward across the cutter head. As the wood passes over the knives, hold it with the right hand, advance the left without

passing it directly over the head, and grasp the wood on the opposite side. As you near the end of the piece, use both hands to press the wood down on the rear table to keep the end from being depressed and knicked at the lower corner. That's all there is to it. Just steady pressure and forward motion.

Planing End Grain. With end grain (which also may frequently become part of a joint) feed the work halfway into the cutter head, remove it, and push through the other end halfway. This reduces the chance of splitting along the grain, just as in hand planing.

Surface Planing. Here the limit of board width may be decided by the jointer size—4 or 6 inches. The purpose is to smooth the flat and wide surface. Lay the board flat, holding it with both hands against the fence and the table. No part of the hands or fingers should extend over the edges of the board. Beginners—and careless old-timers—should use a pusher stick to advance the work.

When planing a board wider than the surface of the jointer, remove the fence and make several passes across the cutter heads, thus covering the entire board surface. Make the first two passes on the outer 3 inches of the two sides before you make the center passes.

Bevel Cuts. Instead of tilting the table, tilt the fence to the desired angle for a beveled edge. Lock the fence in place securely. Wherever possible tilt the fence to a closed angle (less than 90 degrees). You'll have better control of the work when fitting into the closed angle. In most cases this work will require several passes across the cutter heads, reducing the stock a little more each time across, until full depth of bevel is reached.

Rabbeting. This is the only operation where the guard must be removed. Remove the guard, set the fence for the width of the rabbet, and set the front table for the depth of the rabbet to be cut. Hold the wood firmly, and feed it slowly. If the cut is deep, make several passes across the cutters.

In making rabbets across the end grain—a common form of jointing—lay the edge to be cut down and against the fence. Use a form of pusher if at all possible.

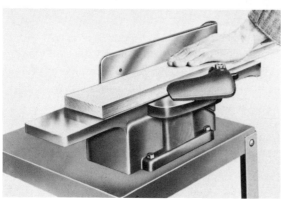

Fig. 2-77. *Top left:* In pushing material over cutters, all parts of hands and fingers should be above the table. *Above:* For wider boards remove fence and guard and pass outer edges, then center, over cutters. *Bottom left:* Correct positioning of hands, guard, and fence in surface planing of boards.

Fig. 2-78. *Top right:* In cutting a rabbet, cutout section is on underside, and fence side, of piece being cut. *Below:* Bolt on fence addition for longer pieces as required for grain-end rabbets and smoothing. *Bottom right:* Eventually you can manage without the stop block, but it is still good for cutting multiple pieces.

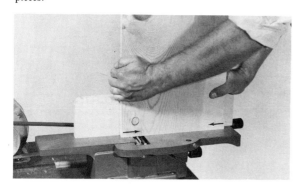

Taper Jointing. This is one of the most interesting jobs your jointer will do. While it's possible to cut a 9-inch taper on a 9-inch piece of wood, it's better to start out with wood that is longer than the taper. All taper cuts start with one end of the piece of wood resting on the rear table, which is raised above the front (infeed) table. The height of the rear table is set to produce the desired angle of taper.

When the length of the taper to be cut is *shorter* than the infeed table, try this method:

1. You want to taper 9 inches of a 15-inch table leg ¼ inch. Mark the work, and set the infeed table ¼ inch lower.

2. Clamp a stop block to the infeed table 9 inches from the cutter.

3. Rest the end to be tapered against the stop block, press down on this end, and feed in.

4. If more than one side is to be tapered, as may happen with a table leg, repeat these steps on the other sides to be tapered.

Eventually you'll become so proficient at this that you can omit the stop block and start from the marked line without the block. If you have the wood to waste on practice, try it right away. But for economy try it the right way first, then work up to the no-block method.

When the taper is going to end up longer than the front table, you'll need to follow this system:

1. Mark off the taper and divide into two equal sections—say each 10 inches long for a 20-inch taper. The taper is to be ¼ inch deep.

2. Lower the feeding table half the depth of the taper—in this case ¼ inch only.

3. Make the first cut, starting at the 10-inch marker point and going to the end of the marked area.

4. Make the second cut, starting this time at the 20-inch mark and running the full 20 inches in length.

5. Repeat for other sides of the taper.

Other Uses. The jointer will also allow you to convert plain stock to tongue-and-groove stock with selected cutter heads. And with combination cuts you can make other interlocking joints for connecting two pieces of wood permanently together with the addition of glue only.

Molder-Planer Machines

Thickness planers are often in a class by themselves. Molder-planers can be converted to other uses, such as jointing, by the addition of other blades. They can also be used to make moldings of various types with these knives. Basically, however, the molder-planer is a thickness planer, a small machine to pass boards *through*, rather than across, to reduce their thickness.

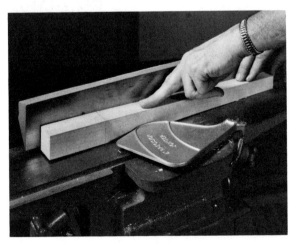 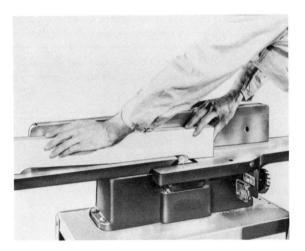

Fig. 2-79. *Left:* The long taper needs no block, runs through from high to low end, and is repeated on all sides. *Right:* More intricate work on tapering can also be handled—here a cutout made as a taper.

Fig. 2-80.   A molder-planer (*left*) and a thickness planer (*right*).

A curious feature of the molder-planer is that its opening is twice the rated capacity; by reversing the board and passing it through twice on opposite sides, a double-width board may be handled.

With this molder-planer you can create from raw stock such materials as door and window casings, baseboards and their trim, tongue-and-groove boards, knotty pine and other ornamented panel stocks (such as the popular V- grooved boards for random-width work), and similar well-known shapes.

All these can be created from rough stock of irregular thickness and shape. Your main limitation is in the amount of wood that can be removed from stock as it passes through the machine and over the knives.

The Thickness Planer

This machine, similar to the others in many respects, is used almost exclusively in making thick wood thinner. Naturally this suggests the salvage job—reduction of rough or irregular thickness. The original thickness planers were heavy, expensive machines. Today lighter-duty, hand-feed types are available and priced right for the average home furniture-maker. The cutter heads are on top instead of underneath the work.

As long as nails are removed, you can salvage secondhand lumber with this device at a great saving. It may have occurred to you already that this is the ideal way to remove old paint from wood and so salvage it without much work. Well, you are right, but you must consider that old paint is partly metallic and raises cain with the blades. If you can afford the time to sharpen the blades or to replace those permanently damaged, it will work. But you'll do better to remove old paint, and old nails, before reducing the wood to desired thickness.

THE LATHE

If you plan to make furniture of other than modern design, you'll need a lathe. Modern wood lathes are available in a variety of sizes and designs. For home furniture-making workshop use the lathe should have a bed long enough to accommodate a turning square 30 inches long. Most machines in this class have a "sweep," or turning swing, of about 12 inches over the bed. However, this is not as important as the distance between centers, since large work can always be mounted on an outboard faceplate. There are some points aside from capacity to consider when choosing a lathe: Will it do other jobs such as boring, sanding, and finishing? Is the construction heavy enough to absorb vibration?

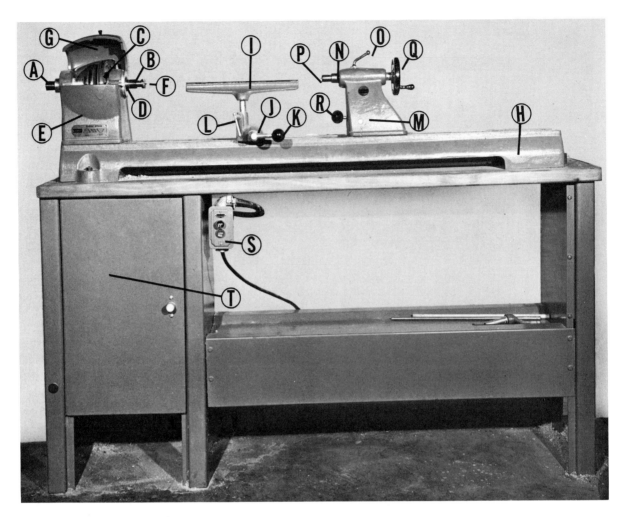

Fig. 2-81.   Nomenclature of a lathe. Lathes are available in a variety of sizes and designs, but all share certain common features. Here are the key components of a good modern wood lathe: (A) outboard headstock spindle; (B) inboard headstock spindle; (C) spindle pulley (note cone-pulley arrangement for adjusting belt for various speeds); (D) indexing stop pin (used for faceplate work and for spacing cuts in fluting); (E) headstock; (F) live (spur) center; (G) pulley cover; (H) lathe bed; (I) tool (tee) rest; (J) tool rest base; (K) tool rest base clamp; (L) tool rest clamp; (M) tailstock; (N) tailstock quill; (O) quill clamp; (P) dead (cup) center; (Q) quill wheel crank; (R) tailstock clamp; (S) on-off switch; (T) stand and motor housing.

Does it have a sturdy stand? Does it have a threaded outboard spindle for turning large work? Is the spindle hollow to permit passage of bar stock, if you want to do some light metal turning? And, finally, does it have the little extra features that add versatility and safety—well-covered pulleys, a protected motor housing, a stop pin for indexing the work when grooving, fluting, or drilling?

Essentially, lathe work can be divided into two categories: spindle-turning and faceplate turning.

Spindle-Turning

In turning between centers, the workpiece is referred to as a turning square. To prepare the square for the lathe, first trim it to length (allow a little extra for cutoff) and make sure that the ends are square, then find the centers on both ends by

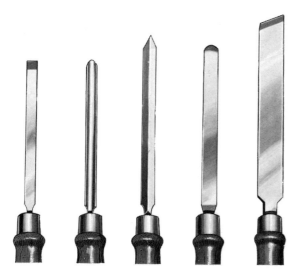

Fig. 2-82. Basic chisels for lathe work. *Left to right:* The squarenose is used for squaring shoulders, forming tapers, forming recesses, and smoothing convex forms; the gouge is used for initial roughing, fast stock removal, forming coves, and, occasionally, finishing; the parting tool is used for sizing cuts, cutting off, shouldering, and detailing; the roundnose is used for finish-forming inside curves and coves and cutting cavities in faceplate work; the skew is for smoothing flats and outside curves, end trimming, tapers, squaring shoulders, V-cuts, and beading.

scribing lines diagonally between opposite corners. To provide a solid bite for the live center (spur), make saw cuts about ⅛ inch deep along the scribed lines on one end. An awl or sharp punch can be used to make a small hole in the other end for the point of the cup center. If the square is a big one, you can ease the job of rough-cutting considerably by trimming the edges of the square with a planer or table saw so that it is approximately octagonal rather than a square.

Mark one of the teeth of the spur with a file, then mark the work correspondingly with a pencil. Thus if you remove the work before it is finished, you can easily reposition it in exactly the same relationship with the spur. Stand the square on end, position the teeth of the spur in the X-cut, and give the tail of the spur a couple of sharp raps with a mallet. This will give the spur a solid bite and ensure

against the work shifting on the center during turning. Never pound the work against the center when the spur is mounted in the spindle—this can cause serious damage to the headstock bearings.

When the spur has been sunk into the square, slip the tapered center into its hole in the spindle. Run the tailstock up to the other end of the square. Don't force it so that it binds, but be sure it's good and snug. After a few minutes of running, the center will "wear and seat," and the slack can be taken up. Be sure to lock the quill, or else vibration may loosen it enough to allow the work to come loose and go flying across the room. A little oil on the cup center will reduce friction and keep the work from burning, particularly when running at higher speeds. If the end is to be part of the finished piece and stains from the oil are a problem, use a dab of beeswax or a bit of graphite.

Adjust the drive belt on the pulleys for the proper speed and position the tool rest. The edge of the rest should be about ⅛ inch below the center line of the work, just far enough back to allow the square to turn without hitting it. Lock the rest firmly, and make a final check for clearance by turning the work by hand a few times. The large gouge is the tool you'll be using most often, and it's the one you need now. Grab the front with your left hand and the very end of the handle with your right. When you make a cut, let your knuckles ride along the back of the tool rest to act as a guide. Keep your thumb on top of the chisel and use it for control. Keep a firm hold on the tool, but don't take a death grip; that will only give you muscle cramps. Your right hand braces the tool and controls depth of cut by changing the angle of the tool.

Make a series of nicks all along the piece to prevent long splinters from breaking off during the roughing. Start the cut an inch or so in from the end; holding the gouge flat, bring the cut across. As you gain experience, you will find that cutting speed can be increased by rolling the gouge over slightly in the direction of the cut. The reason for not starting at the end, incidentally, is to eliminate the possibility of digging the chisel into a corner and knocking the work out of the centers.

Fig. 2-83. *Top:* The first step in roughing down a turning square is to nick the corners with a small gouge or parting tool. This eliminates the danger of breaking off long splinters. *Center:* Use calipers and parting tool to make guide cuts every few inches along the work. *Bottom:* Use a large skew or squarenose chisel to turn work to size.

It may surprise you, but to achieve top results, you should spend almost as much time whetting your chisels as cutting with them. At 3,000 rpm a 6-inch-diameter workpiece produces about 4,400 feet of shavings every minute. At that rate even the finest steel doesn't hold its edge for long. For whetting chisels, we prefer India or Arkansas stones that have been soaked in light oil. Both are much harder and will hone a far keener edge than conventional sharpening stones.

Table 2-3

RECOMMENDED LATHE SPEEDS FOR SPINDLE AND FACEPLATE WORK

Diameter of work	Roughing		Finishing	
	Min.	Max.	Min.	Max.
under 2 in.	900	1,500	2,500	4,000
2-4 in.	600	1,000	2,000	3,000
4-6 in.	600	800	1,800	2,500
6-8 in.	400	600	1,200	2,000
8-10 in.	300	600	900	1,500
over 10 in.	300	600	600	900

To determine the speed of the spindle, multiply the speed of the motor pulley by its diameter, then divide by the diameter of the spindle pulley. Larger motor pulley and smaller spindle pulley will increase spindle speed; smaller motor pulley and larger spindle pulley will decrease spindle speed.

An old pair of heavy leather gloves will save a lot of wear and tear on the fingers when sanding produces high frictional heat. Straight edges and shallow curves can best be finished with sandpaper cut in strips 2 to 3 inches wide. After removing the tool rest, hold one end of the paper and let the other end follow under the work so that it bears on about half the work diameter. Use the gloved hand to work the paper against the turning. Start with

Fig. 2-84.   *Left:* An effective and easy way to turn down a straight section is with a wood plane. Set the blade for a very fine cut, hold the plane at an angle to the work, and move from end to end. *Right:* Sand a finished spindle with sandpaper cut in strips. The position shown allows pressure to be applied without tearing paper. Glove protects hand from friction.

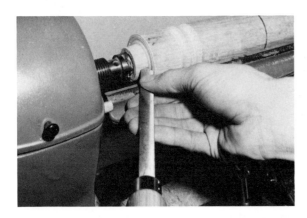

Fig. 2-85.   *Left:* To true up the ends of a spindle, use a spearpoint chisel and a scraping cut. The pencil marks were made on the stock to indicate locations of further cuts. *Right:* To eliminate chatter and whip when turning fine work between centers, support the work with your free hand. Leather glove protects hand from heat and splinters.

coarse paper, changing to progressively finer grits until you achieve the desired finish. Remember, speeds that are too high will cause the paper to burn the work.

When you're ready to cut off the work, turn down the tail stub to a little less than ½ inch and smooth the end down to it. Belt the lathe down to its slowest speed. Hold the headstock end of the work loosely with one hand while you slowly cut the piece through with the parting tool. When the cutoff is finished, the workpiece will drop free.

Faceplate Turning

Faceplates are available in sizes ranging from about 3 to 9 inches in diameter. The larger ones are drilled so that the work can be attached with wood screws, while the smaller ones have their own single screw center. Unless the workpiece is very small, the first step in faceplate turning is to remove the corners from the blank, making it roughly octagonal. On larger work use a band- or scroll saw to cut the blank in a circle. This not only saves time but is highly important from the standpoint of bal-

Fig. 2-86.   *Right:* On inboard faceplate work use gouge and scraping cut for all roughing. Keep tool rest as close to work as possible, and make cuts from center toward outside edge. *Far right:* Turning back of inboard faceplate project is made easier by using short tee rest that can be moved in closer to the work. Bowl is being finished at high speed with skew.

Fig. 2-87.   *Right:* Right-angle rest allows two surfaces of turning to be worked on without repositioning the rest. This is the proper position for a scraping cut. *Far right:* For really big work a special faceplate is mounted on the outboard end of the headstock spindle and a floor-stand tool rest is used.

ancing the work. When the blank is prepared, center the faceplate and attach it with large, short wood screws. If you plan to cut deep enough into the work for the screws to present a problem, glue a piece of scrap backing stock to the work and run the screws into this. If you sandwich a piece of paper between the two pieces of wood when you glue them together, the scrap backing can be easily split off with a chisel after the project is completed.

Clean the spindle threads (so the faceplate doesn't bind) with a small brush, and screw on the plate and work. The first step in turning a disk is to true the edge, so adjust the tool rest accordingly. Use a small skew, and cut in from the front. If you leave a small fin at the back, you will greatly reduce chances of splitting a big chunk out of the work.

Now set the tool rest so that you can make your finishing cuts (and also remove the fin) from the edge.

The job of hollowing out the inside may now be started, so reposition the tool rest once more. Use the large gouge for roughing. The technique is exactly the same as for spindle-turning except that all cuts must be started at the center of the work, then continued toward the outside edge. As stock removal progresses, the tool rest should be moved, keeping it as close to the work as possible. Finish by scraping with a roundnose chisel.

Make the final finishing cuts on the outside by shearing with the skew. A folded pad of sandpaper and a leather glove to protect the fingers from the heat are all you need to do the fine finishing.

Chapter 3

NAILS, SCREWS, GLUES, AND OTHER FASTENING METHODS

If the piece of furniture is to be durable, it must be made out of sturdy material and with secure joints. To accomplish the latter, the material should be held together or fastened by nails, screws, glue, or a combination of any of these. But whether you fasten with nails, screws, dowels, splines, bolts, or adhesives, three basic principles must be considered:

1. Fasteners must be strong enough to support both external and internal stresses.

2. Fasteners must be placed so as to overcome any tendency of the wood to bend, belly, or buckle.

3. Fasteners must be of a type to compensate for any potential movement. Movement must be anticipated where there are extreme fluctuations in moisture content or where wood parts are fastened to supporting members of different material.

NAILS

While nails are not the prime fastening devices in furniture-making that they are in most other phases of woodworking, they *are* used, and their proper selection is important. One of the major sources of confusion is the method of naming the sizes of nails in terms of pennies. We hear about 4-penny nails, 10-penny nails, even 60-penny nails. Things are confused a little more by the practice of abbreviating penny as *d*, the English sign for pence, so that sizes are written 4d, 10d, and 60d. This nomenclature originated when nails were sold by the hundred, the number of pence being the price per hundred. Today most nails are sold by the pound (weight, not currency), but the penny designation has stuck. The four most frequently used types of nails—"common" nails, box nails, casing nails, and finishing nails—come in penny sizes, but many other kinds are designated simply in inches.

The kind of nails you buy depends on what you want to use them for.

The four types mentioned here are multi-purpose nails that can be used for most nailing jobs. The main distinction among them is that common nails and box nails have flat heads, while casing nails and finishing nails have narrow heads that sink into the work and can be concealed easily. There is also a variation in diameter for a given length; common nails are thicker than box nails, although they have the same basic shape; casing nails are about the same diameter as box nails in each length; and finishing nails are thinner than casing nails. This is worth knowing when you need a nail of a certain length but want to make sure it will not be so thick that it will split the wood.

A nail must be properly selected for the work it is to do so that it will not split the wood or distort the fibers. The type of nail that distorts the fibers of the wood the least will have the greatest holding power. When nailing two pieces of wood together, you should use a nail that will *practically* go through both pieces. The length of the nail should be about $\frac{3}{16}$ inch less than the combined thickness of the two pieces. This is true only when surface-nailing, that is, driving a nail through the thickness section of both pieces. In edge-nailing, the nail size should be three times the thickness of the first piece of lumber through which the nail is being driven. Whenever possible, you should nail through the thinner piece into the thicker one. Otherwise the nail might be too thick and split the second piece into which it is being driven.

Hammers

While all hammers are pounding tools, each member of this prolific family has its specialty. Fortunately for the budget of the home furniture-

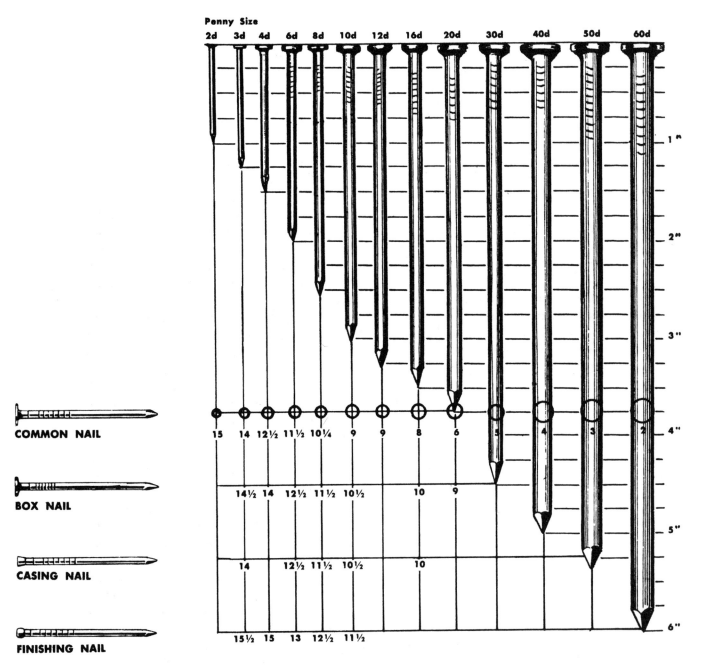

COMMON NAIL

BOX NAIL

CASING NAIL

FINISHING NAIL

Fig. 3-1.   Chart of nail dimensions (see Table 3-1).

maker, the number useful around his shop is relatively limited.

Nail or claw hammers, the kind most frequently used, are available in head weights of 7 to 20 ounces; 13 to 16 ounces is more or less standard. A good claw hammer has a smoothly crowned face to allow driving nails flush without marring the surface. The face and edge of the poll are hardened to resist wear and marring; the center of the face is slightly harder than the rim to prevent chipping.

Table 3-1

NAILS

COMMON NAILS					FINISHING NAILS				
Size	Length	Diameter gauge no.	Diameter of head	Approx. no. per pound	Size	Length	Diameter gauge no.	Diameter of head gauge no.	Approx. no. per pound
2d	1″	15	$^{11}/_{64}$″	830	**2d**	1″	16½	13½	1,351
3d	1¼″	14	$^{13}/_{64}$″	528	**3d**	1¼″	15½	12½	807
4d	1½″	12½	¼″	316	**4d**	1½″	15	12	584
5d	1¾″	12½	¼″	271	**5d**	1¾″	15	12	500
6d	2″	11½	$^{17}/_{64}$″	168	**6d**	2″	13	10	309
8d	2½″	10¼	$^{9}/_{32}$″	106	**8d**	2½″	12½	9½	189
10d	3″	9	$^{5}/_{16}$″	69	**10d**	3″	11½	8½	121
12d	3¼″	9	$^{5}/_{16}$″	63					
16d	3½″	8	$^{11}/_{32}$″	49	**16d**	3½″	11	8	90
20d	4″	6	$^{13}/_{32}$″	31	**20d**	4″	10	7	62

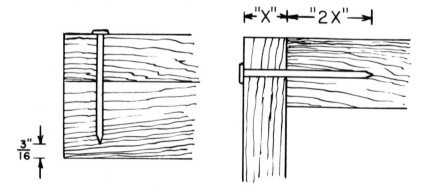

Figure 3-2.   Surface nailing (*left*) and edge nailing (*right*).

The claw is also hardened and has sharpened inner edges that bite into nails which must be pulled.

There's no magic in using a claw hammer—or any other type, for that matter. Grasp the handle near the end. Hold it firmly, but don't choke it to death. Position the nail, holding it with thumb and forefinger. Lay the face of the hammer squarely on the nailhead, raise the hammer a few inches with a *wrist* movement, and give the nail a light swat. Depending on the force needed, the correct swing is

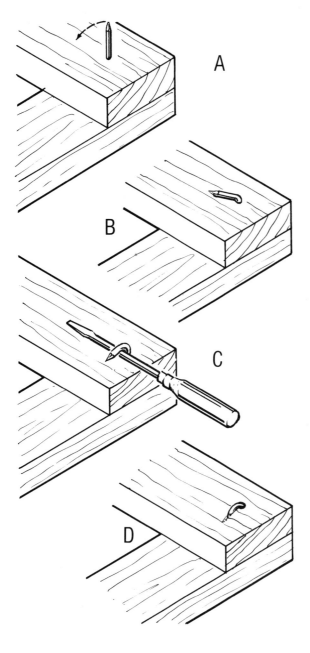

Figure 3-3.   How to clinch nails.

Clinched nails have more holding power than those that are driven straight. To clinch a nail, drive it through both boards so that one-third of the nail extends beyond the board. If you hammer the excess and the point down with the grain, it is possible to drive the nail below the surface of the board (Fig. 3-3, A). For a stronger joint, however, the excess of the nail and the point should be hammered down across the grain (B). This provides maximum strength but requires heavier blows of the hammer to depress the point. A quick and easier way to do this job is to bend the nail over an old screwdriver (C). Hammer the point of the nail toward the wood. (You can use a triangular file, but files are brittle and are likely to break.) Remove the screwdriver, and hammer the excess projecting upward from the board (D). Make certain that the head of the nail (on the other side) is flush against a sturdy surface such as a metal block.

To pull a nail, slip the claw under the head hard enough to let it bite. Then, holding the workpiece

Fig. 3-4.   When pulling a long nail, use a wood block under the hammerhead for better leverage and to avoid marring the work surface.

wrist alone, wrist and arm, or wrist, arm, and shoulder. You'll do better with a series of light blows instead of one or two smashing whacks. The nail will hold better and there is less chance of missing your mark.

Fig. 3-5. *Left:* When there is danger of splitting, especially in end grain, drill a pilot hole a little smaller than the nail diameter. *Right:* When nailing and gluing, start nails in upper piece, then apply glue to the surfaces. Place pieces in contact and drive the nails home.

steady, pull the handle until it points almost straight up. Don't force it beyond the vertical. The hammer loses its leverage at this point, and further exertion will bend the nail, mar the work, or even break the hammer handle. Instead, ease up on the claw higher, then repeat.

In fastening hardwoods, bore holes slightly smaller than the diameter of the nail and to a depth two-thirds of its length. In nailing a board end, blunt the tip of the nail to prevent it from splitting the end. A few staggered nails are stronger than a large number of nails in a row. If one of two pieces of wood to be joined is thin, use nails that will penetrate half to three-fourths of the second piece.

In fine work, where the nailhead must not show or must be inconspicuous, it is driven well below the surface with a nail set. The hole in the wood over the nailhead can then be filled with putty, plastic wood, or sawdust mixed with glue.

Nail sets are made in several sizes, usually $\frac{1}{32}$, $\frac{2}{32}$, and $\frac{3}{32}$ inch, the size being the diameter of the small end of the tapered shank. The end of a nail set is often "cupped," or hollowed, which prevents

it from "walking," or slipping, on the nail. Use a nail set of a size that won't enlarge the hole made by the head of the nail.

Blind Nailing. Blind nailing is an old craftsman's trick that is used where a clear-finished piece of wood may show its filled-in nail holes. To accomplish this trick, start by gouging up a sliver in the surface of the wood with a small chisel or carving gouge. The narrower the sliver the better, although it should be wide enough so that the nail-head can be buried beneath it. Drive a finishing nail at a slight angle into the wood behind the sliver. Sink it beneath the surface of the wood and below the bottom of the sliver, using a nail set. Next apply any good wood glue behind the sliver, and use masking tape over the sliver to hold it tightly down in place, flush with the surface of the wood, while the glue sets. If the wood is to be finished clear, keep the glue clean or else it will leave a dark outline around the sliver. Allow the glue to set and dry before removing the tape. A light sanding with a fine-grain paper will smooth out the sliver's edges until they are invisible.

Fig. 3-6. *Left:* On surfaces to be finished, exposed nailheads should be set in with a nail or nail set. Use size corresponding to type of nailhead. *Right:* Conceal counterset nails with paste filler or wood putty. Allow filler to dry, then sand smooth before applying finish.

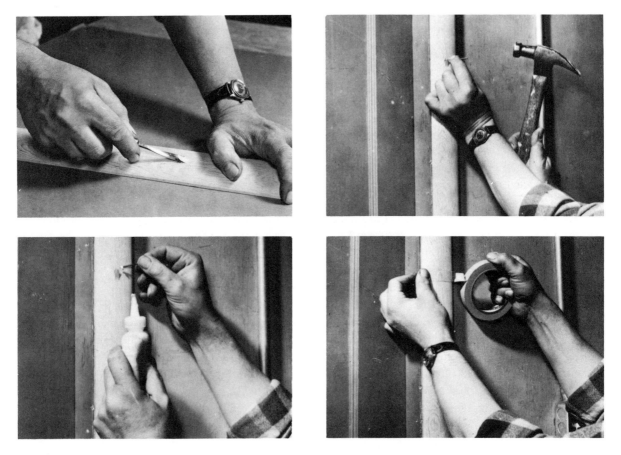

Fig. 3-7. *Top left:* To blind nail, gouge out a thin sliver of wood. *Top right:* Drive in and countersink a nail. *Bottom left:* Glue sliver back down. *Bottom right:* Tape sliver in place until glue dries. Sand area smooth with fine-grain paper to complete job.

Nailing Plywood. Plywood holds nails well, and they can be placed near the edge of a panel without splitting it. For finish work casing nails hold better than finish nails. Nailheads can be driven flush or slightly set and filled with wood filler, spackle, or putty. When this is done, the nail holes will be nearly invisible and the panels will be ready for finishing. If appearance is not important, box or common nails should be used. Spiral or ring-barbed nails give extra holding power. For exterior work use hot-dipped zinc-coated nails to avoid rust.

The thickness of the plywood you are using should determine the size of the nails. For ¾-inch plywood use 6*d* casing or 6*d* finish nails; for ⅝-inch, 6*d* or 8*d* finish nails; for ½-inch, 4*d* or 6*d*; for ⅜-inch, 3*d* or 4*d*; for ¼-inch, use ¾- or 1-inch brads, 3*d* finish nails, or (for backs where there is no objection to heads showing) 1-inch blue lath nails. Although proper spacing depends on the job, nails should be about 6 inches apart. Closer spacing is necessary only with thin plywood, where there may be slight buckling between nails. Nails and glue together produce a strong, durable joint.

Before nails are placed on, or very close to, an edge, drill a pilot hole slightly smaller than the nail diameter at each spot where you want a nail to go.

SCREWS

Screws are recommended over nails in furniture construction in the following cases: (1) when the work may have to be taken apart at some future date; (2) when greater holding power is required of the joint; (3) when it is important that the finished job be unmarred by such accidents as misguided hammer blows; and (4) when appearance of the finished project must be as neat as possible.

Screws should always be used when the pull of the load is to be directed along the length of the fastening devices. A nail in this position will pull out; a screw will hold tightly.

Choosing the Right Screw
Since there are literally hundreds of types of screws, selection of the right one can be difficult. Screwheads are made round, flat, and beveled.

Fig. 3-8. Space nails about 6 inches apart for most work. Closer spacing is necessary only with thin plywood.

Shapes are long and thin or short and squat. The materials of which the screw can be made range from mild steel, blue steel, and galvanized steel to brass, copper, and cadmium-coated steel. Further, unlike nails, screws are not identified by length alone. A screw has two dimensions—diameter of the shank just below the head, which is the number of the screw, and the length, which is indicated in inches or fractions of an inch.

In choosing a screw for a specific purpose, first select the proper head style for the job. Round heads will remain exposed, and can become a part of the decorative scheme or must be used where they will remain unobtrusive. Flatheads will either be countersunk flush with the surface or buried deeper, where the screw itself will be concealed by a hole-filling material, such as plastic wood or putty, or by a wood plug.

When selecting a screw by its number, remember that the number indicates thickness only, and the length must be specified, too. Use a thin screw for hardwood, a thicker-shank screw for softer wood. A flathead screw is measured by its overall length; a roundhead screw is measured from its point to the base of the slot in the screwhead. Select a maximum length that will not protrude entirely through the wood. At the same time remember that, as with nails, the maximum area of wood fiber gripping the screw provides the maximum holding power.

In determining the safe load to be placed on a single screw, consult Table 3-2, which provides a

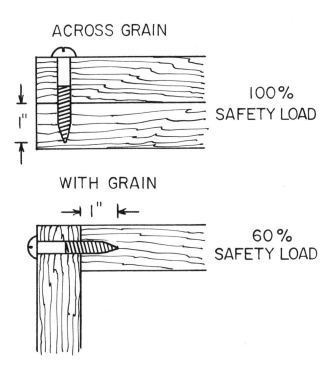

Fig. 3-9.   To determine load a screw will carry, refer to Table 3-2, Safety Load for Wood Screws. This table assumes that 1 inch of the screw thread is embedded in the wood across the grain. That is, 1 inch is inside the piece of wood to which another is attached. But if the screw is set with the grain, use 60 percent of the safety-load factor noted in the table. If only ½ inch is set into the second piece of wood, use half the safety-load factor, but if 2 inches are embedded, double the load factor.

guide for selection where 1 inch of screw thread is embedded in wood across the grain. This, of course, means 1 inch in the *holding* piece of wood of two pieces. For ½ inch of embedded screw use one-half of the load shown. For 2 inches of embedded screw thread double the load value. When the screw is set with the grain, use 60 percent of the indicated load figure.

Using Screws Correctly

In softwood it is necessary only to make a short indentation as a starting hole for the screw; your screwdriver plus wrist action will sink it into place.

In hardwood and for deeper holes where the screw length exceeds 1 inch, a drilled hole is

Table 3-2

SAFETY LOAD FOR WOOD SCREWS— CROSS GRAIN—IN POUNDS

Screw Number	4	8	12	16	20	24	28	30
White oak	80	100	130	150	170	180	190	200
Yellow pine	70	90	120	140	150	160	180	190
White pine	50	70	90	100	120	140	150	160

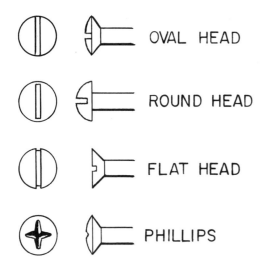

Fig. 3-10.   Various types of screwheads used in furniture work.

necessary. Perhaps the handiest invention on the market today to speed this process is the one-shot drill that makes pilot hole, shank hole, and countersink hole for flathead screws all in one operation.

In woods that are soft or medium-soft a pilot hole will serve for all purposes but countersinking. In hardwood a drilled hole similar in shape to the screw is needed. It is also necessary to drill the hole through both pieces of wood to be joined. Two boards cannot be drawn together by screw action alone because wood shreds will pile up between the boards and prevent a tight joining action.

In hardwood lack of a pilot hole and a secondary hole for the shank will invariably result in a splitting of the wood by the thickness of the screw.

Screws hold well in most types of plywood (for exceptions see pages 9-10). Table 3-4 contains the recommended screws for plywood under normal furniture applications.

Driving the Screws

To speed up the driving action on setting screws and to reduce palm blisters, it has long been customary to soap the threaded end of the screw. The idea was that this made driving the screw easier. This idea is correct, but in this situation,

Table 3-3

PILOT HOLE CHART

No. of screw	HARDWOOD	SOFTWOOD	Shank clearance holes
	Drill gauge No. to be used for maximum holding power		
0	66	75	52
1	57	71	47
2	54	65	42
3	53	58	37
4	51	55	32
5	47	53	30
6	44	52	27
7	39	51	22
8	35	48	18
9	33	45	14
10	31	43	10
11	29	40	4
12	25	38	2
14	14	32	D
16	10	29	I
18	6	26	N
20	3	19	P
24	D	15	V

Table 3-4

RECOMMENDED SCREWS FOR PLYWOOD

Plywood thickness	Flathead Screws		
	Screw	Length	Pilot hole
$\frac{3}{4}$ "	#8	$1\frac{1}{2}$ "	$\frac{5}{32}$"
$\frac{5}{8}$ "	#8	$1\frac{1}{4}$ "	$\frac{5}{32}$"
$\frac{1}{2}$ "	#6	$1\frac{1}{4}$ "	$\frac{1}{8}$"
$\frac{3}{8}$ "	#6	1"	$\frac{1}{8}$"
$\frac{1}{4}$ "	#4	$\frac{3}{4}$ "	$\frac{7}{64}$"

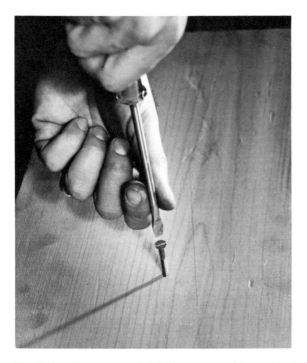 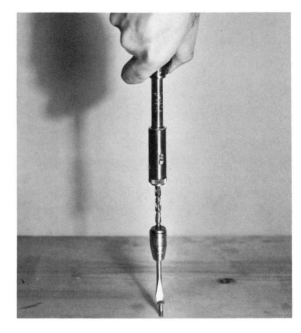

Fig. 3-11.   Proper method of driving a screw with a standard screwdriver (*left*) and with a spiral ratchet screwdriver (*right*).

soap turns to a form of glue and cements the screw into the hole. It also produces rust on steel screws and corrosion on brass screws. As a result withdrawing the screws later is almost impossible. Use candle wax or graphite instead of soap. Oil will stain and penetrate wood grain for some distance.

The second important consideration in driving screws is the use of the proper size screwdriver bit. If your screwdriver bit doesn't fit the screwhead slot, you will probably chip off bits of metal from the head, making it difficult or impossible to withdraw the screw and leaving a marred and broken screwhead. Failure to use steady, even pressure as you turn the screwdriver will produce a similar result.

For difficult-to-turn screws there are several possible driving techniques. If possible, use a hexagonal-shaft screwdriver over which a wrench may be fitted for those final difficult turns. Better still, especially where you have many screws to sink, use a special bit in your brace.

Don't use a hammer to drive screws. This is done often, of course, but it is a poor practice. The thread of a hammer-driven screw must force wood fibers out of its way to enter, and these shreds pack tightly deep in the hole and reduce the gripping power of the wood around the screw. If you're going to handle a screw in this fashion, you might as well use a nail.

When two pieces of wood are to be fastened tightly together with screws, two sets of holes must be drilled. The holes are drilled so that the threaded portion of the screw "bites," or takes hold, only in the underpiece of wood. The piece on top is clamped to the lower piece by the pressure of the screwhead. There are five steps in the operation:

1. Locate the position of the screw holes and mark them with a brad awl. The awl mark will center the drill and prevent it from "walking" away with the spot.

2. Bore a pilot hole, slightly smaller in diameter than the threaded portion of the screw, all the way through the upper piece of wood and into the lower piece, half the length of the threaded part of the screw.

3. Enlarge the pilot hole in the upper piece of wood by drilling it out to the same diameter as, or slightly larger than, the shank, or unthreaded portion, of the screws.

4. If flathead or ovalhead screws are to be used, countersink the clearance hole in the upper piece of wood to match the diameter of the heads of the screws. If roundhead screws or cup washers are used, don't countersink.

5. Drive all screws firmly in place; after they are all in, tighten each of them.

Screws are sometimes set below the surface of the wood and concealed by a wooden plug. Plugs cut in various diameters from mahogany, oak, pine, white cedar, and cypress can be purchased from dealers in boat supplies and at some hardware stores. Of course, plugs should match the wood in which they are to be inserted as closely as possible. You can also cut your own plugs, matching kinds of wood and grain. They should be cut so that the grain runs across the plug, not lengthwise. Sometimes dowels may be cut off for use as plugs.

To install a plug, first bore a hole at least ⅜ inch deep with an auger bit the same size as the wooden plug. Then bore the proper pilot and clearance holes. Drive the screw in as far as it will go with a screwdriver. Select a suitable plug, put some glue on its sides, and insert it in the hole, with the grain on the end of the plug running in the same direction as the grain on the surface of the work. Drive the plug in as far as it will go. When the glue has dried, use a chisel or a plane to pare off the plug level with the surface.

Screw Replacement. Since it is understood that a screw is used with the idea that it may later be removed and replaced several times, it is well to bear in mind that a screw that is withdrawn leaves a much larger hole than an extracted nail. Before it can be replaced, the hole must be rebuilt around the screw again for equal strength to result. You can follow one of two courses—use a longer screw for replacement, giving new gripping area, or fill the hole with plastic wood and reset the screw in this new material. Plastic plugs driven into the old screw holes form an excellent base for replaced screws.

Screwdrivers

Screwdrivers are sized according to the length of the shaft, which is measured from the tip to the bottom of the handle, and the width of the tip. The following sizes will be a good match for the average slotted-head screw: $\frac{7}{32}$-inch tip with 3-inch shaft; ¼-inch with 4-inch shaft; $\frac{5}{16}$-inch with 6-inch shaft; and ⅜-inch with 10-inch shaft. You also should have a stubby 1½-inch screwdriver

Fig. 3-12.   *Left:* Plug-cutter in operation. *Right:* The plug is used to conceal a screw.

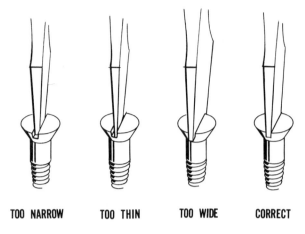

TOO NARROW   TOO THIN   TOO WIDE   CORRECT

Fig. 3-13.   Screwdrivers vary in blade width and blade length. They are usually specified by their blade length (from ferrule to tip). When selecting a screwdriver, be sure that the blade tip matches the slot of the screw. If the blade tip is too thin, or narrower or wider than the slot, the screwhead or the surrounding wood is likely to be chewed up before the screw is finally driven home.

with ¼-inch tip. It's excellent for working in very tight places.

If you do a lot of cabinetwork, you can speed up the task of driving screws by using a screwdriver bit in your electric drill. The best drill for the purpose is a ⅜-inch, variable-speed model, which has double-reduction gears that give the required torque, or turning power, needed for driving screws. The variable speed gives you the slow speed necessary for this kind of work. But even at the relatively slow speed used for driving screws (350-400 rpm) you may find it difficult to keep the screwdriver bit in the slot. The answer to this problem is the screwdriver bit with a finder sleeve, a metal, spring-loaded sleeve that helps you find the slot as you press the drill down on the screwhead. Its greatest value is that it helps keep the screw bit in the slot. Also very useful is a combined clutch and bit-holder that you can put in the chuck of your drill. The screwdriver bit and its finder sleeve can be snapped into the bit-holder of the clutch. When you press down with the drill, the clutch takes hold and the bit turns the screw. If you pull

back the drill slightly, the clutch disengages and the bit stops turning. You can thus stop to see what progress you are making without turning off the drill. The clutch also helps you to disengage quickly when the screw is driven home; without this element the drill can twist out of your hand.

OTHER FASTENERS AND HARDWARE

Metal fasteners, generally called mending plates and angle irons, can be used to reinforce wood joints. Available in many shapes and sizes, they can either be set into the wood or on its face. A mending plate recessed into the wood has more holding power than one placed on the surface. Half of the plate is first centered on one member of a joint and screwed in place. The second member of the joint is then held tightly against the first, and the other half of the fastener is screwed fast.

Corrugated fasteners, often called wiggle nails, are used for holding two wood surfaces together side by side. They can be used on miter joints, on edge-to-edge joints, to assemble frames with butt joints, or for tightening loose joints or cracks in woodwork. They are made with a plain edge for

Fig. 3-14.   Corrugated fasteners can reinforce miter joints and hold joints together while glue sets.

Fig. 3-15.   Two-hand staplers are excellent for nailing cabinet backs. They drive long staples, setting them below the surface if desired, and greatly speed up the work. They are sometimes available on loan or rental.

hardwoods and a saw edge for softwoods. They are generally used with glue for better holding power.

There is a trick to driving corrugated fasteners. Use a medium-weight hammer and strike light blows, evenly distributed over the outside edge. It is essential that the pieces that are being fastened together rest on something solid while the fastener is driven in.

Another steel fastener, the clamp nail, is new in woodworking. These nails are used only on miter joints. The wide end of the clamp nail is driven into a saw cut ³⁄₁₆ inch deep on both edges of the miter, and the joint is held more firmly than with corrugated fasteners.

Other furniture-fastening hardware on the market serves many special purposes. For example, there are steel-table or chair corner braces that enable you to pass a lag screw into the inside corner of a leg. Taking up on the screw locks the leg and rails firmly together.

GLUING

Gluing is the most common joining method in furniture construction. Actually glue is the neatest, most durable, and strongest wood fastener when properly used. Here is a summary of the most common wood furniture glues.

Plastic-Resin Glue. Excellent for fine furniture work, plastic resin glue is very strong and water-resistant. Used correctly, it will produce joints stronger than the wood itself, but to achieve this result the joints must be smooth and close-fitting. Another good quality is that it will not stain such hardwoods as mahogany and oak. It is very resistant to mold and rot. Plastic-resin glue is sold as powder and is mixed with water. Wood parts must be held in clamps for about ten hours at a temperature not less than 70°F.

Resorcinol Adhesives. For any good job that requires completely waterproof wood joints the best adhesive is resorcinol. This is a two-part adhesive that comes in twin cans. The two components must be mixed in precise proportions—usually four parts powder and three parts liquid. Resorcinol adhesives must be used at room temperature, and the wood parts must be kept in clamps overnight. If the room temperature drops below 70°F., however, the glue will still harden but the joint will be weaker. Glues of this type tend to shrink as they dry, so joints must be smooth and fit closely.

Polyvinyl Glue. One of the most widely used glues available to the general public, polyvinyl white glue is inexpensive, nontoxic, and nonflam-

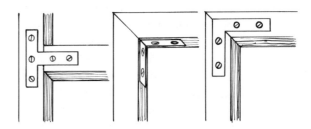

Fig. 3-16.   Mending plates are useful in furniture construction.

mable. Although milky white in color, it dries clear and is usually sold in plastic squeeze bottles with a nozzle that makes for convenient application. Although polyvinyl is primarily a wood glue, it can also be used for gluing paper, fabrics, leather, and cardboard. It is excellent for interior woodwork when used with nails or screws. It is nonstaining and can be used with most porous materials. A moderate amount of pressure is needed while it is setting. The glue hardens in about thirty minutes and attains full strength in about twenty-four hours. Polyvinyl glue is not meant for joints that have to withstand great pressure.

Casein Glue. A powdered wood adhesive that you mix with water before use, casein glue is ideal for heavy-duty work where strong joints are required. It works very well on loose-fitted joints because it fills voids and gaps by supplying needed bulk. For best results this glue requires firm clamping while it sets. It is the only woodworking glue that permits you to glue wood at low temperatures in an unheated garage or basement workshop. On the other hand casein glue is not recommended if a waterproof joint is necessary, and it may stain some dark woods. It is highly recommended, however, for use on such oily, hard-to-glue woods as teak.

Contact Cement. Because it bonds instantly—on contact—and without clamping, a contact cement is perfect for many awkward gluing jobs around the house. It is used for bonding broad surfaces to each other where strength is *not* important, such as gluing plastic laminates to countertops, tabletops, and other flat surfaces. In addition it may be used for such light jobs as adhering leather, linoleum, thin-gauge metal, and many other dissimilar materials in situations where clamping is either impossible or difficult. Both a highly flammable, solvent-thinned cement and a newer, water-thinned kind are available. The latter is nonflammable, quick-drying, and gives off no toxic odors as the solvent-thinned cements do. Although the newer type generally costs more, it covers a bit more area. Regardless of type, all contact cements are used in a similar manner; the adhesive is applied to both surfaces to be bonded, then allowed to dry from

five to forty minutes, according to the manufacturer's directions. The parts are then pressed together, bonding instantly. Once the surfaces come into contact, they can't be shifted around. Therefore, when bonding large surfaces such as plastic laminate to countertops, a slip sheet of wrapping paper can be used while aligning the two parts; after they are lined up, the sheet can be slid out of the way and the surfaces pressed together.

Epoxy Resin Glue. Originally developed for joining nonporous materials, epoxies have been recently found useful in making wood furniture. Since they don't shrink appreciably on curing, they can be used in thick glue lines. Their sticks-to-anything quality makes them the choice in building projects that utilize different materials, such as wood and metal or glass. Epoxies are among the strongest wood glues available, but they are in the higher price range. They come in two-part formulation and must be mixed before use. At normal room temperatures the mixture has a working life of about two hours. Total setting time is about eighteen hours, but this can be accelerated by the application of moderate heat, such as from a lamp.

Liquid Animal Glues. Liquid animal glues, also called liquid hide or fish glues, are light brown or amber organic glues that are good for most general woodworking repairs where a strong bond is needed. Because they are not waterproof, damp

Fig. 3-17.   Electric glue gun is ideal for light bonding tasks.

conditions can hinder their effective use. They also do not stand up well where there is a great amount of heat, and some types will stain light-colored woods. You can use them on wood and leather in addition to cork, paper, fabric, and other similar porous materials. They are very useful in filling small gaps and rough areas in poorly fitted joints. Clamping is necessary for about an hour. Remember that these glues thicken at low temperatures. You may have to apply heat to gain a better consistency for spreading when the temperature is less than 70°F. Their slower setting time makes them advantageous for furniture work, where parts have to be positioned before clamping.

Hot Hide Glue. This animal glue is an excellent adhesive but it is generally not too popular with the home furniture-maker. You can buy hide glue in flake, cake, or ground forms. Soak the glue in lukewarm water overnight, being sure to make it according to the manufacturer's instructions. Use glass ovenware or metal containers, double-boiler fashion, to keep it below 150°F., and apply hot. Heat only the quantity needed; frequent reheating weakens the glue. It sets fast but requires tight clamping for proper bonding.

Hot-Melt Plastic Glue. This material isn't actually a glue but a thermoplastic that acts like a glue when it is melted and then hardens. Sticks of solid plastic (ethyl vinyl acetate) are inserted into the magazine of an electric glue gun. The gun is pointed directly into the joint between the parts to be bonded, and as the trigger of the gun is squeezed, the plastic is melted at the front of the gun. The gun is moved along the joint, and the plastic is automatically distributed. No clamping is necessary, and the plastic hardens in one minute. This plastic will securely bond any combination of wood, tile, leather, plastics, fabrics, metal, and masonry. Although it is not meant for major adhesion jobs, it is ideal for light bonding tasks because it provides a quick, very strong, waterproof bond.

Gluing Technique

Regardless of the type of glue you use, be sure to mix and/or apply it according to the manufac-

turer's instructions. But before gluing any part of a project, carefully inspect each part to make sure that all sandpapering has been completed and that all joints fit properly. Put all the items together (without glue) to make sure that the joints come together as they should and that the parts line up square and true. Then with a soft pencil clearly mark all companion pieces as 1 and 1, 2 and 2, etc.; then indicate front right, front left, etc. Once this is done, the different pieces will fit together as they should for the actual gluing without further adjustment; this is important since the assembly period (the time between spreading the glue and application of pressure) should not exceed fifteen minutes. The clamp should also be set to the correct size beforehand to facilitate the final gluing.

Now put all hand screws and clamps in position (no glue yet); remember to put scrap blocks of wood under the clamps so that they won't bruise the veneer. Inspect the work once more, for it is not too late to trim a joint a little or make a necessary alteration. Planning pays off in assembly, just as in cutting. Frequently you can break down complicated projects into subassemblies that are easier to handle and make joints more accessible.

Apply glue with a brush or stick to only one of the surfaces to be bonded (except when using contact cement). Use plenty of glue; do not starve the joint. End grain absorbs glue so quickly that it is best to apply a preliminary coat, allow it to soak for a few minutes, and then apply another coat. Gluing must be done in a warm, dry, draft-free room. Apply clamps with full jaw length in contact, making sure that jaws are parallel; otherwise, pressure is applied to only part of the joint. Nails, screws, or other fasteners may also be used as temporary clamps. After the clamps have been applied, test the job for squareness. Wipe off excess glue, since some glues stain wood and make it difficult to achieve a good finish. If you throw sawdust over the glue as it oozes out of the joint, the sawdust will absorb the moisture of the glue, making it easier to peel off the excess. Never wash off excess glue with water. This would only coat the wood with a thin layer of glue that might show

Fig. 3-18.   *Left:* Apply glue with brush or stick. Avoid excess glue when project is to be finished with stain or varnish. *Right:* For this reason it is sometimes a good idea to apply the glue from a squeeze bottle.

when it dries; it might also make the wood swell, which is very undesirable. The work must be held together under pressure until the glue is hard, which will take anywhere from one to twenty-four hours, depending on the temperature and type of glue.

When working with a glue that has to be mixed before use, make certain to measure ingredients carefully, then take the time to mix them thoroughly. This is particularly true with the two-part synthetic resins. Thorough blending is required to start the chemical reaction that makes them harden. With some, temperature limitations must also be carefully adhered to. Using these glues at temperatures well below recommended limits may not necessarily interfere with their hardening, but it will greatly weaken the resulting bond.

One more important point to remember is that all porous surfaces need special treatment. Spread a thin coat of glue on both surfaces to be joined; let it stand until tacky. This first coat will dry partly by evaporation, partly by being drawn into the pores of the material. Spread on the second coat and join, then clamp in place.

When preparing wood for gluing, remember that shrinkage and a tendency to warp are greatest at the ends of the pieces. To join long pieces, take an extra shaving from the middle section so that greater pressure will be applied at the ends by the clamps. Flat boards should be glued together with the sap sides back to back to equalize the strain of this warpage tendency. Boards glued side by side to form wider boards should have heart and sap sides turned up alternately so that warpage will be held to a wavy pattern rather than bowing from the outer edges.

As discussed later in this chapter, special clamps frequently save work and help you do a better job. Keep in mind that heavy pressures will crush the softer woods. To prevent injuries of this sort, place hardwood blocks of wood between the faces of the clamps and the work's surface to distribute the pressure over a wider area. For very delicate work you can make up blocks of wood with felt or foam rubber strips cemented to one face and use these between the work and the clamps. If possible, use clamps in pairs on both ends of the work to prevent one end from separating while the other is being joined. For large surfaces additional clamps are needed. Apply even pressure on all clamps and tighten as far as possible by hand. After a few minutes take a few extra turns on the clamp handle, if possible. However, avoid pressing in the sides of the work. If you have a job that requires pressure and the workpiece is too wide for any of the clamps you have available, just open one clamp to approximately its full length and hook its jaw

Fig. 3-19.   C clamps in use. A handy, little-known trick for clamping miter joints in cabinets is shown here. Glue triangular blocks to the ends of each mitered piece, with a piece of paper between the block and the mitered piece to permit easy removal. Let glue set. Apply glue to mitered ends and pull together in alignment with clamps. Remove clamps after glue has set, pry blocks away, and sand off paper.

over the jaw of a second clamp. Then tighten the second clamp to the tension desired, and your problem is solved. Regardless of which clamps are used, there is usually a tendency for long-glued joints to spring apart at the ends. Greater clamping pressure should therefore be applied to the ends than to the center, and the center clamps should be tightened before the end clamps.

Powdered glue is often difficult to mix in small quantities. For small jobs and fast gluing moisten the edges of the wood to be joined and sprinkle some powdered glue onto these moistened areas. Spread the resulting glue mixture along the joint and then apply clamps.

When it is dry, carefully remove the clamps and start on the final cleaning job. Use a sharp chisel. Holding it with the bevel side up and cutting across the grain (where possible), remove all glue that still remains. Follow this with a thorough sandpapering of all such parts. Give a final sanding to all parts of the furniture with fine and then very fine sandpaper (see Chapter 8).

Clamps

Here's a listing of the various types of clamps used in furniture-making and where they are used. To start your shop you don't need them all but you nevertheless know about them.

C Clamps. Perhaps the most widely used of all clamps, the C clamps are inexpensive, long-lasting, quick-acting, and easy to use. They come

Fig. 3-20.   Two styles of bar clamps.

in a wide range of sizes and shapes, differing in the depth of throats and the widths of jaws. They are adaptable to many uses, some of which include holding edging on veneer strips, clamping on a drill press, and holding rabbeted glue corners. A C clamp can also be used as an auxiliary vise.

Bar Clamps. These make up an entire category of useful tools, complete in themselves. Generally used for clamping over relatively long lengths, they are made as complete steel-bar clamps or as fixtures to be put on ordinary steel black pipe of various diameters, on special wood bars of various thicknesses, or on ordinary 2x4's. Most bar clamps can be had with different heads—fixed, sliding, or eccentric—and different handles—crank, wing-nut or hand-wheel. They are unexcelled for gluing large surfaces such as tabletops, for joining large frames holding furniture sides and backs, for gluing shelves into position, and for holding large workpieces on workbench or steady under a power tool.

Cross Clamps. Used in conjunction with bar clamps, these are ideal for edge-gluing and other jobs for which longer clamps are either unavailable or impractical to use. The cross clamp fits over the shank of the bar clamp and provides a means of

Fig. 3-22.   Universal clamps have many uses around a home furniture workshop.

applying pressure at right angles to the axis of the clamp.

Universal Clamp. This tool has movable swivel plates that adjust easily to curved or beveled edges and horizontal spindles that enable side adjustment for pulling the pieces together. It can be used for miter work, corner work, and irregular frames. Once the clamp is set, the pieces can be pulled apart for gluing and pressed together again without removing the clamp. The big advantage is that you can have one hand free for gluing while you close the joint.

Handscrews. The aristocrats of all clamps, handscrews are considered the most satisfactory for holding wood, plastic, metal, or fabric. They can be used on flat or irregular shapes. In relation to their weight they provide powerful, even pressure without slipping or twisting the work. To use the handscrew, adjust both spindles so that the jaws grip the work lightly (the ends of the jaws should be lightly open). The jaws of the handscrew should be kept parallel at all times, both for clamping efficiency and for preservation of the tool. A narrow paint line or register mark applied to the handle grips when the jaws are closed will do the trick. If

Fig. 3-21.   Special cross clamps in use.

Fig. 3-23. Handscrews are possibly the most helpful clamps for a woodworker.

Adjustable Corner Clamps. These are used to hold two pieces of wood together at any predetermined angle to produce miter or butt joints. One screw clamp is stationary, while the other swings a full 180 degrees. It also has clearance for a saw blade, which allows you to correct inaccurate miter cuts.

Press Screws. These are used for making up special clamping jigs or press frames for veneering work. A veneer press consists simply of 2x6-inch pieces bolted to 2x4-inch top and bottom members. The top members have holes drilled in them to receive the press screws, which apply the

you keep these colored lines or registers in the same relationship to each other when working, the jaws will always remain parallel. Then turn the end spindle counterclockwise to tighten the grip on the work. Since the middle spindle acts as a fulcrum, all final pressure should be applied by means of the end spindle only. If glue is apt to touch the wood jaws and complicate removal, you can use the type of handscrew that has soft metal faces, which make for easier removal and cleaning of the clamp.

Spring Clamps. These light, inexpensive clamps have many uses. It pays to have a few of them around the shop for quick clamping jobs. Their pressure is limited to the strength of the steel spring in the handle, but they're ideal where light pressure is adequate. The maximum jaw opening of the larger clamps is about 4 inches. Their biggest advantage is fast application and removal; you can apply or remove a dozen of them in less than a minute.

Band Clamps. For clamping round or irregular sections, such as furniture frames, columns, rail spindles, and other odd shapes, band clamps are used. A canvas belt distributes pressure evenly on all sides of the work.

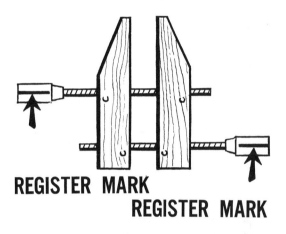

REGISTER MARK
REGISTER MARK

Fig. 3-24. Keep handscrew jaws parallel.

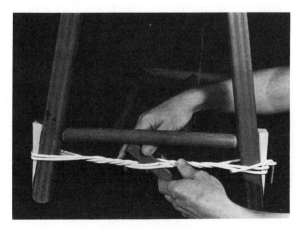

Fig. 3-25. A single tourniquet being applied.

pressure. A few 3x8-inch boards laid across the bottom 2x4 make a flat bed for the work.

Tourniquets

Frequently it's necessary for you to design and make your own clamps to secure the work. For instance the homemade wedge clamp shown in Fig. 5-10 is excellent for bonding boards that are to be glued together edge to edge. Also the use of a so-called tourniquet is often more satisfactory than a mechanical clamp when properly applied, as it distributes the pressure more evenly. There are two basic types of tourniquets used in furniture work, the single and the double.

A single tourniquet is made by placing a rope once around a furniture piece, while in the double tourniquet the rope is passed around twice. The ends of the rope are tied together (a bowknot is good) and a stick (a short dowel or large spike is good) is twisted in the rope until the desired tension is obtained.

Many craftsmen use the single tourniquet, but the double type is better because when the stick or spike is twisted between the two turns of the rope, it can be pushed in back of some portion of the furniture piece to maintain the tension. In the single type the stick or spike must be tied in position. Moreover, the double type gives more even distribution of pressure.

The best rope to use is a heavy cotton clothesline that is soft, strong, and closely woven. There is no need to cut the rope to the size needed. When two tourniquets are needed on a single job, each end of the rope may be used.

DOWELS AND SPLINES

In almost every furniture project it becomes necessary to make a firm joint between two pieces of wood where their narrow edges meet. Frequently the bulk of the furniture pieces prohibits the use of nails or countersunk screws. The answer lies in the use of dowels. Also, many joints—miter, edge, butt—are greatly strengthened by installing dowels.

Dowels are hardwood rods—generally maple or birch—and are available in diameters from ⅛ to 3

Fig. 3-26.   Specially designed clamp blocks such as those shown here often come in handy, especially when making duplicate furniture pieces.

Fig. 3-27.   *Top left:* Professional doweling machine is equipped with two fixed drills for producing accurately aligned holes. *Top right:* Holes for dowel joints can also be made with a portable drill, but this takes a lot of care. *Bottom left:* Spiral-groove your own dowels by passing the length across the spinning blade, twisting the shaft as you go. *Bottom right:* Bevel ends of individual pins cut from shaft, apply glue, and tap into holes with mallet.

inches, with either a plain or grooved surface. The latter surface allows the glue to run more freely into the joint. It's good practice to have a stock of dowels on hand at all times.

In selecting the size of a dowel rod to use, a general rule is that the diameter should be no more than half the thickness of the stock. The depth of the hole will vary with the type of joint. The length of the dowel rod should always be cut about ¼ inch shorter than the total of the two holes. Cut the ends of the dowel pins with a bevel. Remember that a dowel inserted in the drilled holes of a joint adds considerably to the strength of the joint. The dowel's hard qualities and the fact that it is laid with the grain at right angles to the materials joined are the reasons.

There are two methods used in doweling, the open method and the blind method. In the open method a hole is drilled completely through one piece of wood and deeply into or through the one to be joined. The dowel is coated with glue and pushed completely through the drilled holes, joining the pieces, and the remainder is sawed off flush with the outer surface.

Fig. 3-28.   Cutting for a spline in a miter joint.

In the blind method holes are drilled partway into each piece from the joined faces. A dowel cut to the combined length of both holes is then glue-coated and inserted in one hole, and the second piece pressed onto the protruding dowel end. To ensure adequate glue on a snug-fitting dowel, some are spiral-grooved and others are provided with a lengthwise slot. When filled with glue, these indentations assure a firm grip. In most joints two or more dowels are used in place of one to prevent the pieces from twisting on the dowel.

When using the open method of doweling, the problem of aligning the drilled holes does not occur. Even when poorly centered, the holes match and the dowel can be driven through both holes. In the blind system, however, two separate holes must be drilled—and here trouble can develop unless a jig is used. Don't let the word "jig" throw you. This is any type of device that holds several successive pieces of wood in position so that holes can be drilled equidistant from one or more edges of the several pieces.

In some instances the drilling device is clamped in position and the wood is guided to it along measured channels to ensure proper centering of the holes. In others the wood is clamped and the drilling device is guided along identical channels for all holes drilled. In either case the guide is actually a jig. Furthermore it is also possible to arrange the jig so as to control the depth of the hole drilled.

For further insurance against dowels turning or becoming loose and permitting the joint to crack or spread as the surrounding wood shrinks, set small finishing nails or brads through wood surfaces into the dowels.

Should it ever become necessary to remove dowels and reinforce the joint, there is but one possible method—drill out the old dowel, enlarging the hole by ⅛ inch, and replace with a new dowel of larger diameter adequately glued. More information on dowels can be found in Chapter 4.

SPLINES

A spline is a thin strip of hardwood inserted in a groove cut in the two adjoining surfaces of a joint. It is a popular means of strengthening miter joints. The groove is cut with a saw to a specific width and depth (page 125). A thin piece of stock is then cut to fit into this groove. This stock should be cut so that the grain runs at right angles to the grain of the joint. Various types of joints employing splines are illustrated in Chapters 4 and 5.

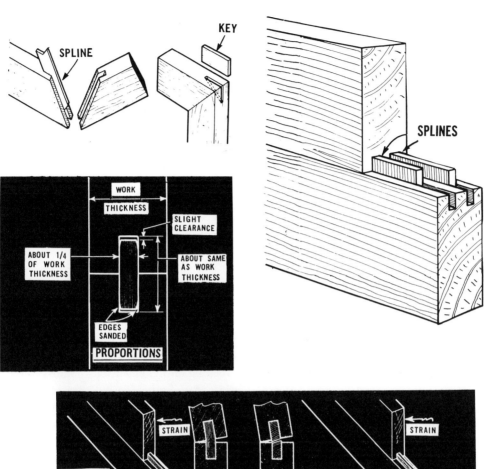

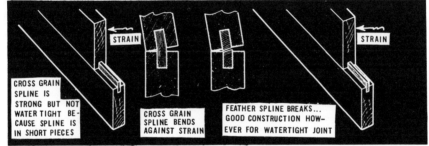

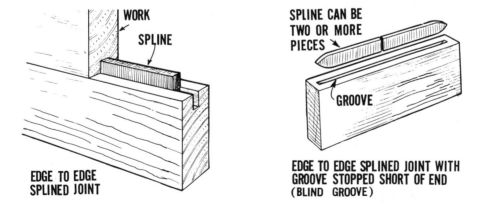

Fig. 3-29. Splines.

Chapter 4
FURNITURE JOINERY

Joinery in furniture construction is a series of proven methods for putting two or more parts together permanently and, for appearance's sake, pleasingly. It is fine work, done mostly by professionals. Every home workshop enthusiast ought to aspire to professionalism, but too few ever make it or even try to make it, possibly because of disappointing experiences, mistaken notions, or both. This leaves the confirmed woodworker without one of his strongest shop assets and with the necessity of sticking to simpler projects, and never really advancing.

To set the record straight, there is nothing in joinery the professional can do that the handyman can't do, although it will obviously take you longer. As you may have supposed and as you will see throughout this chapter, specially tooled factory equipment makes the pros' craft easier to execute. But that's all it does. Planning a project still requires the same study, and conventional shop power tools (and regular accessories) can prepare any joint as well as their factory counterparts.

Measuring and Laying Joints
Before any sort of furniture joinery work begins, measurements must be made. The home furniture-maker who wants his project to turn out well must first learn to measure materials accurately and mark lines where the cuts of that material must be made. Shoddy measuring and layout means inaccurate cuts and poor furniture joints.

The measuring and laying-out tools used most frequently in furniture-making include rules, straightedges, squares, and marking gauges.

Rules. Rules are used for measuring material to exact dimensions. Those most frequently used in furniture-making are the metal tape and the zigzag folding wood rule.

The *metal measuring tape* is reel-fed and spring-loaded, with a locking button that securely holds

the tape at any point. Some metal tapes have a specially treated surface that allows pencil marks to be made and later rubbed off. The average length is 12 feet, or twice as long as the average folding rule. The tape measures regular and irregular shapes, and inside measurements can be taken simply by adding 2 inches to the reading on the blade.

The *zigzag folding rule* is an ideal complement to the tape measure, handy for taking or laying off long or short measurements; it is stiff enough to measure across openings with ease. The thin metal extension rule built into one of the end sections is particularly useful for inside measurements; the reading on the extension is added to the length of the opened rule. To measure accurately with any rule, hold it on its edge so that the measuring marks are in contact with the work. Be sure that the end of the rule is even with the edge of the stock, with your thumbnail fixed to the exact measuring mark.

Another marking device that will come in handy is the *combination caliper ruler*, which has jaws designed to make either inside or outside measurements. If you are measuring the diameter of a hole, you should read the scale mark that lines up with the in mark. But when you measure the diameter of a shaft, you should read to the out mark. Actually a caliper rule is very useful for fine measurements. It can be used to determine the exact size of dowels, rocks, bits, screws, square thickness of boards, etc. It is also used to measure thickness within the limits of its jaws. Furthermore it can be used to take measurements of slots, grooves, and openings and for confirming dado measurements.

Straightedges. While a straight and square piece of wood is often used, it is a good idea to have available a strip of hardened, tempered steel—in a length of 1 to 6 feet—in order to check the linear accuracy of work and as a guide for scribing

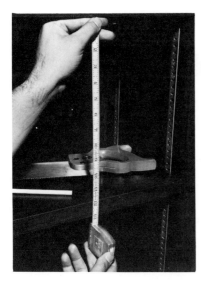

Fig. 4-1.   Metal measuring tape (*left*) and zigzag folding rule (*above*) are must items for any furniture-making shop.

Fig. 4-2.   A *try square* (*left*) and combination or miter square (*right*) perform many useful tasks in woodworking.

working lines with a knife or pencil when extreme accuracy is required.

Squares. Squares are sometimes used for making measurements, but they are used mainly for laying out and checking angles. The *steel square, try square,* and *double square* are all designed to check right angles (90 degrees). Squares must be handled carefully so that they will stay square; a square that isn't true is worthless.

Combination or *miter squares* are designed to handle, in addition, the measurement, layout, and checking of angles other than 90 degrees. Thus the square stock may be used as a regular square for 90-degree angles or as a miter square for 45-degree

angles. The center head is used with the blade for marking the centers of round objects. (The two intersecting lines are marked to establish a center.) The protractor head is used with the blade to measure any angle. It has a circular scale marked off in degrees, and the blade may be set and locked at any desired angle.

To square a line with a square, press the stock of the square firmly against the edge of the board and mark the guideline along the blade with the point of a pencil, knife, or scriber. In squaring a line across a board, one edge and one face of the board should be marked with light pencil marks so that they can be distinguished as the working face and edge. Then square a line from the working edge across the working face. Make sure that the working edge is absolutely flat so that the square cannot move about. Make it a practice to square the lines from the working face across both edges. Then, holding the stock of the square up against the working edge, square a line across the face on the side of board opposite the working edge.

To test a board or joint for squareness, place the inside edge of the stock of the square in contact with one surface. Face the light so that it will shine on the work. Slide the square downward and observe where the blade first comes in contact with the surface of the work. If the angle is square and the surface of the work is true, no light will be seen. If the angle isn't square, or if the surface isn't true, light will shine through between the work and the blade.

Marking Gauges. Furniture layouts are usually marked off with a chisel-pointed pencil. Extremely accurate layouts, for cutting special types of joints, are made with a sharp knife-point or steel scriber. Lines parallel to edges and ends are quickly marked with a *marking gauge*. Keep the spur point of this gauge sharply pointed so you will get a clean, fine line.

The marking gauge marks best when it is pushed with just enough pressure to make a distinct line.

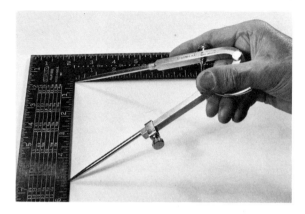

Fig. 4-4.   Dividers are most useful in furniture layout work.

Keep the face of the gauge head pressed snugly against the edge, or the marked line will be wobbly and inaccurate. To obtain an accurate marking line, follow these steps:

1. Set the marking gauge by measuring from the head to the spur pin or joint. Although the gauge usually has its own scale, check the measurement with a ruler after you tighten the thumbscrew.

2. Hold the gauge as you would a ball. Advance your thumb toward the pin so as to distribute the pressure evenly between the pin and the head.

3. Lay the beam flat on the wood so that the pin drags naturally as the marking gauge is pushed away from you. Do not roll the gauge; the pin and the line should always be visible as you mark.

4. To make the gauge line, push the unit forward with the head held tight against the work edge of the wood. The pressure should always be applied away from you and toward the edge of the board, in the direction shown by the arrows in Fig. 4-3.

When making a mortise-and-tenon joint, you can use a mortise gauge, which is a marking gauge with two spur points instead of one. The two points, one of which can be set independently, are used to score parallel lines. This gauge is used in about the same way as the standard marking gauge except that before the head is adjusted, the two spur points are set the required distance apart by securing the movable one with the thumbscrew in the end of the beam.

Dividers. Dividers have many uses in furniture

Fig. 4-3.   For accurate layout work be sure to use a marking gauge.

Fig. 4-5.   Both a carpenter's level (*left*) and a small torpedo level (*right*) have a place in your home furniture-making shop.

Fig. 4-6.   Two methods of laying out a circle.

layout work. They are necessary to scribe a line when matching a workpiece to an irregular edge such as in brick or stone masonry. Dividers can also be used to step off a measurement several times accurately, as well as for scribing circles or arcs.

Levels. While not a measuring or layout tool in the true sense of the word, a level indicates true vertical and true level position. It may have either a wooden or aluminum frame in which two or four glass liquid-and-bubble tubes are mounted. (When there are four tubes, they are mounted in sets of two, each set at right angles to the other.) For larger work the so-called carpenter's level should be employed. But for average furniture work the smaller torpedo level has two advantages over the larger model: a bevel bubble for checking 45-degree angles and a grooved base for unassisted positioning on shafts and similar rounds. When using any type of level on either a flat or a vertical surface, the work is level if the bubble in one of the tubes is absolutely in the center—that is, between indicated lines on the tube. If the bubble is off-center, the work isn't level.

HOW TO MAKE FURNITURE JOINTS

In furniture-making the importance of making well-fitted and properly constructed joints cannot be repeated often enough. Although nails, screws, and other fasteners are sometimes used, glue with properly constructed joint is the most common form of joinery.

The common joints in furniture-making are the butt mortise-and-tenon, dado, miter, rabbet, dovetail, and lap joints.

Butt Joints

The butt joint is the simplest of all joints. Though it is extremely simple to make, the edges to be joined must be tested with a square for absolute squareness before the pieces are fitted together. Actually, to fit a butt joint properly, proceed as follows:

1. Square the end of one piece of wood, using a try square and pencil to mark all four sides.

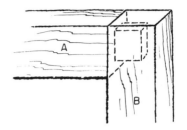

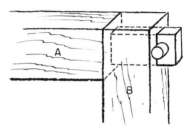

Fig. 4-8.   *Top:* In the blind mortise-and-tenon joint the tenon piece A extends partway through piece B. Secure with glue; if stronger joint is needed, dowel or finishing nail is set through B into the tenon. *Bottom:* In the case of a key mortise-and-tenon joint the mortise or square hole in B goes all the way through. Tenon of piece A extends beyond outside edge of piece B. Hold the same as blind mortise or with dowel peg set through tenon.

Fig. 4-7.   Dowel-pinning provides you with the tightest possible butt joint. It is also a concealed form of joining wood.

2. Use a crosscut or backsaw to cut the wood along these lines.

3. Take the end just cut and set it against the piece of wood to which it will be fastened.

4. Secure the pieces together with glue, nails, screws, or corrugated or other fasteners.

5. If an exceptionally strong joint is required, you can combine any of the previously mentioned methods or use them in conjunction with dowels, angle irons, mending plates, or a T-strap. Even a combination of any of these methods with gluing will result in no more than about 25 percent of the tensile strength of the wood parallel to the grain.

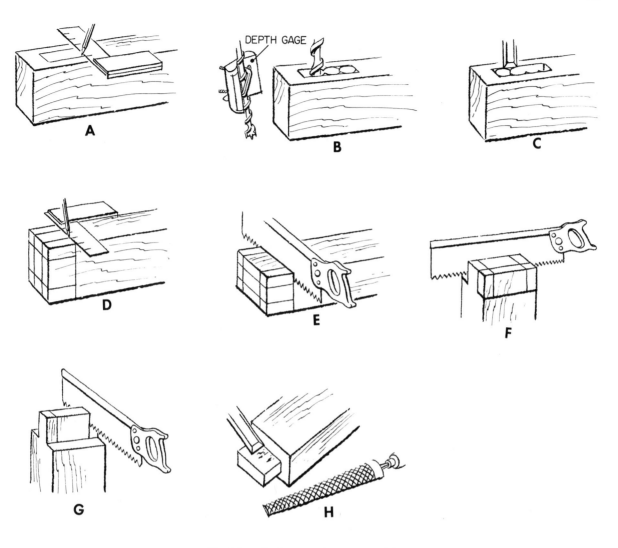

Fig. 4-9.   Cutting a mortise-and-tenon joint.

Mortise-and-Tenon Joints

The mortise-and-tenon is a very good joint, stronger and more widely used than the dowel joint, and about the best technique you can use in fine furniture-making. You have probably seen the keyed mortise-and-tenon on heavy-stocked tables (where the tenon protrudes and a plug or wedge pierces it), but the blind mortise-and-tenon is much more widely used, although this is not apparent because it does not generally show.

Essentially, the tenon is what is left of the end of one workpiece after cutting away part of two or four sides, and the mortise is the matching through-slot or blind pocket of the adjoining workpiece.

The big question to many beginning woodworkers is how to make the mortise. The tenon is less of a problem—although equal care should be given to both. To cut a mortise-and-tenon with hand tools (see Fig. 4-9), measure and mark location of mortise, using a square to make certain of perfect alignment (A). With brace and bit drill a series of holes in area (B). For blind mortise, use a depth gauge set for proper depth. (C) Clean excess wood out of mortise with a sharp chisel. Make sure corners are cut square and are even. (D) Mark

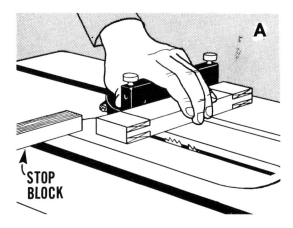

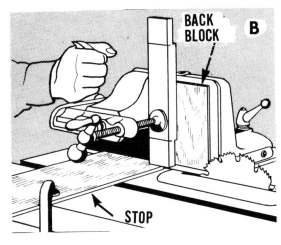

Fig. 4-10.   Method of cutting a tenon with a power table saw. When you have a choice of faces that are to be mortised, selection should be made with a view to hiding any blemishes in the wood. Unmortised faces will show on the outside of the frame. For more details on tenon-cutting device, see Fig. 4-11.

tenon, drawing all lines square with edge of board. Mark on all sides to avoid error. (E) Use backsaw to cut "shoulder" of tenon. Cut across board first to exact depth, keeping saw perfectly aligned. (F) Turn board in vise and cut down edge to the two points cut in previous step to form a square corner. (G) The other parts, called cheeks, are cut in the same manner as the wide sections. Add guidelines before cutting. (H) With sharp chisel and file, smooth the surfaces of the tenon and check fit in mortise. Sandpaper smooth afterwards.

Ideally, what you need for this joint-making is a table saw and a drill press with a hollow-chisel mortising bit. The table saw will see you through exact tenons (a radial arm saw is good for only two of the four or four of the eight cuts that produce a tenon), and the mortising bit will cut square corners and straight sides for a blind pocket or through-slot in no time at all. If you don't have this kind of equipment, hand tools will do, but the job will take longer and you will really have to watch yourself.

The tenon for the mortise-and-tenon joint can be cut in a number of different ways, depending on equipment available and the nature of the joint. For instance, tenons are easily produced with a backsaw, notching two sides of one end or four sides, as the case may be. Mortises can be made with a chisel and mallet all the way or with a chisel for finishing off a mortise started with a brace and bit.

With power equipment, an accurate method for regular work is shown in Fig. 4-10. This makes use of a base stop and a backing block, both of which should be made up and kept as regular fixtures. The shoulder cuts are made first, as shown in A. The first cheek cut is then made, using a backing block of a thickness equal to the thickness of the tenon plus the thickness of the saw blade. After the first cheek cut is made, the backing block is removed and the second cheek cut is made (C), keeping the same face of work against the jig. The base stop shown in C is the same thickness as the baseplate of the tenoning jig. This system of cutting eliminates any possible error due to variations in work thickness. If only one or two joints

Fig. 4-11.   Steps in cutting a tenon with a double saw-blade arrangement.

are to be made, the simpler procedure of working to pencil lines and turning the work over for the two cheek cuts can be used, eliminating the base and backing blocks. Fig. 4-11 shows the tenon being cut with a double-saw-blade arrangement, which is a useful technique assuring constant accuracy. For example, if you're working with ¾-inch stock on a furniture project, you will want a ⁵⁄₁₆-inch spacer, and run the stock through to the depth (or length) you want, usually a 1¾-inch tenon if you are working with a 2-inch material. Cut off the scrap later, using one blade on the machine. If you do not have a spacer or if you have only one blade, you can still make the basic cuts, one at a time.

When joining the mortise and the tenon, apply plenty of glue, nail the pieces together with sash nails (they have no heads), and clamp.

Dado Joints

The dado joint is no more than a groove, called a dado, into which the end or side of a companion piece is fitted. This remarkably practical, workmanlike, and easy to make joint is a favorite for construction of shelves, bookcases, and drawers.

In times past, you made two cuts across the grain—representing the overall thickness of the piece to be joined—with a backsaw, then chiseled out the groove. This required constant checks with

Fig. 4-12.   The mortise-chisel attachment for your drill press lets you cut a square hole or a clean mortise without using a hammer and chisel. *Top left:* Matched sets of hollow chisel and special bit are available in $\frac{1}{4}$-, $\frac{3}{8}$, and $\frac{1}{2}$-inch sizes. *Top right:* Remove the geared chuck of the drill press by loosening its retaining collar with the handle of the chuck key. Replace the stop rod collar with the mortising housing and refit the chuck. *Bottom left:* Secure the hollow chisel in the housing and insert the bit through the bottom of the chisel and lock it in the chuck. *Bottom right:* When cutting a mortise, make the end cuts first, then work toward the center, overlapping preceding cut.

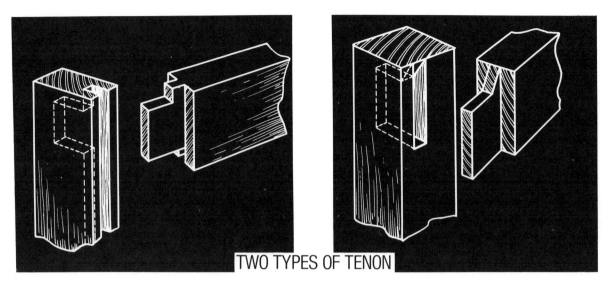

TWO TYPES OF TENON

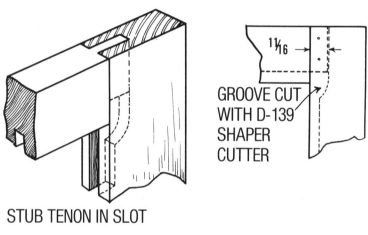

STUB TENON IN SLOT

GROOVE CUT
WITH D-139
SHAPER
CUTTER

$1\frac{1}{16}$

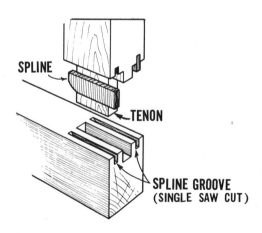

SPLINE

TENON

SPLINE GROOVE
(SINGLE SAW CUT)

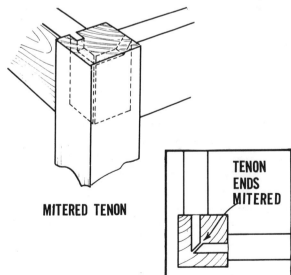

MITERED TENON

TENON
ENDS
MITERED

Fig. 4-13.   Various types of tenons and methods of fastening.

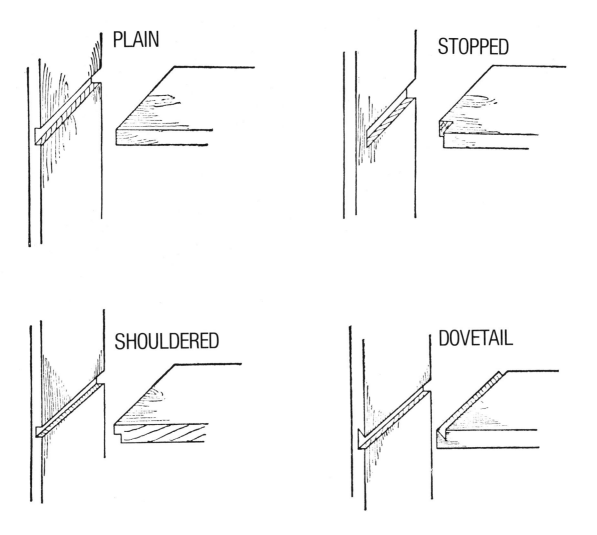

Fig. 4-14.   Various types of dadoes.

a depth gauge to make sure the groove was flat at the bottom.

There is nothing to stop you from this hand-worked approach, however, even if you use power tools. With the portable circular saw set to the necessary depth, the two outside or limit cuts are made first, then the area between is reduced by repeated passes of the single blade. This can also be accomplished with a radial arm saw and a table saw, the latter being a tricky method because of working upside-down.

The dado adapter, or dado blade, set (see pages 30-31) is the smart way to make fast dado grooves. Consisting of two outside blades and one, two, three, or four inside cutters (depending on how wide you want your groove), the dado can be made in one pass, or swipe, of the blades. As a guide, when using ¾-inch stock, a groove of ¾ inch is standard.

When assembling, glue the entire joint and hold the workpieces together with a bar clamp. Drive nails or screws and countersink them, patching the holes.

The Blind Dado. A groove cut with the dado

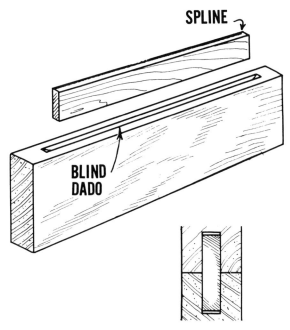

Fig. 4-15.   A splined joint employing a blind dado.

made in any suitable size on a circular saw fitted with a dado head.

To set up for the work, it is necessary to have an auxiliary wood fence, which can be screw-fastened to the standard miter gauge (see Fig. 4-17). After sawing this piece, remove the saw from the arbor and mount a dado-cutter of the thickness selected for the joint. In most cases the width of the cut is equal to, or slightly less than, the thickness of the stock. Hold the fence firmly against the miter gauge and run it across the dado head somewhere near the center. Remove the fence and mark the position of a second cut, D, spacing this from the first cut, C, the same width as the groove. At the same time mark the lines A and B, centering them as shown. Nail a little square of wood in the first dado cut and then make the second dado cut, D, with the fence screw-fastened to the miter gauge. You are now ready to make the box joint.

To make the joint, set two pieces of stock that are to be joined against the fence. Set the edge of

head that stops short of one or both ends of the work is called a blind dado. Cuts of this kind are commonly used in making splined joints. Stops to locate the beginning and end of the cut are necessary, the position of these being determined by holding the work alongside the saw in the required position. In some cases the end stop can be eliminated by using just a pencil mark, but the starting stop is always needed. The reason for this is that there is a fairly strong kickback of the work when it is lowered over the saw, and the stop is needed to support the work and prevent it from being thrown off the table. If the groove is in a long piece of work, it is necessary to clamp an auxiliary wood facing of suitable length to the regular fence and then to clamp the stop blocks to the auxiliary fence.

The Box Joint. This familiar joint, which is seen on many varieties of small boxes, can be used to advantage for much of the work that falls within the scope of the home or production furniture workshop. Besides being neat in appearance, the joint presents lots of gluing surface. It can be easily

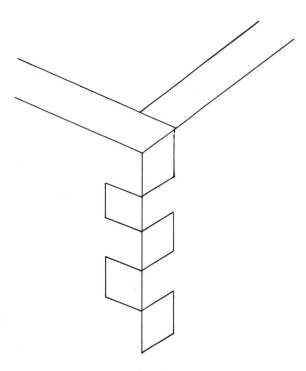

Fig. 4-16.   A box joint such as this usually is cut with the dado head and is easily made with the automatic spacer.

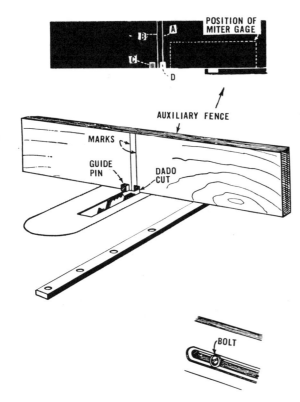

Fig. 4-17.   The setup for cutting box joints.

between the side of the cutter and the side of the guide pin is the same as the width of the cutter. A small guide pin serves for all sizes of cuts, each groove being set tight against the side of the pin nearest the cutter. This type of fence is recommended for all-around work, since it permits any width of dado-cutter to be used. Another worthy feature is that any box joint can be made either a driven or loose fit by simply setting the fence a fraction of an inch one way or the other.

The Lock Joint. This dado-type joint requires precision cutting but makes a very strong joint. The cuts are all made with a dado head on the saw. Allow a little tolerance between the tongues and grooves so that you can assemble the joint by sliding the pieces together.

one piece even with line A, the edge of the other piece even with line B. Push the work across the cutter and then shift it so that the groove just cut sits over the locating pin. Make the second cut. Place the second groove over the locating pin and make a third cut. Continue in this manner until the whole width of the work is cut. It is important that the two pieces of stock maintain the same position throughout the operation. This is easily effected if the guide pin is made long enough to catch both pieces. If desired, the two pieces can be lightly nailed together. Adjustments can be made by moving either the guide or the fence itself.

In order to make adjustments simple and to accommodate a wide variety of work, many craftsmen prefer the arrangement shown in Fig. 4-17 or something on the same order. In this case the fence is held to the miter gauge by means of bolts inserted through a long slot. After selecting the cutter to be used, set the fence so that the distance

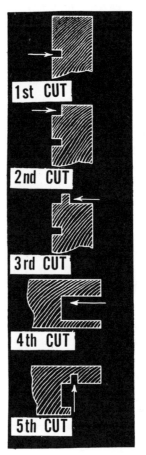

Fig. 4-18.   Steps in cutting a lock joint.

Fig. 4-19. *Top:* Cutting a miter with a saber saw. *Bottom:* Checking the joint with a square.

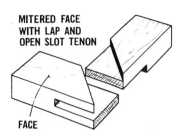

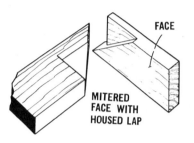

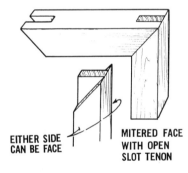

Miter Joints

The miter joint is primarily for show—when, for example, you want uninterrupted wood grain around edges (side-to-top-to-side of a cabinet) or at corners (a picture frame). The joining ends or edges are usually cut at angles of 45 degrees, then glued, clamped, and nailed. Cuts slightly less than 45 degrees are often necessary when fitting new moldings on settled window casings, but the differences are hardly noticeable, once they are up and painted.

There is a definite finished look to a mitered joint, whether it is left natural or painted. The planning of the cut and the assembly of the joint, however, need more care than the actual cutting. What with the miter box for molding or trimming stock and the radial arm saw for sheet work, the cuts are highly systematized. And to scribe a 45-degree angle on your work, all you have to use is a combination square, try square, miter square, or bevel as a preset, sure guide. Assembly can be heartbreaking, though, unless you control your work every step of the way. The joining of the two

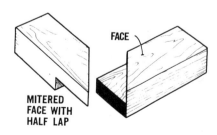

Fig. 4-20. Various types of mitered joints.

Fig. 4-21.   Miter corner clamps in use.

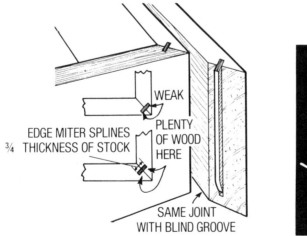

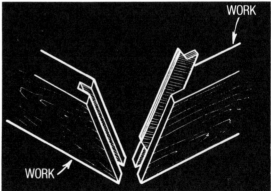

Fig. 4-22.   Splined miter joints on the edge (*left*) and on the flat (*right*).

ends or sides must be precise, neat, and trim—and add up to an exact 90-degree turn.

On corner work involving molding or trim pieces use miter corner clamps specially made for the purpose. These devices assure a square set after you have glued.

The Splined Miter Joint. The splined joint is simply a plain miter with a spline (see page 108) to give it added strength. The spline, which can be either masonite or plywood, should always run the full length of the joint. The miter is cut with the saw blade tilted to 45 degrees, using either the rip fence or the miter gauge to guide the workpiece. Use the tenoning jig to cut the slot for the spline; leave the blade at the same angle but adjust it for height. When both pieces are mitered and slotted, the spline is glued in place. Reinforced in this manner, the miter joint is very strong. You can use the same technique in a different correlation of the parts or, where practical, you can use corrugated nails.

The Blind Splined Miter Joint. In this construction there is one edge, as can be seen in the open view of the joint (Fig. 4-22). Stop blocks are needed to control the length of spline groove. A test block of same thickness and width as the work provides an accurate means of setting the stops and also shows the exact shape of spline when sawed apart on the bandsaw. The complete schedule for cutting the joint is described here and illustrated in Fig. 4-24.

1. Cut work to net length for plain miter. Miter test block about 6 inches long. Arrange work four-square, and number joints.

2. Cut through groove on test block.

3. Split groove on bandsaw. Make pencil marks ¼ inch from edge.

4. Use test block to determine forward travel of miter gauge. Clamp stop in place.

5. Cut joints 1, 3, 5, 7. Also make same cut on opposite end of test block.

6. Use test block to determine backward travel of miter gauge. Clamp stop in place.

7. Cut joints 2, 4, 6, 8, pulling work backward over saw blade. Watch for slight kickback. Miter gauge clamp must be used.

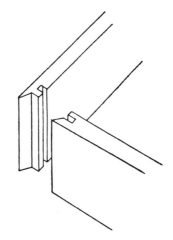

Fig. 4-23.   A lock miter joint.

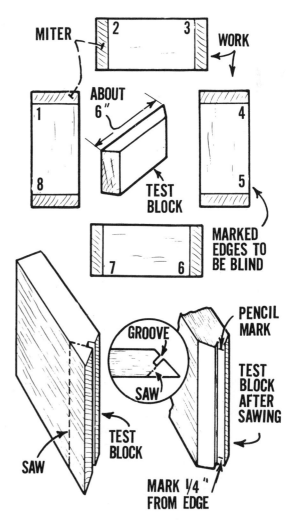

Fig. 4-24.   The steps in making the blind splined miter joint.

8. Split groove in test block on bandsaw and reassemble to show shape of spline.

The Slip Feather Miter. Similar to the splined miter, except that the splines are placed in the outside edge of the corner, this joint is generally used when making something wide and flat. The two miters are cut in the conventional manner, then the pieces are clamped together in a tenoning jig and one or more slots are cut across the end of the joint. The slip feathers (triangular splines of plywood) are then secured in the slots and sanded

smooth. This gives a strongly reinforced miter joint.

The Lapped Miter. This miter-type joint is also used when jointing frames, but when it is desirable to have the miter show on one side only. This joint will give the appearance of a conventional miter from one side, yet will be considerably stronger because of the increase in area of contacting surfaces.

In every instance of mitered construction always use corner clamps, web clamping devices, or plain old rope to hold your workpiece in square when drying. Mitered articles, more than any other jointed project, have a tendency to shift without your knowing it, so you have got to keep a sharp eye.

Rabbet Joints

The rabbet joint is like a dado except that it has only two surfaces (a bottom and one side) and therefore has to be made at the edge of your workpiece (unlike the rabbet, the dado occurs anywhere, except along an edge).

In making a drawer, for example, rabbet joints are extremely practical, allowing sides to be jointed at the ends of faces (recessed sides would have to be dado-jointed). You probably have also seen rabbet cuts (not rabbet joints) used as lips on kitchen cabinet doors.

The cleanest, quickest way to cut a rabbet is with a dado head. Or you can use a notching technique with a single blade—on a radial arm or bench saw (Fig. 4-26). When ready to assemble, glue well, nail, and clamp the parts for twenty-four hours.

Rabbeted Miter Joint. This joint is excellent for cabinet bases and is easily cut by following the schedule given here. The square-cut section simplifies gluing or nailing operations. As a cabinet base joint piece B should be the end or side, and nails, if used, should be entered from this piece. In heavy work the joint is sometimes assembled with dowels fitted across the square step in the same position as the nails that can be seen here. A more complicated variation of the joint is the lock miter, as shown in Fig. 4-27, which is sometimes used for drawer or furniture box work. This construction is usually

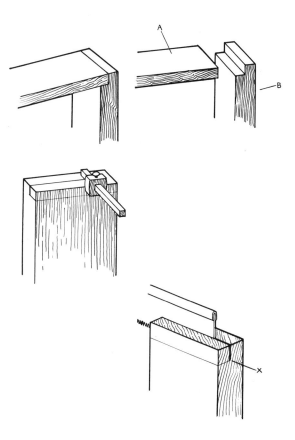

Fig. 4-25.   To make a rabbet joint with hand tools: Make certain that the ends of both pieces are square. Take piece B and use a try square to make a line across it; the distance from the end of the board is the thickness of the piece. Next, using a marking gauge, draw a line across the end of piece B. This distance is one-third or one-half the thickness. Then, using the backsaw, cut along line of the board's end to the depth of the draw line, point X. Using the same saw, cut along the other line to meet first cut. Then place boards in position and fasten.

Fig. 4-26.   To make a rabbet joint with power tools: *Left:* Using a table saw, first put very firm pressure against the fence and then make a cut across the grain. *Center:* Having adjusted the fence for the second pass, turn the workpiece on end and cut away the scrap to form the rabbet. *Right:* Glue the component pieces (one side is the rabbeted stock) and clamp firmly, making sure to check for square.

worked with the use of the dado head, following the same general principle of dado and double-dado dimensions as described for drawer joints (see pages 117 and 120). However, for most work the simpler rabbeted miter is both neat and strong.

The following is the cutting schedule for the rabbeted miter joint:

1. Set the saw projection at one-half the work thickness, checking on a piece of scrap stock. Next, using a scrap piece of stock or one of the workpieces, set the fence at a distance equal to the thickness of the stock, as measured from the free side of the blade. In other words, the saw blade is flush with the face of the work, as shown. Be sure

both adjustments—saw height and fence setting—are exact.

2. With the depth and fence setting made, make the first cut. Pencil marks on the work are not essential as far as actual cutting is concerned, but they are useful to show which piece is which. If more than one joint is required, all similar pieces should be cut before advancing to the next step. Pencil-marking to identify face surface and edge is always good practice and will ensure more accurate work.

3. With the saw at the same depth, walk across the joint with about four saw cuts. The exact width of the groove cut in this manner is immaterial so

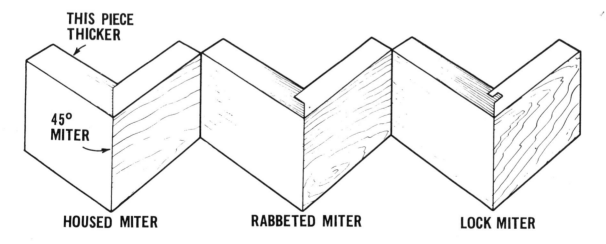

Fig. 4-27.   Popular rabbeted miter joints.

long as it extends a little more than halfway to the end of the work. Also, on the first piece cut make a single saw cut at the extreme end. This cut, which serves as a guide in the next operation, is not essential and can be omitted if desired.

4. Using the step at the end of the work as a guide, set the fence so that the distance from fence to the open side of blade is equal to half the thickness of the work. Measure the distance by holding the work in contact with a raker tooth. Piece B is used to make the saw setting, but the operation is on piece A, as previously described.

6. Fasten an auxiliary wood fence in place and adjust the fence so that the saw cut will come exactly on the corner of the work. Make the cut, lowering the saw table as required. Run the same cut on piece B to complete the joint.

The Rabbet and Groove Joint. Neater and stronger than the plain rabbeted joint, the rabbet-and-groove, or milled, joint is popular for drawer construction. The joint with average dimensions is shown here. The dimension DD means double dado and represents a distance equal to twice the width of the dado combination being used. The ¼-inch dado combination is commonly used, making DD equal to approximately ½ inch (dado

saws are usually a trifle scant on their named size). The fit of the joint depends on getting the dado groove exactly DD distance from the inner face of the front, and the same DD distance from the end of the side. This is best accomplished by using the same stop block for both cuts. Start by mounting the ¼-inch dado combination in place. Use a thin metal collar or several paper collars behind the innermost saw so that the outer edge of the combination will be DD distance from the edge of the tenoning jig baseplate. Set the depth of cut to a trifle less than one-half the thickness of side stock. Using the edge of the tenoning jig baseplate as a stop, cut the groove in the side piece. This completes the side. Reset depth of cut to the same depth as thickness of side stock. Mount the front stock in the tenoning jig, with the inner side of the front against the baseplate, and cut the groove in front. The joint will now assemble as shown and needs only the cutting off of the tenon to bring it to a perfect fit. A slight amount of clearance at the tenon should be allowed.

Both drawer joints—straight rabbet and rabbet groove—are sometimes worked with the front overhanging the sides by about 1/32 inch, the same as in Fig. 5-33. This is easily managed by varying the saw setting slightly. The purpose of the overhang is to allow a neat closing fit of the drawer without binding the sides.

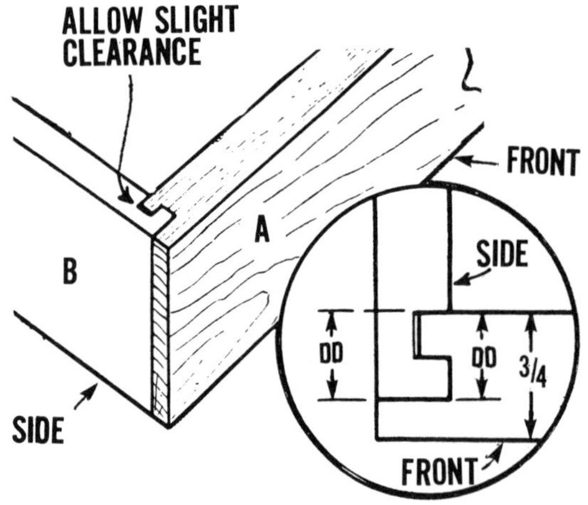

Dovetail Joints

The interlocking of two pieces of wood by a special fan-shaped cutting is called a dovetail joint. It is used extensively by skilled craftsmen in making fine furniture and drawers and in projects where good appearance and strength are desired. A dovetail joint has considerable strength because of the flare of the projections—technically known as pins—on the ends of the boards, which fit exactly into similarly shaped dovetails. The spaces between the pins are called mortises or sockets. The dovetails are visible on the face, or flat, side of one of the pieces being joined, and the pins are visible on the end of the other piece.

Dovetail joints are made in a variety of ways. A

Fig. 4-28.   Details of rabbet and groove joint.

Fig. 4-29.   Cutting dovetails with hand tools can be a lengthy task. Glue can be used to lock dovetails together.

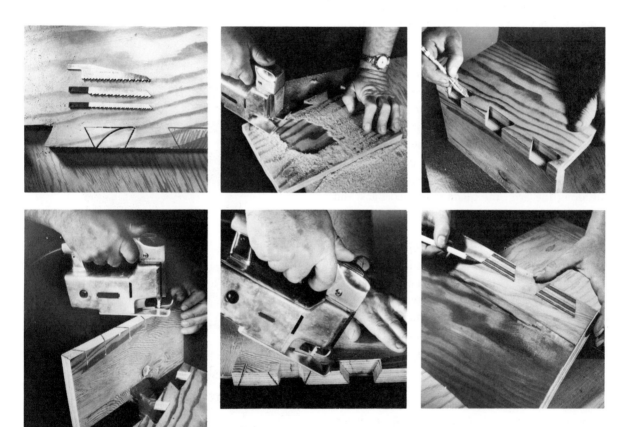

Fig. 4-30.   In cutting dovetails with a saber saw, first draw your marks with a soft pencil. If you are new at the job, pencil in the part to be cut out so you do not cut out the wrong section. When making the cuts, make the angled side cut first. Then bring the saw in on the curve to meet the side cut at the corner, removing section. Then run the saw back along the rear line of the dovetail to the opposite corner. To remove remaining section, run the saw in on the other angled side cut. Trace cut dovetails on second component to joint to ensure a perfect fit. Cut and fit joint together. Blades shown (*top left*): Top blade is for flush cuts up to wall or joining surface. Note that teeth protrude ahead of shank. Middle blade is coarse-tooth, hollow-ground, for long, fast cuts. Bottom blade is fine-toothed for fine-detail, smooth-edge cabinetwork. Blade-change time is less than ten seconds.

major breakdown can be made according to appearance:

1. Through dovetails are joints where the dovetail and pin are clearly visible from two sides of the joint.

2. Stopped dovetails or half-blind dovetails are joints where the face of one board is perfectly smooth and the pins and dovetails are visible on the face of the other.

3. Blind dovetail joints are those where all the cutting is done without marring the outside face of either of the two pieces.

Cutting dovetail joints calls for precision craftsmanship. They can be cut by hand using a dovetail saw and small chisel or with a special template or pattern with a router. The latter is highly accurate and considerably faster than cutting by hand.

Home furniture-makers who own a radial arm saw can make a modified dovetail joint, sometimes called a finger joint. It is easy to cut with this type of saw. Actually, to cut this joint, the saw arbor has to be tilted so that the blade is parallel to the tabletop. After a saw cut is made by pulling the saw out along the arm, the blade is pushed back and the entire motor, arbor, and blade are lowered or raised, depending upon whether you started making the cuts at the base or top of the board. It is sometimes necessary to support the board being cut so that it does not rest directly on the table. As long as one face of the board rests against the table fence, you should be able to cut this joint.

Perhaps the most direct way to a dovetail is the dovetail kit, useful to you as an accessory if you own a router. One kit, for example, makes joints in stock from $7/16$ inch to 1 inch and contains: (1) a $7/16$-inch template guide; (2) a dovetail fixture; (3) a finger template; and (4) a $9/16$-inch dovetail bit. Working with thinner stock—from $5/16$ inch to $5/8$ inch—there is still another kit containing: (1) a dovetail fixture; (2) a smaller finger template; (3) a $5/16$-inch template guide; and (4) a $9/32$-inch dovetail bit.

Lap Joints

Bring two workpieces together, notch them equally where they overlap, and you have got either a cross-

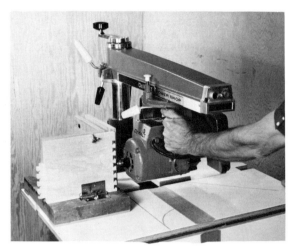

Fig. 4-31. *Top:* Cutting dovetails with a radial arm saw. *Center:* Components of dovetail router kit are shown, including alternate finger template, for joints $7/16$ to 1 inch. *Bottom:* Router is at work shaping characteristic dovetails, following fingers of the template as a guide.

Fig. 4-32. *Top left:* To make a cross-lap joint, mark the workpiece (stock next to fence is guide only) and make the two limit cuts. *Top right:* Remove the scrap between the two limit cuts by jockeying work beneath saw, taking successive bites. *Bottom left:* The inner surfaces of finished lap-cuts are serrated by the repeated passes of the saw blade. *Bottom right:* The cross-lap joint is glued and screwed, the two pieces now overlapping one another within a single thickness.

lap joint, a half-lap joint (end-to-end, at right angles), or a tee half-lap joint (end-to-side, at right angles). The desired visual effect, of course, is that the two thicknesses overlap within a single thickness's tolerance.

Grooving for the lap is simple enough with power. A bench saw, radial arm saw, or portable circular saw equipped with a dado head will clear the necessary grooves in no time. Just remember to limit your dado passes to a ¼-inch depth-of-cut at

a time. For instance a 1-inch groove in 2-inch stock should take you four passes; never overload the dado head with any deeper cut. There is no limit to the width of any groove you make. All you have to do is keep repeating the basic cut until you are finished.

You can, of course, make the grooves with a single blade in repeated passes; i.e., the measure of the blade's kerf divided into the width of the groove. Without power you can make your two

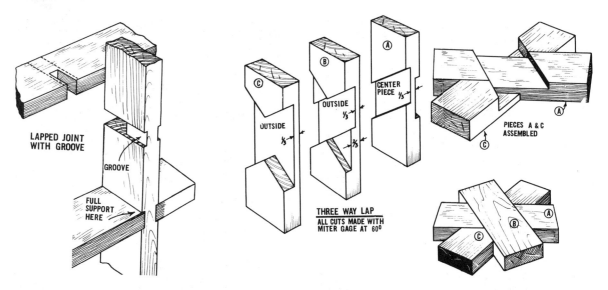

Fig. 4-33.   Lapped joints can be made in other forms, as shown. The plain style (Fig. 4-32) is useful for a wide variety of furniture work.

limit cuts with a backsaw, then chip out the stock between with a chisel. In this case use a depth gauge as you near the bottom of the groove, checking for an even, flat bottom surface.

The fit of the two pieces should be snug. Test for surface evenness of the lap with a steel straightedge. Preparatory to assembling, drill pilot holes for the screws, then glue and clamp the parts, inserting the screws after the lap has been positioned.

The End Lap or Corner Lap. This lap joint is made by halving and shouldering the opposite sides of the ends of the workpieces and then joining them at right angles. When one of the cuts is made at a point other than the end of the workpiece, you have a *center*, or *middle, lap*. This joint is most commonly used when joining a rail to an upright.

The Edgewise Cross-Lap. This is another joint that is made by halving the two pieces at right angles, but in this case the notches are cut in the edges rather than the surfaces of the two members. This is particularly useful when making framing or partitioning, and often both cuts can be made at the same time.

The Open Mortise-and-Tenon. This arrangement, which makes a corner joint a bit stronger than the corner lap, is used on the corners of cabinet doorframes. A variation of the open mortise-and-tenon can be used in place of the middle lap to join rails and crosspieces or uprights.

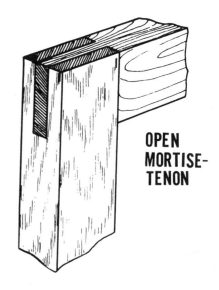

Fig. 4-34.   Details of the open mortise-and-tenon joint.

The Half-Dovetail Lap and the Full-Dovetail.
These fancier versions of the corner and cross lap are often seen in old cabinetwork. In both these joints the dovetail is half-lapped into a rail, cross-piece, or upright, and the two pieces are joined at right angles. The main difference between the two is that the half-dovetail lap is only half as difficult to make.

Where a tee half-lap with strong resistance to separation is required, the dovetail is a logical form of construction. Piece B is cut first (Fig. 4-35, *left*). Where the work permits, it is best to make the angle of the dovetail equal to half the thickness of the work, since this eliminates one setting of the saw. For example, if ¾-inch stock is being worked, the dovetail should be ⅜ inch. The angle setting for piece B is obtained by holding the work against the miter gauge and rotating it until a measurement taken off the end of the work measures ⅜ inch. The saw is set to cut the half thickness of the work, and many saw cuts are made to clean one side of the joint. The opposite side is worked the same way, with the miter gauge swung to the same degree setting on the opposite side. Piece A is made by cutting the shoulder cuts on three sides. Surplus wood can be removed by walking across the cut. Alternately, the wood can be removed in one pass if mounted in the tenoning jig. The sloping shoulders of the tenon are cut last, tilting the saw table the same number of degrees as previously used for the miter gauge setting. The same joint is satisfactory with only one side dovetailed, leaving the other edge square, as in the common lap joint (Fig. 4-35, *right*).

There are other useful furniture joints, and several of them will be shown in later chapters. Actually there are hundreds of different joints and variations of each. All have their advantages and particular applications, and even though you may never have need for some of them, it is good practice occasionally to take scraps of wood and see how many you can cut and fit properly.

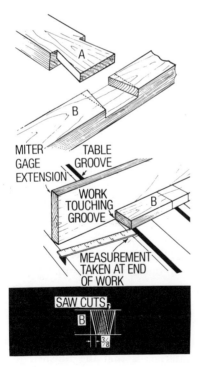

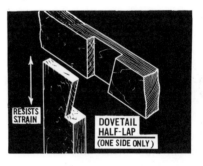

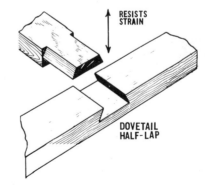

Fig. 4-35.   Details of the full-dovetail lap (*left*) and the half-dovetail lap (*right*).

Chapter 5
FURNITURE-MAKING TECHNIQUES

Furniture-making or cabinetmaking is an extension and refinement of finish carpentry. It requires skill, precision, and knowledge of construction techniques. Regardless of the design of your furniture projects, you should follow these six major procedures:

1. Lay out the project by measuring, diagramming, and estimating the quantity of materials needed.

2. Mark the materials for length, width, and shape. Use a well-sharpened pencil, knife, or metal scriber for marking out lines. Be sure that the point of the pencil or scriber is as close to the edge of the rule or square as possible. The thickness of a blunt pencil point can often mean the difference between a good fit and a poor one.

3. Cut the material to the exact size required. Always make your cut on the outside, or waste side, of the line marked on the board. The blade of the saw has some thickness, and if you saw on the finish side, or inside, of the line or along the line itself, you may find that, in spite of your accuracy in measuring, the piece of wood is cut too short.

4. Join the cut parts into the desired assembly by nailing, screwing, or gluing and by using the most appropriate of the wide variety of joints available.

5. Prepare the surface for finishing.

6. Apply the finish material selected to give the project its final appearance.

To get the best results from any furniture project, there are also certain other fundamental principles that must be followed:

1. Be accurate when taking measurements and laying out work.

2. Lay out the job clearly by marking the different pieces—front, back, side, etc. Also mark all companion pieces as 1 and 1, 2 and 2, etc.

3. Plan ahead as each step is completed.

4. Be orderly and neat. Take pride in turning out a fine job.

5. All lumber must be squared so as to find any deviation from a right-angle, straight-line, or plane surface, and it must be trued to the required size before proceeding with the actual work.

6. Joints must be made to fit together; never make them too loose or too tight. Remember, your finished furniture piece is only as strong as its weakest joint.

7. Wherever possible, duplicate pieces should be laid out and cut at the same time.

8. Keep all tools in good condition. A sharp blade or cutter makes work easier, safer, and more accurate.

TABLETOPS AND OTHER LARGE SURFACES

Tabletops, desktops, chest tops and large surfaces may be made of plywood, solid lumber (usually made by edge-gluing separate pieces of stock), or a framed-panel construction such as a flush door.

Plywood

Plywood is ideal for large surfaces and is available, as stated in Chapter 1, in various sizes and thicknesses. To use plywood panels most efficiently, cut cardboard pieces to represent the various furniture parts and plan the cuts beforehand on paper. Thus you can plan the best utilization of the panel and the grain direction. Except where indicated otherwise in the plan, you will want the grain to run the long way of the piece. Keep in mind that the arrangement of prominent grain-pattern effects can change the appearance of your furniture piece. If you run the grain horizontally, the furniture piece appears shorter; vertically, it looks taller. A desk or coffee table looks longer when the grain of the top runs parallel to the front edge.

Another point to remember when combining any wood materials is that the finished job must be harmonious. Of course, in some locations this is not so important. For example a dresser back doesn't have to match the surface veneer or the solid-lumber material of its top. Drawer bottoms and dust panels don't have to match materials used in visible areas.

Working with Plywood. Try to work it out so that your first cuts reduce the panel to pieces small enough for easy handling. Most important, watch in planning your sequence of operations so as to cut all mating or matching parts with the same saw setting.

When hand-sawing, place the plywood panel with the good face up. Use a saw having ten to fifteen points to the inch. Support the panel firmly so that it won't sag. You can reduce splitting out of the underside by putting a piece of scrap lumber under the panel and sawing it along with the plywood. It also helps to hold the saw at a low angle. Most important of all: use a sharp saw.

On a radial or table power saw work should be done with the good face of the plywood up. Use a sharp combination or a fine-tooth blade without much set. Let the blade protrude above the plywood just the height of the teeth. You'll find handling large panels an easier one-man job if you build an extension support with a roller. It can have a base of its own or may be clamped to a sawhorse.

A portable power saw should be used with the good face of the plywood down. If you tack a strip of scrap lumber to the top of each sawhorse, you can saw right through it without damaging the horse.

Planing plywood edges with a plane or jointer won't often be necessary if you make your cuts with a sharp saw blade. For a very smooth edge that won't even require sanding use a hollow-ground blade. Remember that if you do any planing, work from both ends of the edge toward the center to avoid tearing out plies at the end of the cut. Use a plane with a sharp blade and take very shallow cuts.

Sawing and drilling of overlaid (*H*igh-*D*ensity) plywood should always be done with the cutting edge of the tool entering the face of the panel. Tools should always be sharp and fed easily into the wood. Any chipping at the point of tool exit can be minimized by using a piece of scrap wood as a backup or, in the case of sawing, by stripping tape along the line of the cut. Before surface-gluing HDO plywood, it is important to roughen the surface by a light sanding.

When using plywood (especially the lumber-core type) for a furniture project, the craftsman may employ any of the conventional joints used in making furniture (see Chapter 4). The dowel-and-spline joint is the most commonly used in joining panels. The spline, usually about ¼ inch thick and

Fig. 5-1.   *Left:* Butt joints work well, but reinforce them with glue blocks if you use thin stock. *Right:* When possible, save on lumber by using frame construction and thin sheets.

Fig. 5-2.   There are two ways to conceal edge grain. *Left:* Thin strips of matching wood veneer are available, already coated with pressure-sensitive adhesive. *Right:* Matching wood strips can be glued to edge in a V.

⅜ inch wide, is continuous and may be made from plywood. The dowels (usually No. 7 or 8 spiral dowels) are on centers anywhere from 4 to 10 inches. The tongue-and-groove joint is a standard treatment. The tongue is usually ¼ inch wide and approximately ⁵⁄₁₆ inch deep. It is used when bowing panels into place, with the sides of the tongue slightly chamfered. The groove is always made a little larger than the tongue. Dowels are often used to provide extra joint security, too. The offset tongue-and-groove joint is a variation of the standard tongue-and-groove type. While it has greater strength, it is more difficult to make. For thinner plywood, joint treatments recommended for wall paneling can be used. Reinforcement strips must be used behind the thinner materials (it's a good idea for thicker material, too). Glue should be used on all panel joints.

Corner butt joints are the easiest to make and suitable for ¾-inch plywood. For thinner panels use a reinforcing block or nailing strip to make a stronger joint. In both cases glue will make the joint many times stronger than would nails or screws alone. Frame construction makes it possible to reduce weight by using thinner plywood. Dado

joints, which can be quickly made with a power saw, produce neat shelves. Use a dado blade shimmed out to produce these grooves in a single cut. Rabbet joints are neat, strong, and easy to make with power tools; they are ideal for drawers, buffets, chests, or cupboards.

When making miters of plywood, there is sometimes a swelling of the wood that causes the joint to open, especially when water-base glues are used. To solve this problem, cut the miter so that it is left slightly open at the back. Although this necessitates a corner strip to reinforce the joint, the little extra work pays off in a perfect fit and a good-looking corner. The miter corner is more difficult to make, but it needs clamping pressure from only one direction instead of both, as in a regular miter. The hardwood corner is another possibility. This method depends on the availability of matching hardwood. It is advisable to keep the dimension of the piece such that stock wood sizes can be used, such as ⅞ or 1⅛ inches.

Edge-Grain Treatment. Plywood edges can be a problem. Unless you are careful, the finished job will be bonded with raw edges that resemble half-healed scars. First check the design of the piece to

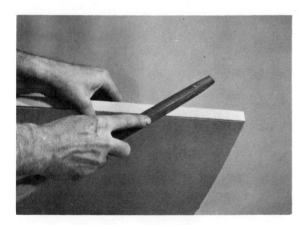

Fig. 5-3. *Top:* When covering an edge with plastic laminate, the top piece of the laminate should be cut to overlap the strip used for edging. *Center:* Using contact cement simplifies the job. Allow cement to dry on both surfaces, then align carefully and press together. *Bottom:* Use a file to smooth edges. File on forward stroke only and in a direction that doesn't cause the laminate to pull away from the edge.

be built. Even with plain butt joints there is an astonishing number of ways to assemble a simple box, and in each one the number or position of visible edges is different. If your equipment will make rabbets and miters, a little thought at the design stage will simplify the problem. You should also consider where the furniture will be located, what surfaces will be visible, and what finish you'll use. It may sometimes help to use lumber-core plywood.

There are many ways to finish plywood edges. You can achieve handsome, solid results by cutting a V groove and inserting a matching wood strip, but this method is comparatively difficult. This and other suggested edge treatments are shown here.

Thin strips of real wood edge-banding now are available, already coated with pressure-sensitive adhesive. You need only peel off the backing paper and apply it to the edges according to the manufacturer's recommendations. These tapes are sold in several different kinds of wood by lumber dealers.

You can apply laminated plastic-surface materials to table edges with the same contact cement used in applying them to the tops; apply first to the edges, then to the top. A thicker effect can be secured by nailing a 1- or 1½-inch strip all around the under edge.

Fig. 5-4. Laminated plastic is applied to edges first, then to countertop or tabletop.

End grain on edges that are to be painted can be filled with any of several varieties of wood putty—some powdered to be mixed with water, others sold ready for use. Plaster spackling also works well. Sand smooth when thoroughly dry and then finish.

Working with Laminated-Plastic Material

Decorative laminated-plastic materials are available in sheet form or already glued to ¾-inch plywood. If the material is in sheet form, you must apply it yourself to a plywood base. The development of contact adhesives (see page 100) makes this application possible without clamps, presses, or other pressure devices. While you should follow the manufacturer's instructions to the letter, the following four basic steps will help you do a perfect

bonding job with contact or pressure-sensitive adhesives:

1. Be sure the surfaces are clean prior to covering with a glossy film of adhesive. (When the adhesive is dry, the entire surface should look glossy. Dull spots mean that another coat of adhesive is necessary.)

2. Apply cement to both surfaces and allow it to dry. (Test dryness by pressing a small piece of heavy kraft paper onto the cemented surface. If no cement sticks to the paper, it is dry.)

3. The temperature of both cemented surfaces must be 70°F. or above at the time of bonding.

4. Apply the sheet to its proper location; roll the surface thoroughly, using heavy pressure on a hand roller. Make certain the two surfaces are brought

Fig. 5-5.   *Right:* Filling end grain on plywood edges that are to be painted. *Far right:* A molding can also be glued and nailed to the plywood to conceal the edge grain.

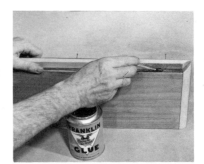

Fig. 5-6.   To apply laminated plastic material in sheet form. *Left:* Spread the adhesive. Contact cement is spread with a toothed trowel to the thickness recommended by the product's maker. *Center:* Slipsheet the surface. Kraft paper is laid on the cement when dry enough (time required varies), and plastic is positioned. *Right:* Remove kraft paper a few inches at a time. Roll plastic on tight. An ordinary rolling pin applied from center outward to edges will ensure best possible contact and adhesion.

into contact in every part. No sustained pressure is required to create a permanent bond.

The plywood used for tables and cabinet tops is usually ¾ inch thick, whether of interior or exterior grade. The exterior type should definitely be used for sink and vanity countertops. Interior, non-waterproof types may be acceptable for furniture shelves, coffee tabletops, etc.

Although laminated plastics are harder than marble, they are surprisingly easy to cut. The edge will be cleanest and the physical effort required at a minimum if you use suitable tools. As a general rule carbide-tipped or hardened-steel blades are the most durable, but they must be handled carefully because they tend to be brittle.

A standard wood saw gives a virtually chip-free edge, but such a saw dulls easily on this material and requires sharpening often. If you plan to cut much laminated plastic, a plumber's saw with twelve teeth per inch would be a good investment. This kind of saw is about 18 inches long, and its width tapers from about 3 inches at the handle to 2 inches at the tip. Since it is tempered to cut through hard flooring, cables, lead pipe, and similar materials, the steel is better suited to saw the hard plastic than the steel used in regular saws.

Hand-cutting can also be done with a straight-toothed, twenty-four-to-the-inch hacksaw or a fine-toothed coping saw. Feed the sheet slowly and hold the saw at a low angle to avoid chipping.

For home furniture-makers who have portable power saws cutting laminated plastic panels is easy. When you use an electric saw, always have the blade cut into the decorative side so that the decorative edge will not chip. Carbide-tipped blades do the best job. A portable router may also be used to cut the material.

Always drill into the decorative side, as some chipping out can be expected where the bit comes out, unless the material is firmly backed up with hardwood. Give the drill a start by punching the surface with a nail point, which drills small neat holes. First remove the head so that the nail can be held firmly in a hand drill. For larger holes use regular metal drills. (Wood bits can also be used, but chipping must be allowed for.)

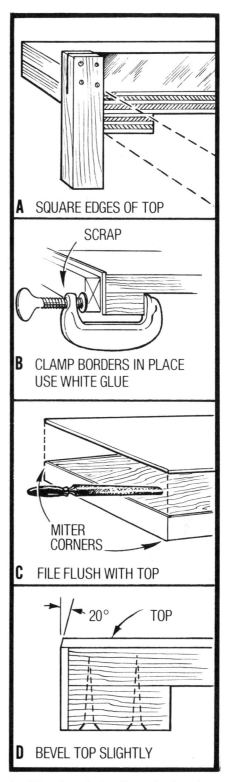

A SQUARE EDGES OF TOP

SCRAP

B CLAMP BORDERS IN PLACE
USE WHITE GLUE

MITER CORNERS

C FILE FLUSH WITH TOP

20° TOP

D BEVEL TOP SLIGHTLY

Fig. 5-7.   Steps in installing a hardboard top and edge.

Exposed edges of laminated plastic should always be given a slight bevel, as a sharp edge is dangerous and susceptible to chipping. Beveling also corrects any unevenness resulting from the sawing operation. Use either a fine-toothed flat file or a fine-set plane, and cut down from the decorative side.

All panel edges—whether painted, stained, or covered with molding—should be given a generous coat of urea-resin glue, resorcinol-resin glue (rubbed in), or any other material which will seal the pores to prevent moisture absorption. Where moisture will be excessive, a waterproofing compound should be used under a suitable molding.

For painted or stained edges plug any voids in the core veneers with wood slivers or wood putty; then seal the edges with a presealer such as waterproof glue; sand and then stain, paint, or enamel in the desired color. This is the easiest and most economical edge treatment, but should be used only where the edge will not be subjected to severe abuse.

Solid-wood molding makes an attractive finish for the edges. The wood can be painted or stained any color. It is usually best to give the laminated-plastic panel a slight bevel and to apply the mold-

ing with its top surface flush with the bottom of the bevel.

One way to finish the edges of particleboard is to fill them with wood putty, sand smooth, and paint. Another simple, easy way is to glue wood tape slightly wider than the edge to the edge and then shave or sand it down to a perfect fit. You can finish edges with more expensive solid wood strips, mitered where they meet at the corners, as shown in Fig. 5-8, and glued on. Another way to finish edges is with any one of a number of commercial edgings. One of these is plastic in the form of a T whose stem is burred or barbed, hammered into a saw kerf slightly narrower than the thickness of the stem of the T. All these methods work for shelf and table edges, but wood filler and wood tape or strips are preferred for doors, since they do not interfere with operation of the hinges.

Of course, the most professional way to finish off laminated edges is with a router, as described on pages 65-69.

SOLID LUMBER TOPS

While plywood is more often used in making a large slab or tabletop, many craftsmen prefer to use solid lumber, especially for early American pieces. There are several ways boards can be joined to form a large one.

1. The straight-butt joint is one of the simplest and most frequently used. All boards are jointed, that is, the edges are planed so as to be square with the face, or flat side, of the board. Adhesive is applied along the edges, and the boards are locked together with clamps until the adhesive has set.

2. Rabbet joints are more difficult to make and, therefore, less frequently used. To make this joint, joint all boards and cut a rabbet on each edge, except for the outside edges of the first and last board. The individual boards are secured with adhesive and clamps.

3. Dowel-joining of individual pieces to make one large board is often done, especially with large surfaces. A blind-dowel technique is employed to join the boards edge to edge (see page 108).

4. Tongue-and-groove joints are best cut with a

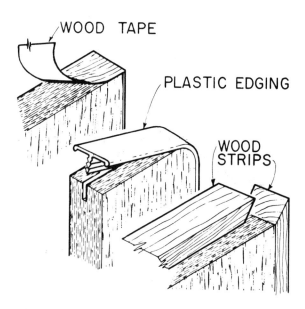

Fig. 5-8.   Finishing laminated edges.

shaper or shaper attachment so they can be cut along the edges of each board. The pieces are joined with adhesives and clamps.

5. The feather-joint and the spline technique are the most practical ways to join small individual boards. This joint requires the use of power tools. Each cut has to be exact, and hardwood must be used for the feathers or splines. Again, it is necessary to use adhesive and clamps.

6. A modified tongue-and-groove technique can be used. Cut the ends of the boards with a tongue and cut a narrow end piece or cleat with a groove. This transverse rail, which runs at right angles to the boards, tends to eliminate any tendency toward warping. It is fastened with adhesives to the boards and adhesive is also used between the edges of the boards.

When jointing in the planks in any of these techniques, cut the original boards ½ to 1 inch longer than the finished length and width to allow for trimming and necessary square. Lay the boards side by side with the grain of all stock running in the same direction. Check the end grain of each board and alternate the direction of the annual rings. This will help to keep warping to a minimum.

While large slabs may be clamped in the conventional methods described in Chapter 3, a homemade wedge clamp is excellent for binding boards that are to be glued together, edge to edge. It is easy to make and use, as shown in Fig. 5-10. Here is how it is done:

1. Construct this clamp from scrap lumber ¾ to 1 inch thick and 2 to 4 inches wide. You will need two pieces of wood (A and B) about half as long as the boards to be glued. With a third piece (C), form an H frame that is just slightly larger than the total width of the boards you are gluing (allow approximately one-half the width of your wedge piece—D —as the extra length).

2. On the wide side of a fourth, smaller piece of wood (D), mark each end at the midpoint from the sides. Now measure up and mark a point ½ inch above the center on one end and ½ inch below the center on the other end. Connect these two points by a diagonal line and saw through the material

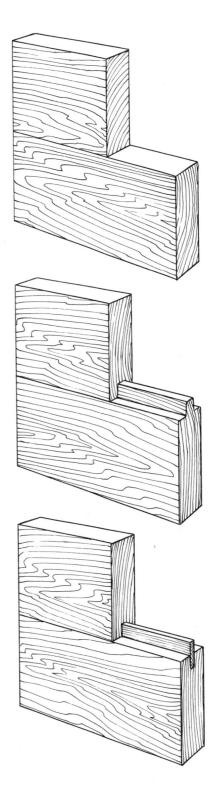

Fig. 5-9.   Three techniques of forming a solid lumber top. *Top to bottom:* Butt, tongue-and-groove, and spline.

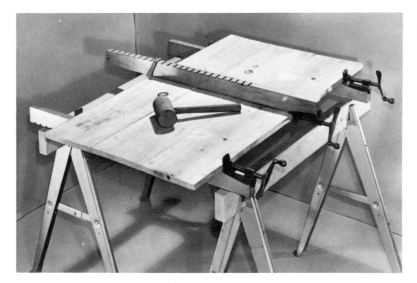

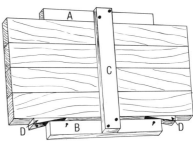

Fig. 5-10.   Two ways of clamping a large slab are (*left*) conventional bar clamps and (*above*) a homemade wedge clamp.

lengthwise along the line. This will give you two wedge-shaped pieces of the required angle, regardless of the length of the material.

3. Apply glue to both contact edges of the boards to be glued and place these edges in the correct permanent position on a level wood surface, over waxed paper, and under the H frame, making sure the boards butt up against board A. Board A, in turn, should be pushed tight against a surface perpendicular to your work surface.

4. Secure the construction by driving two nails that are at least one and one-half times the thickness of board B through it into your work surface. As shown in the drawing, allow the nailheads to remain above the surface in order that they may be pulled out easily later.

5. Now insert one of the wedges into the space on the left between the frame and the glued boards, hammering it lightly so it is tight. Drive a nail through the wedge and into the edge of the board, again with the nailhead well away from the surface.

6. Place the second wedge in the remaining space and pound it tightly into place, creating a strong tension against the glued boards. If the boards to be glued are thin, it will be necessary to place a weight on them to keep them from buckling.

7. Using a damp cloth, wipe off any excess glue

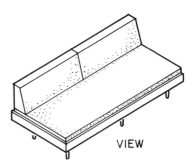

VIEW

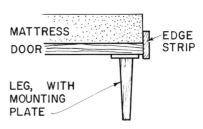

MATTRESS
DOOR
EDGE
STRIP
LEG, WITH
MOUNTING
PLATE

Fig. 5-11.   A sofa can be made from a flush door. Use a foam rubber mattress 4 inches or thicker that will fit the door size. Cover it with a box-type cushion cover. Mount the door on six legs—the short, fat, perpendicular wooden ones are probably best here. If you want to keep the mattress in place, edge it with a 1x4 and set it against a wall, as shown. Use bolsters along the back. If you use a 7-foot door, the couch can serve nicely as an extra bed.

Fig. 5-12.   Steps in making mosaic tabletop. (A) Lay out design on a large piece of paper, then trace it onto the plywood base. (B) Purchase tiles mounted on paper sheets with the finish face down. When tiles of the same color are used to cover large areas, they may be laid in sheets; remove paper later by soaking. For designs, soak the sheets in water to free the tiles. (C) Individual tiles for the design are "buttered," then set in place. (D) Where tiles must be fitted, mark with a pencil, then (E) snip off with end-cutting pliers. (F) When the design portions have been completed, use a sawtooth spreader to apply adhesive in the remaining areas, then place tiles. (G) Roll the mosaic firmly and smoothly to set and level all tiles. (H) Grout comes in powder form and is mixed with water to a creamy consistency. Spread grout over the surface and work it into the joints. (I) Wipe off grout with a damp cloth before it hardens completely. When dry, polish briskly with a soft cloth.

squeezed out on the upper surface and keep the boards clamped for forty-eight hours. A knife may be used later to clean any excess glue off the bottom. When using wedge clamps, remember that the work must be done on a level, clean surface such as a workbench with a back wall to butt against. A section of a wood floor adjoining a wall is an excellent spot, provided you don't object to nail holes in the flooring.

Circular Tabletops. It is best to cut circular flat surfaces with a bandsaw or a saber saw. The techniques of cutting with these two useful tools are given in Chapter 2.

FLUSH-DOOR AND FRAME CONSTRUCTION

It's easy to make a fine table- or desktop with an attractive flush door. For example a large modern coffee table can be constructed merely by adding four wrought-iron legs to a flush door. Or for a spacious desk add an unpainted cabinet plus wrought-iron legs to a flush door and the job's done. You can build the drawer section yourself,

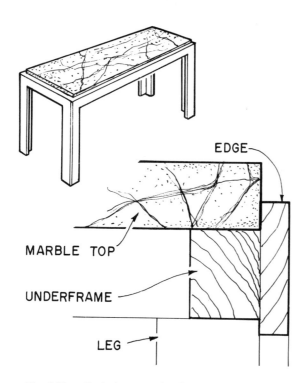

EDGE

MARBLE TOP

UNDERFRAME

LEG

Fig. 5-13.   Typical construction for a marble-top table.

but it's quicker to use unpainted furniture finished in a color that contrasts with the attractive wood grain of the door.

Flush doors are available in an assortment of hardwoods—oak, walnut, mahogany, gum, maple, birch—and several softwoods including fir and pine. They range in width from 1 foot 6 inches to 4 feet in 2-inch intervals and in two standard lengths—6 feet 8 inches and 7 feet. Flush doors are made in two styles, solid-core and hollow-core. The former is filled with solid lumber while the latter is not. The open space in the hollow-core door, however, has a system of bracing that prevents warpage and adds rigidity and strength. The hollow-core door is much lighter and less expensive than the solid-core, but it has the disadvantage of a limited screw-holding area. Unless you do either of the following, the only place for leg attachment is along the outer edges where the solid framing is:

1. Fasten the legs to cleats that are glued to the surface of the door and screwed to the stiles.

2. Attach the legs to rails, and glue the latter to the surface of the door.

The legs can be attached at any point on the underside of solid-core doors. But both hollow- and solid-core doors are unattractive on the edges, and therefore should be given one of the edge treatments recommended for plywood on pages 136-138.

LEGS

Furniture legs may be straight, tapered, or turned, and may be made in your home furniture shop or purchased ready-made. Legs may be of wood or metal. With the latter type, if you don't have welding equipment, take the plans to a welding shop and ask them to build the frame or legs. They will usually drill the parts for screws and file the welds for clean, neat joints. When you get the pieces back in your shop, smooth the wrought iron with fine abrasive cloth. Then give the metal one coat of metal primer and at least two coats of flat black or other colored enamel.

Ready-made furniture legs can be used in many projects. They are sold in a wide variety of lengths

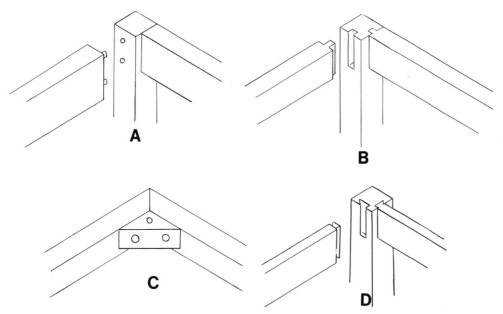

Fig. 5-14   Four methods of adding legs to a frame: (A) dowel joint to hold a leg; (B) open mortise and tenon, which is a stronger joint than the simple butt type; (C) a gusset or glue block, used to fasten two rails together; (D) the dovetail corner joint, exceptionally strong and recommended if proper tools are available.

and styles at local hardware stores or lumber dealers. Some legs are supplied with metal brackets that allow either angled-out or square mounting. Most ready-made legs come prefinished. Follow manufacturer's instructions for positioning and fastening details.

For wooden legs you can purchase a steel plate which is fastened to the underside of the furniture unit with screws; the wooden leg is fastened to the steel plate with a hanger bolt. Here are several ways to add legs to units when you cut the furniture leg yourself.

1. A simple butt joint can be used at the corner to join the two rails and the leg. Blind dowels plus adhesive will make for a good job. This is the joint most handymen prefer to make because of its simplicity and ease in assembly.

2. A well-fitted open mortise-and-tenon makes a stronger joint. Tenons are cut on the ends of both rails, and the adjoining faces of the leg are mortised to receive the rails. This type of joint should be secured with adhesive, plus nails or screws when necessary.

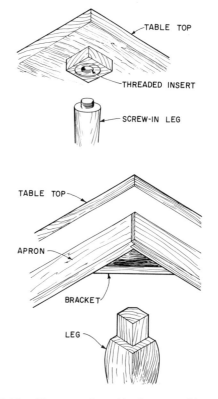

Fig. 5-15.   Two ways of attaching legs to a tabletop.

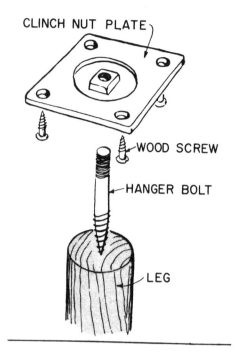

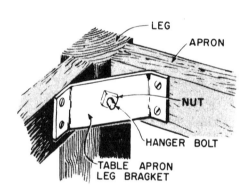

Fig. 5-16.   Furniture hardware may be used to make legs solid. *Top:* For example on a thick top screw a clinch-nut plate to the table and a hanger bolt to the leg. Attach the leg to the plate. *Bottom:* With an apron table use a metal bracket instead of a wooden comer block for installing legs.

3. The dovetail corner joint is exceptionally strong and is one of the best for the handyman to use. This joint, however, should be cut with power tools. While it is possible to cut the joint by hand, it must be so precise that only an experienced woodworker can do the job.

4. A gusset or glue block set in the corner not only joins the two rails but in some cases provides a larger surface to which to attach a leg. This method can be used to make a base, which is then secured to the underside of the furniture unit by flathead screws driven upward through the gusset.

Other possible methods of leg jointery are given in Chapter 4.

Making Tapered Legs

Legs may be tapered by hand, using a plane and drawknife, or by employing such power tools as a table saw or a planer. The latter method is much easier, and the result will, of course, be more uniform.

Tapering with a Table Saw. When taper-ripping furniture legs, a special jig must be made up to suit the work, as shown in Fig. 5-18. With the work dressed to net size and perfectly square, the saw fence is set to equal the combined width of work and guide board. The leg is then placed in the first notch of the jig, and the combined jig and work are pushed into the saw. An adjacent side of the work is cut in the same manner, while the two remaining sides are cut with the work in the second notch. No change is made in the fence setting.

Various styles of tapered legs are shown in Fig. 5-18. Straight tapers, styles A, B, C, D, and G, are cut with the saw, while the spade foot, styles E and F, are worked on the shaper. The various shapes are often ornately carved, fluted, or inlaid. Style B has the corners planed off, while C is rounded on the outer corner after sawing. Style A is tapered on two sides only. A planer blade is the best saw to use for this work, since it cuts more smoothly. However, if another saw is used, the taper cuts can be smoothed by taking a light jointer cut on each of the four surfaces. The adjustable type of tapering jig shown in Fig. 5-19 can be set to produce any required taper.

Tapering with a Jointer. Taper-jointing is one of the most useful jointer operations and can be used to good advantage on a wide variety of work. The furniture legs shown here are typical examples. The simplest kind of tapering involves stock that is shorter in length than the front table. On the

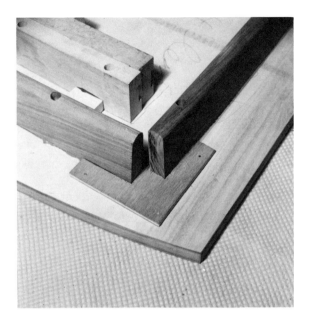

Fig. 5-17.   *Left:* Framing is necessary when leg is to be installed with a lag screw. *Right:* After the glue block has been fastened in place, the lag screw is fastened through the block into the leg.

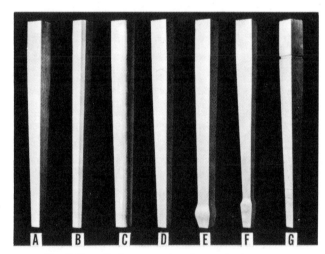

Fig. 5-18.   Various examples of taper-ripping.

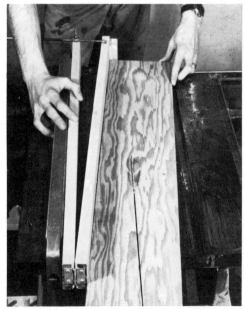

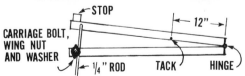

Fig. 5-19.   The taper jig.

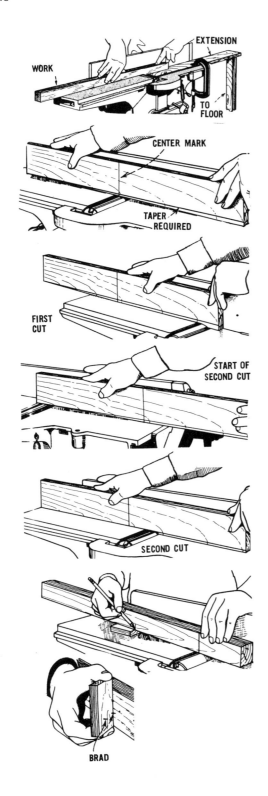

Fig. 5-20.   Steps for making a long taper on a jointer.

6-inch jointer this takes in stock up to about 14½ inches long. In making the cut the front table is lowered to the necessary depth of cut. The stock is then placed against the fence. The far end of the board is in such a position that it will land on the rear table at the start of the cut. From this position the board is moved forward to cut the taper. Work longer than the length of the front table can be handled similarly by making a front-table extension.

Where long tapers are to be cut without the use of an extension, a slightly different procedure must be followed. The basic rule is that the stock must be divided into a number of equal divisions, each slightly less in length than the length of the front table. For example, a 28-inch board would have two divisions. The depth of cut must be divided into a corresponding number of equal parts, which in this case would be two. Thus if a 28-inch board was to be tapered ⅜ inch from end to end, the board would be divided into two equal parts and the front table would be set to a depth of 3/16 inch. Two cuts are necessary, the first cut being started by dropping the mark over the knives. Fig. 5-20 shows the completion of this first cut. The second cut is started at the far end of the board and proceeds its full length to complete the ⅜-inch taper. Any length of board can be handled in this manner. A 36-inch-long board, for example, would be divided into three spaces of 12 inches each. If the taper required ¾ inch, the front table is set to one-third of this, or ¼ inch.

Very short and fast tapers are best cut by pulling the work over the knives. In setting up for the cut, the front table is lowered to the desired depth. Then place the stock on the table so that the point at which the taper is to start comes over the knives. Push the board so that the end contacts the front table, and slip a suitable block under the free end of the stock to maintain this position. Mark the position of the block so that it can be lightly bradded in place. The start of the cut is shown here; it is from this position that the stock is pulled over the knives to cut the required taper. In a variation of this method the block is not bradded to the work but is clamped to the rear table, the result

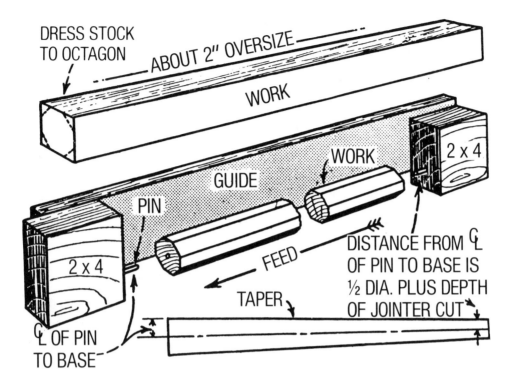

Fig. 5-21.   Tapering in the round setup.

being a slightly curved surface throughout the length of the taper. Short tapers demand a stop block against which the work can rest at the beginning of the cut; otherwise the slight bite of the knives in making contact will pull the work.

Tapering in the round requires a setup such as shown in Fig. 5-21. The stock is dressed to an octagon shape—not tapered—and is then mounted between the two end blocks. The pin in the block which is to rest on the rear table is located at a distance of one-half the diameter of the large end of the required taper, measuring from the base of the 2x4 block. The distance of the other pin from the base of the block is one-half the diameter of the small end of the taper, plus the depth of cut, which is quite deep, usually ½ inch. One screw through each end of the guide board holds the two end blocks snugly in place. In operation the two end blocks are considered as opposite ends of a long board, the cut being made in the same manner as

for ordinary tapering. Successive cuts, turning the work about 15 degrees for each new cut, results in a taper that can be readily sanded to a perfect finish.

Turned Legs. Round and other legs of similar design can be produced on the lathe. (Full details of lathe work are found in Chapter 2.)

Compound Angles on Legs. Legs on tables and chairs are sometimes splayed outward, and this construction demands a compound cut at top and bottom. Work of this kind usually has less than a 15-degree tilt, and for these small angles direct setting to the work tilt gives a satisfactory joint. If there is a 5-degree tilt as seen from the front and a 10-degree as seen from the end, the saw table is tilted for one of the angles and the miter gauge is swung for the other. If the tilt is 10 degrees and equal, the saw is tilted 10 degrees and the miter gauge is swung 10 degrees. The cut surfaces are parallel, so both cuts are made at the same setting by simply sliding the work along the miter gauge

Fig. 5-22.   Here are several furniture ideas that use ready-made spindles (available at most lumberyards) and lumber slabs.

facing. The list below gives the correct angle of set for the three major types of tables:

Type of table	Maximum angle of slant
Coffee	15 degrees
End	10 degrees
Dining	5 degrees

Casters and Glides

Put casters or glides on those items that are fairly light and often moved. Rollers, of course, work better on movable tables, caddies, and serving devices. For heavier pieces that are sometimes moved—particularly over hard-surfaced floors like tile and polished hardwood, use glides. Fixed pieces such as pianos and heavy dining tables can be fitted with cups into which legs or casters are set to distribute the heavy load over the widest possible area.

Glides. One type of glide is held in place with a pin used as a prong. To install, tap it into the center of the leg with a mallet or with gentle hammer blows. While this type of glide will give good service, it may eventually come out due to wood shrinkage. For a more permanent job you can drill a hole in the leg, insert a socket by driving it in, and

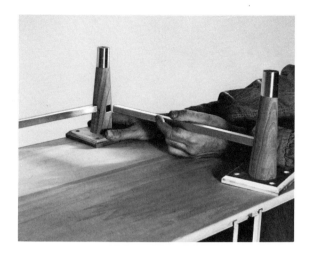

Fig. 5-23.   Legs can be braced with supports.

fit the glide into the socket. If a hole is already drilled in the leg, and it is too large for the socket, you can use an expansible socket that will grip the inside of the hole and stay in place. There are special glides made for tubular metal legs, which expand and grip the inner surfaces of the tube. Incidentally most glides add about ½ inch to a furniture piece's height, which must be taken into consideration when designing an object.

Casters. Casters come in various sizes, so it is important to measure them accurately when planning a leg's length. Many casters are made to fit into sockets. Others are mounted on flat plates that may be screwed to the bottom of a wooden leg. Casters are made in many different varieties, including ball bearing casters, which turn and move more easily than standard casters. These are more effective with furniture that must be frequently moved. Most casters are made with black, hard-rubber wheels. While these work very well on carpeting, they tend to leave black marks on hardwood floors. To avoid this, buy casters with steel or plastic wheels. Some casters come with brakes to keep the wheel from turning. These are particularly valuable with light pieces that need to be kept stationary.

Cups are made in two different styles. One is made of soft rubber and fits tightly on the legs of a chair or table. It has a broad, flat base to spread out the weight, and the resiliency of the rubber prevents the sharp leg edges from digging into the floor. The harder types are usually made of plastic. They are used mainly for heavy pieces such as dining room tables. Hard cups hold casters steady and distribute weight over a larger area of flooring.

Rollers are larger wheels that give serving tables, caddies, and the like maximum mobility.

HOW TO JOIN A CORNER

Making a corner is an elementary part of furniture-building. No matter what type of furniture you are making, you will encounter numerous corner joints. Of course a simple butt joint where one piece fits flush against the other can be used. However, this is not a good furniture joint. There is a wide choice of corner joints (see Fig. 5-25):

A. Although the end-lap joint is easy to make, it is rarely found in good furniture. The joint is often reinforced with screws, or even bolts, plus adhesive.

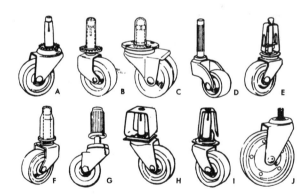

Fig. 5-24.   Caster stems and sockets vary widely, but most of them used on wood furniture have grip-neck (A), top-bearing (B), or friction-grip (C) stems and sockets or drive stems (D). Spring-clip sockets (E), pivots bearing stems and sockets (F), and plastic sockets (G) are used with metal tubing legs. Interchangeable sockets (H and I) make it possible to adapt almost any type of caster to metal furniture. Threaded-stem casters (J) are also available.

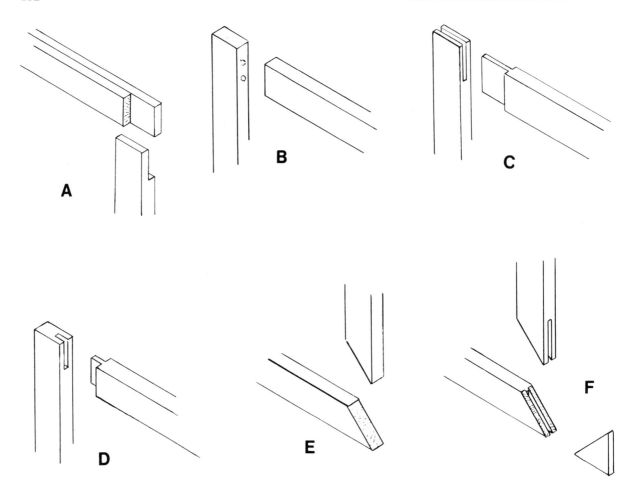

Fig. 5-25. Methods of forming a corner: (A) end-lap joint; (B) dowel-butt joint; (C) through mortise-and tenon; (D) open mortise-and-tenon; (E) conventional mitered joint; (F) miter joint with a spline or key.

B. Dowel joints are fairly common and frequently used to attach a leg to a frame. While the dowels can be driven in from the outside edge, it is best to use the blind-doweling technique for furniture-making.

C. A through mortise-and-tenon is often used by the handyman. However it is less frequently found in professionally built furniture. This joint is easy to make with a power saw that has a dado head.

D. The open mortise-and-tenon looks more professional and is stronger than the through mortise-and-tenon. The mortise can be cut with a mortising chisel on a drill press.

E. The conventional mitered joint with its 45-degree angle isn't a good choice for any corner that will be subject to unusual strain or excessive weight. This joint is best to use on trim around cabinet doors and elsewhere, rather than at the primary corners of the furniture piece.

F. A miter joint with a spline, which is much stronger, is easily made. The joint is cut in the regular manner, then a groove is cut in each end and a spline inserted. Secure with adhesive.

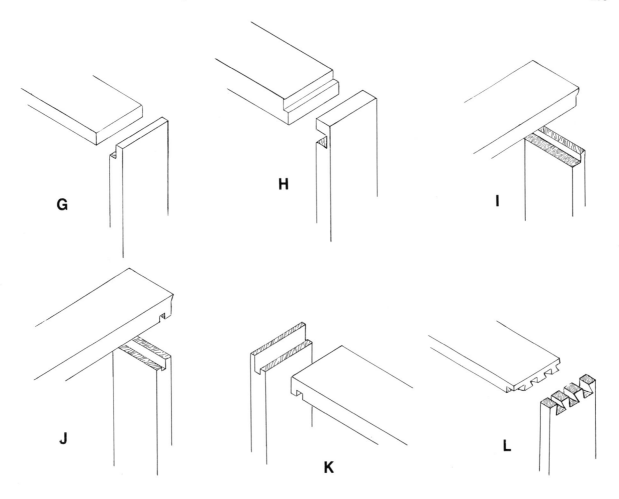

Fig. 5-25.   Methods of forming a corner: (G) conventional rabbet joint; (H) box-corner joint; (I) mitered-rabbet joint; (J) lock-miter joint; (K) milled-corner joint; and (L) half-blind dovetail.

G. A rabbet is frequently used for joining the top of a piece of furniture to the sides. Whether cut in the sidepiece or the top piece, the rabbet leaves only a narrow strip of end grain visible.

H. A box corner is sometimes used when making furniture, but the home furniture-maker is advised against this type of joint because there is always a strong possibility of cracks along the edges.

I. A mitered-rabbet joint is easy to make with a power saw and looks professional. The pieces may be secured with dowels, screws, or nails in addition to adhesive.

J. A lock-miter joint is one of the better types for the experienced handyman to use when making furniture. The pieces must be cut accurately on a power saw. They are held securely with adhesive.

K. A milled-corner joint is used extensively in making drawers. It is much stronger than the box-corner joint and less subject to cracking; it has closed edges.

L. A half-blind dovetail isn't recommended for the handyman who does not have power tools. This joint is often used when making drawers and is very strong when held with adhesive.

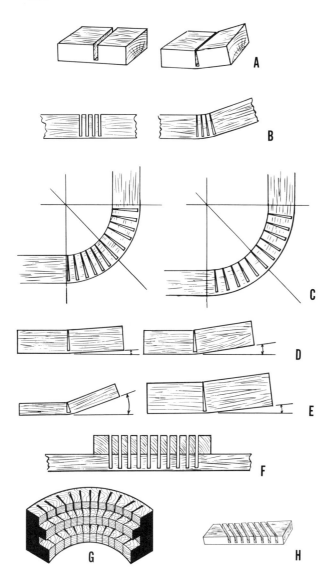

Fig. 5-26.   Steps in bending wood by cutting kerfs.

KERFING OR BENDING WOOD

If you rip a piece of wood thin enough, it will bend quite easily. If you wet this piece, it will bend even more easily and have less tendency to crack. By cutting a slit cross-grained and leaving a thin piece of wood on the bottom (see Fig. 5-26), you can bend the wood at this cut until the slit, or kerf, is closed at the top (A). By cutting several slits one alongside the other, the piece will appear to bend (B). To calculate the number of slits required to

bend the lumber 90 degrees, measure the angle of the first bend and divide it into 90 degrees. An easier method is by trial and error on a piece of scrap of the same thickness. Once you determine the number of cuts, you will always get a blend of 90 degrees regardless of the distance between cuts. The wider the cuts are spaced, the larger the arc (C). When the kerf cuts get wider than ¼ inch, the effect of the curve changes to straight sections at an angle to each other. If wide arcs are desired, the number of kerf cuts needed can be increased by one of two methods or by a combination of both: use a blade with a thinner kerf (D) or use a thicker piece of lumber (E). By gluing an extra piece of lumber to the back of the section to be kerfed, you can artificially increase the thickness of the lumber only at the place you want it thickened (F). The piece to be curved can be mitered, rabbeted, or grooved on the inside, but this must be done before you cut it (G). Once the piece is bent, the holes from the kerf cuts are filled with sawdust and glue. When the glue has hardened, you have a solid, curved piece of lumber. All sides of the curved piece can be veneered to give a smooth, solid appearance. If the cuts are made at an angle, the piece of lumber will spiral at a pitch that is the same as the angle you cut (H).

ADDING CENTER BOARDS

When making a bookcase or a frame for a sofa, shelves or center support boards must be added. Here are four ways to do this:

A. A dado joint is much stronger and looks more workmanlike. The dado can be cut with a dado head on a power saw, a dado plane, a backsaw, chisel and mallet, or with a router. The center board or shelf is held with adhesive and, if necessary, countersunk screws or counterset nails.

B. For a butt joint cut the shelf or center board to fit between the two sides. The board is then secured with nails or screws and adhesive. This type of joint is not very strong and will not support any extensive weight.

C. A stopped-dado joint is more difficult to

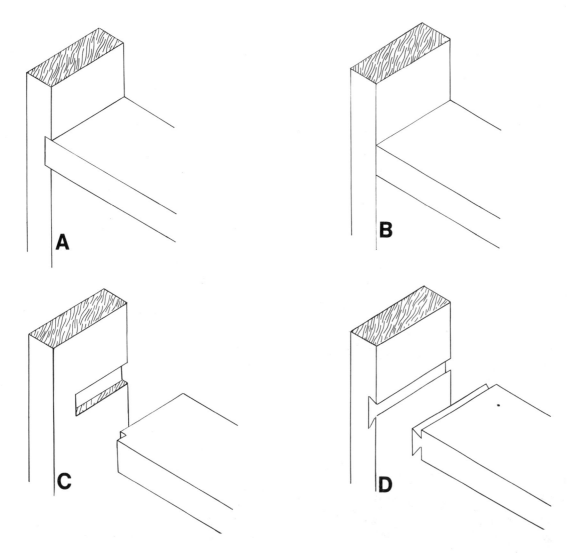

Fig. 5-27.   Four methods used to add center boards: (A) dado joint; (B) butt joint; (C) stopped-dado joint; and (D) dovetail-slip joint.

make by hand. It looks better than the ordinary dado because the front edge of the side upright is uncut. It combines the finished appearance of a butt joint with the strength of a dado joint.

D. A dovetail-slip joint is exceedingly strong and is best cut with a power saw. If this method is used, there is little chance of the sides pulling apart.

BACK PANELS AND DIVIDERS

The standard method of applying backs to cabinets and other furniture units calls for rabbeting sides.

The cabinet at the left in Fig. 5-28 has a rabbet that is just deep enough to take the plywood back. (Hardboard or particleboard may also be used as back panels, and the thickness rarely runs over ¼ or ⅜ inch.) For large units that must fit against walls that may not be perfectly smooth or plumb, the version at right in this photograph is better. This rabbet is made ½ inch or even ¾ inch deep. The lip that remains after the back has been inserted may be easily trimmed wherever necessary to get a good fit between furniture unit and house wall.

Fig. 5-28. Standard methods of applying backs to furniture pieces call for rabbeting sides.

Fig. 5-29. When hand tools are used, attach strips of ¼-inch quarter-round molding for the back to rest against. Glue and nail back to molding.

Nail the back panels into the rabbet by driving the nails at a slight angle. Use 1-inch brads or 4d finishing nails. Where the back won't be seen, 1-inch blue lath nails may be used. Two-hand staplers like the one illustrated in Fig. 3-15 are excellent for nailing cabinet backs. They drive long staples, setting them below the surface if desired, and greatly speed up the work. They are sometimes available on loan or rental.

When hand tools are employed, attach strips of ¼-inch quarter-round molding for the back to rest against. Glue and nail the back to the molding.

Fig. 5-30 shows two methods of applying cabinet backs without rabbets or moldings. The back can be nailed flush with the outside edge or, by setting the back ½ to ⅞ inch away from the edges, it becomes inconspicuous when the cabinet is against the wall. Of course bevel cabinet backs must be applied without a rabbet to make them less conspicuous. Install ⅜-inch plywood back flush with the edges of the cabinet, then bevel with light strokes of a block plane.

Furniture dividers, either horizontal or vertical, are usually set in dadoes cut in the opposite cabinet member. It's important that these dado cuts be properly located before the assembly begins. It is a good idea to use a blind dado when installing dividers.

If power tools are not available, small channels can be hammered into the sides or bottom and top of the unit to hold ¼-inch dividers of plywood or hardboard.

DRAWER CONSTRUCTION

One of the indications of how well furniture is constructed is how the drawers are made. Since a furniture-maker can save a good amount of material and time by skimping on drawer construction that doesn't show, the degree of quality here is a good indication of the quality of the furniture piece as a whole. Yet there is a sound reason for good quality in drawer construction; drawers take a beating and must hold together.

What type of drawer you make depends to a large extent upon its use and the tools available.

Fig. 5-30.   Two methods of applying furniture backs without rabbets or moldings.

Further, what size lumber you use depends upon the height, width, and depth of the drawer. But the thickness of the lumber is more uniform; it should be: (1) about ½ to ¾ inch thick or thicker for the front end; (2) about ⅜ to ⅝ inch thick for the two sides and back end; (3) ⅛ inch or more for the bottom.

Drawers Made with Hand Tools
The basic form of a drawer is a box without a top, and the simplest way to make a drawer is with ordinary butt joints at each corner. The bottom fits inside the opening formed by the front, back, and sides. Another way to make a butt-type drawer is to permit the drawer front to extend down to cover the front edge of the drawer.

As illustrated in Fig. 5-31, an additional strip of wood, glued and nailed to the front panel, will

Fig. 5-31.   *Top:* This drawer, shown upside-down, is easily made with saw and hammer. *Bottom:* Additional strip of wood, glued and nailed to front panel, reinforces the bottom of this second type of drawer made with hand tools.

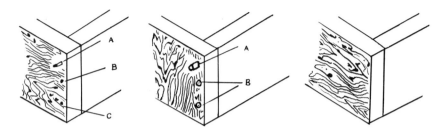

Fig. 5-32.   *Left:* Nails or screws (A) hold corner; head is countersunk (B); hole is filled (C).
Center: Dowel with glue (A) to hold corner; dowel flush with drawer front (B). *Right:*
Blind-dowel method; dowel from side goes halfway through front end.

reinforce the bottom. Reinforcing permits use of economical ¼-inch plywood or hardboard for drawer bottoms. Actually all drawers can be held together with finishing nails, screws, or dowels. Where the finished drawer front is to be painted, nails or screws should be countersunk and holes filled with wood putty. But where a natural wood finish is desired, another technique must be used if the front surface is to remain unmarred. There are three ways to do this.

First, nails, screws, or dowels can be used, as in the case of painted drawers, but they should be countersunk ¼ inch. The holes are then closed by means of wood plugs that can be cut out of the same type of wood.

Secondly, a "face," or extra front end, can be attached to the original front end. To attach this piece, use screws that pass through the front end and go into (but not through) the face piece.

Third, blind doweling, or dowels that do not go straight through to the front surface, can be used. To hold a drawer together with blind dowels, first mark off the center of the edge of the sidepiece. Next mark off the location of dowels along this line. Use at least three dowels if the drawer is 4 inches high and at least four dowels if the drawer is 6 inches high. Hand-drill holes for dowels in the edge of the sidepiece. These holes should be about 1 inch deep. Use a try square to make certain that each drilled hole is straight. Insert dowel centers

(these can be bought in many hardware stores) in the holes just drilled. Take the front end and lay it back-side-up on the workbench. Take the sidepiece with dowel centers in place and place it in position over the front end. When all edges are aligned, tap the sidepiece gently with a hammer, and the dowel center points will mark position for drilling into front end. Use a drill the same size as the dowel and drill holes in the front end, making certain that you do not go through the entire thickness of the piece. Remove dowel centers and cut dowels to size (the depth of the hole in the sidepiece plus the depth of the hole in the front end minus ⅛ of an inch). Apply glue liberally to the dowel and force it into the sidepiece. It is best to hold the wood in a vise and hammer the dowels in. Then position the front end and force the dowels into the already-drilled holes.

Drawers Made with Power Tools

As Fig. 5-33 shows, this drawer uses a ¾-inch or thicker frontpiece, from which most of its durability comes. Regardless of the number of identical drawers you're making, every individual frontpiece should be fitted to its own opening in the project— allowing a ¹⁄₁₆-inch clearance all around for a flush-front drawer and the same for a lipped drawer (lips on a rabbeted drawer should extend ⁵⁄₁₆ inch to ⅜ inch all around, and they should be from ¼ to ⅜ inch thick).

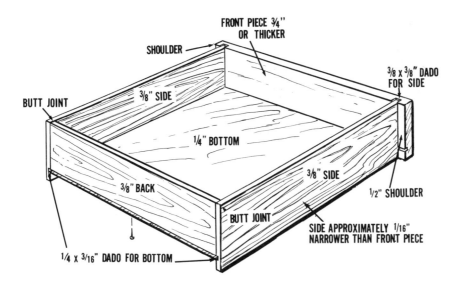

Fig. 5-33.   Details of making a drawer using power equipment.

The drawer sides are of ⅜-inch stock, dadoed ¼ inch wide and ³⁄₁₆ inch deep, beginning ½ inch in from one of the long edges (the ½-inch setback is called a shoulder). The same kind of dado can be made on the back of the frontpiece, but if you're using a radial saw, you'll have to raise the blade to compensate for the thicker (¾-inch) dimension. The back is cut last. Its height is ¾ inch less than the sides (½-inch shoulder + ¼-inch dado), but it can also be measured directly and ripped to fit as you're assembling the drawer.

The vertical cuts for the side-to-frontpiece joints will be either rabbets or dadoes, depending on how the drawer is to be mounted. Using no hardware, the back edges of the frontpiece are simple rabbeted ⅜ inch deep and ¹⁵⁄₃₂ inch wide (the ⅜-inch thickness of each side plus the ³⁄₃₂-inch required clearances). If side-mounting sliding hardware is to be used, dadoes will have to be cut ⅜ inch deep times ⅜ inch wide), after first providing for a shoulder, or setback, designated in inches by the manufacturer's instructions—usually ½ to ⅝ inches. But this is no set rule.

Make the drawer bottom, using ¼-inch stock or hardboard, cutting the width at ¹⁄₁₆ inch less than the space it will slide into. With all parts ready

assemble the drawer, using glue and finishing nails, checking at every step for squareness. Finally clamp the drawer in square. When you are placing the bottom of a drawer in place, keep in mind that it is best to leave some room for shrinking and swelling. This usually isn't necessary when either pressed wood or plywood is used, but even in these cases it is best to allow for some freedom of movement.

Therefore, when attaching the bottom to the fronts and sides:

1. Make certain that the grain of the lumber used for the bottom runs parallel to that of the front end.

2. If the bottom is held by a dado, glue it to the front end only.

3. The back end of the drawer should rest on the bottom; or

4. The dado cut in the back end should be wide enough to permit free movement of the bottom if it swells or shrinks.

Making a Dovetail Drawer

The dovetail is the strongest of all types of drawers (Fig. 5-34). Dovetail joints can be cut with power

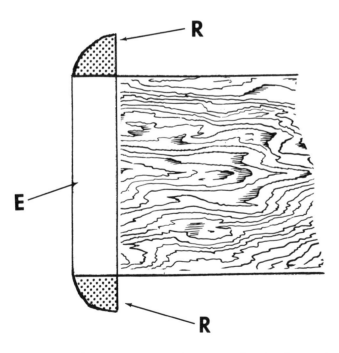

Fig. 5-35.   Quarter-round (R) cut and mitered to fit around all four sides of front end (E).

tools, as described in Chapter 4, with hand tools, as follows:

1. Take the front of the drawer and hold it so that you are looking at it from the side.

2. Divide the board height by two—that is, divide a 4-inch board in half; a 6-inch board in thirds; an 8-inch board in fourths, etc. Mark these points off on the outside and inside edges of this front end.

3. Along the front or outside edge mark off ¼ inch from top and bottom. Also mark ¼ inch on either side of the marks positioned in step 1 above.

4. Along the inside edge or the back edge mark off ½ inch from the top and bottom; also mark ½ inch on each side of the marks indicated in step 1.

5. Join each pair of points (one on the front edge and one on the rear edge) by drawing a line through them.

6. Trace this on tissue paper or measure off with dividers, and mark the same pattern on the outside edge of each sidepiece.

You now have the narrow pins, as they are technically called, on the front edge and the wide tails. With a crosscut or backsaw, cut along all diagonal lines. Remember that the depth of the cut on the front edge should be equal to thickness of the sidepiece. Then use a keyhole or coping saw or a chisel and mallet to cut out white portions of both the front edge and the sides.

Adding a Face

The drawers thus far discussed are general-purpose but not dust-free. To make the front end dust-free—that is, to make the front end cover the opening provided for the drawer—you can:

1. Make the front end wider and higher than the side so that it is close up to, in fact flush against, the drawer-opening frame; or

2. Add four pieces of quarter-round around all four sides of the front end; these corners should be mitered (see Fig. 5-35). The molding should be the same thickness as the front end.

3. Add an extra-large piece of lumber as a face over the front end (see Fig. 5-36). This method is often used to conceal homemade dovetail joints. It can also be used when decorative drawer fronts are

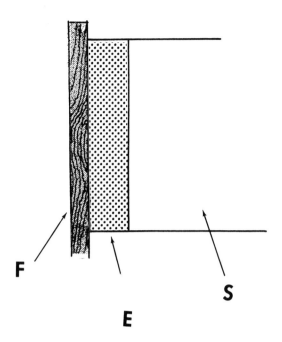

Fig. 5-36.   Decorative face (F) held by screws through front end (E) after sides (S) are attached.

support to the cabinet sides. In this way the drawer slides along this unit and is easy to move.

Adding wheels along the bottom-outside edge of the drawer makes it easy to roll back and forth on a board set between the two sides of the cabinet. It is best to rabbet-cut the bottom-outside edge of the drawer to provide space for the wheel.

2. Rail. To keep the drawer level while it is moving in and out, you can cut a dado in the side of the drawer and add a cleat to each side of the cabinet. This keeps the drawer bottom off the shelf and puts all the weight on the trim (Fig. 5-39, *left*). When the added strips are made of hardwood, you should encounter little difficulty in opening and closing the drawer. Incidentally the dado need not be cut into the drawer front if the cleat doesn't

desired. The face is attached to the front end by screws from the inside of the drawer, through the front end and into the face. The screws don't come through the face.

Getting Drawers to Slide

Sticking drawers are one of the most common complaints around the house. In any drawer the sides generally ride on pieces of wood anchored to the frame. Warping, shrinking, and swelling all make for trouble, but there are many ways to make drawers slide more easily.

1. Base. If the drawers are fitted between a series of shelves, the drawer can ride on the lower shelf. There is nothing special that the furniture-maker has to do except to see that both surfaces are smooth. This is the simplest way to do the job, but the drawer isn't free-moving.

It is possible to extend the bottom piece and have it slide in a dado in the side of cabinet, as shown in Fig. 5-37.

Another way to suspend the drawer is to add a cleat to the outside-top edge of the drawer and a

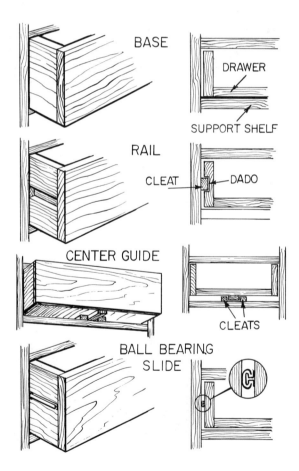

Fig. 5-37.   Drawer-sliding methods.

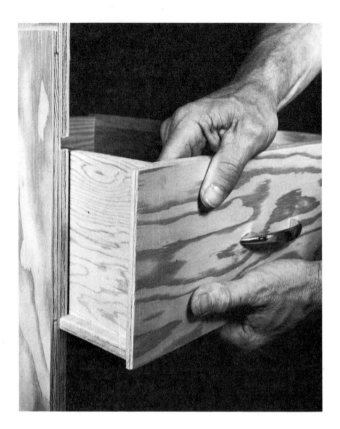

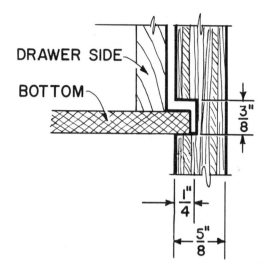

Fig. 5-38. *Left:* Extended bottom of drawer fits into slots formed by gluing pieces of ⅜-inch plywood to the inner surface of each side of the furniture piece. Gap just wide enough to take the lip is left between the drawer on each side. *Above:* Extended bottom of drawer is set in slot dadoed in the side panels.

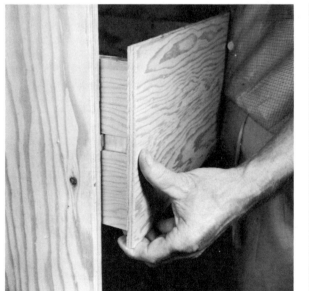

Fig. 5-39.   Two types of guides calling for use of power tools. *Left:* Drawer side has been plowed before assembly to fit over a strip glued to the side of the cabinet. *Right:* Procedure is reversed and cabinet side has been dadoed before assembly.

extend all the way to the front of the unit. Even heavy drawers slide easily on guides like these if they have been waxed or lubricated with paraffin after finishing.

In Fig. 5-39 (*right*) the procedure is reversed, and the cabinet side is dadoed before assembly. A matching strip is glued to the side of the drawer.

3. Center Guide. To keep the drawer straight and to prevent side-sway binding, a special cleat with a dado cut its full length will act as a drawer guide. A special trim strip is attached to the bottom of the drawer, and the cleat is attached to a board set between the cabinet sides. This method can be used with any of the above to prevent the drawer from shifting from side to side when being opened and closed. Remember to countersink all nailheads or to recess flathead screws; otherwise they will interfere with the smooth opening and closing of the drawer.

A modification of the tongue-and-groove method just described is a dovetail slide that serves the same purpose. It is used primarily by professionals and advanced craftsmen, since it requires precise cutting.

4. Ball Bearing Slide. Special hardware, often called phonograph slides, make opening and closing a drawer very easy. Furthermore they prevent the drawer from coming out all the way. These units are fastened to the side of the drawer and the side of the cabinet. Many different types are available, and they are desirable where any sub-

stantial weight will be placed in the drawer. As a rule the unit comes in two sections, one attached to the cabinet side and the other to the side of the drawer.

A modified form of the phonograph slide is mounted on the bottom of the drawer. It is necessary to use two slides for the easiest movement of the drawer. This type of drawer mounting is generally used for phonographs set into cabinets.

When planning drawers, keep in mind that they can be great space-wasters. It is important that their size be based on what is to be stored in them. Of course drawers can be partitioned or fitted with special trays to make them more efficient. In other words consider the depth of the drawer in relation to its ultimate use.

DOORS

Doors for furniture pieces can be swung on hinges, made to slide, fold back on themselves, or even disappear.

Hinged Doors

There are only two types of hinged doors, panel and solid. In either type the edge of the door may be set in flush with the case edges or butted against the case edges (flush overlay). The door edge may also "lip" over a portion of case edges. This cabinet-door lip is just a rabbeted edge.

Flush doors, which are the easiest of the hinged

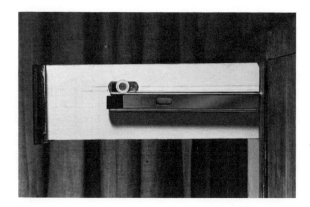

Fig. 5-40.   Two types of ball bearing slides.

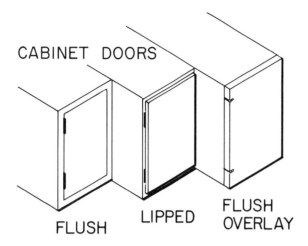

CABINET DOORS

FLUSH   LIPPED   FLUSH OVERLAY

Fig. 5-41.   Methods of setting doors.

constructed by assembling the boards vertically and securing them across the back with horizontal battens or cleats. In this construction the boards are not edge-glued, but the mating edges should be matched to minimize any separation that might occur. Actually it is best, when matching, to use rabbet cuts, tongue-and-groove construction, or any of the other joints detailed in Chapter 4.

Solid doors can be decorated by fastening trim to their fronts. Sometimes a slab-on-slab construction is used as a form of decoration. A slab of solid lumber is cut to fit inside the door opening, and a second, of thinner material, is cut to overlap the opening. When the two pieces are glued together, the finished door gives a lipped effect.

Panel doors consist of a frame and a panel. The frame can be made with mortise-and-tenon joints, doweled butt joints, or lap joints. The panels can be made of joined boards, hardwood-veneered plywood, decorative hardboard, corrugated fiberglass, or plate glass. The panel may be solid or louvered. There is a hardboard pattern that looks like louvers that can be mounted like an inset panel if you want to save yourself some work and don't care if the louvers operate or not.

Here are but a few of the ways in which panels can be secured to a frame:

1. The panel can be mounted flush with the back, extending to the outer edges of the sides top and bottom. The panel can be fastened with adhesive, nails, or screws.

2. The rear pieces can be cut with a rabbet to

type to install, are sometimes desirable to give a uniform appearance to a series of furniture units. Unfortunately they often increase the possibility of construction errors. Hinged flush doors have a tendency to sag, and when this occurs, the doors will jam against the cabinet form or show an open space along the door edges. Sometimes this problem can be minimized by recessing or attaching the doors so that they project slightly.

Rabbeted edges give a better appearance and keep sagging problems to a minimum. By cutting a ¼- or ⅜-inch rabbet on the lip, plus the ⅛-inch clearance around the open door, the cabinet opening will be completely covered at all times, and minor sags won't be noticed. The rabbeted edges may be cut with a saw blade, shaper, or router.

Solid doors consist of a simple slab of suitable material—plywood, particleboard, or solid lumber. A hollow-core frame door can also be used with thinner plywood, laminate, or hardboard (plain, perforated, or textured). These materials can cover both sides of the wood frame, or you may cover just one side with the more expensive material and the other with a less expensive one.

Solid-lumber doors may be made in the same way described for making solid-lumber panels or slabs (see pages 140-141). But in doing this, remember that narrow pieces should be avoided because they tend to warp. Solid-lumber doors may also be

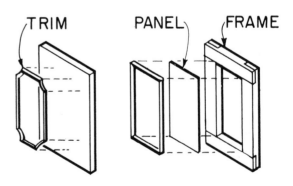

TRIM   PANEL   FRAME

Fig. 5-42.   Solid door (*left*) and panel door (*right*).

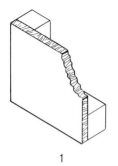
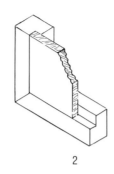
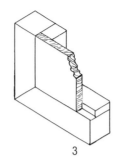
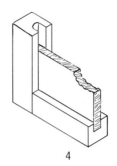

1   2   3   4

Fig. 5-43.   Methods of adding door panels: (A) flush mounting; (B) rabbet cut; (C) cleats; and (D) dado cut.

receive the panel. It is best to cut all the pieces—top, sides, and bottom—before they are assembled. With a router, however, this job can be done after the pieces are securely joined.

3. It is perhaps easier for the home furniture-maker to use cleats attached to the inside of the sides, top, and bottom. The cleats can be made out of finished molding, ½ x ½- inch or larger, or quarter-round molding. The panel fits flush within the opening made by the top, sides, and back.

4. The panel can be set in a simple dado or groove cut into the top, sides, and bottom edges of the frame. The width of the dado should be the same as the thickness of the panel used.

Hinges and Their Installation. The edge of the door, lipped or flush, will determine the type of hinge to use. In fact there are many different styles and designs of hinges from which to select when you mount swinging doors on a cabinet. Usually the better hinges come with mounting instructions, some even with templates or patterns, to make attaching the doors a simple job. Here are several different ways in which hinges can be added to swinging doors and cabinets:

1. Butt Hinge. The quickest and easiest door hinge is a butt hinge, which is usually employed with a flush door. It is attached to both the side and edge of the door with screws. Both the side and door can be mortised for the hinge, but if you don't mind the gap, no mortise is necessary. When the

hinge is mounted inside, the door can open only 90 degrees before the side edge prevents it from opening farther.

2. Surface or H-Hinge. A decorative form of butt hinge, the surface hinge can be mounted on the outside of the door. The other section of the hinge is attached to the edge of the side, which permits the door to open almost 180 degrees. Surface hinges are quickly mounted and require no mortising. A pair of H or H-L hinges will do for most

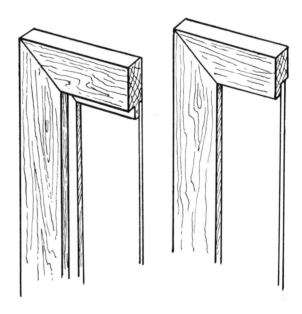

Fig. 5-44.   Other methods of installing a panel.

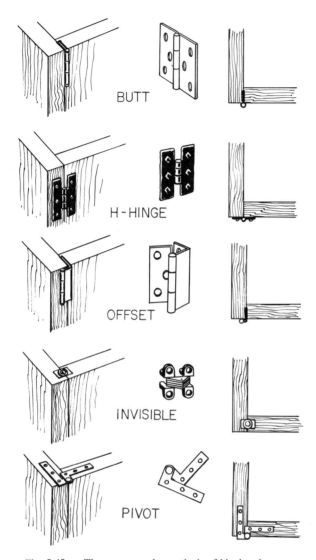

Fig. 5-45.   The more popular methods of hinging doors.

closed. Use a pair for small doors, three (a pair and one-half) for larger doors. Note: Doors are easier to hang if at least one side of the hinge mounts from the front, so that you can see what you are doing.

4. Semi-concealed Hinge. Semi-concealed, loose-pin hinges offer the same appearance when the door is closed as ordinary butt hinges, since only the barrel shows. They're much better, though, for flush plywood doors because screws go into the flat plywood grain. A variation called a chest hinge may be used in the same way.

5. Offset Hinge. With an offset hinge the door is rabbeted and the hinge is recessed in the door next to the cabinet or case side. Since offset hinges are

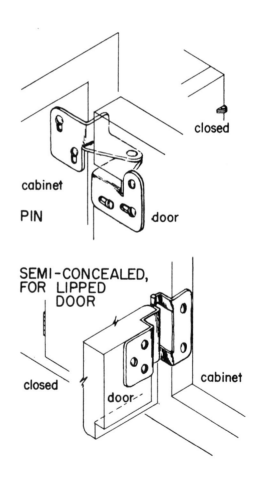

Fig. 5-46.   The pin (*top*) and semi-concealed for lipped door (*bottom*) types of hinges.

doors; for larger doors, or to add rigidity to smaller ones, use a pair of H-L plus one H or use three of the H type. Tee or strap hinges help prevent sag in large doors. On tall doors one or two added hinges between those at top and bottom help to minimize warping.

3. Pin Hinge. Concealed pin hinges give a neat, modern appearance to flush doors. They mount directly onto the cabinet side. Construction is simplified because no face frame is necessary. Only the pivot is visible from the front when the door is

made in different sizes, it is wise not to cut the lip or rabbet until the hinges are on hand. These hinges are available in many styles and finishes, with semi-concealed or surface mounting.

6. Invisible Hinge. When you don't want any part of the hinge to show, you can use the Soss invisible hinges. It is necessary to cut a mortise (which can be done with a drill and chisel) in both the edge of the door and the support side. These hinges come in different sizes, depending upon the thickness of the door.

7. Pivot Hinge. Unlike the other types of hinges, the pivot hinge, also called the knife type, is attached to the top and bottom edges of the door and the top and base of the cabinet. With this type of hinge the door opens all the way.

When hanging cabinet doors, first plumb the hinge edge of the door true. Then square the top and bottom edges to fit the opening. Finally plane the edge opposite the hinge joint. This edge should have a slight bevel to give clearance when closing the door and thereby make possible a tighter fit. Wedge the door up from the bottom by forcing a chisel or screwdriver under it, until it almost touches the top of the opening. Using the hinge itself, lay out its position on both the door and the frame. If lead holes for the hinge screws are needed, be sure to keep them as small as possible so that the screws will grip with maximum strength. While two hinges are usually sufficient for most furniture installation, a third hinge should be installed at the center if the door is unusually large or heavy. Once the hinges are installed, check the door for smooth operation.

When hanging matching doors, allow for complete freedom of movement both between the paired doors and around the hinge. The easiest method of determining the space required between matching doors is by inserting a paper match between them and then setting the hinges. This clearance allows for free movement and prevents the doors from sticking together if they are not perfectly set.

How to Add a Doorstop. Hinged doors require a doorstop that will prevent the door from being pushed into the cabinet and possibly pulling out

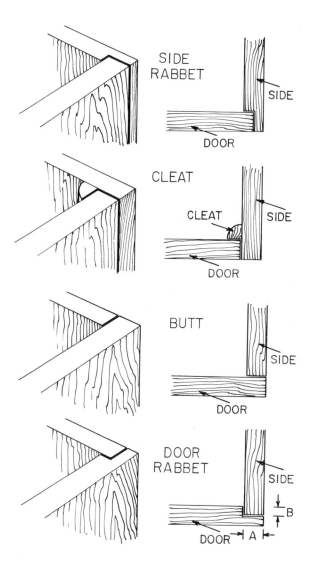

Fig. 5-47.   Several doorstop arrangements.

the hinges. Some ways this can be accomplished are as follows:

1. *Butt.* The easiest method is to have the side opposite the hinge act as the stop. The door fits over the side. When closed, it can't go any further.

2. *Cleat.* Another simple way to add a doorstop is to nail or screw a cleat to the side of the cabinet so that when the door is closed, it is flush against the cleat.

3. *Door Rabbet.* By cutting a rabbet along the inside edge of one side of the door, it can overlap

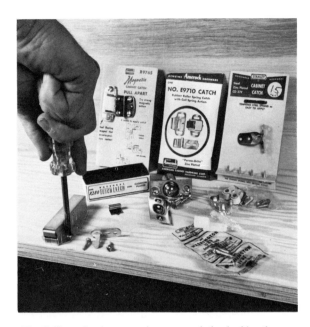

Fig. 5-48.   Catches come in many varieties besides the conventional friction type, shown at extreme right, and the bullet type, center. The touch type being installed here lets the door open at touch. A magnetic catch has no moving parts to break. Roller catches and the new ones made of polyethylene are smoother and more durable than plain steel friction catches.

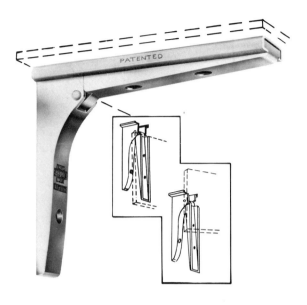

Fig. 5-49.   Load-bearing folding brackets will safely support up to 200 pounds on an 18-inch-wide shelf. Of course these shelves may also be used as tables, seats, counter space, etc. When not in use, the shelf may be dropped against the wall, or the whole unit can be completely removed from the wall or supporting structure.

the side and thus it can be stopped when it is closed (see Fig. 5-47). When cutting the rabbet, its width (A) should be the thickness of the door if the remaining extending part of the door is thicker than ¼ inch.

4. *Side Rabbet.* This is merely a modification of the door rabbet. In this instance the rabbet is cut into the side rather than the door.

How to Install Door Catches. To keep hinged doors shut, you should attach a catch. Catches come in many varieties, but most fall into one of the following three categories:

1. *Bullet.* Most common of all catches is the bullet type, a shell-like unit sold in hardware stores. The strike plate is nailed to the top or bottom, and the catch is force-fitted into a small drilled hole.

2. *Magnetic.* This catch consists of two parts, a small metal plate that is screwed onto the door and a magnet unit that is attached to a shelf or the top

or bottom of the cabinet. The magnetic force keeps the door tightly closed.

3. *Friction.* This type of catch is often used and is easily available. The rigid section is attached to the door, and the spring catch is anchored to a shelf or the top or bottom of the cabinet.

How to Make a Desktop Door. When making furniture, you may want to provide for a writing surface—a desktop—that is not visible when the cabinets are closed. The basic unit is similar to any other type of cabinet construction. The door, instead of being hinged at the side, is hinged at the bottom.

Regular butt hinges or a piano hinge—a continuous hinge strip—is fastened to the cabinet base and the lower section of the door. When the door opens forward and downward, it becomes a desktop. To keep the desktop door level with the floor, support braces are added. These are made of steel or solid brass and are available in many dif-

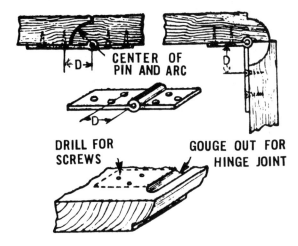

Fig. 5-51.   Detail of installing a drop-leaf hinge.

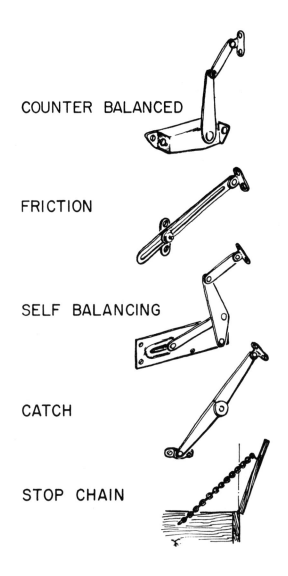

Fig. 5-50.   Various types of lid-supporting devices.

ferent styles. A support on each side will support the desktop as a writing surface.

Installing Drop-Leaf Hinges. Drop-leaf hinges are used in good furniture construction for drop leaves of tables and cabinets. The longer half of the hinge must be long enough to reach across the joint and have the screws set in the drop leaf, as shown in Fig. 5-51. The center pin is in line with one face of the hinge, so that it may be set without gaining

or cutting out for the whole hinge; however, it is necessary to gouge out a groove for the hinge joint. When these hinges are set, the center line of the pin must coincide with the center of the arch that marks the rule joint.

Door and Drawer Locks. Some furniture pieces have drawer and door locks as part of a decorative scheme. To fit a typical till or drawer lock, first lay out the dimensions of the faceplate and make the required recess cut. Then position the case of the lock so that the body can be placed in position and the faceplate can be checked against the marks made on the top edge. After all cuts have been made, tap the lock into position; after the keyhole has been finished, the lock case can be screwed in position.

To mark the position of the striking plate, place a piece of carbon between the lock body and the other surface. Then turn the key and the bolt position will be registered. To complete the job, cut out the underside of the striking plate and install the plate.

Sliding Doors

Sliding doors are very popular in contemporary furniture. The use of this type of door makes it

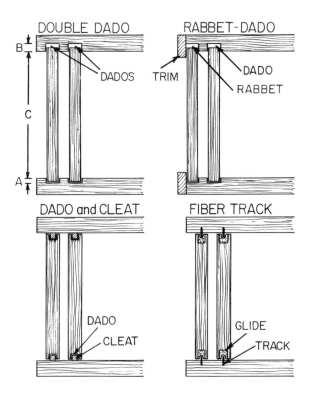

Fig. 5-52.   Various methods of installing sliding doors.

possible to open a cabinet without having the doors swing out where they may get in the way.

Whether or not you have power tools, it is simple to make sliding doors for a cabinet. You have a choice of many materials to use for sliding doors—tempered hardboard, perforated hardboard, plywood, flat, reinforced fiberglass, mirror, glass, and particleboard. One important point to remember about sliding doors is that you must use a material that will not warp.

How thick the door material should be depends upon the size of the door and the method used to make the doors slide. Normally, ½- or ¾-inch material presents no problem in cabinet doors. However, ⅛-inch tempered hardboard or ¼-inch plywood may buckle or warp if the door is of any substantial size. Select the material for the door carefully before you start to make the necessary provisions for installation. Here are several ways in which you can install sliding doors in cabinets or built-ins. Some require the use of power tools;

others need nothing more than simple hand tools.

Double Dado. Two dadoes cut into the bottom surface of the cabinet top and two dadoes in the top surface of the cabinet base provide the grooves in which the doors will slide. Here are several pointers to help you make the proper size cuts (see Fig. 5-52, *top left*):

1. The width of each dado should be equal to the thickness of the sliding door plus ¹⁄₁₆ to ⅛ inch.

2. The forward edge of the front dado should be no less than ¼ inch, but preferably about ½ inch, from the edge of the board.

3. The space between the two dadoes should be no less than ⅛ inch, but preferably ¼ inch.

4. The depth of the dado cut into the top of the cabinet (B) should be double the depth of the dado cut in the bottom of the cabinet (A).

5. The height of the door should be the distance from the top surface of the bottom of the cabinet to the bottom surface of the cabinet top (C), plus the depth of the top dado.

6. The width of each door should be one-half the distance between the two sides of the cabinet plus at least ¼ inch and a maximum of ½ inch.

7. When installing the doors, set the rear one in place before the front one.

8. To set a door in place, insert the top into the top dado and then lower it into the bottom dado.

9. To remove a door, lift it all the way up into the top dado and pull the bottom edge forward.

You can also use this technique to set metal track or ball and roller track into the groove and slide the glass or wood doors on the track.

Rabbet Dado. A modified method of the double dado, this is used when a picture-frame trim is to be added to the outside of the cabinet. In this way only one dado is cut, while a rabbet is cut along the edge.

Dado and Cleat. A single dado is cut into the top and bottom of the door itself rather than into the top and bottom of the unit. This groove in the door rides on a ½ x ½ cleat that is nailed or screwed and glued into the cabinet's top and bottom.

A variation of this technique is to cut dadoes in the underside of the cabinet top and the top surface of the cabinet base to provide tracks in which the door rides. Cut the top and bottom edges of the doors with a tongue to fit into the dado grooves.

Fiber Track. Narrow fiber or plastic track is available in some hardware stores. Dadoes that are the thickness of the track are cut into the top and bottom of the cabinet. Special glides that are recessed in the door itself ride on these tracks. It is necessary to mortise in the doors to insert the glides.

Metal Track. There is available metal track on which the doors may slide. Dadoes or grooves are cut in the top and bottom edges of both doors to enable them to ride on the track.

Double-channel track of plastic, fiber, or metal is also available for glass sliding doors. This track does not require the bottom surface of glass to be beveled, as is normally the case with other sliding arrangements. At the top of the door you can use the same channels inverted, with wood stops, or you can use dadoed slots. When using glass doors, be sure to allow enough clearance at the top so that you can push them up and remove them for cleaning.

Cleat Method. If you don't have power tools, it is possible to make sliding doors by using pieces of ¼- or ⅜-inch square trim molding as guides. Following is a description of this method, based on using ¼-inch quarter-round molding, ¼-inch square molding, and ⅛-inch clearance for each door to slide freely:

1. Measure the thickness of the door and double that figure. Add 1 inch and measure off this distance from the front edge of the cabinet along the underside of the cabinet top and the top surface of the cabinet base.

2. Cut two pieces of ¼-inch quarter-round to the proper length to fit between the cabinet sides, and nail them so that the back edges are flush with the lines drawn.

3. Measure the height and width of the door and cut to size.

4. Measure ⅜ inch from the forward edge of the quarter-round, and draw a line along the top and bottom.

5. Cut a piece of ¼-inch square molding the width of the cabinet.

Fig. 5-53. Only hand tools are required when this version of the sliding cabinet door is used. Front and back strips are stock ¼-inch quarter-round molding. The strip between is ¼-inch square. Use glue and brads or finishing nails to fasten strips securely.

6. Set the rear door in place, and nail this ¼-inch square strip so that the rear edge is flush with the lines drawn in step 4.

7. Cut two more pieces of ¼-inch quarter-round to the cabinet width.

8. Set the front door in place, and position the forward quarter-round so that the front edge is flush with the forward edge of the cabinet. Then nail in place.

How to Make a Lift and Sliding Door. Another variation in attaching a door is the lift and sliding unit. The door can be mounted in different ways: it can lift up and slide back, drop forward and slide back, or swing forward and slide back. In all three of these types the door disappears into the cabinet. This is a more advanced method of installing a door and is best done with power tools. It is

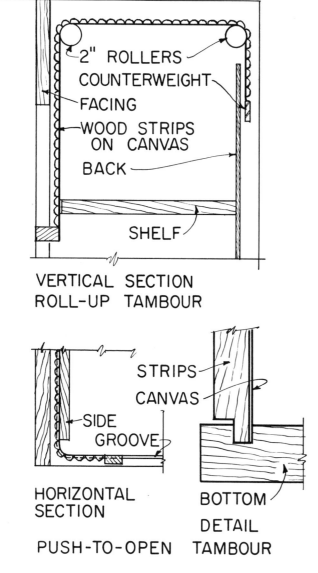

VERTICAL SECTION
ROLL-UP TAMBOUR

2" ROLLERS
COUNTERWEIGHT
FACING
WOOD STRIPS ON CANVAS
BACK
SHELF

HORIZONTAL
SECTION

STRIPS
CANVAS
SIDE GROOVE

BOTTOM
DETAIL

PUSH-TO-OPEN TAMBOUR

Fig. 5-54. Here are details for making a roll-up tambour door. Further details on this type of door can be found in Chapter 7.

necessary to use pivot hinges and to rout out the sides so that the hinged door can slide back into the cabinet.

This type of door is particularly useful when a radio is mounted inside the cabinet together with its speaker, or when a TV set is installed and you want to get the doors out of the way. It is neces-

sary, however, to add a false top, bottom, or sides—depending on the way the door is hung. The false section should be equal to the inside depth of the cabinet less the thickness of the door plus ⅛ to ¼ inch.

A router will cut the grooves necessary for the pivot hinge to move in when the door is being pushed back into the cabinet. The groove can be cut with a router bit on a drill press or even with an electric drill, but do not use these tools until you have had sufficient experience to cut along a straight line and at a constant depth.

How to Make Tambour Doors. Rolling doors that disappear within a cabinet are not difficult to make. They take time but can be built with simple hand tools.

The doors are made by attaching half-round to canvas with adhesive. False sides and back must be added, for the doors will ride between the false side and the cabinet side and then disappear between the false back and the cabinet back.

Use a piece of finished molding stock at each end of the door, and rabbet-cut the rear side to attach the canvas. It is best to use adhesive and tacks to hold the canvas to the molding stock. A groove must be cut in the underside of the cabinet top and the top surface of the cabinet base for the door guides to slide in. The door guides can be finished

Fig. 5-55.   The simplest drawer pull is a notch cut into the top of the drawer front.

nails hammered into the end molding pieces on each door. To keep the door from buckling and to make it ride easily, door guides should be added to every third half-round as well. For more details on making tambour doors see pages 215-217.

How to Add Pulls

Drawer pulls and door handles are widely available. Use them in metal or wood to give style accents to your furniture piece. They come in a variety of traditional and "ranch" styles as well as in many modern designs.

Knob. Handles and knobs can be attached by setting bolts through predrilled holes. You can cut your own pulls out of lumber of decorative trim and then nail or screw them in place on a drawer or door.

The simplest drawer pull of all is a notch cut into the top of the drawer front. It may be rectangular, V-shaped, or half-round. You can omit the notch from every other drawer, opening it by means of the notch in the drawer below, as shown in Fig. 5-55. By sloping drawer fronts, the drawer may be pulled out by grasping the projecting bottom edge.

Finger Grip. To avoid pumping of pulls on sliding doors, you can either drill a finger hole

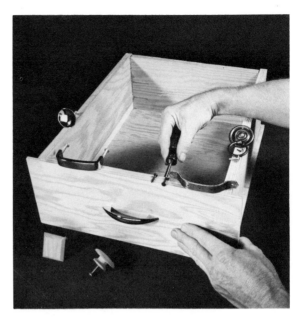

Fig. 5-57.　Drawer pulls and door handles of the types shown here are widely available.

through the door (a 1-inch-diameter hole is sufficient) or you can insert a small metal cup (a finger grip available in hardware stores) into a predrilled hole in the door. These are held in place by force-fit and glue. For large doors use the rectangular or large, round cups that are fastened in with screws.

Built in. If you wish to avoid exterior hardware on a drawer or door, you can cut a slot in the bottom as long as the door or front of the drawer extends somewhat out from the cabinet. This slot is simple to make with a power saw but difficult by hand.

Invisible. For those without power tools who do not want exterior knobs the "touch-latch" is easy to install. A slight pressure on the door releases the lock mechanism and the door swings open. To close, merely push door shut. This eliminates the need for a door catch as well.

SHELVES

The usual construction of shelves merely requires the fitting of boards together at right angles in good

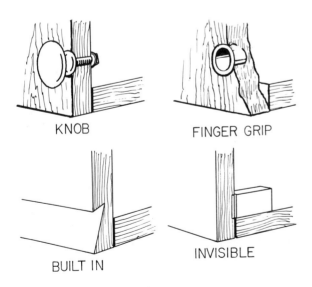

KNOB　　　　FINGER GRIP

BUILT IN　　　INVISIBLE

Fig. 5-56.　Popular door-pull arrangements.

and practical proportions. When designing your bookshelves, make them as close as possible to the actual width of the books, because this reduces the amount of exposed shelving to be dusted. For this reason, shelving is generally 1x8 or 1x10 inches. Shelves spaced 9 inches apart will accommodate most books, and a shelf or two with 11- or 12-inch clearance will take care of the larger ones. One-inch boards can support spans of about 3 feet without sagging. For 2-inch boards the span is approximately 5 feet. Longer spans require additional support such as toenailing into the backing of the bookcase. Popular methods of supporting shelves in furniture are as follows:

A. *Butt.* Shelves inside the furniture piece that are the exact width of the inside can be held by nails or screws set in through the sides.

B. *Cleat.* Where it's not possible or desirable to drive nails or screws through the side, a cleat (½x½ or 1x1 or quarter-round) can be nailed or screwed to the side and the shelf nailed to it. The cleats may be masked from direct view by installing vertical molding strips along the side edges of the shelves.

C. *Dado.* A stronger and neater way to support an inside shelf is to cut a dado in the sides. The dado should be as thick as the shelf, which can be held in place by glue and/or screws. A blind dado (see pages 120-121) gives a neater appearance.

D. *Dowel-Peg.* On the other hand you may want adjustable shelves. The dowel-peg technique can be used for short shelves that won't be supporting heavy loads. Merely drill a series of holes in a straight line about 1 inch from each edge of the sides. A short length of dowel, extending halfway into the side and an equal distance under the shelf, is used in each hole for the shelf to rest upon.

E. *Metal-Clip.* The metal-clip technique is similar to the dowel-peg. The only difference is that these metal clips can be purchased in many hardware stores. They carry more weight than the dowel; besides, there's no work in making them.

F. *Adjustable Strip.* For heavier loads on shelves you can use adjustable metal strips. These units, available in hardware stores, are screwed to the insides of the sides. A small clip snaps into the opening and supports the shelf.

FASTENING FURNITURE UNITS TO A WALL

You can hang cabinets on frame walls by using long wood screws driven through the cabinet backs and into wall studs, where they secure good holding power. Locate the first stud by tapping the wall; then measure off 16- to 24-inch intervals to find the other studs.

To hang units on hollow masonry walls, you need toggle bolts or molly fasteners. First drill a hole with a star drill or carbide-tipped bit; then insert and tighten the molly. After that you can remove the bolt and use it to hang the cabinet. Concrete, stone, or other solid masonry walls require anchor bolts. You can also use toggle bolts in expansion shields.

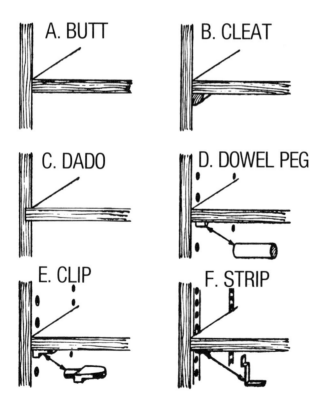

Fig. 5-58.   Ways to support inside shelves.

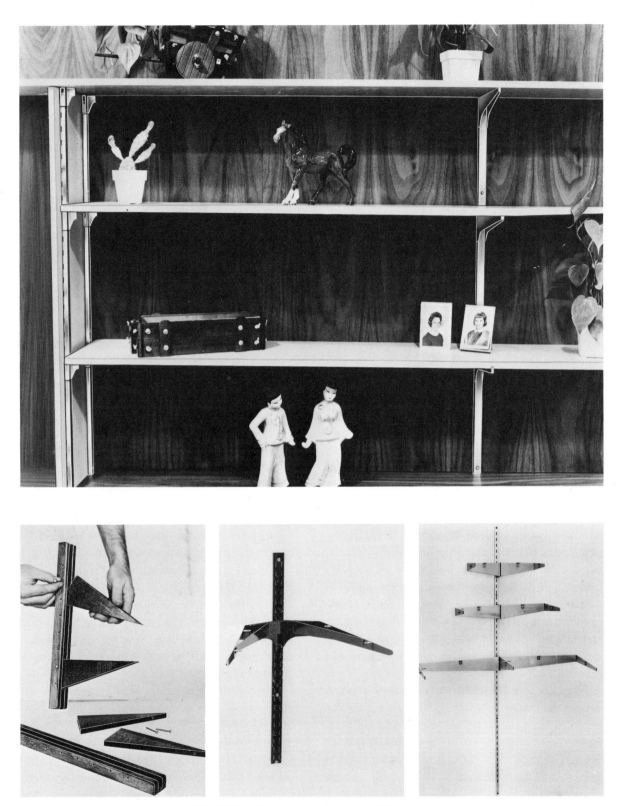

Fig. 5-59.   Various mechanical means of shelving.

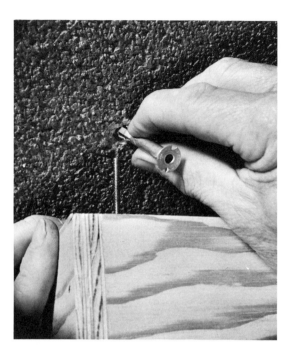 

Fig. 5-60.   *Left:* Hollow masonry walls call for use of toggle bolts or molly fasteners. *Right:* Concrete, stone, or other solid masonry walls call for anchor bolts.

VENEERING

Practiced by the ancient Egyptians, the art of veneering came into high repute, via France, during the eighteenth century under the skilled hands of such furniture-makers as Hepplewhite and Sheraton. Nowadays the availability of plywood surfaced on one or both sides with a wide selection of native and imported veneer woods has relieved home furniture-makers of much of the time-consuming gluing and pressing required for a satisfactory veneering job. In fact about the only veneering practice left for this type of craftsmen is inlaying.

Inlay Borders. Narrow borders or bands of inlays $\frac{1}{8}$ to 1 inch wide in hundreds of patterns can be obtained from supply houses or craftsmen in yard-long lengths. As a rule these are fabricated from pressed "sandwiches" of various layers of veneer about 10 inches wide and 36 inches long that are sawed into slices $\frac{1}{20}$ inch thick, thus giving an allowance for sanding when they are applied

around or between sections of standard veneer $\frac{1}{28}$ inch thick.

To apply veneer borders to solid stock, dadoes are usually cut along the traced pattern in a drill press or hand router with a single- or double-flute router bit of the same diameter as the width of the banding. To prevent the wood from tearing, it is best to cut across the grain first, with the speed no less than 5,000 rpm. The depth of the cut should be slightly less than the thickness of the border, to allow for sanding after it has been glued into position. Corners should be cleaned out with a chisel. Fig. 5-61 shows several examples of popular inlaid border corners.

When fitting the border into its groove, select pieces that will match when the corners are mitered. Moderate curves can be inlaid with banding that doesn't exceed $\frac{1}{4}$ inch in width. Fairly sharp curves can frequently be installed by heating the inlay banding or by wetting it and separating the outer strips so that they can slide past each other as they are pressed into the curved recess.

Fig. 5-61.   Examples of typical border designs.

Inlays. Completely assembled inlays in various colors and designs and mounted on paper backing are also available at craftsmen supply houses. There are paper-backed inlays made so that the exposed, or finish, side is glued to the paper. The entire inlay is enclosed by a frame of inferior wood, which must be carefully cut away.

Application of these inlays to solid stock is effected in much the same manner that a border is set into place. The cutout inlay is placed in position with the paper side up, and its contour is accurately traced with a slight bit pencil. The recess is then routed a slight bit short either with a hand router or freehand, in the drill press, preferably with a carving cutter.

APPLYING SEATING MATERIAL

Once you have completed a chair or sofa, there is a problem of applying seating material or upholstery. Following are some of the methods of applying such seating materials.

Rush Seats for Chairs

Many chair seats are designed for rush. Real rush, or cattail, is better than imitation fiber for chairs of good design, although more skill is required to weave it.

The kind of rush used for chair seating is known as cattail. Cattails grow in shallow fresh water, swampy places, along the banks of streams, and in lowlands and marshes. Commonly found in most parts of the northern states, they can be gathered easily and with little or no expense. If properly chosen and prepared, they are easy to use. Rush also may be bought. Stock ordered from a reliable dealer is usually well cured.

How to Collect and Dry Rush. You can tell cattails from other plants by their round spikes of flowers—the "bobs," or "cattails." The leaves are in two rows, with their flat sides back to back. There are two kinds, the broad-leafed (about 1 inch wide) and the narrow-leafed. The broad-leafed is more common; the narrow-leafed grows in lowlands and has much longer leaves. Choose the narrow, long leaves (about 7 feet) for making chair seating.

Gather the rush when the leaves are full grown, when the stalks are still green and the tips are beginning to turn brown. Late July, August, or early September is the usual time. Select perfect leaves and those from the stalks that do not have "bobs." Cut the stalks just above the surface of the water or ground. Gather an ample supply, since leaves shrink at least one-third of their weight as they cure and there is waste in weaving as well.

Pull the leaves from the stalks. Sort the leaves, placing together those of about the same width and length, and tie them in loose, flat bundles. Be careful not to bend or break the leaves. Dry them thoroughly for at least two or three weeks in a dark, airy room. An attic or storeroom floor is a good place for drying. Don't put the leaves in a damp room, such as a celler, where mildew might form, or in a hot, sunny room where leaves might become brittle.

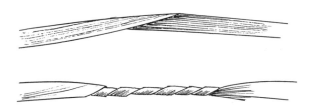

Fig. 5-62.   How to make the twists for rush seats.

Rush that has been carefully dried and stored should be usable for a year or more.

Getting Ready to Weave. Smooth any uneven places in the wood, and round the edges if they are sharp and likely to break the rush.

Dampen the Rush. Dampen the rush until it is workable enough to twist and weave without cracking or breaking. This may take one hour in warm water in a trough or eight to twelve hours if spread on the floor and sprinkled.

Fill the trough about three-quarters full of warm water. Add about 1 cup of glycerine, until the water feels soft, or use a solution of urea crystals available at drugstores in one-pound jars, about ¼ cup to 1 gallon of water. Either solution helps prevent the rush from drying out. Glycerine is preferable but costs more. Soak the rush, about a handful at a time, in the solution. You may have to change the solution once before you finish weaving a seat.

You would probably use only water if you dampened the rush on the floor.

Choose and Prepare the Leaves. Choose long, unbroken leaves of about the same length, width, and thickness. The number of leaves to use in each strand depends not only on the leaves but on the size of strand you want. Usually two leaves are twisted together; sometimes, if they are narrow or thin, three may be used. A thin strand is best for a graceful, delicate chair, but many strands are needed to fill the seat. Fewer thick strands would be needed, but they are too coarse for such a chair. It is important to decide what size strands will look best on your chair.

Select and prepare the leaves and make them into strands as you work. Run the leaves through a wringer to remove air from the cells and to make the leaves workable. Set the rollers tight so that the leaves make a sharp crackling noise as they are run through. Good rush, well prepared, seldom stains the rollers. Draw each leaf quickly over the edge of a metal surface to remove any air left in the cells.

Practice Making Twists. Cut off about 1 yard of cord and loop it around the back rail of the seat. Tie the ends of cord in a square knot; keep the loop about 5 inches long. Arrange two leaves with a butt end and a tip end together, with the flat side of one next to the rounded side of the other, like stacked spoons. Put one end of the pair through the loop of cord for about 3 inches. Fold it toward the front rail, and use the ends of string to tie around the bunch, making a square knot near the fold of rush. Tie the string temporarily around the side rail. Twist the leaves together away from you in such a way that the strand is smooth, even, tight, and of good color. Usually the thumb and first two fingers of one hand are used to make the twist, and the thumb and fingers of the other hand hold it. Keep the separate leaves straight and smooth as when making a braid; make long but firm twists, with the thumbs about 2 inches apart. Practice until you can make a smooth, even strand that is of a good size for your chair. Then untie the string around the side rail and take out this practice strand before starting to weave.

Fiber Rush. Fiber rush is made from a very rough grade of paper twisted into a strand to resemble rush. It may be purchased in dark brown in widths of $\frac{3}{32}$ inch, $\frac{4}{32}$ inch, $\frac{5}{32}$ inch, and $\frac{6}{32}$ inch to resemble the rush in antique rush seats; in multicolored strands it comes in a width of $\frac{5}{32}$ inch to resemble new seats.

Buy the fiber in 1- or 2-pound lots or in quantity on a large reel. That in pound lots costs a few cents more; that in reels takes time and patience to unroll and rewind. Handle that on a reel as you would wire; that is, roll and unroll it rather than pull it. Take off about 25 yards to work with at one time. Tie the end to a nearby strand, and wind it in a roll about 6 inches across. Twenty-five yards of $\frac{5}{32}$-inch-width fiber weighs about half a pound.

Tie the string in a slip knot around the roll so that it will not unwind or untwist.

The techniques of weaving fiber rush and natural rush are similar.

How to Weave. Weaving a firm, smooth seat takes much skill and practice. How you do it depends on the way you like to do it and how you want it to look. One satisfactory method is described in the following paragraphs.

Seats Without Corner Blocks. With a carpenter's square as a guide make a second square of stiff cardboard, with the long side about 15 inches. Use this to mark off a square center opening. Place the short side of the cardboard square parallel to either the front or the back rail and the long side against the inner edge of the corner of the back rail. Using a pencil, mark the edge of the square on the front rail. Do the same on the other side of the seat. The two corner measurements may not be the same, but the distance between pencil lines on the front rail must be the same as between posts on the back rail.

Weave the corners first, until you reach the marks on the first rail, and then weave as for a square seat. To do this, face the front of the chair and push the loop of string that was used for the practice twist close to the back post on the left side of the seat.

Begin with four leaves, each long enough to reach around three sides of the seat. Make two pairs, each with a butt and tip end together and with the flat side of one leaf next to the round side of the other. Place one end of the pair through the loop of cord for about 3 inches. Fold it toward the front rail, and use the end of string to tie around the bunch, making a square knot near the fold of rush.

Choose one pair of leaves, bring them almost to the front rail, and then twist them into a strand. Turn this twist away from the post; keep all other twists in the same direction, like a rope. Draw the strand over rail 1, close to post A (see Fig. 5-63, *left*), up through the opening of the chair, over the side rail 2, again close to the corner post A, and up through the opening again, thus holding the beginning of the twist. Lift up the strand from the underside of the seat to shorten its length and thus help to make the seat firm. Lay the strands in position to make a square crossing and a seam straight from the corner of the seat.

Without twisting the leaves, pull the strand across the front of the seat. At post B twist the leaves, bring the strand over side rail 3, close to post B, up through the opening of the seat, over front rail 1, again close to post B. Arrange the strands as at post A.

Again without twisting, pull the strand to the back and fasten it firmly by winding the ends around the back rail and tying them together, or by holding them with a clamp clothespin.

The strands should be twisted only over the rails where they will show, not on the underside of the seat.

Weave the second pair in the same way. Loop the ends tightly around the back rail and fasten them with a clothespin to the first strand. Tie more leaves, one pair at a time, in the same loop of string. About five twists fill 1 inch. Use a piece of rush or the cardboard square every two or three rows to make sure that the corners are square and the rows straight. Use the hammer and block of wood to force the strands in place. Keep the seam straight from the corner toward the center of the seat. Make a square crossing; add from 4 to 6 inches of another leaf, if needed, to fill the space.

After the corners are woven as far as the marks on the front rail, fasten the ends on the right-hand side. Take a piece of string about 18 inches long and tie it with a square knot around all the ends of rush. Loop the ends around the back rail and tie another knot. Pull the strands taut, keeping the rows straight and close together. Remove the clothespin, and cut away the rush over the rail.

If the rush breaks, replace it with another piece.

Pad the Seat. After the front corners are filled in, pad them. The padding is put in the pockets on the underside of the seat at each side of the corner seams. Butt ends and short lengths of rush are folded the length of the opening and forced in flat bunches from the center toward the corner posts. To do this, turn the chair over. Using a wooden stuffer, poke a bunch of rush into the pocket on the underside of the seat, from the center to the seam.

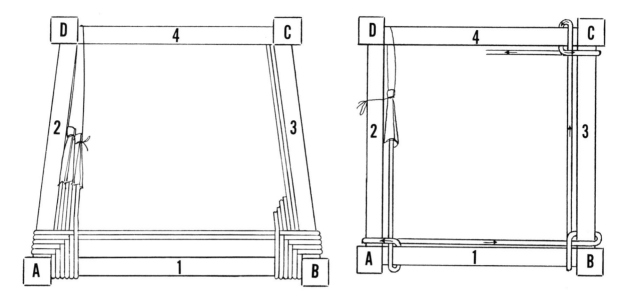

Fig. 5-63. *Left:* Weaving seats without a corner block. *Right:* Square seat weaving.

The finished seat should be hard and flat, or slightly rounded, but not overstuffed. Rush shrinks as it dries, so put in enough padding to make the seat firm but not "fat." Both front corners should be of the same thickness.

As you continue to weave around all four corners, add padding about every 3 inches. Back corners take less padding than do front corners. When you have finished the weaving, add the last padding by poking in bunches parallel to the last strands.

Square Seats. Seat frames may be square or have corner blocks that make the opening almost square. Weave these seats and seats that are wider at the front—after you have filled the corners—as follows:

Weave the first strand, corner A. Use the same loop that is used for seats that are wider at the front, or make a similar loop if you are just starting to weave a square seat. Tie in the butt ends of two leaves, one of which is long and the other short. Twist and weave around post A. Loops of string never have to be cut; weaving covers them.

Join the Rush. As you leave corner A, add a new leaf. Place between the weaving and the strand,

with the butt end hanging down below the underside of the seat for about 6 inches, or the amount of the stiff end of the leaf. Keep the curved side toward you. Twist this new leaf (about twice) with the other two to hold them together. The butt ends make a seam on the underside of the seat and should hang down rather than be caught in the weaving. That is, always add a new piece of rush after you finish each corner so that when you are ready to weave the next corner, the rush will be securely fastened and you will have enough to go around that corner.

Adding Rush. Occasionally you may need to use a third piece of rush to fill out the strand, as when crossing twists at the seam. Weave the first strand to corner B. If the strand is too fat, drop the end of the shortest leaf, which can be cut off or folded in for padding. Twist and weave around corner B. As you leave this corner, again add a new leaf. Then continue to corner C and weave, as shown in the illustration here. Add a new piece of rush, and proceed to and weave around corner D, again adding a piece of rush.

Splicing. If the rush breaks or if you do not have enough to finish weaving the corner, another piece may be spliced in. After you weave the first half of the corner, add a new leaf at the seam with the butt end extending about 6 inches below the seat. Twist the old leaves once around the new to lock it. Then arrange the leaves parallel, and twist all three together. If the strand is too thick, pull out the shortest leaf. Continue weaving the second half of the corner. On the underside of the chair these butt ends will stick down, but at an opposite angle from those used for joining, and will be cut off later.

Weave the rest of the seat. Go on weaving, as for the first strand around post A to posts B, C, and D, until there is only space for two more rows on the side rails. Continue to make the rush workable by running it through the wringer and zipping it with a metal tool. Smooth the twists. Join a new piece of rush after each corner. Pad the seat as you weave. Keep the strands taut and the rows straight by pounding them with the block of wood. Be sure that seams are straight and the opposite sides of the chair are alike. Check as you go along to see that the opposite openings measure the same and that you have the same number of twists over each rail. Occasionally force the metal tool quickly between the rows to straighten them and to smooth the strands. Also occasionally, and before the rush dries out, roll and polish the strands with the round end of the stuffer until the seat is smooth.

If the sides are shorter than the back, fill the sides and then weave from back to front in a figure eight. To help prevent holes near the center, weave around the right side rail twice for the last two strands, then proceed to the left rail and weave around it twice. Then weave in a figure eight over the back and front rails until they are filled in. Sometimes this process is reversed. Join the rush at the center after weaving the front rail or after weaving around both rails.

Pull the last few strands through the small opening with a hook made of wire. Weave in as many rows as possible; when you think the seat is filled, add one more strand. Fasten the last strand

Fig. 5-64.   As successive rounds are placed, a pocket is formed between the top and bottom layers. Pack the pocket with wadded brown paper to form a bulge. Tie on new lengths of fiber with a square knot.

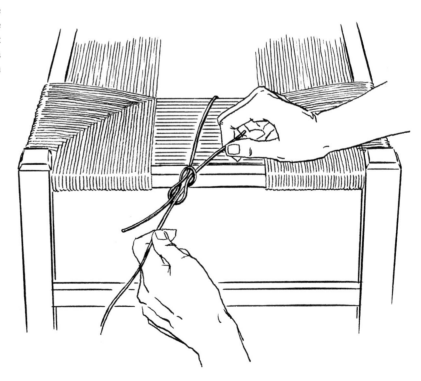

on the underside of the chair by separating the ends, winding each one around a nearby strand, and tying them firmly with a square knot.

If the unfinished seat is left overnight, fasten the last twist to the seat with a clamp clothespin. Cover the seat with wet cheesecloth, to keep the rush from drying out.

Techniques for finishing rush seats are given in Chapter 8.

Splint Seats and Backs

Splint seats and backs are made of wood that has been cut in long, thin strips and interwoven in a pattern. Actually splint is obtained from native ash and hickory and from tropical palm trees. The native splint is cut from selected second-growth timber with straight grain. Ash splints, machine-cut to a uniform width, wear well. Hickory splints often vary slightly in width, giving a pleasing effect. The tropical palm tree from which materials like splints are made grows in the Indian archipelago, China, India, Ceylon, and the Malay peninsula. Without its leaves it is known commercially as rattan. The outer bark, stripped in different widths, is sold as cane; the core, split into round and flat strips of different thicknesses and widths, is called reed. These materials are available from dealers of seat-weaving supplies, mail-order houses, and local stores.

They are all sold either in bunches containing enough for one chair or in quantity lots. Costs per seat are about the same. Real splint makes a better-looking seat than does flat reed, but reed may be easier for beginners to weave.

To Prepare to Weave. Pull one of the strands of splint from the looped end of the hank, near where it is tied. As you pull, shake the hank so that the splint won't tangle or roughen. Bend the piece between your fingers. The right side is smooth; the wrong side splinters. With the smooth or beveled side out, roll the strand to fit the pan or bowl in which it is to soak. Fasten the ends with a clamp clothespin. Prepare three or four strands in the same way.

Soak the splint in a solution of glycerine or urea crystals; either helps to shape the splint. The

crystals increase its strength, but glycerine is preferred because it helps to retain moisture and keep the splint from drying out and cracking. To hasten the soaking process, use warm water in the solution. Lay the roll in the appropriate container and let it soak until it is soft and pliable—about thirty minutes for splint and about twenty minutes for flat reed, flat oval reed, and binding cane. Each time you remove a roll from the pan, put another one in to soak while you work.

How to Weave. Weaving is done in two directions: the first, called *warping*, is the wrapping of the splint around the seat rails. Usually this is done from the back to the front of the chair, or the long way of the opening, so that the second step, called *weaving*, can be done across the open rails, from side to side, or the short way of the opening. Both sides of the seat are woven so that they look alike when finished. All splints woven one way on the top of the seat are at right angles to those woven the other way. If the front of the seat is wider than the back, weave the center first and fill in the corners later with short lengths.

Warping. Mark a center rectangle or square in the following way: Using a carpenter's square, cut a cardboard pattern of a size that will fit within the chair rails. Fit this close against one back post, parallel with the back rail. Mark the front corner of the square on the front rail. Repeat on the other side of the seat. Check to see that you have enough space for the width of the splint. If the two sides vary, adjust by marking a slightly greater allowance on the shorter side and less on the long side. On the front rail mark the center between these two marks. Mark the center on the back rail.

Take the roll of splint from the bowl in which it is soaking, and remove the excess water with your fingers, sponge, or cloth. Put another strand in to soak while you work.

Work with the full length of the strand. Tie one end to the left side rail with string, with the right side of the splint next to the wood, so that you are working with the grain. Pull the strand under, and then up and over, the back rail, close to the post, in the exact position and shape you want it to dry. Pull the strand to the front rail, with the outside edge exactly at the pencil mark. Pull the strand over and under the rail and then return it to the back rail. Continue until you have used all the strand. Force the wet warpers close together so that they will not slip on the rail—strands are apt to shrink more in width than in length—and keep the strands equally taut. Hold the end temporarily with a clamp clothespin.

To join strands on the underside, place a new piece under the old, with the right side down. Lay a stick of soft wood across the rails, under the strands, and staple the strands together in three places, 1 to 2 inches apart, so that at least one of them can be covered when you weave the other way. Pull the strand away from the stick, and use pliers to flatten the sharp ends of the staples. Leave enough of the old strand to support the new, but cut off any that would make a double thickness around the rail. Pull the new strand under and around the rail.

Continue warping strands. When you reach the center mark, count the warpers to make sure you will have the same number on each half of the seat. When you reach the pencil mark on the right side of the chair, use a clamp clothespin to hold the warper. If the work is interrupted, sprinkle the seat and dampen the end to keep the splints pliable.

You may work out your pattern on squared paper, using one square for each warper. In any case count the number of warpers on the back rail. This number may be evenly divisible by the number in the design you want to use: for example twenty strands and a mesh of two over two under, twenty-one strands and a mesh of three over and three under, etc. If the number is not evenly divisible, you may use the same design if you:

1. Plan from near the center of the opening and begin weaving accordingly. Example: If there are twenty-three strands and a mesh of three over and three under, weave over one to start the row, continue across until you have used twenty-one strands, and then weave the single strand as on the first side.

2. Plan to use a diagonal design. Emphasis then will be away from the side rails, where the design may or may not be completed. A diagonal design may or may not be completed, so it is also desirable if the side rails are uneven.

The second row determines how you use the design. You can move one or more strands to the left for a diagonal design from the right back to the left front of the seat, or you may reverse the direction. For a geometric design weave alternate rows alike.

Weaving for the design is frequently:

over two and under two

With finer mesh strands are difficult to push together closely.

Other designs are:

over two and under three
over three and under three

 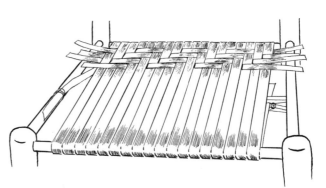

Fig. 5-65.   *Left:* A simple two-over weave. *Right:* A three-over weave.

Large seats or seats using narrow strands, ⅜ inch or less, may be woven:

over four and under four
over four and under two
over five and under three

The above combinations may be reversed, such as

over two and under four

Coarser mesh may be used occasionally if long strands will stay in place and wear satisfactorily.

Weaving. Be sure the strand of splint is long enough to weave across the top of the seat and to join on the underside. Loosen the last warper over the back rail and under the preceding warper. Then bring the strand diagonally in front of the back post, under the side rail and turned so that the right side is down. Pull all strands tight and then weave across, right to left.

Pull the weaver over the side rail and weave the underside like the top, going over and under the same warpers. When you join strands, staple from either side, if you know the staples will be hidden under warpers. Or you can cover staples with short lengths of splint tucked under nearby strands. Flatten the sharp ends of the staples with pliers, as before. Continue weaving, cutting the old strand inside the rail—even if you waste some of it—and forcing the joining in position. You cannot use the warper strand you tucked under until you get nearer the front.

The second row is over two and under three, but with one warper to the left of the first row. Weave to the right if you want the diagonal in the same direction as on the top of the seat. Use a stick or a screwdriver to force the strands together. At the same time pull the strand across the rails so that the seat will be firm.

On the underside plan from near the center of the opening, where the design is established, how to begin the row and so continue the design used on the top. In this way you will weave over and under the same strands as you did on top.

When you have woven far enough to see the design, and when you have space, cut off a length of splint for a warper in the corner of the seat. Hook about 3 inches over the weaver that will continue the design, near the back of the seat, or if it fits snugly, just push the strand in rather than hook it over a weaver. Bring this warper to the underside of the seat and hook it over a weaver there also. The strands may be joined on top of the seat, under the warpers, to save splint. If the joining is secure, cut off the old strand so that two thicknesses do not show. Also cut the string holding the first strand; the weaving will hold this end in place. Add other short lengths in the corners of the seat, as you have room for them. Warpers should also be cut so that the ends can be concealed under the weavers. One or two staples and the weaving will hold the joining. Use a screwdriver or similar blunt tool to help with the weaving as you get near the front of the seat.

Continue weaving to the front rail. Finish the underside by weaving as far across as you can and tucking the end under a warper. If the back of the chair is to be woven, warp strands the long way (up and down). Weave across from the bottom up so that you can push the strands in place easily. Back warping and weaving are done in a manner similar to that for a seat.

Techniques for finishing splint seats and backs are given in Chapter 8.

Webbing Seats

Webbing seats look good on contemporary indoor and outdoor furniture.

The chair on which you plan to use webbing should be simple in line and design and sturdy. Seat frames should be straight rather than noticeably curved. The front of the frame should be no more than 3 inches wider than the back so that the webbing will stay in place without slipping on the side rails. The wood of the frame should be 2 to 3 inches deep to support the webbing underneath. There must be enough space between the seat and the back to bring the webbing through the opening.

Webbing can be used on round seat rails as well as on flat ones. For large openings the frame must be sturdy and the wood able to hold tacks well so that the webbing can support the necessary weight.

Usually wooden chairs with small seat openings are neither comfortable nor attractive with webbing. If webbing is to be used on the back of the chair, the wood in the crosspieces should be thick enough to take tacks without splitting.

Select the Webbing. Webbing is available in both plastic and cotton, 2 inches wide, in a variety of colors. It can be tacked or stapled to wood.

Plastic webbing can be cleaned easily with a damp cloth and used on both indoor and outdoor furniture. Cotton webbing stays in place better than plastic webbing, but it is not as easy to clean or as satisfactory on outdoor furniture. You can buy webbing at chair-seating and craftsmen's supply houses and at certain mail-order houses and department stores.

How to Weave. The following is the way to apply webbing:

Seats with Flat Rails. Measure with a stiff ruler and mark the center of the front rail. Do the same on the other three rails. To plan the number of strips you will need to use each way, place short strips of webbing loosely on the chair or fold a long length and make an estimate. As you plan, avoid the legs and the lower part of the back posts. Use tacks and clothespins to hold the webbing temporarily in place. Arrange crosspieces to see how the mesh will look. Allow space between strips so that the seat will not look solid or bulky.

The correct side is usually on the outside of the roll, is smoother, and has more sheen than the wrong side. Cut the number of strips you'll need back to front. Allow enough webbing for each strip to extend across the top of the seat, down the rails to the underside—or to the inside if there is room to hammer the tacks—and to turn under ½ inch.

Tip the chair so that you can tack easily. The place you begin tacking is determined by the shape and construction of the chair. Tack only temporarily until you are sure the strips are where you want them.

Fasten strips first on the straighter of the two rails or on the one with a crosspiece, where you have less room to hammer. Then you can stretch the webbing and tack it on the more open rail. If the back of the chair is curved, fasten the strips first on the front rail so that they can be stretched taut from the straight edge. Fasten the webbing on the inside of the frame so that the lower edge of the front rail will look smooth rather than bumpy. Fasten the outside strips first, with the webbing close to the chair leg. Or you may find it easier to start in the center.

Put the tape over the end of the strip to prevent raveling. Turn the end under about ½ inch and fasten with five tacks, staggered to help keep the wood from splitting. Tack the center strip next, or those on each side of the center if you have an even number, and then the strips between. When you are sure the strips are evenly spaced and properly placed, pound the tacks all the way in. On the curving rail at the back, tack the center strip first so you can be sure it is straight. Tape the end.

For each webbing strip cut a cardboard strip about ¼ inch narrower than the webbing and the wood. Turn under the taped end, and insert the cardboard to help make the edge smooth. Pull the strip taut, and tack it on the bottom of the seat rail, since this edge shows least. If the wood splits easily, tack it on the inside of the frame.

When pulled tight across the top, the outside strips will be on a slant underneath the rail. Cut the end parallel with the rail. Tape the end, and tack the strip temporarily in place. Do the same on the other side, then fasten the in-between strips in the same way. The strips will be closer together on the back rail because it is shorter than the front rail. When you are sure the strips are placed correctly, tack them permanently.

Measure and cut all the side strips at once. (If you want to save webbing, you may find it more economical to cut each one as you work.) Fasten them together with a clamp clothespin in the order in which you will use them from front to back.

Weave the front strip over and under to determine how you want the design and how the mesh will best be held in place. Weave the next strip under and over, and alternate the rest.

Fasten the strips on alternate sides. Since the side rails slant, the ends of the webbing will slant. Tape one end of each strand and tack the front strip, bringing the edge close to the front legs. Tack

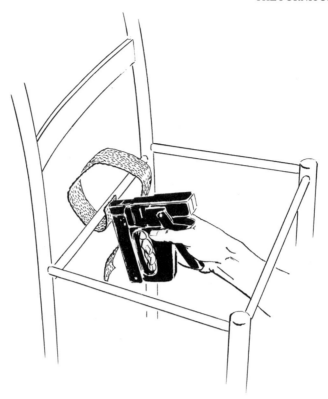

Fig. 5-66.   Stapling plastic webbing to a round rail.

on the inside, if you have space, because the wood splits less, or tack on the bottom edge. Tack the back strip close to the back leg, then tack the center strip and those in between. Pull the strips taut and tack them. When the strips are all in place, evenly spaced and equally taut, pound all the tacks all the way in.

Seats with round rails. Webbing can also be used on chairs with round rails. Paint the chair or refinish with a natural finish. Be sure the chair is thoroughly dry before you weave the seat.

Mark the centers of the four rails as directed on page 185. Plan the number of strips you will use each way, and cut those for back to front.

Since both back and front rails are straight on this chair (see Fig. 5-68), first fasten the strips to the back and stretch them toward the front. The wood does not hold tacks easily, so use a heavy stapling gun to fasten the strips. Use three strong $\frac{5}{16}$-inch staples across the width of each strip of

webbing. There is little room for cardboard strips on round rails, so omit them and turn the webbing under a generous ½ inch. Otherwise the seat is woven in the same way as the one with flat rails.

Backs of chairs. Webbing may also be used for the backs of chairs. Mark the centers, and plan and cut strips as for seats. Allow enough length so that the laced webbing will shape to the back of the person using the chair as well as to the back of the chair frame. Strips are first fastened up and down, then other strips are woven from side to side.

Tack the end of the strip first on the front of the lower crosspiece. Then pull the strip over the top of the crosspiece, down the back, under the crosspiece, and then up the back of the chair and over the top crosspiece, tacking the end on the underside.

The tacking of both ends of side-to-side strips is more difficult to conceal. The left of Fig. 5-67 shows the tacks that fasten the upper two strips.

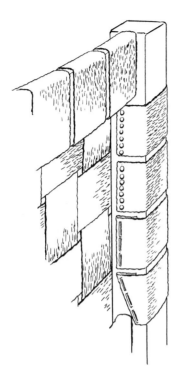 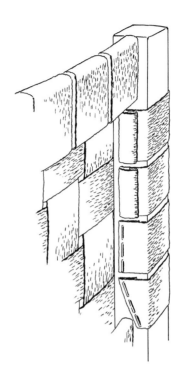

Fig. 5-67.   Two methods of finishing webbing on backs.

The two lower strips are stapled to the chair and are less conspicuous than tacks. At the right of the illustration two fastenings are covered by folds of webbing. Weave the strips first. About 2 inches in from one end, tack near the front of the post. Turn the end under and insert a strip of cardboard. Use 3¾-inch wire brads to hold this fold. The top of these brads can be concealed by forcing apart the mesh of the webbing. The cardboard prevents the brads from going all the way through and also keeps the edge of the fold smooth.

Fasten the other end of the strip to the opposite post in a similar way.

Foam Rubber Upholstery

Foam rubber is one of the simplest materials to work with. No complicated special equipment is needed for upholstering with latex foam. It can be cut, shaped, or trimmed with regular shears, a sharp knife, or razor. The only other items you will need for working are rubber fabricating cement, ordinary tacking tape (or special latex-foam adhesive tape), and soapstone.

Marking Your Pattern. Patterns may be marked on latex foam with a soft lead or wax pencil, with talc dusted through a perforated pattern, or with talc dusted around the edges of a solid pattern.

Cutting. Latex foam can be cut to any desired shape quickly and easily. In general add ¼ inch to your pattern on all sides (including arm and frame posts) for upholstering allowance.

Mounting. On hard surfaces apply latex foam directly on the base and secure it with tacking tape around the edges or by cementing it to the base. In the case of plywood the base should be ventilated, if possible, with very small holes to permit free passage of air through the latex foam. Metal bases need a rust-resistant finish. Apply latex foam directly over webbing (spaced for good ventilation), and secure with tacking tape around the edges.

Fig. 5-68.   Step-by-step procedure for installing webbing.

Fig. 5-69. Mounting foam rubber over (*top to bottom*) springs, hard surface, and webbing.

Using Tacking Tape. Tacking tape serves as an aid to edging, as a means of securing the cushion to the base, and as a handy reinforcement for holding a sharply defined edge. It can be fastened securely to the foam with rubber cement. Regardless of width, tacking tape should be cemented on the foam about 1 inch from the edge of the cushion. Frequently tape is cemented to the edge of a reversible cushion and then sewed into the welt of the cushion cover to prevent the fabric from slipping.

How to Use Cement. Cement may be used for securing the latex-foam padding and cushion to the base of frame, for fastening tacking tape, and for joining sections and fabricating cushions. Cement

should be applied to both sections to be joined and should be allowed to dry long enough to become tacky before the sections are pressed together. Any cement left exposed on surface after fabricating should be dusted with soapstone. Cemented pieces should be permitted to set for several hours before they are used.

How to Make Reversible Cushions. Reversible cushions may be made from two pieces of cored utility stock in one of two ways:

1. Bevel all four edges on the cored side and cement together, smooth side out.

2. Place a smaller piece of 1-inch cored utility stock or plain sheet stock between the two pieces, and cement together. The cushion may be finished with square or rolled edges made from plain sheet stock.

Edging. You can make any type of edge you desire very simply, using either cored utility stock or plain sheet stock. Here are the three most common types of edges:

1. Feathered edge. Cut the stock to the proper

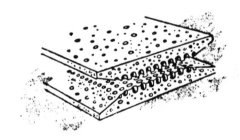

Fig. 5-70. How to make a reversible cushion.

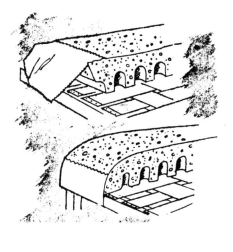

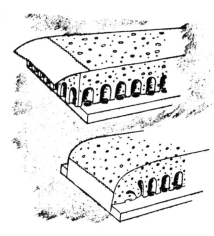

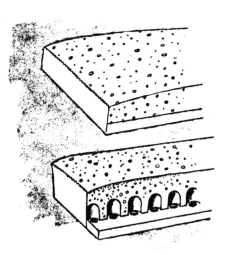

Fig. 5-71. The three types of edging: feathered edge (*top*); cushioned edge (*center*); and square edge (*bottom*).

cushion size, adding the usual ¼ inch all around for an upholstering allowance. Cement the tacking tape to the cushion 1 inch from the edge. Then bevel the lower edge to the necessary degree for the desired contour. Draw the tape down so that the beveled edge of the cushion is flat against the base, and tack in place.

2. Cushioned edge. Cut the stock to cushion shape, adding the usual ¼ inch all around for the upholstering allowance plus ½ inch for the edge (a total of ¾ inch over the base measurement at the cushion edge). Cement the tape to the foam 1 inch from the edge. Tuck the bottom edge of the cushion under so that the edge is flat against the base, taking care to keep the tape taut so that the foam doesn't wrinkle or bunch unevenly. Finally, tack the tape to the base.

3. Square edge. For square edges of different types cut the stock to desired shape and size, adding the usual ¼-inch upholstering allowance all around. Cement the tape flat against the vertical edge, and tack overhang to the base.

How to Cover Latex Foam. Avoid using material that has a tendency to stretch excessively. When using extremely slippery, very loosely woven, or high-pile fabrics, it is generally advisable to cover the foam rubber first with muslin. Where leather, coated fabrics, or plastic materials are desired, the supplier of the material should be consulted. He can recommend the proper material for use with latex foam.

Covers should be cut to fit neatly but not too tightly. Unlike conventional upholstering materials latex foam never packs down, so no allowance need be made for that. Also, covers shouldn't be so tight as to compress the latex foam excessively, since too much cover tension reduces the depth of the cushion and detracts from the resilient comfort of the foam. When covering shaped seats, it is often advisable to cement fabric lightly to the foam padding to keep the cover in position.

UPHOLSTERING WITH SPRINGS

In place of conventional coil springs, which require a great degree of skill and a good amount of work to tie together properly, springs of the so-called no-sag type are designed for easy application to home furniture. The springs come in two different sizes, or gauges. The 11-gauge is used for small chairbacks or dinette chairs, while the 9-gauge (the heavier spring) is used for medium and large chairs as well as for sofas and daybeds.

The springs are installed with a shallow arc so that the center is slightly higher than either end. The ends of the springs are held to the frame with special metal clips. After the springs are in place, crossties—helical springs—are used to connect together. Twine may also be used where necessary.

Burlap or some other strong fabric is applied over the springs and nailed to the frame. Over this a minimum of 2 inches of cotton, rubberized curled hair, or foam rubber should be used as a padding. Manufacturers of these springs furnish complete instructions as to their installation. Follow these to the letter.

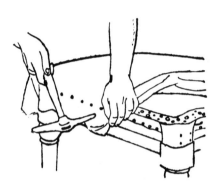

Fig. 5-72.   How to cover latex foam.

Chapter 6
STYLE AND DESIGN OF FURNITURE

Furniture should be suited to its purpose and to the people who will be using it. For instance heights of table, desk, and work surfaces should be comfortable. A chair should fit the individual who will be sitting on it most of the time. For this reason make only furniture that will serve the utmost convenience and comfort of your family.

Ingredients of beauty in furniture include pleasing lines and good proportions. Pieces of similar line and feeling go well together.

Well-designed furniture has harmonious, logical lines. The shape of a piece clearly defines the use to be made of it. As a result horizontal and vertical lines usually predominate. Diagonal and curved lines serve as transitions for horizontal and vertical lines.

Good proportion means that all parts of an article look well together. No part seems too heavy or too light in relation to other parts or to the whole. Proportions of a rectangle approximately two to three or three to five are more interesting.

The principle that a shape is usually more interesting when the length is about one and one-half times the width can be applied to good furniture design. Actually the division of space in a pleasing manner makes a piece of furniture attractive. Even the finest woods, the best finish, and the most painstaking workmanship combined can't make a piece attractive if it doesn't have good proportions. A few of the basic rules for designing and planning the division of space are sketched in Fig. 6-1. They illustrate the following principles:

1. If a vertical line divides the space in two, one method you can follow is to make two sections of equal size.

2. On the other hand you can divide the space in two by a vertical line so that one section is one and one-half times greater than the other.

Anyone who plans and builds his own furniture will find a knowledge of design helpful. Even if you modify a plan you already have, an understanding of design principles will help produce a better job.

Fig. 6-1.   Good proportion in furniture design is very important.

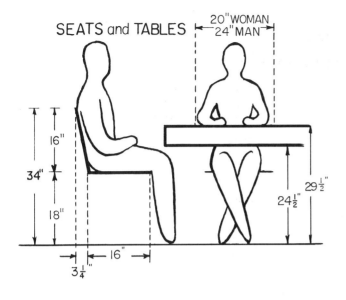

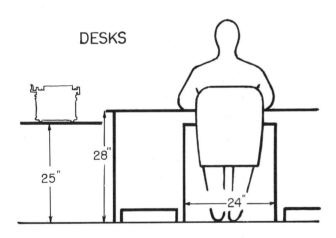

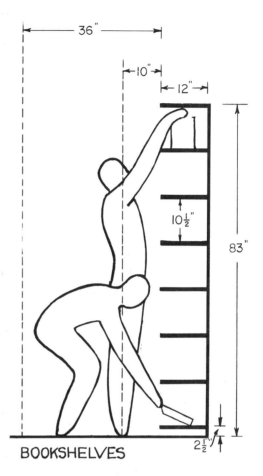

Fig. 6-2.   Proper design dimensions for seats, tables, desks, and bookshelves.

Any piece of furniture you design or build should meet three requirements: It should be durable, useful, and attractive. To be durable, it is necessary to make the piece of furniture out of sturdy wood with secure joints. Since these techniques have been described in previous chapters, let's take a look at the two other requirements: usefulness and attractiveness.

FURNITURE SIZE

The size of a piece of furniture is generally determined by its use. For example a dining table should be approximately 30 inches high; the back of a chair should slope to form about a 105-degree angle with the seat. Anatomical dimensions as well as building standards play a major role in design. While furniture sizes vary a great deal, Table 6-1 gives some standard dimensions.

Of all furniture the chair presents the most difficult in establishing dimensions. It is very important to remember that the purpose of a chair is to support the body comfortably and in a relaxed position. In fact a well-designed chair can reduce wear and tear on the spine, neck, arms, legs, and

Table 6-1

FURNITURE DIMENSIONS

Item	Length in inches	Depth (width) in inches	Height in inches
Dining table	56-62	36-40	29-30
	38-48	72-80	
Kitchen table	30-45	25-30	29-30
	48-58	35-41	
Coffee table	32-36	16-17	12-18
	36-44	18-22	
	48-56	22-32	
	62-80	22-38	
Coffee table (round)	about 36 diameter		15-18
End table	22-28	12-18	20-24
Drum table	about 36 diameter		30
Card table	36	36	30
Lamp table (square)	16-22	16-22	24-30
Lamp table (round)	about 24 diameter		28-30
Snack table	14-17	12-16	17-24
Desk	45-54	20-24	28-30
Secretary	34-38	18-20	78-84
Lowboy	30-32	18-20	30
Highboy	34-38	18-20	60-84
Breakfront bookcase	48-60	18-20	78-84
Sofa	68-72	30	36
Love seat	46-50	30	36
Occasional chair	27	30	36
Occasional chair (armless)	24	30	36
Wing chair	30	30	36
Dining, desk, folding chair	15-18	15-18	30-36 (seat height, 15-18)
Single bed	78	34-36	20-24
Twin bed	78	39	20-24
Double bed	78	54	20-24
Queen bed	86	76	20-24
King bed	86	84	20-24
Dresser	42-60	22	32-38

even eyes. The type of chair design selected depends upon the activities performed in it—working, reading, eating, viewing television, or just relaxing. Regardless of a chair's style or period, its profile is mainly determined by the function for which it is intended.

The size and scale of a chair are determined by the size and weight of the person occupying it. It is difficult to assume that one chair will fit everyone. The best way to test a chair's comfort, of course, is to sit in it. This is rather difficult to do when you are planning the design of a chair, unless you have the time to make a full-scale model first. The furniture-maker can do quite well if the following checkpoints are kept in mind when designing and determining chair dimensions (see Fig. 6-3):

1. A well-proportioned chair allows the occupant's feet to rest flat on the floor.

2. The seat should slant slightly toward the back. A flat seat is often better than a bucket-type seat because it allows freedom of movement. There

should be clearance from the edge of the chair to the back of a person's leg.

3. The chair should curve in the back or have an opening at the point of contact with the body's lumbar region to allow room for the buttocks.

4. The back of the chair should be slanted and support the lumbar region without hitting the shoulder blades.

5. The chair's arms should be of a proper height to support the arms without raising the shoulders.

6. The sitter should be able to get in and out of a chair without difficulty.

When considering the size of any furniture piece, it's important to remember that it must be designed to fit the convenience and comfort of your own family.

DESIGN CONSIDERATIONS

Good design technique is important to assure both usefulness and attractiveness. The design process suggested here is rather fundamental. The steps themselves, though they represent a means of clarifying ideas from the initial concept to the actual building, are not so important as the approach. For the home furniture-maker with experience it's not necessary to follow all the steps faithfully. The extent to which you follow our recommended design process—which is in fact followed by most professional furniture designers—depends upon your own particular interests as well as your experience. Many home furniture-makers are content to reproduce furniture pieces from plans such as those given in Chapter 7 and from the issues of *Family Handyman* and other similar magazines rather than design pieces of their own. For those craftsmen we'll continue to turn out suitable furniture plans. But for home furniture-makers who wish to design and make their own plans, the following three-step procedure should be considered:

1. The Idea. First you must start with the idea itself. This idea may come from a photograph, a piece of furniture already made, or it may be completely original. In many cases your initial thoughts may be rather vague. However, once you start thinking about the basic means of construc-

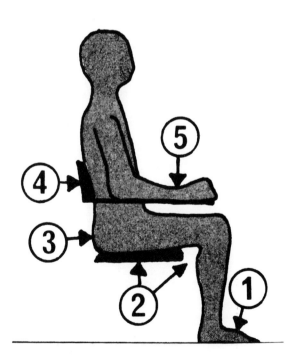

Fig. 6-3.   The check points for determining chair dimensions.

tion or joinery, the size, and the appearance, the plans will start to crystallize. Make several sketches until you obtain the one that appears closest to your original concept.

2. The Model. Once the plan is on paper, the next step is to make a model. Made to scale, the model will permit you to check the appearance and the size and will help you to determine the construction techniques. It is a good idea when making your model to use materials that approximate the material to be used for the full-size piece. For example, if you're planning to use plywood panels, cardboard or thin sheets of plywood will be most useful in making the model. On the other hand, if you're developing your idea around the use of solid-wood pieces, thin strips of cardboard, solid wood, or balsa wood will serve best.

3. The Layout. After your model is found to be feasible and practicable, the final step in furniture design is the layout. This simply means the transferring of your design to the material from which the furniture piece is to be built. The layout is broken down into the various separate components of the furniture piece in much the same manner as a dress pattern. That is, the parts are drawn in full scale on a large sheet of wrapping paper or directly onto the wood itself, with 1-inch squares to guide you in drawing irregular contours or shapes. This method is described and illustrated in more detail in the next chapter.

A final and important thought in the design of furniture: Remember that the time spent in sound planning will save you hours of reworking and correction.

Fig. 6-4.   Why not make the plans for these two furniture pieces?

Chapter 7
FURNITURE PROJECTS

In this chapter we have selected a group of furniture plans—including a couple of built-ins and exterior pieces—from the issues of *Family Handyman*. These furniture pieces were selected to illustrate different methods in which plans are presented as well as to show many of the techniques discussed in previous chapters. There are some new furniture techniques presented in these plans, too. While these projects were basically selected for their educational value, they offer a wide array of practical furniture-making ideas.

Project #1—BUFFET-SIDEBOARD-BAR

By studying the drawings and following these instructions closely as you progress, you'll get as much fun from building this clever cabinet as your family will have when they see it completed. To start, cut and rabbet all vertical pieces, as shown in Fig. 7-3. Cut walnut-faced, ¾-inch plywood ends a full 16x23 inches, with bottom rabbet ¾ inch wide and rabbet for back plywood ¼ inch wide. Plain ¾-inch middle partition of plywood is ¼ inch narrower to allow for the back and ¾ inch shorter to fit above the bottom plywood. Other partitions are of plain fir plywood ½ inch thick and are 2 inches narrower than the middle partition. All interior partitions are notched both front and back to fit the 1x3-inch plates, which butt against the inside of the end panels. Lengths of the bottom and back are 96 inches, less the depth of the end rabbets. Assemble body of cabinet, including the two plates, with No. 6 finishing nails and glue. Construct slope-front drawers, as shown, with ¼-inch walnut-faced plywood fronts cut away in front, and install them with slides, which allow the drawers to open at a touch. Rabbet ¾ x1½ -inch walnut door frames for ¼-inch walnut-faced panels, before cutting the notched corners to assemble them. After assembly cut a rabbet in the

top and bottom of each door to fit the fiber sliding door track, as per drawing detail. All edges that will be exposed when doors are open should be covered with walnut veneer strip and cemented with contact cement. Paint other interior parts white enamel, which gives a pleasing contrast with the walnut exterior. Trim on front of cabinet is ¾x1½-inch walnut, with corners mitered. Cover top with white laminated plastic, and trim edges and shelves with walnut veneer strip. Apply the laminated plastic over a layer of contact cement. Legs are of standard manufacture, from 6 to 10 inches long depending on whether you like the low, low streamlined look or want a higher cabinet.

Fig. 7-1.   The smooth lines of this handsome walnut cabinet conceal behind the double-track sliding doors quite a few conveniences as well as much storage space.

Fig. 7-2. *Left:* Opening the end doors reveals three linen drawers, racks for trays, and shelves aplenty. *Right:* Look what the middle doors conceal—spirits in all flavors, a silver chest, and a drawer for glasses.

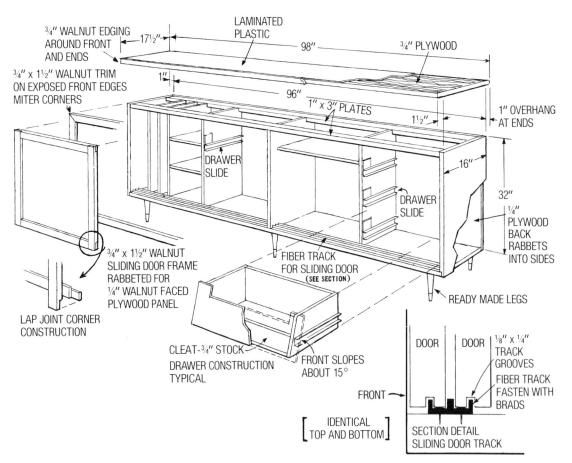

Fig. 7-3.

Fig. 7-4. This china cabinet for your dining room wall is an up-to-date version of an old standby.

Project #2—MODERN CHINA CABINET

This well-designed addition to almost any dining room serves a dual purpose of bringing useful space for china storage to the room where it is needed and adding a note of formal elegance to the decor. The narrow door panels, framed in solid wood and faced with stark white vinyl fabric, are studded with small brass buttons for sharp contrast. The shallow cabinet, which is only 9 inches deep, takes little from the depth of the room, yet provides a round dozen handy shelves for your best china and glassware.

Making the cabinet is easy when this recommended procedure is followed. First comes the frame, a simple rectangular form of ¾-inch hardwood veneer plywood. Rip pieces to size for the two sides, top, bottom, and the two dividers. Dado the top and bottom for the upright dividers. Make rabbet cuts ¾ x ⅜ inch on one edge of each side for

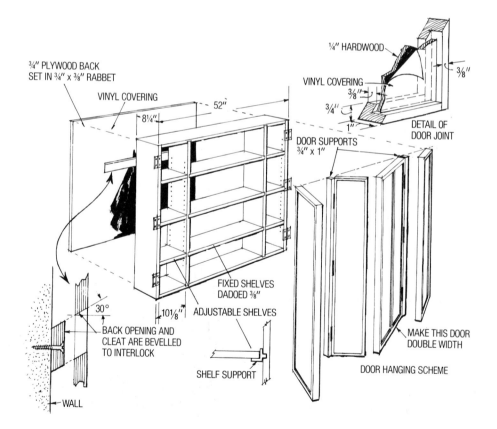

Fig. 7-5.

the ¾-inch back panel. Drill rows of ¼-inch holes in the inner surfaces of the sides for adjustable shelf pegs.

Use a square to make sure that the corners are perfect right angles, and join the sides to the top and bottom with flathead screws. Countersink the heads and fill flush to the surface with wood putty.

On one side of each divider, drill ¼-inch holes to match those mentioned above. On the other side cut three dado grooves for shelf supports. Make the divider ¾ inch narrower than the sides to clear the back panel. Complete the frame by inserting uprights and shelves, fastening them in place with countersunk finishing nails and glue.

As shown in Fig. 7-5, cut out a piece from the back before placing it on the cabinet. The cutout becomes a cleat which will be fastened to the wall and from which the cabinet will hang. Sides of the piece are cut square, but the top and bottom edges should be beveled about 30 degrees. When the cabinet is completed, the back will fit over the cleat and will be held in place by the bevel. After the cutout is made, cover the inside surface of the back with vinyl fabric fastened with wallpaper paste.

Doors are constructed of a frame of ¾x1-inch hardwood stock rabbeted to take ¼-inch hardboard panels that will be covered with vinyl later. The diagram shows their construction and placement.

Mounting the cabinet is simply a matter of locating the studs in the wall, fastening the cleat to them at the proper height, and hanging the cabinet on the cleat. As a final measure drive screws through each corner of the cabinet into the wall to prevent its being lifted off the cleat accidentally.

Project #3—WARDROBE STORAGE CHEST

This combination drawer and wardrobe chest will go a long way toward solving the problem of clothes storage for any home that has a shortage of closet space. Although shown in use as a child's wardrobe, this compact unit is ideal for the grown-ups, too. It has ample depth to hang jackets, shirts, blouses, trousers, and skirts.

Construction details have been kept relatively simple in the design of this unit. After you have studied the details, you will probably agree that this method of drawer construction, which involves projecting bottoms, is the easiest you've seen. The bottom edge of each sloped drawer front forms a finger pull, giving the chest a clean, contemporary look.

1. Using the dimensions given in Table 7-1, lay out the component pieces on plywood as shown on the cutting diagrams. Allow for saw kerfs between adjacent parts.

2. Carefully saw all plywood parts to size and sand the cut edges. Rabbet the rear edge of the sides C to receive the ¼-inch plywood back. To accomplish the rabbet along the inside-bottom edge of the sloped drawer fronts, set the table saw at 10½ degrees off the vertical and make a ⅜-inch-deep saw cut 1 inch from the edge. Remove the excess material with a chisel, and sand the rabbeted cut smooth. Now make a ¾ x 1¹⁄₁₆-inch rabbet on both side edges of all drawer fronts.

3. Nail and glue drawer guides as shown to one face of the middle partition and the inside surface

Fig. 7-6.   This wardrobe storage chest is a fine addition to any bedroom.

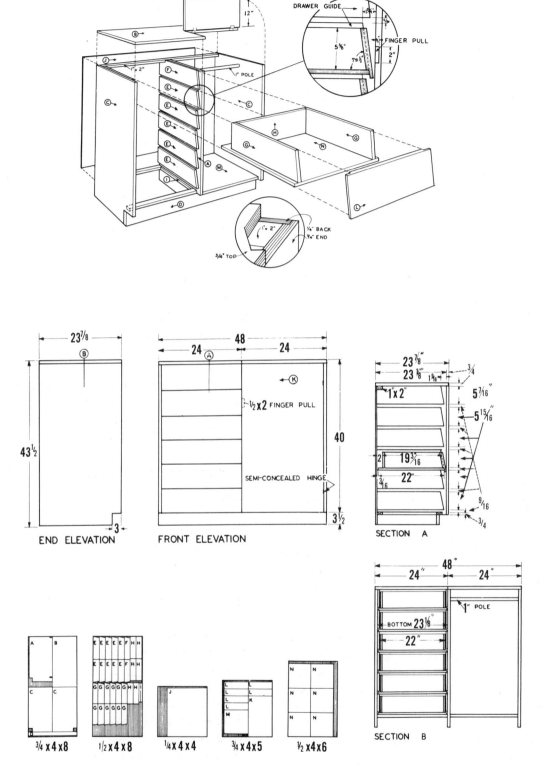

Fig. 7-7.   See Table 7-1.

Table 7-1

PARTS SCHEDULE

Code	No. Req'd.	Size	Part Identification
A	1	22 ⅞″x 42 ¾ ″	Standard
B	1	23 ⅞″x48″	Top
C	2	23 ⅞″x42 ¾″	Side
D	1	3 ½″x48″	Base
E	10	5¹⁵⁄₁₆″x22 ⅛″	Drawer guides
F	2	5 ⁷⁄₁₆″x27 ⅛″	Drawer guides
G	12	5 ⅜″ x20 ″	Drawer side
H	6	5 ⅜″x21″	Drawer backs
I	2	⅞″x18 ⅜ ″	Drawer guides
J	1	42 ¾ ″ x47 ¼ ″	Back
K	1	23 ¼ ″x39 ¼ ″	Door
L	6	6 ½ ″x23 ⅛ ″	Drawer front
M	1	22 ½″ x22 ⅞″	Bottom
N	6	22″x23 ⅛ ″	Drawer bottom
	12 lin. ft.	1″x2″	Stops
	2 lin. ft.	1 ″ diameter	Fir pole
	1 pair	—	Semiconcealed hinges

of one side. Install 1x2-inch stiffeners at the top and bottom to join the sides. Then, using 6*d* nails and glue fasten back into rabbeted sides.

4. Add rigidity and keep in square by installing base strip D and wardrobe bottom M. Now install divider A as shown, and fasten 1x2-inch forward stiffener in place.

5. Drawer assembly goes fast after parts are cut. Nail and glue sides to back, and then attach bottom to front. Cut out lid in top, and hinge as shown. Install wardrobe top last with 8*d* nails, to make it easier to check fit and action of drawers.

6. Install 1-inch pole with ordinary closet-rod ferrules. Fill and sand all exposed edges, and finish as recommended in Chapter 8.

Be sure to seal all door edges well and finish both faces alike.

Project #4—BUNK BEDS

Bunk beds are no longer considered just a temporary sleeping device for children's rooms. Nor need they be planned only for summer cottages or trailer units. The idea of an extra bed somewhere in the average home is a good one.

In addition to conserving space, the bunk bed can take a lot of abuse, is inexpensive, and is easy to build. With a little modification it blends into any decor and can be offered to the most exacting guest.

When building a bunk bed, it's a good idea to get the springs and mattresses first. In this way you can adjust the dimensions of the bunk bed frame to fit these items. If you do the job in reverse, you may end up with a bed you can't fit with springs. Supports for springs and mattresses vary according to their composition. Some have their own framework, others rest on slats. Still others, like a good inner-spring mattress or a foam rubber arrangement, rest on a single plywood sheet. When you are dealing with a hinged, drop-down upper bunk, keep these factors in mind, since they can reduce the weight and make the hinging job easier.

When it comes to selecting materials, choose hardwoods for the supporting members. They'll

Materials Needed
   Lumber
4 pieces, 3″x3″x74″
4 pieces, 1″x8″x80″
4 pieces, 1″x8″x38″
4 pieces, 1″x2″x80″
8 pieces, 1″x3″x38″
4 pieces, 1″x10″x38″
16 pairs of glue blocks to confine slats
8 round dowels ¾ x2 inches (optional)
   Other
32 No. 6, 1½-inch screws
60 No. 8, 2-inch screws
16 ¼ x4-inch carriage bolts
Wood glue
4 hard rubber casters (optional)

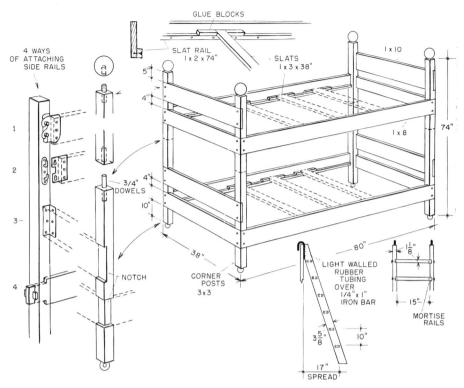

Fig. 7-8.   Basic bunk bed showing standard dimensions. Adjustments may be made to fit mattress size and room height.

stand the frequent assembly and dismounting as well as hard use. Bolts and screws instead of common nails are the best fastening devices. Complicated joints aren't needed; in fact, they should be avoided. This not only speeds construction, lowers cost, and puts the job in almost anyone's hands, it also permits the use of the most common hand tools in construction.

Be sure to round all exposed edges as a safety measure. Use rubber bumpers where possible on ladder legs, over ladder hooks, and where swinging sections make contact with walls and other parts of the bed.

A ladder should have the steps 15 inches long, and there should be about 10 inches between steps. Sometimes a small two-step ladder to the lower bunk will avoid arguments as to who climbs to bed via the ladder. When children reach the right age, a brass pole from floor to ceiling makes descent from the upper bunk more fun.

Project #5—DUAL-PURPOSE TABLE

It isn't often that you can put together a double-duty piece of furniture for your home in just one evening. This modern efficiency unit can be converted from a coffee table to a dining table in a matter of seconds.

If you have a few scrap pieces of hardwood in your shop, it will take literally minutes to saw the legs to shape, cut the supports, and prepare them for joining, sanding, and finishing.

Materials Needed
Each leg, 1 ¼″ x2″ x12″
            1 ¼″ x2″ x30″
Two supports, 1″ x12″ x24″
Two lengths of piano hinge
Dowels, glue, and screws

Fig. 7-9.   The dual-purpose table in its two positions.

The top can be a modern flush door, or you might take a discarded door and resurface it with a plastic laminate. If possible, obtain hardwood legs with a pleasing grain so that a natural finish will emphasize the beauty of its design.

The following is a key to Fig. 7-10:

1. Hinge the leg units to the underside of the tabletop so that the shorter leg ends are recessed slightly from the outer ends of the tabletop.

2. Legs are joined to each other with broad board attached to the outer side of the longer leg of each unit. The board is hinged to the top.

3. Join long and short piece as shown to make each leg. Miter joints, using blind dowels and

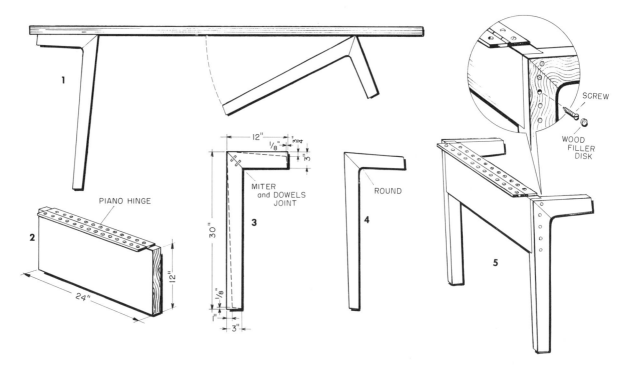

Fig. 7-10.

waterproof glue. Taper legs to shape as shown, and round inner surface with rasp; then sand.

4. Finished leg indicates proper shape. Pitch of leg in either position helps to stabilize table.

5. While butt joints may be used to join legs, setting board in rabbet provides greater strength.

Project #6—WALL STEREO UNIT

The modular system of poles and panels illustrated here is a great way to divide and display, with option for cabinetry in equal units of length. Our sample is one of the most convenient sizes—four poles and three panels jutting about 8 feet into the room, hung with six shelves offering 16 running feet of display. Add to this the stunning hi-fi cabinet described below and you've got a do-it-yourself project that's a real addition.

Following the system described here, the poles are one of the safest, surest ways to support the panels and shelving. Looking at the detail sketch

Fig. 7-11.   A wall stereo unit such as this gives an illusion of space.

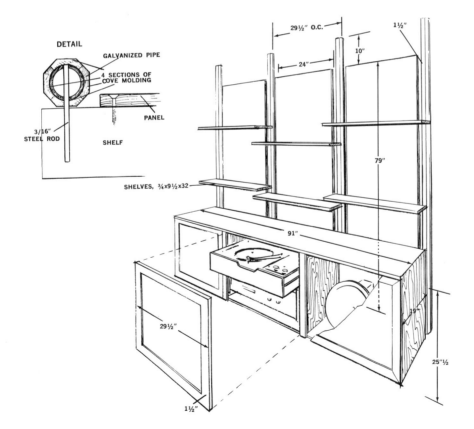

Fig. 7-12.

(Fig. 7-12), you'll see that they are made of a core of 1⅛-inch o.d. (outside diameter) galvanized pipe sheathed in four sections of cove molding, bonded face-down, forming an octagon. First, unsheathed pipe is clamped at the top to the second-floor joists and socketed in the hardwood floor at the bottom. They are set on 29½-inch centers for as many units as you plan to install.

After sheathing, determine the height and order of your shelving and drill $\frac{3}{16}$-inch holes (two per shelf) through the facing molding and the two walls of the pipe, stopping at the rear molding. Next drill $\frac{3}{16}$-inch holes in the shelf edges, insert $\frac{3}{16}$-inch steel rods in the poles, and then jam the shelving into place for a bracketless installation.

The 24x79 panels are secured directly to the back edges of the shelves, centered between the poles. There is a space approximately 10 inches between the top edge of the panel and the ceiling. Being 79 inches long, the panels extend beyond the cabinet's surface to within inches of the floor, so that the back of the cabinet is concealed.

This particular cabinet is equipped with component stereo units, with the two end sections housing speakers and the center section opening to the turntable and tuner.

The basic box design simplifies construction: a top, two sides, two center uprights, a bottom, and a back (the top is ½ inch wider than the sides, uprights center and bottom). Two facing trim slats conceal the leading edges of the center uprights. Six 1-inch-diameter wheel casters raise the cabinet just enough on carpeting to allow free door movement, but are themselves hidden in the pile.

Door frames are of ½-inch clamshell molding, mitered at the corners, with speaker grille cloth stretched and stapled. Concealed hinges provide a clean look; side-mounting sliding hardware supports the phono turntable, allowing smooth, easy access.

Project #7—MODERN DESK

Here's a modern desk that is easy to build of plywood, solid hardwood, or pine—a piece that will be a delight to your eyes and a joy to own and exhibit as evidence of your ability as an all-around handyman.

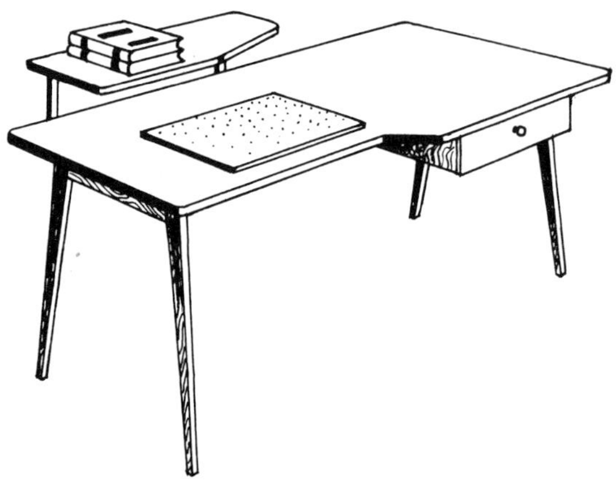

Fig. 7-13. The details for making a modern desk.

To create this piece, cut all pieces to size, as indicated on material list and drawings. Then follow assembly directions.

1. Join E with F; then D with F and E (detail 1).
2. Assemble the drawer H and G and I (detail 2),

Materials Needed

(Plywood or solid wood may be used)

Piece	Number required	Dimensions
A	1	24″x9″x¾″ thick
B	1	48″x24″x¾″ thick
C	2	18″x1″x1″ thick
D	1	40″x3″x1″ thick
E	2	12″x3″x1″ thick
F	4	28½″x2¼″x1″ thick
G	1	15″x4″x¾″ thick
H	2	18½″x4″x⅜″ thick
I	1	14¼″x18″x⅜″ thick
J	1	14⅝″x18″x¼″ thick
K	2	18″x⅝″x⅜″ thick
L	2 metal supports	18″x1″x¼″ thick

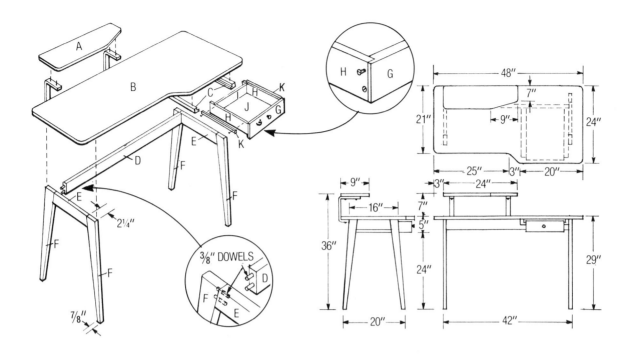

and fasten bottom to sides. Fasten guides K to sides of H (flush with the top of H).

3. Fasten guides C under bottom of top B; fasten top B to frame.

4. Fasten metal support L to top of B, and add shelf A.

5. Smooth all edges and finish to suit.

Project #8—CHILD'S CRAFT DESK AND BENCH

The materials needed are a single flush door, two sets of wrought-iron legs, some lengths of 1x6, 1x4, and 1x2, and a few pieces of hardboard. Begin by cutting out the piece that later becomes the bench. Use a fine-tooth saw to avoid splintering. Both the cutout piece and the area from which it was removed must have their edges filled if your flush door is hollow. Close these edges with strips of 1x2 planed to a snug fit, glued and finish-nailed in

place between the face veneers. Fig. 7-15 shows how the compartments at the rear and the shelf below are assembled.

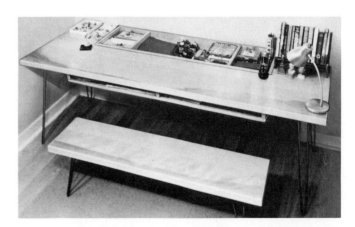

Fig. 7-14.   The dual-purpose desk and matching bench are handsome and useful. Compartments are provided for books and craft materials.

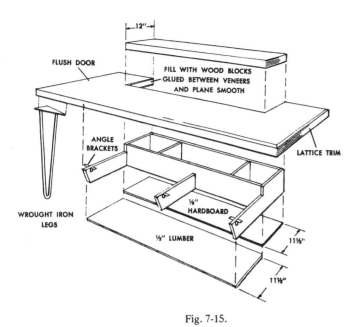

Fig. 7-15.

Project #9—DINING TABLE

This fine, all-teak dining table, inspired by Danish contemporary furniture designs, will whet the appetite of do-it-yourselfers seeking a new, exciting project. Gourmet palate or not, you'll delight in its graceful lines and wide serviceability—as a perfect oval seating four or as an extended oval seating six. Our simplified construction stages show all the vital cuts, while the design allows for personal modifications wherever you may want them.

To lay out a perfect oval shape, draw a 75x40-inch rectangle (overall dimensions of the top with leaf) on your sheet of plywood (see Fig. 7-17). Bisect the rectangle the long way. Locate points A, B, and C. Insert thumbtacks at B and C with the heads almost touching the surface. Tie a piece of thin, strong, nonstretch cord (heavy fishing line is good) into a loop exactly 43⁵⁄₆₄ inches long (the distance from A to C). Place a loop around the tack points. Draw the loop taut with a sharp-pointed pencil, forming a triangle whose three corners are B, C, and the pencil point. Slide the pencil along the fishline while keeping the loop stretched taut, and you will see immediately that the pencil moves in an elliptical line. Draw the ellipse starting at D, through A, to E. The line you've just drawn should just touch the edges of the board at A, D, and E. Repeat the process at the other end of the plywood rectangle to obtain the opposite curve, measuring for new tack points and inscribing another ellipse. Note that the 22-inch-wide center area, when cut out, becomes the leaf.

Fig. 7-16.   The dining table (*left*) and its extension (*right*).

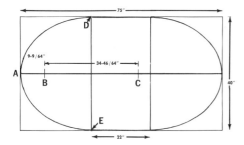

Fig. 7-17.   Details of laying out the oval shape.

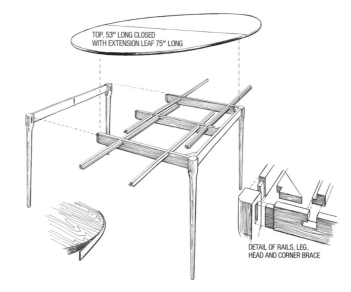

Fig. 7-18.   Details for final construction.

Project #10—COFFEE TABLE WITH
LAZY SUSANS

Offering elegant contrasts in color as well as texture, the coffee table seen in the accompanying photographs will truly become the center of attraction in your living room, for it is as unusual in conception and design as it is in execution. Not one but two lazy Susan turntables allow both the tiled and the top-most surfaces to rotate freely, independently of each other, making convenience in serving guests an outstanding feature.

The beautiful colors of glazed-ceramic mosaic tile may be chosen from a large selection available to provide a bright accent or to blend subtly with any decor, while the gleaming walnut surface of the central turntable gives the piece a look that bespeaks quality. Follow the ten-step sequence outlined below—after first cutting all the wood pieces to size. Refer to Fig. 7-20 for ready identification of the parts.

1. Tile top and outside edges of D.

2. Drill mounting holes for turntable F through top of E., but do not mount turntable. Insert mounting bolts and leave them in turntable holes, loose.

3. Fasten other side of turntable F to underside of G.

4. Now fasten turntable F to top of E, utilizing holes made in step 2.

Fig. 7-19.   A coffee table with two lazy Susans.

5. Turn above assembly upside-down so that it rests on the top face of G. Place tiled ring D (tiled side down) over E.

6. Coat underside of E and part of underside of D (wherever it will overlap C) with a good grade of wood glue. Tack C to D and E with ¾-inch finishing nails. Also use clamps to assure a good bond. Allow glue to dry fully. Drying time will depend on the glue used.

7. Drill mounting holes through A for turntable B, but do not mount turntable. Insert mounting bolts and leave them in the turntable holes, loose.

8. Fasten other side of turntable B to the underside of C (after the glue is completely dry).

9. Now fasten turntable B to top face of A.

10. Fasten legs to underside of A.

Applying the Tile. You will need approximately eight sheets of glazed-ceramic mosaic tile for the surface of piece D, and two sheets for the edge. The tiles used here, called Lurano, are imported from Italy in 12x12-inch sheets, pasted to a cloth net backing. Each tile is ⅜ inch square. Although larger tiles are also available, this size is best to work with when covering circular objects. The larger sizes leave too much space between tiles.

Start tiling by sealing the disk-shaped surface of D with one or two coats of shellac thinned with an equal amount of alcohol. Allow to dry fully. Then cut ⅛-inch tempered hardboard into strips about 1½ inches wide, and tack the strips around the entire outside rim of the circle with wire brads to make a small fence whose top is ⅛ inch above the surface to be tiled. This serves as a temporary form against which you will start to tile. It is later removed.

Next apply special tile adhesive (Surebond is one good variety) to an area equal to about a square foot. Slit the sheets of tile with a kitchen knife into strips two tiles wide, and press them into the adhesive, net side down, starting at the outer rim against the little hardboard fence. Place each strip in a curve that follows the fence. Continue to apply

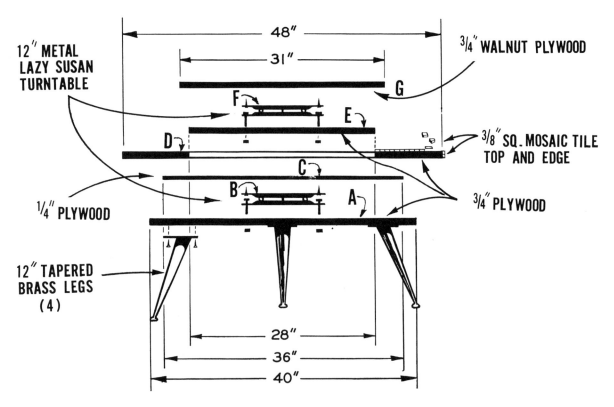

Fig. 7-20.

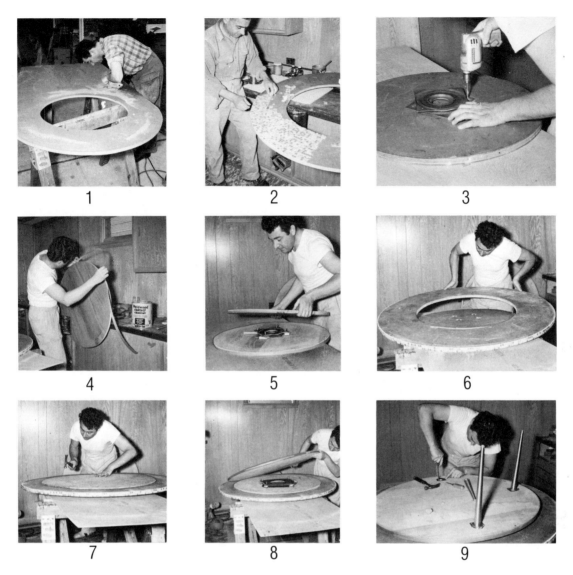

Fig. 7-21.   Major steps and details of making the coffee table with two lazy Susans: 1. A saber saw make an easy job of cutting the wood into disks of the proper size. 2. The open disk (piece D in Fig. 7-20) that is tiled is first to be worked on. Place tile in strips following the curve of the edge as closely as possible. See text for details. 3. Using lazy Susan as a template, drill screw holes through piece E, but do not fasten the turntable in place until after completing steps seen in next two photos. 4. Cut a 31-inch-diameter circle from ¾-inch walnut plywood for disk G. Sand edges smooth. Cover edge with flexible wood tape that has adhesive back, or use contact cement. 5. Fasten turntable to bottom of G with flathead wood screws. Then insert bolts through turntable, wedge them in place, and position E. Tighten bolts to hold E. 6. Next turn tiled ring D upside-down. Lay it over E so that surfaces of both are flush. They will fit together nicely because E is a cutout from the center of D. 7. Take disk C (¼-inch plywood, 36 inches in diameter) and center it over E and D. Nail together, using ¾-inch finishing nails, after coating opposing faces with glue. 8. Repeat turntable-fastening steps detailed previously to join pieces C and A to second turntable. Piece A is ¾-inch Duraply. Cement wood tape to the disk's edge. 9. Legs are the final touch. Brass was used here, but you can substitute any material that may be more appealing to your own taste. Legs should be 12 inches high.

strips, working in toward the inside rim of the circle—the hole in the doughnut. When one portion has been completely tiled, coat an adjacent area with adhesive and repeat the process until the entire circle is covered. If you're using Surebond, do not attempt to spread more adhesive at one time than you can easily cover in forty-five minutes, for that is the longest time you can count on its remaining tacky enough to be workable. Adhesives differ widely, so be sure to check the label on the one you are using.

When the surface is completely covered, allow the adhesive to set for as long as the manufacturer recommends in the directions you'll find on the package. Now you can turn your attention to the edge. First remove the hardboard fence. Spread adhesive along the edge, and then tile with strips cut two tiles wide. Place the strips so that the edge is flush with the top of the surface tiles. Work your way around the perimeter of the circle until it is completed, adjusting the space between tiles, if necessary, to make an even fit possible. Again, allow the cement to harden for the recommended period.

Grouting the tile is the final step here. Grout is a variety of cement that is mixed with water to a creamy consistency. It is usually white, but water-base colors can be added to it to give unusual and interesting effects. When the grout is mixed, spread it over the surface of the tile and work it into every crevice carefully. A sponge will help to spread it evenly. Any excess can be wiped off with a damp cloth. Later, when the remaining grout has dried thoroughly, the tiles can be polished with a soft, clean cloth to remove any film.

Assembling the Table. With the major part of the job done, there now remains only the assembly of the pieces in the order already given, starting with step 2, and the table will be complete. If you've been puzzled about the second and seventh steps in the sequence of assembly, here's why.

When the table is completed, both the turntables are sandwiched between two relatively large pieces of wood, with too little space between them to allow reaching the screws that fasten the turntables in place. This is why it's necessary first to prepare

holes in one side and then to separate the pieces. When fastening them later, as you must do in steps 4 and 9, the boltheads are held in place temporarily with small wood wedges while the nuts are turned on from below. Be sure to examine photo 5 in Fig. 7-21 carefully for a clear understanding of these steps.

Locate the positions for mounting the legs by drawing two diameters at right angles to each other on the underside of A. Then measure and mark a spot 8 inches in from the outside edge on each of the four segments. The four spots marked are the center points for mounting the legs, which are attached with screws. Although turned-brass legs were used here, any style—wood, wood with brass tips, or wrought-iron—may be used instead.

Project #11—COLONIAL TRESTLE TABLE

An attractive, easily made workshop project consisting of only thirteen parts, this Early American piece can serve as an occasional table, gaming table, or "showcase" for knickknacks. Although pine was used in this example, cherry, birch, or maple may be substituted.

Boards for the top are doweled and edge-glued to

Fig. 7-22.   A Colonial trestle table will add charm to an Early American setting.

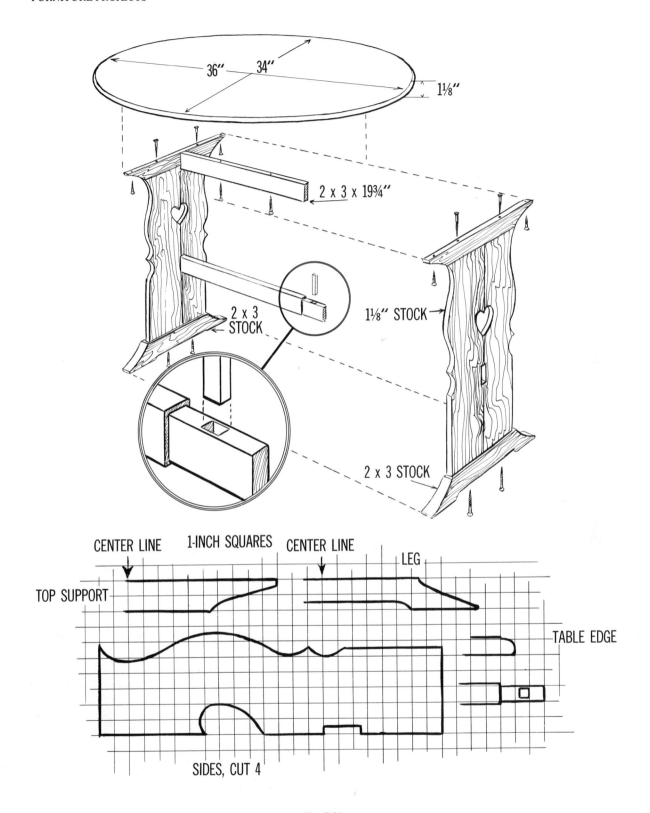

36″

34″

1⅛″

2 x 3 x 19¾″

2 x 3 STOCK

1⅛″ STOCK

2 x 3 STOCK

CENTER LINE   1-INCH SQUARES   CENTER LINE   LEG

TOP SUPPORT

TABLE EDGE

SIDES, CUT 4

Fig. 7-23.

form a single piece from which an oval is cut with a saber saw. Its molded edge is finished with a router or shaper (if you don't own one, rent one from a hardware store or take the tabletop to a local lumber mill). Each leg is made from two pieces of stock, with the butt joint running vertically on the leg center line (see Fig. 7-23). Before doweling and edge-gluing the leg halves, cut heart shapes and notches (for stretcher joint). Add top and bottom horizontal members with screws and glue.

The lower stretcher is 25 inches in length. Tenon the ends of the lower stretcher to fit the leg slots. After the holes in the lower stretcher have been made (using a mortising attachment or by drilling holes and squaring the slot with a chisel), cut wedges with a slight taper. This will tighten the joint, assuring a solid assembly.

Assemble the legs and stretchers, gluing all joints. Attach the tabletop to the legs and the upper stretcher with six screws and glue. Plug all six screwhead holes, and sand smooth. Finish the entire piece as suggested in Chapter 8.

Project #12—BOOK AND MAGAZINE TABLE

The low lines of this occasional table integrate well with contemporary furniture. An interesting surfboard shape and a slight tilt to the end panel give this useful piece character and grace. The sturdy, unusual wrought-iron legs can be easily secured from any metal-working shop. The legs can be painted black or in a color to contrast with the shelves of the table.

Give the drawings for this table (Fig. 7-25) some study before beginning construction. Assembly is easy when you take it one step at a time.

1. Have a metal-working shop fabricate the wrought-iron legs for you. This plan gives all the information required. To take care of minor variations in angles and dimensions, you probably will save yourself extra work by having the legs bent before beveling and drilling the bottom shelf and cutting partition C to proper height. Paint the legs with flat-black enamel or in a color to contrast with the shelves.

2. Using a large steel square, lay out the parts on

a panel of ¾-inch-thick plywood as shown on the cutting diagram. Remember to allow for saw kerfs while laying out the parts.

3. Saw out all parts to size, drill holes to receive legs, and then dado bottom shelf to receive part C. Make an angular cut on the wide end of shelf A to fit the rabbet on end panel D. Rabbet the end of the top shelf to receive partition C.

4. Using glue and 6d finish nails, fasten end D and partition C to bottom shelf A. Then support shelf B on a block while attaching it to C. Some adjustment for the length of the legs can be obtained by drilling blind holes on the underside of the top shelf; plates can be threaded up or down a few turns to bring the top shelf level. Use screws to fasten leg frames and plates as shown.

5. Smooth all edges and joints with coarse sandpaper on a block, and fill nail holes and plywood edge grain with wood paste filler. Then smooth the table with fine sandpaper, rounding sharp edges and corners slightly.

Fig. 7-24.   The book and magazine table is detailed here; the couch may be constructed as described in Chapter 5.

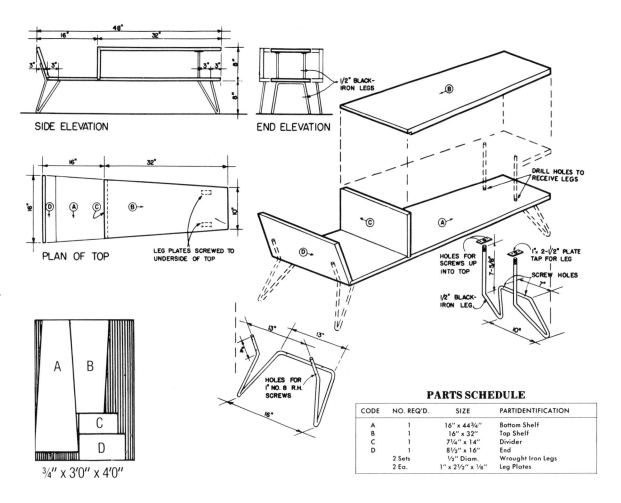

SIDE ELEVATION

END ELEVATION

PLAN OF TOP

LEG PLATES SCREWED TO
UNDERSIDE OF TOP

½" BLACK-
IRON LEGS

DRILL HOLES TO
RECEIVE LEGS

HOLES FOR
SCREWS UP
INTO TOP

½" BLACK-
IRON LEG

1" 2-½" PLATE
TAP FOR LEG

SCREW HOLES

HOLES FOR
1" NO. 8 R.H.
SCREWS

¾" x 3'0" x 4'0"

PARTS SCHEDULE

CODE	NO. REQ'D.	SIZE	PART IDENTIFICATION
A	1	16" x 44¾"	Bottom Shelf
B	1	16" x 32"	Top Shelf
C	1	7¼" x 14"	Divider
D	1	8½" x 16"	End
	2 Sets	½" Diam.	Wrought Iron Legs
	2 Ea.	1" x 2½" x ⅛"	Leg Plates

Fig. 7-25.

6. Apply an enamel undercoat, then two coats of semigloss enamel. For an inexpensive blond finish follow the recommended finishing procedure in the next chapter.

Project #13—TAMBOUR DOOR STORAGE WALL

The roll-top covers used for desks at the turn of the century are still favored by many people when they can find these antiques, in spite of the clumsiness of the early tambour materials. Lately the material has come into favor again with furniture and cabinet designers in a much more streamlined form than the original. However, it is as yet unavailable to the do-it-yourselfer. This project brings you an easy method to build strips of tambour, using commonly available materials: standard molding shapes, canvas, and fast-setting contact adhesive. Also other bugaboos like curved grooving have been eliminated in this design.

Since this unit is to be built clear up to the ceiling, no exact overall height can be specified, although the height of the middle shelf, which divides the tambour-covered upper area from the lower cabinet, is 40 inches so that the tilt-out shelf will clear the knees of the person working at it. Cut all uprights to ceiling height, and estimate how many shelf spaces can be divided into the remaining distance after allowing for the bottom

Fig. 7-26.   Open or closed, the tambour doors over the book-shelves in these cabinets are never in the way and serve to keep out dust.

part of the cabinet. Deduct the thickness of one shelf from each space, and cut ¼-inch plywood spacers to that length. Since spacers above the top shelf will contain axle holes for the tambour rollers, drill all of them together to assure proper alignment. The plywood spacers also form the inside of the channel in which the tambour will run, so round the upper corners of the top ones to match the 2-inch rollers used. In assembly, space uprights as indicated, then build in shelves and spacers from the bottom up. Continue building progressively to the top space, where you install the axles of each pair of rollers into the predrilled holes before nailing in the top pieces of plywood in each section. Roller "axles," as shown in Fig. 7-27, are ordinary wood screws with their heads cut off.

To make tambour doors: A. Square one end of the canvas backing material working from side nearest you, and mark it for the wider starting strip. B. Lay a 1x4-inch straight board parallel to the other edge of the canvas at the proper distance, and clamp it as a guide to width. C. Coat surface of

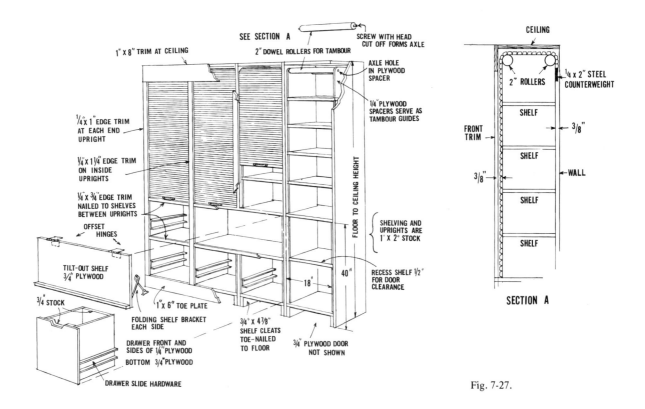

Fig. 7-27.

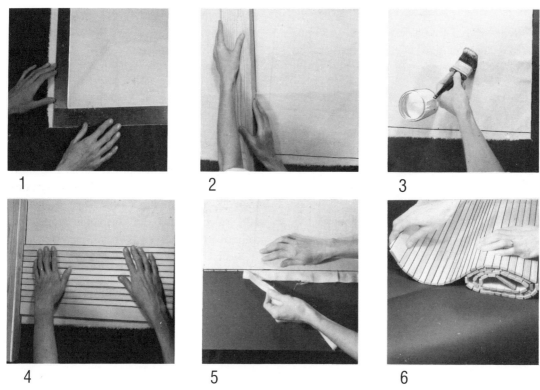

Fig. 7-28.   Steps in making tambour doors.

canvas with a good grade of contact cement, then apply cement to each strip as it is used. D. Starting with the starter strip squared by the mark, strips of tambour lay up easily to the desired length. E. When cement is thoroughly dry, remove guide board and invert tambour material. Canvas is scored with sharp knife to trim. F. Narrow strips of molding make flexible tambour, as shown here. Mount a suitable handle or "starter," and paint to suit.

Tambour door material, built as indicated in Fig. 7-28, is to be counterbalanced by steel weights. Dimensions shown in Fig. 7-27 are for ¼x2-inch steel, which is an approximate dimension since different ceiling heights for the cabinet will require different door lengths. To determine the proper weight of counterbalance for your doors, weigh one length of the tambour after it is made up. The counterweight should equal two-thirds of that weight in order for it to balance when the door is about half-closed. Once the weight is known, your

local supplier (usually a sheet-metal shop) can cut strips to your requirements. Do not go beyond 18 inches in length or ¼ inch in thickness; the width of the strips is immaterial. Drill the weights and fasten them to the end strip of the door with short lengths of wire. Ordinary metal drawer handles are mounted on the lowest strip of each tambour door, which is of ⁵⁄₁₆x1½-inch stock rather than the ⅝-inch width of the other strips. This handle also acts as a top stop for the tambour material after the front-trim board at the top of top cabinet has been nailed fast.

The working shelf is hinged with offset hinges to the middle shelf and supported in the raised position by folding shelf brackets. Drawers, constructed as shown, slide at a touch thanks to regular drawer slides.

Project #14—COLONIAL KEY-TENON BED

Because of its honest craftsmanship and functional simplicity of design, Colonial furniture has endured through the centuries to become about the most popular single furniture style in America today. Take the Colonial key-tenon bed as an example. Here we have the typical Colonial scroll-

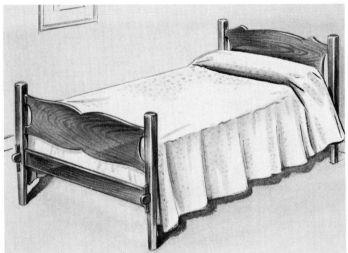

work applied as tasteful embellishment to solid wood construction. Here, too, authentic hand-pegged mortise-and-tenon joints and sturdy keyed tenons guarantee permanent workmanship. In fact not a single bit of hardware (which was scarce in the early days) is called for in this entire construction.

The Colonial key-tenon bed is essentially a hand-made piece of furniture. Of course, it is even simpler to make with power tools. But if you use machinery, be sure to apply those important hand touches, those rounded and softened edges that add so much to the authentic appearance of antique design.

Basic Construction. The basic construction procedure is as follows:

1. Start by making the four posts. As shown in Fig. 7-30, each post is tapered at the foot end on

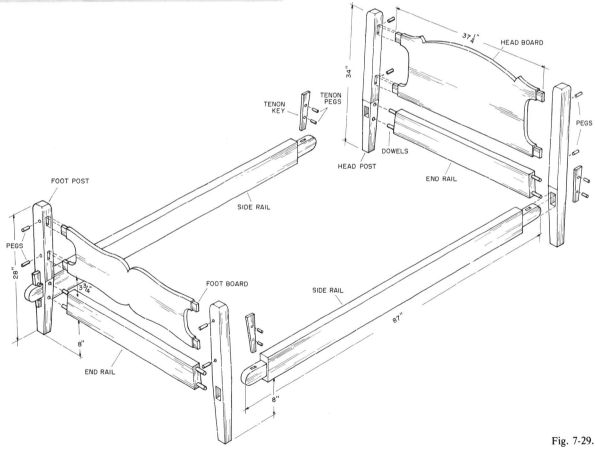

Fig. 7-29.

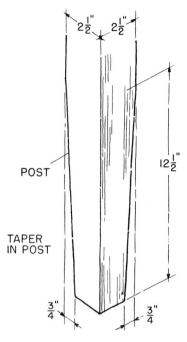

Fig. 7-30.   Post taper.

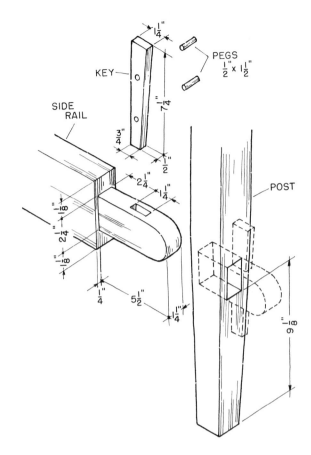

Fig. 7-32.   Key-tenon construction.

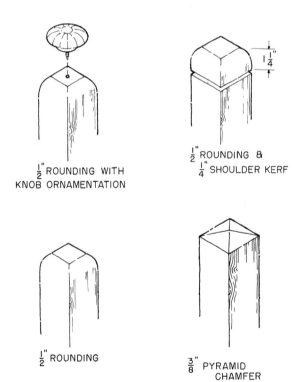

Fig. 7-31.   Variations of Colonial post tops.

the two inside surfaces. Mark and cut the ¾-inch taper to a line 12½ inches from the end. Post tops are then shaped as shown in Fig. 7-31.

2. Extreme care must be exercised to ensure accurate cutting of post mortises. Bore and chisel out the through mortises, which receive the protruding keyed tenons of side rails as shown in Fig. 7-32. Cut blind mortises for tenons of headboards and footboards (Fig. 7-33).

3. Bore ⅝-inch holes, 1½ inches deep, for dowel connections of posts and rails (Fig. 7-34). It should be noted that posts are tapered where dowel holes are bored. Be sure, therefore, to bore holes square and perpendicular to outside straight edge of posts. A doweling jig will help if it is adjusted off the taper to assume a face position parallel to the outside straight edge of the post.

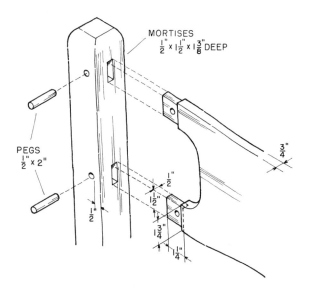

Fig. 7-33.   Blind mortise-and-tenon.

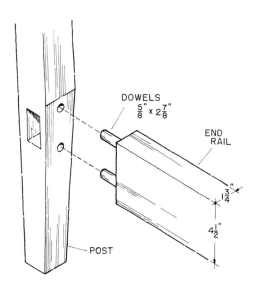

Fig. 7-34.   Dowel assembly of bedpost and end rail.

4. For shape of headboard and footboard make a full-size paper pattern from the accompanying graphs of the scroll design (Fig. 7-35). Cut and smooth the scrollwork with spokeshave, file, and sandpaper. Cut headboard and footboard tenons as shown.

5. Cut end rails to size. Rail ends are beveled to assume the same angle as the bottom taper of posts. Thus rails connect at right angles to the outside straight edge of the posts. Bore perpendicular ⅝-inch holes, 1½ inches deep, for doweled connections of end rails and posts. (Caution: Bore in line with straight edge of rail.)

6. Cut side rails to size. Mark and cut the protruding key-tenons as shown in Fig. 7-32. Mark and shape full half-rounding at tenon tip. Bore ½-inch holes for slot of tenon keys.

7. Cut and shape hardwood tenon keys as shown in Fig. 7-32.

Assembly. To assemble the Colonial key-tenon, follow this procedure:

1. Before assembling your bed, be sure all exposed edges are carefully dulled and rounded with a spokeshave, file, and sandpaper.

2. Start assembly by gluing and clamping together the mortise-and-tenon and dowel joints of the

footposts and the rail and footboard. Follow with assembly of the headposts, end rail, and head-

Materials Needed
(*White pine, maple, cherry, or walnut*)

Piece	No. Required	Size in Inches
Footposts	2	2½x2½x28
Headposts	2	2½x2½x34
Footboard	1	¾x9½x37¼
Headboard	1	¾x17x37¼
End Rails	2	1¾x4½x35½
Side Rail	2	1¾x4½x87
Tenon Keys (hardwood)	4	½x1¼x7¼
Tenon Pegs (dowel)	8	½x1½
Rail Dowels	8	⅝x2⅞

Note: Dimensions specified are for 3-feet-3-inch-wide bed. For a full-size bed all *width* measurements must be increased 15 inches.

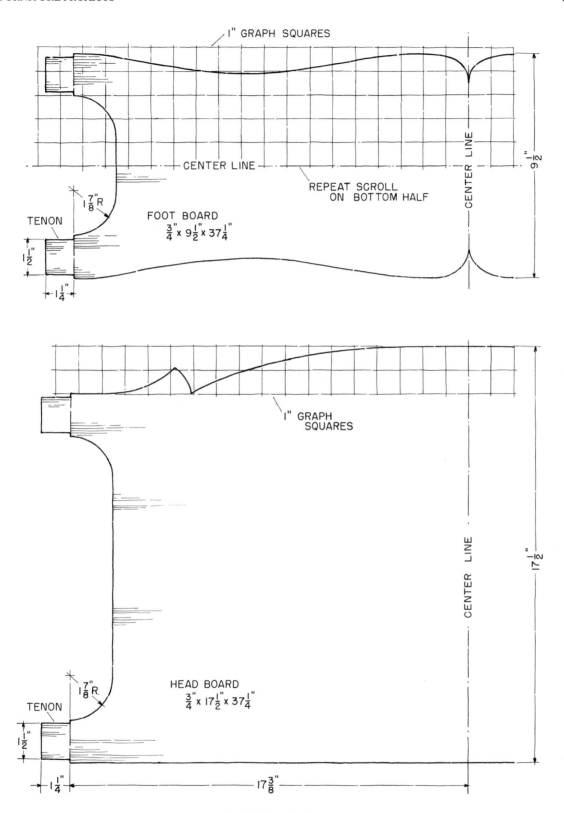

1" GRAPH SQUARES

CENTER LINE

REPEAT SCROLL
ON BOTTOM HALF

CENTER LINE

$9\frac{1}{2}$"

$1\frac{7}{8}$" R

TENON

FOOT BOARD
$\frac{3}{4}$" x $9\frac{1}{2}$" x $37\frac{1}{4}$"

$1\frac{1}{2}$"

$1\frac{1}{4}$"

1" GRAPH
SQUARES

CENTER LINE

$17\frac{1}{2}$"

$1\frac{7}{8}$" R.

TENON

HEAD BOARD
$\frac{3}{4}$" x $17\frac{1}{2}$" x $37\frac{1}{4}$"

$1\frac{1}{2}$"

$1\frac{1}{4}$"

$17\frac{3}{8}$"

Fig. 7-35. Scrollwork pattern.

board. When clamping, be careful to place work on a flat surface. Check for squareness as clamp pressure is applied, and be sure posts are exactly parallel when measured from the outside edges at top and bottom.

3. After the glue is dry and the clamps have been removed, bore ½-inch holes, 1¾ inches deep in the posts for tenon pegs. Pegs are made of ½-inch dowels rounded at the end for a craft effect. They are glued and driven into the holes to secure the tenons.

4. With assembly of the two bed ends you have only to connect them with the side rails. In fastening the keyed mortise-and-tenons of side rails, caution should be exercised not to force the keys in their tenon slots. Normal pressure will suffice, and thus avoid splitting the tenon.

The bed may be finished as described in Chapter 8.

Project #15—HEADBOARD

You can enjoy a whole weekend of laziness with this headboard, for it has room for music, books, a coffee percolator, a lean-back headboard, and even swing-down shelves to sup from. Harvard swing bed hinges will delight your wife, for either pin may be pulled to swing the bed out for cleaning, yet when fastened, the hinges keep the bed from rolling when you lean back against the tilt-out headboard.

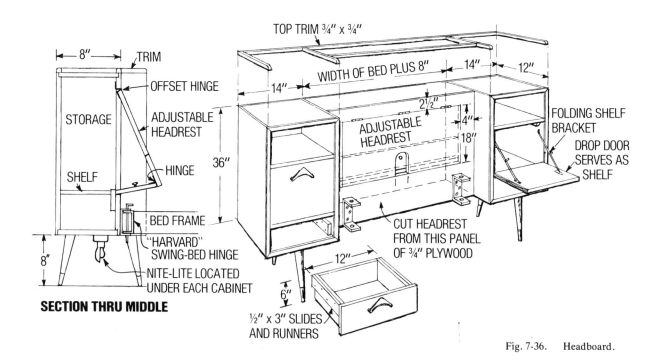

Fig. 7-36. Headboard.

Build the side cabinets—except backs—first, bearing in mind that though they are similar in plan, they are pairs, one left-hand, the other right-hand. The full-length backboard of stout ¾-inch plywood ties the cabinet together so that it will be rigid for the balance of the construction period. With the exception of the shelves major construction here is of ¾-inch plywood rabbeted at the corners, with the edge of the plywood concealed at the top by a ¾ x ¾-inch molding stripe.

The tilt-out headrest, which also acts as a door to the storage compartment, is a trick, though a practical one indeed. Hinged 1 inch from the bottom edge of the headrest is a full length of 1x6-inch board that, when lowered, rests against a doorstop strip at the bottom of the opening. When this board is up—and it is handled easily through an access cutout in the headrest—it is above the stop strip. The headrest is hinged with offset hinges at the top so that it may be swung up high enough for extra blankets or pillows to be deposited in the storage

space behind it. The headrest is 18 inches high, and the length is to match the width of the bed. Allow 4 inches between the rest and each cabinet at the end so that you may reach the Harvard swing bed hinge. Drop doors are operated by folding shelf brackets installed inside each door, and a friction catch at the top of each holds it closed. Reading light is a standard two-post, desk-type fluorescent lamp, and the night-lights are small—5- or 10-watt units. If hardwood plywood is used, either use hardwood strips for the trim molding or paint the unit to match the room decor. Drawers are conventional construction, with their pulls, and those on the doors, of a modern metal finish to match the modern style of the headboard. Legs are ready-made of metal or wood to suit.

Project #16—DRY-SINK BUFFET

One aspect of Colonial life that no one would wish to duplicate today is the absence of plumbing. Yet

Fig. 7-37.   A dry-sink buffet can serve many purposes. As shown at the right, it makes a good home for stereo equipment.

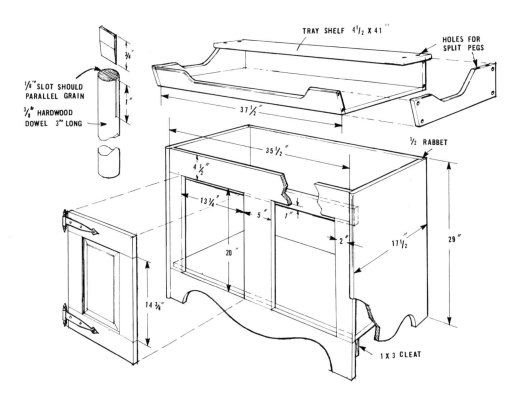

Fig. 7-38.

even this inconvenience made an enduring contribution to the furniture of that period—the dry sink. This was the name given to the humble washstand of New England homes. Since the water supply was usually a distant well, ample space was provided to store two full buckets underneath. Though its original function is happily obsolete, this sturdy little piece can find a place in contemporary dining or living rooms as a small serving buffet, bar, cabinet, or storage chest.

A good grade of 1-inch solid pine (boards are actually ¾ inch thick), is used throughout, except for three plywood panels—the tray bottom and the cabinet back and shelf (see Fig. 7-38). The back can be a ⅜-inch panel and should extend to the floor. The tray bottom can be either ½- or ¾-inch plywood. Since the leading edge will have to be cut at approximately a 15-degree slant, the width of the panel should be a bit over 18 inches to allow for this

bevel. The width of the shelf panel is 15⅞ inches and should be accurate, since the front edge serves as the lower doorstop. The 1x3-inch top cleat is dropped to provide the upper doorstop. If you can't get boards of sufficient width for the sides of the base, edge-join two 1x10's with glue and ⅜-inch dowels.

Project #17—FURNITURE THAT GROWS WITH THE CHILDREN

Flexibility is the outstanding characteristic of this child's storage wall. Although only three types of units are displayed in Fig. 7-40, the same construction methods can be used to provide additional pieces. For example a top could be fitted to the desk, with drawers inserted in each of the two resulting niches. If the shelves with their attached bookends were to be covered, one would have a useful

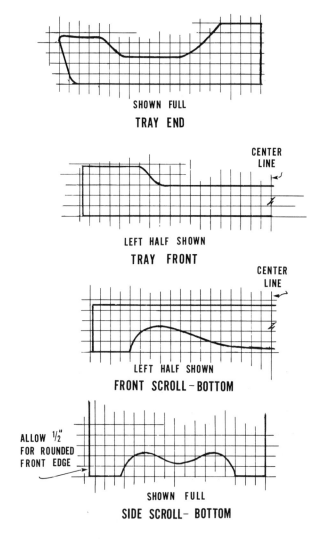

SHOWN FULL
TRAY END

LEFT HALF SHOWN
TRAY FRONT

CENTER
LINE

LEFT HALF SHOWN
FRONT SCROLL – BOTTOM

CENTER
LINE

ALLOW ½"
FOR ROUNDED
FRONT EDGE

SHOWN FULL
SIDE SCROLL – BOTTOM

Fig. 7-39.   Cutting patterns. Each square is equivalent to 1 inch.

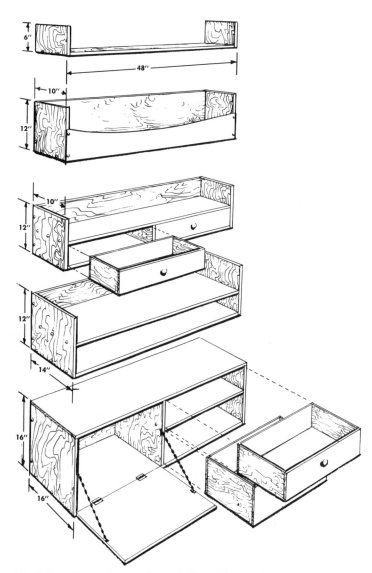

Fig. 7-41.   *Top to bottom:* Open shelf, toy bin, two-drawer display shelf, double shelf, and desk and all-purpose storage unit. Combine features of any or all units as you desire.

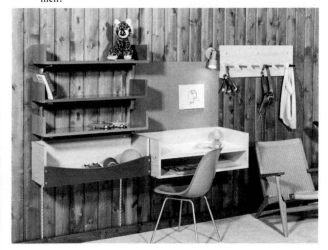

Fig. 7-40.   *Left:* Since you can't stretch wood, the next best thing is to use an expandable modular method of construction.

shadowbox for displaying hobby projects. Additional ideas appear in Fig. 7-41. Others will suggest themselves.

No matter what units or combinations you choose, the system remains flexible because it is mounted on adjustable brackets and wall standards, making movement of any piece a moment's work.

Use ¾-inch pine throughout or, if it's available, ¾-inch fir plywood. Assemble by butting pieces together, gluing, and then fastening with chromed ovalhead screws fitted with matching shoulder

washers. Finish with at least two coats of high-quality, high-gloss enamel. Contrasting colors and the highlights provided by the chromed hardware make an attractive combination.

Project #18—COLONIAL DROP-LEAF TABLE AND CHAIRS

The Colonial drop-leaf table detailed here has a long rectangular top and broad side leaves that open up to a width of 38 inches, yet take up little space when closed.

Fig. 7-42.   *Left:* Drop-leaf table with leaves lowered. *Right:* Completed table with leaves raised can seat eight.

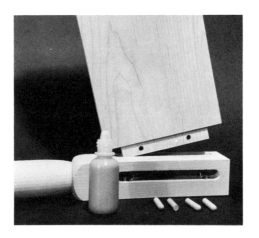 

Fig. 7-43.   *Left:* Close-up of mortise-and-tenon between skirt and legs shows predrilled holes for dowel pegs. *Right:* Final assembly begins by placing the top and the leaves top-down on the floor. Hinges are attached with ½-inch screws into predrilled screw holes.

Assemble the legs and skirts first. Place one right leg and one left leg so that they face each other. Apply glue to the mortises in each leg. Do *not* apply glue to the tenons of the skirts as they may swell rapidly and make it impossible to get them into the mortises. Line up the holes bored through mortise-and-tenon joints, apply glue, and insert the ¼-inch pegs. Start with one of the short skirts. Repeat this procedure with the remaining short skirt and the other two legs. Then add the long skirts to the remaining mortises in the legs already glued to the short skirts, pinning them with pegs as described above.

Note that all of the skirts have screw holes bored at a slant through the upper edges. These edges will be in contact with the underside of the tabletop. When assembling the skirts and legs, it is very im-

portant that all these skirt edges with holes face *upward*. Also be sure that all these screw holes face *inward*. Remove all excess glue at once with a dry cloth.

Because of the size of this table it is suggested that the legs-and-skirt assembly, drop leaves, and top and support slides be stained and finished before complete assembly. Instructions for finishing can be found in Chapter 8.

Attach the leaves to the tabletop, using three hinges for each leaf. The holes in the hinges should line up with the predrilled pilot holes in the undersides of the leaves and the tabletop. Use the ½-inch screws in the kit, and be sure to attach the long side of each hinge to the leaves.

Place the assembled tabletop and leaves face down on the floor. Now place the legs-and-skirt

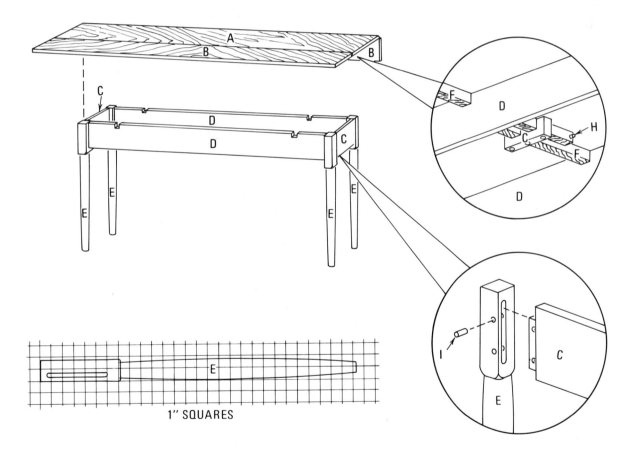

1″ SQUARES

Fig. 7-44.

Materials Needed for Table

A. One piece, 19″ x 72″ x ¾″
B. Two pieces, 10⅛″ x 73″ x ¾″
C. Two pieces, 6⅛″ x 14¼″ x ¾″
D. Two pieces, 6⅛″ x 57½″ x ¾″
E. Four pieces, 1¾″ dia. x 28¼″
F. Four pieces, 1¼″ x 16½″ x 1″
G. Two pieces, 2″ x 5½″ x 1″
H. Four pieces, ⅜″ dia. x 1¼″
I. Sixteen pieces, ⅜″ dia. x 1⅜″
J. Six pieces, #10 2″ screws
K. Ten pieces, #10 1¼″ screws
L. Thirty-six pieces, #8 ½″ screws

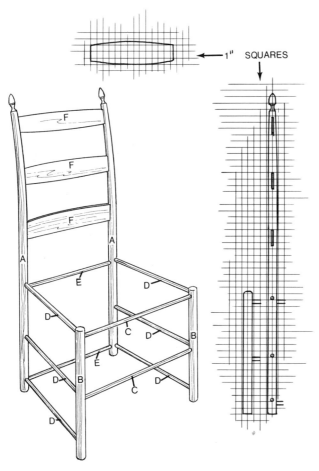

Fig. 7-45.

assembly exactly in the center of the underside of the table, facing up toward you.

With a pencil or nail inserted in the holes of the skirts, mark the underside of the table for pilot screw holes. Using a ⅛-inch bit, drill holes not more than ½ inch deep at the same angle as those in the skirts. Do not drive screws without pilot holes into the bottom of the tabletop as this may cause it to split. To achieve the proper angle, get a ⅛-inch drill bit that is longer than usual for this size, and use the holes in the skirts as guides. The skirts should be fastened with ten 1¼-inch screws.

The final job is the installation of the support slides that hold up the hinged leaves and their guides. There are two support slides under each leaf. Insert these slides in the holes in the skirts. The guides for these support slides have three holes in them and notches that fit the slides. The guides are placed equidistant from the long skirts, with their notches, or dadoes, over the slides. Mark spots on the underside of the table through the holes in the guides. Drill pilot holes at these spots, which are no deeper than ½ inch. Attach the two slide guides with 2-inch screws. Now glue and insert the ⅜-inch slide stopper dowels in the holes in the sides of the slide bars. Make certain that these stop dowels face away from each other as shown in Fig. 7-44.

The chair in Fig. 7-45 is rather simple as far as chair design goes. One-and-one-half-inch-diameter turned stock is employed for the legs, while ¼-inch-diameter stock is used for supports. The back pieces are made from ⅜-inch material. The seat can be woven as described on pages 180-182.

Materials Needed for Chair

A. Two pieces, each 1½″ dia. x 50½″
B. Two pieces, each 1½″ dia. x 19½″
C. Two pieces, each ½″ dia. x 16″
D. Six pieces, each ½″ dia. x 14″
E. Two pieces, each ½″ dia. x 13½″
F. Three pieces each ⅜″ x 3½″ x 13½″

The armchair shown in Fig. 7-46 is very similar in construction to the straightback chair just described. Several of the important steps in the armchair's assembly are illustrated.

Fig. 7-46.

Project #19—PATIO FURNITURE

You don't need a huge collection of tools to duplicate these three items of outdoor furniture. Nor do you have to be skilled in putting pieces of wood together. Easy cutting and simple joining will

Fig. 7-47. *Left:* Garden furniture is most important to outdoor living.

Fig. 7-48. *Below:* Details of the lounge.

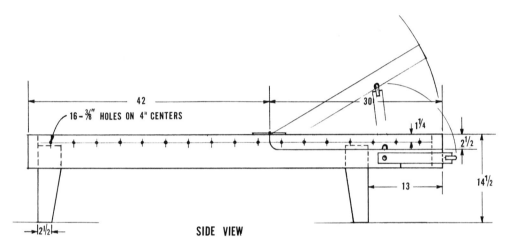

SIDE VIEW

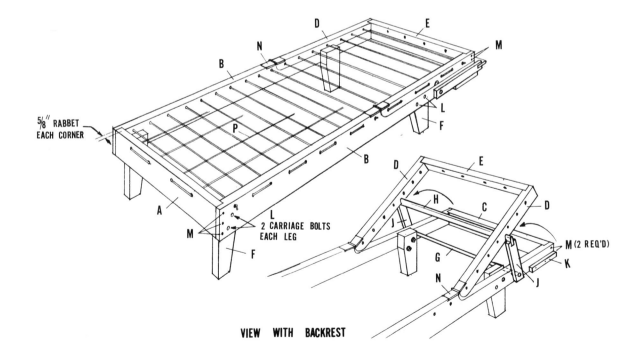

VIEW WITH BACKREST

produce excellent work from even the relatively untrained amateur.

For lumber, you can choose redwood, if it is available at your local lumberyard, or substitute pine (which is as easy to work with) and stain it to resemble redwood.

Cut all the pieces to sizes shown for each piece of furniture. Then put them together. It's a good idea to give all wood a coating of preservative before you put any of it outside. If a chance rainstorm soaks it, it will take weeks to get it in shape to apply a finish.

In finishing, you can first stain and then use two coats of synthetic varnish for a natural finish. Or you may prefer one of the resin-base clear finishes. And use of old reliable outdoor enamels on a suitable undercoat-sealer allows the introduction of any selected colors.

Note that the lounge has holes drilled through the rails for insertion of rope "springs." A good idea here would be to use nylon rope, which doesn't shrink and stretch when humidity changes. Plastic-coated cotton rope can also be used. Neither will

rot out or let you down suddenly due to prolonged exposure to the elements.

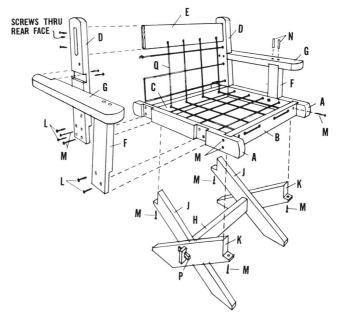

Fig. 7-49.   Details of the chair.

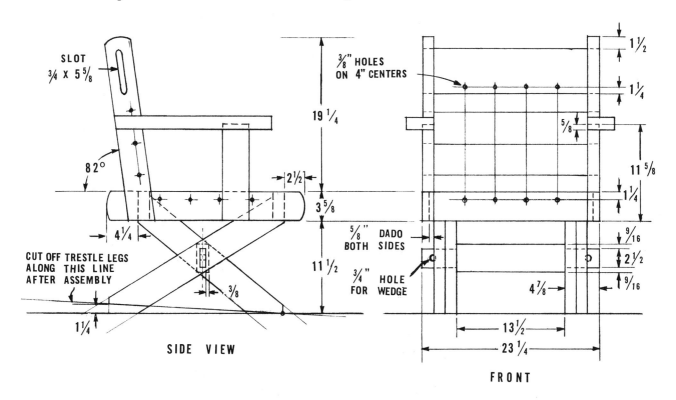

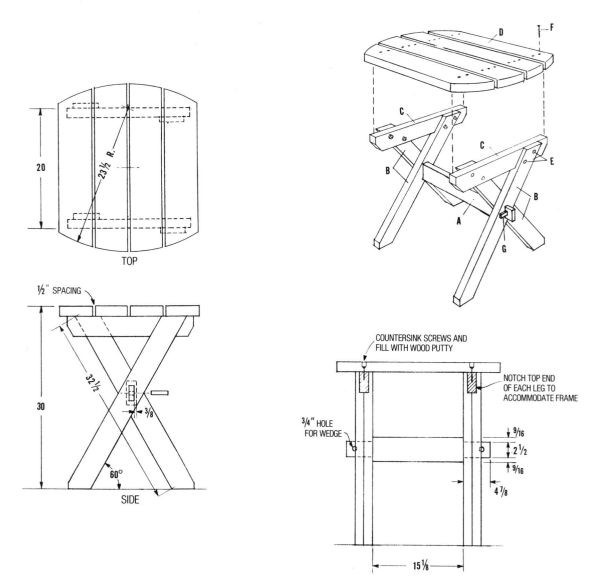

Fig. 7-50.   Details of the table.

Materials Needed

LOUNGE

Piece	Description	No. req'd	Dimensions (in inches)
A	End	1	1⅝x5⅝x21¼
B	Sides	2	1⅝x5⅝x72
C	End	1	1⅝x3⅛x21¼
D	Backrest	2	1⅝x2½x30
E	Backrest end	1	1⅕x2½x21
F	Legs	4	1⅝x3⅝x13
G	Dowel	1	1x23½
H	Backrest support	1	¾x2x23½
J	Backrest frame	2	¾x2x13
K	Stops	2	¾x¾x8

Piece	Description	No. req'd	Dimensions (in inches)
L	Carriage bolts	8	⅜x3½
M	C S wood screws	14	¼x3
N	Hinges	2	1½ strap
P	Clothesline		Approx. 65 feet

CHAIR

A	Seat sides	2	1⅝x3⅝x26
B	Seat front	1	1⅝x3⅝x21¼
C	Seat rear	1	1⅝x3⅝x20
D	Rack uprights	2	1⅝x3⅝x23
E	Back	1	¾x5⅝x23¼
F	Arm supports	2	1⅝x3⅝x11⅝
G	Arms	2	1⅝x3⅝x21
H	Trestle stretcher	1	1⅝x3⅝x23¼
J	Trestle legs	2	1⅝x3⅝x24 (overall approx.)
K	Trestle legs	2	1⅝x3⅝x26 (overall approx.)
L	Carriage bolts	8	⅜x2
M	C S wood screws	20	¼x3
N	Wood dowels	4	⅜x2½
P	Wood wedges	2	taper 3″ length to wedge ¾″ hole
Q	Clothesline		approx. 35 feet

TABLE

A	Trestle stretcher	1	1⅝x3⅝x24⅞
B	Trestle legs	4	1⅝x3⅝x35 (overall)
C	Top frame	2	1⅝x3⅝x21½
D	Top slats	4	1⅝x5⅝ (see drawing for length)
E	Carriage bolts	8	⅜x2¾
F	C S wood screws	20	¼x3
G	Wood wedges		taper 3″ length to wedge ¾″ hole

Project #20—INDOOR-OUTDOOR TABLE AND BENCH

Some ceramic tiles and select wood offer an economical and simple way to make eye-catching tables that will add beauty to outdoor or indoor living. And it's just as easy and inexpensive to make beautiful matching benches.

Making the Table. The table is composed of a frame around a mosaic of broken pieces of tiles of different colors set in grout on a backing. The legs are attached to the backing. You can arrange the broken pieces of tile in any pattern you wish, but a free-form design like the one shown here has been found to look best.

First sketch the desired pattern on a piece of white butcher paper tacked to a piece of plywood; label the sections of the sketch according to the colors of the tile that belong in each. Next break the tile into irregular pieces with a tile clipper or by simply pounding with a hammer. Then place the pieces in position on the sketch (Fig. 7-52, *left*). To ensure straight borders, you should have nailed on thin strips of wood as guides; they make it a simple matter to butt the edge pieces against the strips.

With the pieces in proper position lay a piece of contact paper on them, adhesive side down (*center*). Press the paper on smoothly and firmly, making sure it contacts every tile. The paper should overlap the borders about an inch. Since the table is about 26 inches wide, and contact paper rarely comes wider than 18 inches, you'll have to splice pieces together to make one big enough to cover.

Now place a table-size piece of plywood on the contact paper, creating a sort of sandwich. At this point help is needed. With a partner turn the sandwich over and remove the top piece of ply. What you'll have now is the loose contact paper with the pieces of tile stuck to it. Slide the contact paper onto a solid, level base. Center the frame around the tile, and snugly clamp the frame to the base. The area inside the frame should be ¼ inch larger on all sides than the tile; when you pour the grout, you'll automatically create a border.

One more point about the frame: Use stock of

Fig. 7-51.   In addition to its being a good model for colorful outdoor tables (*left*), this design can also be used indoors (*right*).

Fig. 7-52.

your choice, but miter the corners for good craftsmanship. If you like the frame we used, it's simple to duplicate. It is mahogany, and the inlay is alternate strips of ash and mahogany glued into a groove around the frame.

Mix the grout to the consistency of thick cream. (If you like, you can color it to suit.) Let the grout stand for three or four minutes, then pour it over the tile. With your hands, a sponge, or a spatula spread it evenly over the tile so that it fills all the spaces between the pieces (*right*). As shown in Fig.

7-53, the frame is made with a ¼x¼-inch lip (to provide a solid base for the back) on the inside around the top; use just enough grout so that it is level with this lip.

After the grout has dried completely, install the back. It is made from ¾-inch exterior-grade plywood cut to fit inside the frame. To install it, apply a liberal amount of contact cement to both the tile and frame lip, then simply set it in place. The contact cement will hold it well, but you can also nail or screw it onto the lip.

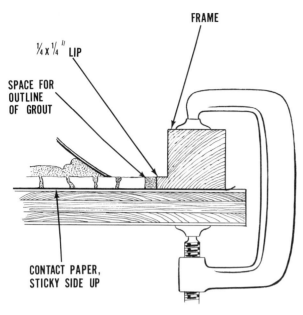

¼ x ¼ " LIP

FRAME

SPACE FOR
OUTLINE
OF GROUT

CONTACT PAPER,
STICKY SIDE UP

Fig. 7-53.

Turn the top over and strip off the contact paper. Be prepared for an unpleasant surprise here. The face will have the texture of the moon, with numerous bubbles and pockmarks. Expect it.

What is important is that every piece of tile is level.

Now perform some cosmetic surgery. Clean out all bubbles and pockmarks until you have a surface of solid grout. A beer-can opener is the best tool for this job.

Next regrout the face, being careful to fill in all holes. Let the grout dry for about a half-hour, until it's fairly stiff, and then remove the excess and smudges with plenty of water and a sponge or cloth. Polish each piece of tile with a soft cloth, and before you know it the tile will be sparkling with beauty.

When the grout is completely dry, apply several coats of a clear finish to protect the tile. A clear floor finish works well.

The legs for the table are optional. There are many good-looking styles available in stock sizes. Or you can use wrought iron, as we did, made as described below.

Making a Bench. To complement the table, we made the benches of ash and mahogany. They are 5 feet long and 13 inches wide.

First cut seven strips of wood, each 10x1½ x¾ inches, four of ash and three of mahogany. Set them parallel on a flat surface, alternating them so that the ash is at the outer edges. Cut spacers of ash

Fig. 7-54. *Left:* First step in making a bench is to align the pieces of wood. Here spacers are placed to fill in one end. *Center:* Next glue and clamp pieces together. A good quality resorcinol glue is recommended. It is strong and weatherproof. *Right:* Legs of your choice can be added to filled-in sections.

and mahogany 11 inches long to fill in sections 6 inches from each end. This provides a solid surface for attaching the legs. Next glue and clamp the pieces together. When the glue is dry, plane or sand the benchtop smooth.

The wrought-iron, hairpin-style legs are made from half-inch mild steel rod. To assure uniform shape, bend the pieces all at once in a vise or press. Then spot-weld the legs inside 9x10 rectangles of ¾-inch angle iron, which are later screwed to the underside of the bench. Of course with both the bench and the table you can also use stock legs of your choice.

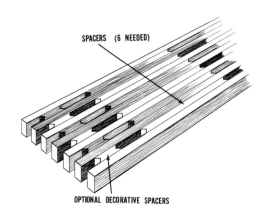

Fig. 7-55.   How the bench should look at each end.

Chapter 8

FURNITURE FINISHING

After the furniture project has been made, the final step is finishing. The importance of proper finishing is obvious; without it the project will fall short of what it should be.

Wood can be finished in a number of ways. It can be varnished, shellacked, lacquered, painted, or waxed. A paint suitable for furniture, such as an enamel, may be used when the wood is unattractive or when color fits into your decorative scheme. If the wood grain has a pleasing appearance, a natural finish may be used, or the wood can be bleached out and given one of many attractive modern finishes.

First, however, the surface must be prepared for finishing. All marks left on the wood after construction must be removed. The rough edges left by the saw should be sanded until they are perfectly smooth. If they are very rough, touch them up with a plane or a rasp before sanding. Small dents may often be removed by placing several thicknesses of moistened cloth over the dent and then pressing with a hot iron. The steam swells the wood fibers and brings them back to their original position. The process may have to be repeated several times to remove the dent completely. Sandpaper the surface when it is dry. Holes, cracks, and other imperfections should be filled with stick shellac, wood putty, or plastic wood. Since none of these will take water stain or oil stain, whichever one you choose must be the same color as the final finish. With shellac coloring is simply a matter of making the right selection; plastic wood can be colored with colors in oil or japan. If the work is to receive an opaque finish, patching is best done between coats. Some workers also prefer this method on bright work, but it is apparent that sanding to a smooth surface is much simpler on bare wood than over the stain. Instead of stick shellac plaster of Paris or a prepared cabinetmaker's cement soluble in hot water can be used for filling cracks.

Nailheads should be punched below the wood surface and the resulting hole filled with wood filler. Screwheads that have been countersunk can be treated in the same manner. However, a more professional method is to glue a wood plug on top of the screwhead. Cut the wood plug off flush with the wood surface after it is in place (see page 97).

Check all the joints on the piece to be sure they are solid. If they do not appear to be strong enough, additional nails or screws may be necessary. In some cases metal angle irons or wood blocks may be required.

SANDING

Any job is easier and less time-consuming if you first familiarize yourself with the tools and materials you are working with—and this is particularly true of most sanding chores. Regardless of whether you will be rubbing by hand or using an electric sander, a knowledge of sandpaper grades and types will enable you to pick the abrasive that will work fastest and give you the smoothest finish. If you acquaint yourself with the pros and cons of the different kinds of portable sanders that are available, you will be able to select the machine that best can meet the needs of the job.

Sandpaper Selection

Although we call them sandpapers, sand is actually not used on any of them (that is why manufacturers call them abrasive papers). The least expensive kind and the one that most people think of when they mention the word sandpaper is *flint paper*. Its sandy-looking color and texture is undoubtedly the reason it was first called sandpaper, but it is actually made of white quartz, a natural mineral that is one of the oldest and cheapest of abrasives, but one that dulls and wears rapidly.

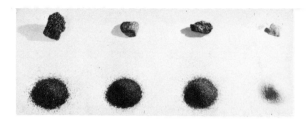

Fig. 8-1. Most "sandpaper" is made of one of these four minerals. *Left to right:* Silicon carbide, aluminum oxide, garnet, and flint.

Garnet paper also uses a natural mineral abrasive, a form of red quartz or garnet that is the hardest of all natural abrasives. Much sharper than flint paper, garnet paper has long been popular with commercial finishers for use with power tools, as well as for hand sanding, because it cuts faster and lasts much longer than flint paper. It does cost more, however, and tends to fracture easily, so many local stores no longer carry it. It has been replaced to a great extent by the newer *aluminum-oxide papers.*

A man-made synthetic abrasive that is sharper and longer wearing than either flint or garnet, aluminum-oxide paper costs only slightly more than garnet. It is actually the best all-round abrasive paper for shop use because it wears from five to ten times longer than flint paper, stands up better than garnet paper, and cuts faster than both. It can be used for hand or power sanding with every type of machine, and it will work on metal, plastics, and other materials, as well as wood.

Silicon carbide, another synthetic mineral, is actually the hardest abrasive of all, but it is very brittle and tends to fracture rather easily. It is widely used on abrasive papers that have a waterproof backing (wet-or-dry sandpapers), especially in the finer grades, which are used for rubbing down varnish, lacquer, or enamel finishes on furniture.

About the only place where flint paper is still useful is for hand-sanding jobs (you can't use it with power tools) where you may be rubbing off old

paint or working on sappy wood that tends to clog the paper so rapidly that you have to throw sheets away before they're really worn out. The low price of flint paper may save some money on jobs of this kind.

Grading of Abrasives

Almost all of the large manufacturers of abrasive paper now grade them according to grain size by using numbers that indicate the size mesh through which the grains will fall. Thus a number-100 paper has grains that will pass through a screen with 100 openings per square inch; a number-220 paper's finer grains will pass through a mesh with 220 openings to the inch. In other words the larger the number, the finer the grit. This method of grading is fairly standard now and has almost completely replaced the old-fashioned system of 1/0, 2/0, etc.

In an effort to make things still simpler for the occasional purchaser most manufacturers also mark the backs of their papers with descriptive grades or names, which vary from Very Fine to Very Coarse, as indicated in Table 8-1. However, remember that these terms are not yet standardized with all manufacturers. Fine, for example, may vary from 180 to 120, and others can vary by the same amount. For casual sanding this will

Fig. 8-2. Open coating (*left*) removes old paint finishes; closed coating (*right*) smooths wood surfaces, hard finishes.

probably make little or no difference, but for the careful worker who insists on consistent results, purchases should be made on the basis of grade or grit numbers, not on descriptive names.

While many abrasive papers are made in both closed- and open-coat form, chances are that you won't have much choice at your local store, since he will probably stock only the most popular numbers. As a rule open-coat aluminum-oxide papers are more popular, and more useful, because the grains are more widely separated and thus the paper has less tendency to clog. Closed-coat papers will cut a little faster, but they also clog more rapidly since there is no space between the grains where sanding dust can accumulate.

Most abrasive-paper manufacturers also make a variety of backings, but here again you'll find that you have to take what is available locally. However, this should pose no problem since they usually match the backing to the grit number so that the finer grades will have a thinner and more flexible backing, while the coarser grades will be stiffer and heavier. The Very Fine grades of silicon-carbide paper that you'll want for polishing and smoothing of final finishes will come on a waterproof backing that can be used wet for finest results.

Hand Sanding

The general rule in all sanding operations is to work from a coarser grit through progressively finer grits until you get the degree of smoothness you require. To avoid doing any more work than is absolutely necessary, never start with a grade that is coarser than it has to be. In other words, if the

Table 8-1

ABRASIVE PAPER GRADES AND USES*

Descriptive name and old rating no.	Grit nos. or grain sizes	Principle uses for this grade
Very Fine 6/0 to 10/0	220 to 600	Light sanding between coats; extra-fine finish on raw wood; final sanding of sealer coat; finishing metal that will not be painted (not garnet)
Fine 3/0 to 5/0	120 to 180	Final finishing of bare wood prior to painting
Medium 1/2 to 2/0	60 to 100	Average sanding to remove minor imperfections and light scratches; light stock removal before final sanding
Coarse 1 to 2	36 to 50	Heavy sanding to remove deep scratches; heavy stock removal
Very coarse 2 1/2 to 4	12 to 30	For smoothing extremely rough wood

*Above grades apply to aluminum-oxide, silicon-carbide, and garnet papers.
Flint papers usually carry only name designations or may use old-style numbered ratings.

surface is not in too bad a condition, start with Medium or possibly Fine and finish up with Very Fine. There's no sense in starting out with a coarse paper that leaves deep scratches that you'll only have to rub out later on.

Always sand parallel to the grain; sanding across the grain tears and roughens the fibers and leaves scratches that will ruin the final finish, especially if the wood is to be stained. Wherever possible use a sanding block or holder of some kind, instead of holding the sandpaper in your hand. When you sand with your fingers, you are bound to apply more pressure with your fingertips than with the rest of your hand, so if you're not careful, you may wind up with gouges or wavy marks in the finish. You can simply wrap the sandpaper around a scrap piece of wood, or you can fasten the sandpaper to the sides or top of the wood block with tacks or staples. For best results, however, face the block with a small piece of carpet or felt to give it some resiliency. In this way if any grits break loose or if there are any high spots on either the block or the surface being sanded, you won't wind up with glazed marks and scratches when loose grit gets caught between the two hard surfaces. The resilient backing absorbs the loose pieces and does a better job of rubbing down high spots without skipping.

Even better than a homemade wood block are several different types of commercially made sandpaper holders. Made of metal, wood, plastic, or hard rubber, they all provide a means for gripping a sheet of sandpaper securely while providing a comfortable grip for your hand.

When you get down to the final rubbing, judge the smoothness of the surface by feeling lightly with your fingertips rather than by merely looking. Examining the surface with an oblique light aimed at a low angle across the surface also helps. To keep edges square, use a small block and keep it flat against the edge by letting your fingertips ride against one side of the piece. In this way you can tell whether or not the block is being rocked to either side as you rub.

If you sand the surfaces and edges properly, you should wind up with a sharp, square edge—but don't leave it this way. Professional cabinetmakers

always give sharp edges and corners one or two light strokes with a fine-grit paper to soften them slightly. This not only makes the corner less susceptible to chipping or splintering, it also helps the finish coats of paint or varnish to stick on the corners.

For a really super-smooth finish on many softwoods or hardwood, try wiping the surface with a damp cloth before the final sanding. Allow the surface to dry thoroughly—overnight, if possible—then sand again with number-220 paper. Since the dampening process raises the fibers that normally tend to swell when the first coat of sealer or paint is applied, sanding after it dries removes this slight fuzz before you start the finishing process. Some professional finishers go one step further. After the raised fibers have dried, they stiffen them by brushing on a very thin coat of shellac (one part shellac to four parts alcohol) and then allow this to dry before going ahead with the final sanding. The shellac hardens the surface so that it can be rubbed even smoother (particularly on softwood), yet it will not interfere with application of stain, varnish, paint, or other finish.

Power Sanders

Hand sanding is sometimes essential on small jobs and may be required in some places where a machine cannot reach, but for stock removal, for smoothing down really rough surfaces, and for fast smoothing and polishing operations on furniture you can't beat the time- and work-saving advantages of a good power sander. That's why most experienced woodworkers and home furniture-makers feel that there should be at least one power sander included in every workshop.

Electric sanders vary widely in price, quality, size, and style, but generally speaking they fall into three broad categories; disk sanders, finishing sanders, and belt sanders.

Portable Disk Sander. Portable disk sanders are seldom used in furniture work since they tend to leave swirl marks and scratches and, unless carefully handled, can gouge the surface severely. When used for such jobs as removing blistered or cracked paint, however, or on heavy work, they

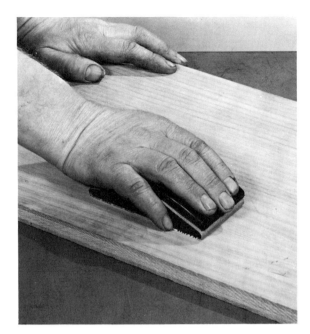

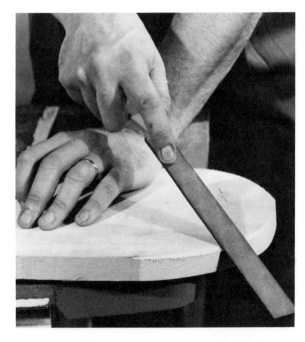

Fig. 8-3.   Hand application of abrasive in sheets is well known to all craftsmen. Wrapped around a block of scrap (*top left*) or a pre-shaped block that grips the paper (*top right*), it is a finger-saving step. More recent is the attachment of abrasives to the threads of coarse cloth (*bottom left*). In this form the abrasive applicator is less apt to clog, and the fabric does not fall apart as does the standard paper backing. Still another device is the grit shaper—fine and medium grits on opposite sides of a file-shaped hand tool (*bottom right*). "Open" spacing or grit prevents clogging of the tool in most uses. This is a fine tool for shaping.

work fast and are easy to handle. In addition, equipped with a lamb's-wool bonnet instead of a sanding disk, they do a fast job of polishing and waxing.

When using a portable disk sander, remember always to hold the tool so that the disk contacts the surface at a slight angle, with the outer half of the abrasive sheet doing most of the work. Keep the disk moving continuously as long as the motor is on by sweeping it back and forth with a gliding motion. Exert only a moderate amount of pressure so that the edge of the disk doesn't gouge the surface.

Portable Finishing Sanders. Finishing sanders are probably the most practical and most popular of all portable sanding machines, since they are the ones that are most useful. They take flat sheets of sandpaper that are clamped to a pad on the bottom of the machine. This pad usually has either a felt or rubber facing to provide a cushioned backing for the sandpaper, and the machine is designed so that the pad is driven with either a straight-line (back-and-forth) or orbital (oval) action. Straight-line action with the grain gives the smoothest final finish, but it is generally slower working. Orbital action cuts faster, but since the oval motion means

that some part of the stroke is crossing the grain, its finish is not quite as smooth—although on most machines the short stroke gives a fine enough finish to satisfy all but the most finicky.

Nowadays there are comparatively few machines that provide only a straight-line action; most are orbital. However, a number of the newer models also give a choice of both actions in the same machine, so that you can change from straight-line to orbital motion by simply flicking a lever or turning a key. These enable you to start with an orbital action for fast preliminary sanding and smoothing, then switch to straight-line action for the final sanding.

Most finishing sanders are motor-driven, but there are a number of smaller, less-expensive units that are driven by a magnetic-vibrator mechanism rather than by a motor. Although they cost less, they have much shorter strokes and are obviously slower working. Nevertheless the better-quality vibrator units are handy for small smoothing and finishing jobs. But don't count on them to do rough work.

Although you can buy strips of sandpaper in the exact size to fit most finishing sanders, you can also cut your own out of ordinary sheets of aluminum-

 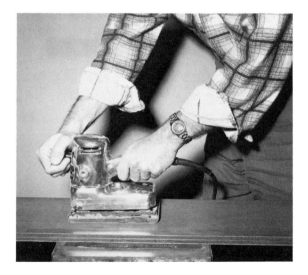

Fig. 8-4. *Left:* A typical portable disk sander. *Right:* A typical portable finishing sander.

oxide paper. For most models you can cut three strips out of a regular-size sheet.

As with many of the other newer power tools that have been introduced in recent years, you can also buy finishing sanders in shockproof or double-insulated versions. (Most have a virtually indestructible plastic housing and all use a conventional two-wire cord and plug so that you don't have to worry about grounding, or about using adaptors to make them fit standard two-hole outlets).

Another refinement you may be interested in is a dust-catching attachment. Some have an apron or skirt that fits down over the body of the machine to cover the sanding pad. An outlet on the back is attached to a flexible hose that is hooked onto a conventional vacuum or shop vacuum; this sucks up the dust as fast as it is created. The system works fine on large, flat surfaces, but it is not fully effective on narrow surfaces that do not cover the full width of the sanding pad and its attached apron. There are also models that have systems built in with their own bag attached, much like that of a miniature vacuum cleaner. All dust is caught in the bag without need for hooking up to a separate vacuum cleaner.

When using a finishing sander, remember that you're not supposed to press very hard. The weight of the machine is usually all you need on horizontal surfaces to ensure firm contact between the abrasive paper and the work. If you press too hard, you'll slow down the machine and thus slow down the cutting action—and you may overload the motor and cause possible overheating and premature wear. On vertical or overhead surfaces, where the weight of the machine will be of no help, you should still press only hard enough to ensure firm contact with the work without slowing down the machine's normal cutting speed.

Portable Belt Sanders. Portable belt sanders are the fastest and most powerful of all portable sanding machines. They are preferred by experienced woodworkers and furniture-makers for working on large flat surfaces and for a really fast job of smoothing down rough or irregular surfaces. As its name implies, a belt sander has a continuous abrasive belt that runs over two drums, or cylinders, one at each end of the tool. A flat, spring-mounted plate between the two drums provides a firm backing to keep the abrasive belt in contact with the surface being sanded. The machines are rated according to the width of belt they take, and these generally vary from 2 to 4 inches, with the

 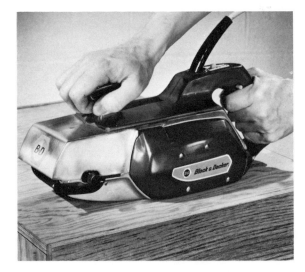

Fig. 8-5.   Portable belt sanders are available with a sawdust pickup bag (*left*) or without one (*right*).

3-inch size being the most popular for general home use. Since they are larger and heavier than finishing sanders, most people buy them as a second machine, for use on large jobs. However, they will do just as good a job of final finishing on most jobs, since the abrasive moves in a straight line, and abrasive belts are available in all the popular grades. You can also buy special nylon mesh belts impregnated with a fine abrasive, which are excellent for polishing and very fine finishing.

Belt sanders cut so fast that you have to handle them with more care than you would a finishing sander. Never let the machine stop moving while the belt is in motion, since holding it in one place for even a few seconds will quickly cut into the surface and cause a depression or shallow spot. When you work near the edges, use extra care to avoid letting the heavy machine rock forward over the edge, since this will round off and ruin an otherwise square edge. All belt sanders have a built-in tracking adjustment so that you can keep the belt centered between the two pulleys. If you find it moving to one side or the other, make the necessary adjustments promptly, otherwise you'll wind up with either a belt flying off and ripping itself to pieces on one side or creeping over and cutting into the housing on the other side.

Like the finishing sanders, belt sanders are also available in dustless models. These usually have a vacuum bag attached and are designed so that dust created by the moving belt is caught in its own bag attached to the top of the sander. On most well-designed machines this bag can be swung through an arc of approximately 180 degrees so that you can get it out of the way when working in tight corners.

Bench-Mounted Belt and Disk Sanders. Power sanding takes in more than just smoothing a finish, as is shown by the stationary belt and disk sanders used to trim individual workpieces. For example, take the disk sanders that are outfitted with tilt tables, for angle and bevel work. While the disk is unsuitable for surface sanding, it's excellent for end and edge work.

In operation the workpiece is always placed on the down side of the disk to prevent its being lifted or flung from the table. Feed should never be

forced (the paper will clog and burn), so gently engage the moving disk, applying only enough pressure to keep the abrasive cutting.

When you are sanding edges longer than the diameter of the disk, take particular care to prevent the disk's edge from digging into the work. The best approach is to start the end of the workpiece at the down side of the disk and, with gentle pressure, feed the full length across the face. Keep the work moving at all times when it is in contact with the disk.

Corner-rounding is easily done by resting one side of the work against the disk, then turning the piece 90 degrees. If necessary, you may have to repeat the turn, but be sure to maintain the same gentle pressure every time.

It is usually a good idea to have a spare disk. Equip one with coarse paper for rough work (good for $\frac{1}{16}$-inch stock removal per pass) and the other with fine abrasive for refinishing ($\frac{1}{32}$-inch stock removal per pass). Change the disks, as needed, rather than the paper; it's easier and you'll get maximum use from every sheet of abrasive.

Many of the bench-type disk sander models can convert to belt sanders, all in the same unit. Of course the tools are also available separately. The belt sander is a larger version of the portable type, having adjustable belt tension and tracking. Its adjustable tilt table operates like the one on the disk sander model. On combination machines, of course, one table serves both sanders.

Most of the belt sanders can be positioned either horizontally or vertically. The horizontal position is best for surface sanding, and the vertical is best for end sanding. With the belt in vertical position and the guard removed, the end drum or turn can be used for shaping curved edges.

One of the most useful accessories for the belt sander is an adjustable fence, which acts as a guide and rest for edge jobs, straight or beveled. In fact you can't afford to do without it.

Of the two, the belt sander is somewhat more versatile than the disk model because of its straight-line action. When you have access to both, however, there isn't any job you can't tackle.

Sanding Attachments. Among the many acces-

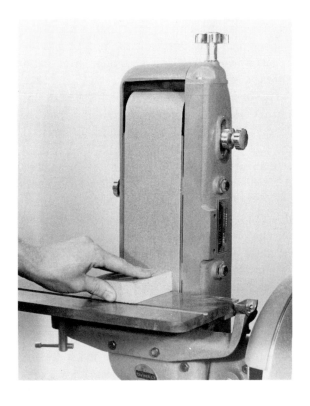

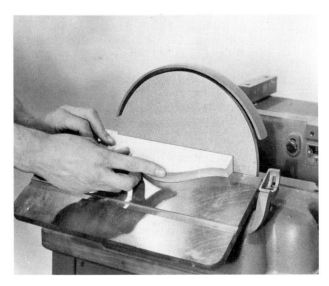

Fig. 8-6.   A combination bench-mounted belt sander (*left*) and disk sander (*above*) in operation.

Fig. 8-7.   Sanding accessories such as these can make a drill press (*above*) and a radial arm saw (*right*) very versatile.

sory sanding devices available today is the drum unit, which is easily chucked into a drill press or portable power drill—it can even be secured to a radial arm saw. As a bench or portable setup, it can be used to sand freehand. In combination with a drill press or radial arm saw and a guide fence, it can accurately edge-trim long pieces with very little effort.

Treatment of Veneers

Veneers require careful sanding to avoid going through to the core stock. No. 1 paper is coarse enough to cut off the tape if the work is a built-up pattern with sand-off tapered joints. This should be followed with 3/0 or 4/0 garnet or aluminum-oxide abrasive paper, using fresh stock to ensure clean cutting. On veneers it is often impossible to follow the grain of the wood, and in this case it is best to disregard it entirely. In hand sanding veneers or other flat surfaces the paper should always be backed with a wood, cork, or felt block in order to ensure cutting to a level surface. Veneers, particularly mahoganies, will often stain if too thin a glue is used or if too much pressure is applied in clamping up. Don't try to sand out these marks. The only way to correct such spotting is to paint the area with a suitable bleaching solution. Proper veneering technique will eliminate staining.

BRUSHES AND BRUSHING

Brushing is the commonest method of applying finish materials. It is slow compared with the spray gun, but has the advantages of simplicity of equipment and ease of application. With paint, varnish, and other brushing mediums the quality of the brushed finish, as judged by durability and appearance, is equal and in some cases superior to the same finish applied by spraying.

How to Choose a Good Brush

When finishing furniture, you must use good brushes. The reason is simple: A good brush picks up a fair amount of finishing material and lays it on smoothly with almost no drag, pull, or brushmarks remaining in the finish coat. A good brush also doesn't lose bristles or wear out after a few finishing jobs and repeated cleanings. In addition it makes work less arm wearying, gives better coverage, and saves you money.

Thickness. Feel the brush for thickness, or fullness. A good brush feels thick; if it's thin and skimpy, it won't hold enough finishing material, and you'll be constantly dipping. Pull the bristles, or filaments, apart so that you can look at the plugs just under the metal band (ferrule). These plugs run across the width of the brush and separate rows of bristles. In cheap brushes the plugs are thick and there are fewer filaments; in quality brushes the plugs are narrow and there is therefore room for more bristles.

The Tapered Brush. Brushes of good quality taper from the heel (the part next to the ferrule) to the tip. This tapering is accomplished in two ways: (1) by using bristles of different lengths; and (2) using filaments that taper from the heel to the tip. Bend the filaments down and release them slowly as you pass your hand down to the tip. If they are not full-length filaments, they will pop up as your hand moves toward the tip. Brushes with filaments of all one length do not pick up and release properly. Filaments in a variety of lengths permit a gradual release of paint and allow it to flow smoothly off the tip of the brush.

If you look closely at a good-quality brush, you will note that the bristles are thicker at the heel than at the tip. To perform properly, a good brush should be stiff at the heel and flexible from the middle down toward the tip. This combination of stiffness and flexibility adds to the ability of the good brush to release the finishing material gradually. To cut costs, some manufacturers add level (nontapered) bristles to the more expensive tapered ones in their cheaper lines of brushes. Such brushes leave brushmarks and tend to release the finishing material too rapidly.

To test a brush for proper flexibility, move it back and forth on a dry surface as if you were finishing, then stop the brush while still applying ordinary finishing pressure. It should bend in a long, even curve with almost no spread at the tip. A poor brush with not enough tapered filaments will "break" or bend deeply in the middle and spread widely at the tip.

Thin Tips and Flags. Tapering alone does not produce the fine tip at the end of a bristle that is required to minimize brush strokes. In high-quality brushes the filament tips are sanded or ground to make them very thin and soft. This gives the brush a delicately fine, soft edge that leaves almost no marks. Depending on their quality, about 45 to 55 percent of the tips are flagged (split). Flagging not only makes the tips of the bristles finer, it also provides a greater surface area to pick up and hold more paint. This means that the brush can be used for longer intervals before dipping into the finish material again.

Nylon or Polyester. At one time all brushes were made of imported hog bristle. But with the decline in the supply of these natural bristles, most brushes are made of nylon filaments. Nylon works well in most wood finishes, with the possible exception of lacquer, where cheaply made nylon may dissolve (see pages 258-259).

In recent years Orel polyester filament brushes have been the best available to home craftsmen.

Wood-finishing brushes vary in size from 1 to 4 inches. The 2½ -inch brush is the best for general furniture work.

Brushing Technique

The proper handling of a brush is largely a matter of common sense coupled with a little practice. Use the tip or edge of the brush to work into corners or to make a line or edge. Cross-brush all large areas for good coverage and to eliminate any skinned places, or "holidays." Turn the brush round and round and then use light lengthwise strokes where possible. For general brushwork the bristles should be dipped to a little over one-third of their length. Surplus paint or varnish should be wiped off on a strike wire or on the edge of the can.

Finishing materials are either brushed out or flowed on. Materials such as varnish and shellac should be flowed on and allowed to level off. In finishing flat surfaces, brush out toward the edges; this will prevent the drips that invariably occur when a loaded brush is pulled over a sharp edge.

Where a uniform coat must be applied using stain, shellac, lacquer, or similar materials, exercise care to prevent double-coating any areas; start the loaded brush on bare wood and brush into the lap left by the previous brushful. This is good technique in applying any finishing material.

Taking Care of Brushes

Brushes should be cleaned immediately after use. The best way to do this is to soak them in several changes of whatever solvent is used in the finishing material and then to wash them in a mild detergent and water. Rinse the brush thoroughly in water, wipe clean, and hang up to dry.

For acrylic and vinyl paints the solvent is water. If you have been using oil paints, enamel, varnish, or alkyd, soak the brush in turpentine, mineral spirits, or naptha before washing with detergent and water. Shellac brushes are cleaned with alcohol; for lacquer use lacquer thinner. After the brush has dried, wrap it in brown paper and let it lie flat or hang from a hook.

Brushes that were cleaned poorly and have hardened paint, shellac, or lacquer on them can be restored by using the appropriate cleaner or solvent followed by detergent and water. Hardened water-base paints, oil-base paints, enamel, and varnish can be removed with paint remover or trisodium phosphate, which is a powder that is mixed with water and is usually available in paint stores. Hardened shellac is easily dissolved in alcohol and old lacquer thinner.

SPRAY GUNS AND SPRAYING

The basic equipment needed for spray-finishing is a gun, air compressor, and hose. There are two types of spray guns to choose from, suction and pressure-feed. The suction-feed gun, as its name implies, works by suction, the nozzle being so constructed as to create a vacuum that sucks the fluid from the paint cup to the nozzle. Suction feed is ideal for small units in connection with lacquer, varnish, and other fairly thin materials. Its only disadvantage is that it will not pull heavy materials to the nozzle. The pressure-feed gun is made with

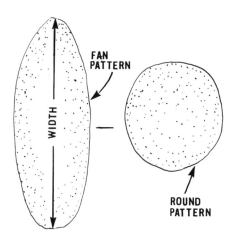

Fig. 8-8.   Standard spray patterns.

external-mix type have an adjustment for spraying a round pattern, which is useful for concentrated flow of material and for small areas.

Preparing Materials. Before undertaking any spraying job, it is advisable to strain all finishing materials. The oversight of this small detail can sometimes ruin an otherwise perfect job. Ordinary fine wire screening or nylon stocking makes an excellent strainer.

We might also mention that it is not always necessary to thin materials to water consistency for spraying. As a rule materials should be used at either can consistency or no thinner than brush consistency. Excessive thinning of materials plus too-high air pressure are two common violations of good spraying practice.

Any brushing material for furniture-finishing can be applied by spraying. However, the gun is at its best when used with quick-drying materials. Both non-grain-raising and pigment stains can be obtained in quick-drying products, which can be recoated in ten to thirty minutes.

As far as surface stains—that is, pigment stains—are concerned, almost identical effects can be obtained by simply spraying the work with a thin coating of diluted lacquer enamel.

Good fillers can be obtained that dry for recoating in two hours. In top coats nothing beats lacquer for speed—if you finish maple natural with a double coat of lacquer, the work will be dry to the touch in a manner of minutes. Spraying synthetics are fast, too, with many good one- and two-hour air-dry products available.

Spraying Technique

For average work the gun is held about 8 inches from the work, and a fan pattern is used. The stroke should be straight across the work; arcing causes uneven distribution of the coating. Proper triggering of the gun is easily learned after a little practice. The ends of the strokes are easily feathered out: start the stroke before pulling the trigger, and end the stroke before releasing the trigger. Overlap each stroke about one-half. Keep the gun in motion. If the fluid mixture is right, the fan pattern produced by the gun at a fixed spot will

an airtight container. Air directed into the container puts the fluid under pressure and forces it to the nozzle. This type of gun is intended for use with heavy-bodied materials like enamels and house paints.

At the nozzle of the gun lies another variable construction feature, the air cap, which is either internal- or external-mix. The external-mix cap has a center hole and two horn holes, and the fluid is mixed with the air outside the nozzle. The internal-mix cap has a long, narrow slot, and the fluid is atomized inside the cap. The slot shapes the spray to the familiar fan pattern. External-mix caps are used on both suction- and pressure-feed guns. Internal-mix caps can be used only with pressure-feed systems. It requires less pressure, hence is popular on small units. The principal disadvantage of internal-mix is that fast-drying materials atomized inside the cap tend to dry in and around the slot.

Pattern and Stroke. The air cap forms the fluid into a definite pattern, the most common being the fan pattern (Fig. 8-8). All guns make this pattern, usually with an adjustment to control the width (the long dimension) of the pattern. The fan pattern is usually 6 inches wide and is used for coating all flat surfaces. Better guns of the

be an even shape with the edges finely blended. A poor pattern with heavy center and coarse edges is usually caused by lack of air pressure. It can usually be corrected by increasing the air pressure or thinning the material. Don't continue spraying if the pattern is poor or if the gun spits or sputters. Stop immediately, clean the gun, and check the mixture. On all large areas better coverage is secured by double-coating.

An important factor in spraying furniture is setting up the job beforehand to get it done with the least effort and without overspraying parts already coated. Work on such parts as legs, stretchers, and other slender members is best done with a small spray pattern 3 to 5 inches wide. This small pattern is dense at the edges, permitting close control of overspray.

Chairs and tables are easily handled on a pedestal turntable. If you have an outboard turning stand for your lathe, it can be used as a base. Chairs are usually turned over when the legs are sprayed. Some sprayers also work on table legs upside-down, since this position gives the best spray angle.

There are three common methods of painting chair and table legs. Most beginners like the four-square method, in which the operator stands opposite each of the four sides of the leg in turn and sprays everything facing him. A faster method is the diagonal system, which employs two work positions. In one you face the corner of the table or chair and aim the gun at the corner of each leg, covering two of the facing surfaces with one stroke. In the second position the object is turned and you spray the other two surfaces of each leg in the same manner. If the work has round legs, the usual system is to spray the inside of all legs first and then spray each leg complete.

To spray an entire table, use a vertical fan pattern and spray all the inner sides of the legs first. Then spray four-square, that is, spray all of the other outer surfaces and edges facing you in a systematic manner. Spray the top last. If you're using lacquer, take care not to overspray surfaces already coated. If you like the faster system of spraying legs two sides at a time, use a horizontal

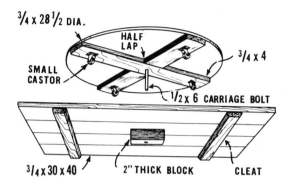

Fig. 8-9.   A turntable is an aid to good work.

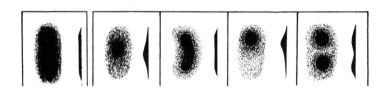

Fig. 8-10.   The correct spraying pattern is at the extreme left. The other patterns are poor—resulting from incorrect pressure, dirty spray gun, and other causes.

fan for good coverage. In this case spray the legs inside and out and then change to the vertical fan required for the rest of the job.

In casework and cabinet pieces the inside is always sprayed first. Then the outside is worked four-square, the right end is first, followed by the front, left end, and top. On some jobs it's practical to leave drawers in place, although the usual practice is to remove them for spraying separately.

STAIN AND STAINING

The first operation is to apply a transparent or semitransparent finish to new wood if the natural color of wood is not desired. The craftsman has considerable latitude in the selection of a stain, since there are hundred of types and colors. Though many different kinds are available, water stains, oil stains, spirit stains, and acid stains are

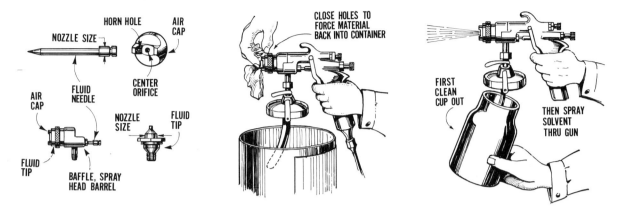

Fig. 8-11.   Details of nozzle and steps in correct cleaning of spray gun.

Fig. 8-12.   *Left:* Mix stains to obtain the right color, then test on scrap wood before using. *Right:* Hold brush at this angle for staining.

the most common. The latter two are seldom used by home furniture-makers.

Water Stains. Water stains may be purchased in powder form in a variety of colors and mixed as needed by dissolving the powder in hot water. Water stains can be sprayed or brushed. Since the water in the stain raises the grain of the wood, a preparatory sponging of the workpiece with warm water is advisable. Some workers prefer a small amount of dextrin (2 ounces per gallon) in the

sponging water to stiffen the wood fibers. Dextrin, also known as starch gum, can be easily obtained at any wallpaper store.

When the wood is dry, sand it with fine paper. Then apply the stain freely and rapidly. Better penetration is obtained if the stain is used warm. Brush on the stain in long, smooth strokes, moving with the grain. Wiping the end grain with a cloth will prevent its darkening. Other methods used to prevent darkening of end grain include: (1) previous treatment with a thin glue size; (2) sponging with water immediately before staining; and (3) using a separate light stain.

Water stain will dry overnight or in twelve hours. A wash coat of seven parts alcohol to one part shellac can be applied when the stain is dry. A light sanding will then remove any remaining traces of raised grain.

Manufacturers have developed stains in which water-soluble powders are dissolved in a solvent other than water. Stains of this kind are known by various descriptive trade terms, such as non-grain-raising stain, fast-to-light stain, non-sand stain, etc. They are more expensive than regular water stains because of the solvent used, but offer one of the best stains for new work. Their rapid drying makes brushing difficult, but smooth coats are easily applied by spraying. They are nonbleeding and can be used under any type of finish coat. They dry in anywhere from ten minutes to three hours, depending on the type. Ready-mixed colors are numerous. Primary colors are available for mixing tints to suit individual tastes.

Oil Stains. The most commonly used oil stains are those made from colors, or pigments, ground in linseed oil. Oil is non-grain-raising, and oil stains do not require previous sponging. They can be brushed or sprayed. The main difference in technique between water and oil staining is that oil stain is wiped with a rag to remove the surplus and equalize the color. Wiping is done while the stain is wet, but time should be allowed to ensure good penetration. Immediate wiping of the end grain will eliminate darkening. Since oil stains will bleed into finishing coats of varnish and lacquer, always seal the stain with a wash coat of shellac.

If you wish to mix your own oil stain colors using tubes of colors in oil, the basic colors are:

Red—burnt sienna.

Yellows—raw sienna, yellow ocher.

Browns—burnt umber, Vandyke brown, raw umber.

Table 8-2

COLOR GUIDE FOR MIXING COLORS IN OIL

Color you want	Use base of	Add to base very small amount of
Cherry (light)	Burnt sienna	Raw sienna
(dark)	Burnt sienna	Burnt umber
Maple (yellowish)	Raw sienna	Raw umber
(reddish)	Burnt sienna	Burnt umber
(blend)	Raw sienna	Burnt sienna plus raw umber or burnt umber
Oak (light)	Raw sienna	Raw umber
Pine (warm brown)	Raw sienna	Ultramarine or deep Thalo green
(honey)	Yellow ocher	Raw sienna
Walnut (dark brown)	Burnt umber	Vandyke brown
(reddish brown)	Burnt umber	Burnt sienna
(yellowish brown)	Burnt umber	Raw umber

Greens (to dull reds)—deep green, medium green chrome.

Blacks—lampblack, ivory black.

Combine the colors-in-oil according to the color guide (Table 8-2). Soften the pigments in turpentine and slowly add in small amounts to a mixture of three parts commercially boiled linseed oil, one part gum turpentine, and one-half part japan drier. Mix thoroughly until the desired color is attained. Avoid the use of oil stains on birch, maple, gum, cherry, or mahogany.

FILLERS AND SEALERS

A filler is used to fill the pores in coarse-grain woods before applying the final finish. A sealer is any liquid finishing material used as a first coat on close-grain wood or over the filler on coarse-grain woods.

Prepared paste filler is generally the best for home craftsmen. It may be purchased in a number of colors; select a shade slightly darker than the color of your wood, for the wood will gradually turn darker as it ages. If the desired color cannot be obtained, get a light color and add colored pigment in oil.

Liquid filler is generally a cheap varnish with a small amount of silex added. It is used on cheap work in medium close-grain woods. For a better grade of work a thin paste filler is more satisfactory. Table 8-3 lists the various woods and the type of filler, if any, required for each.

Before using paste filler, thin it with a small amount of turpentine or naphtha until it is of the proper consistency to brush. Wood with coarse pores will require a thicker filler than wood with small pores.

To apply the filler, use a fairly stiff brush. Brush with and across the grain in order to pack the filler into the pores. In five to twenty minutes the filler will start to lose its wet appearance. As soon as spots begin to flatten out, take a piece of burlap and pad the filler into the pores. Clean off the surplus by wiping across the grain, and finish wiping with clean rags, this time stroking with the grain. If the filler sets up too hard for easy wiping, moisten the wiping rag with benzine.

Table 8-3

FILLER FOR VARIOUS WOODS

No Filler Needed	Liquid or Thin Paste	Paste Filler
Aspen	Alder	Avodire
Basswood	Beech	Ash
Cedar	Birch	Beech
Cypress	Boxwood	Chestnut
Ebony	Cherry	Elm
Fir	Cottonwood	Hickory
Hemlock	Gum, red	Kornia
Holly	Gum, black	Lauan
Larch	Maple	Locust
Magnolia	Sycamore	Mahogany
Pine, white	Redwood	Oak
Pine, yellow		Orientalwood
Poplar		Primavera
Willow		Rosewood
		Satinwood
		Teakwood
		Walnut
		Zebrawood

Fig. 8-13. Filler may be applied in its natural color to bare wood or may be colored and applied after staining. Coloring filler to match the stain will deemphasize pores; contrasting filler, either darker or lighter, creates novelty effects.

Inspect the entire project thoroughly. If the pores are not filled level, immediately apply a second coat of slightly thinner filler, wiping off in the same way. Paste filler should dry for twelve to twenty-four hours, unless it is a fast-drying type, which takes three to four hours. In any case it is of the greatest importance that the filler be bone-dry before any other coating is applied. The dry filler should be sanded lightly with fine or very fine garnet or aluminum-oxide paper and wiped off with a rag moistened with benzine.

Whether or not you seal the filler is largely a matter of preference. The same applies to sealing the stain coat before applying the filler, except in the case of softwoods, such as fir, which must be sealed before staining. Generally it is good practice to seal both stain and filler. A special resin sealer is best for the job, but for many people shellac is the old standby—white shellac for light finishes and orange shellac for browns and mahoganies. The shellac is reduced with alcohol (four to one for filler sealer, seven to one for stain sealer) and then poured slowly into an equal amount or less of mixing lacquer. This mixture can be brushed on more easily than straight shellac, is almost waterproof, and dries to permit recoating in about two hours. Any type of sealer coat over the filler should be sanded with fine paper when dry, after which the work is ready for finishing coats of varnish or lacquer.

Sealing Fir and Other Softwoods. Fir and some other softwoods need a good sealer because of the special character of the grain figure, which is made up of alternate hard summer growth and softer spring growth. If you don't use a sealer, the first coat of paint or finish penetrates unevenly and results in a wild, overconspicuous grain.

To tame this grain, several special types of resin sealers have been developed. These are usually the same type that are used for sealing fillers and may be purchased from lumber, paint, or hardware dealers. If the resin sealer is used properly, it allows the stain to soften the darker markings and deepen the lighter surfaces. The finish will be soft and lustrous, and the wild grain figures pleasantly subdued. For application details follow the manufacturer's directions.

BLEACHES AND BLEACHING

Bleaching lightens the color of woods by means of chemicals. Not all woods can be bleached. Easiest to bleach are the naturally light-colored woods like oak and birch. Next in line are walnut, mahogany, ash, maple, and beech. Cherry, chestnut, and poplar can be bleached but with much difficulty. How satisfactory the job is depends on the power of the bleach and the condition of the wood. Douglas fir plywood and white and yellow pine may not be bleached. However, you can achieve a blond finish on these woods by another method, which will be covered later in this chapter.

Fig. 8-14. *Left:* Bleach is applied according to manufacturer's directions. Be sure to wear gloves to protect your hands. *Center:* When bleach has remained on surface for required time—usually five to fifteen minutes—apply neutralizer as directed. *Right:* Allow wood surface to dry for at least twenty-four hours. A light sanding with a block will be necessary, for bleaching raises grain.

Table 8-4

BLEACHING QUALITIES OF WOODS

Wood	Bleach	* Blond
Ash	Fairly easy	Preferably not
Basswood	Difficult	Yes
Beech	Fairly easy	Yes
Birch	Easy	Maybe
Chestnut	Difficult	No
Cyprus	Difficult	No
Douglas fir	No	Yes
Gum	Fairly easy	No
Mahogany	Fairly easy	No
Maple	Fairly easy	Yes
Oak	Easy	No, when the oak is old
Pine		
White	No	Yes
Yellow	No	No
Poplar	Difficult	Yes
Red cedar	Difficult	No
Redwood	Difficult	Maybe; preferably not
Rosewood	Difficult	No
Southern elm	Difficult	Yes
Walnut	Fairly easy	No

*A light finish with white undercoater, without bleaching
(see page 259).

Types of Bleaches

There are several different types of bleaches that will work well on wood. They are:

Prepared Commercial Bleach. The simplest method of getting a good bleach is to buy a prepared bleach, which usually comes in the form of two solutions that may be applied successively or mixed together, according to the directions on label.

Laundry Bleach. Sometimes a laundry bleach in which sodium hypochlorite is the bleaching agent is effective for such woods as maple, walnut, and gum. Use in full strength as it comes from the bottle, and rinse with clear water. A milder bleach is a 10 percent solution of sodium hydrosulfite in water, used by wetting the wood repeatedly. No final rinsing necessary.

Oxalic Acid. This bleach, once so popular, is losing favor because it works only when a mild bleach is needed. Under this condition it can be used quite successfully for such open-grained woods as oak, and ash.

To make this bleach, dissolve from 11 to 16 ounces of crystalline or powdered oxalic acid in 1 gallon of hot water. Apply with a brush or sponge while hot. Use as many applications as needed, and then wash the surface thoroughly with clear hot water. Sometimes the acid is neutralized with a solution of 3 ounces of borax in a gallon of water, applied cool, then washed with hot water.

Hydrogen Peroxide. Probably the most satisfactory bleaches are those based on a strong solution of hydrogen peroxide (30 or 35 percent).

To use this bleach, first coat the surface evenly with a solution of caustic soda—1 pound of soda to 2½ gallons of warm water. When this has dried, apply an even coat of hydrogen peroxide. The caustic soda causes the peroxide to decompose and liberate a large amount of oxygen in a chemically active condition. This does the actual bleaching. When the surface is dry, wash it thoroughly with cold water. To neutralize any remaining trace of caustic soda, wash the surface with a solution of ¼ pound of acetic acid mixed in 2½ gallons of water. Allow the solution to remain for fifteen minutes, then wash with warm water.

Regardless of the type of bleach used, the wood must always be washed with warm or hot water after the bleaching is completed. After this washing, let the wood dry at least overnight. If a powerful bleaching agent is used, allow it to dry for as long as forty-eight hours—longer in humid weather. As a final step, sand the wood lightly to remove the raised grain caused by bleaching.

Bleaching will usually make your wood lighter than the required final finish. The color is brought back to the desired shade with a light application of stain, followed by a wash coat of shellac. Following this, a neutral filler is applied. You can then use shellac, varnish, or wax as desired. Many of the new, modern finishes combine a light stain coat with a white filler. This results in seafoam and driftwood finishes, which are most attractive for modern decor.

Blond Sealers

Excellent blond finishes can be obtained without bleaching by using a surface color or blond sealer. This is a very satisfactory method of treating naturally light woods. Add white lacquer enamel to clear lacquer, or if an amber effect is desired, add tan to clear lacquer. Blond sealers of this kind can be purchased ready-mixed. A uniform, light coat of the sealer will produce a satisfactory blond color without obscuring the natural grain of the wood. This blonding technique is perfect on maple and birch and can be used on walnut to produce a pleasing tone that is a little lighter than the natural color of the wood. When overdone on dark-colored woods, however, it gives the wood a painted appearance and the effect is not pleasing.

TOP, OR FINISH, COATS

The top finish best suited for a particular piece depends upon several factors:

1. The wood from which the piece is made.

2. What the piece is and what it will be used for.

3. The quality of the workmanship or fineness of the piece—a highboy as compared with a cobbler's bench.

4. The customary finish for the type or period of the piece, as for example a crude piece of pine furniture as compared to a mahogany dining room table that has been smoothed with a paste filler.

It is just as bad to overfinish as to underfinish, depending upon the factors just outlined. There are, however, many cases that are not in the extreme, and it is in these areas that a worker should use good judgment.

You were also instructed to plan ahead any change of color or degree of smoothness desired, in order to decide on a stain to be used (for color) or whether to apply a paste filler (for smoothness). This work must be completed, and a sealer coat applied after each application, before putting on a finish coat.

When all the work of preparing for a new finish has been successfully completed, you are then ready to apply a previously chosen finish material.

High-gloss finish. The natural gloss left after the application of several coats of finishing material is of a high gloss. This finish is seldom desired for indoor furniture.

Satin-rubbed finish. A finish secured by smoothing a high-gloss finish with abrasive papers of steel wool and then waxing is satin-rubbed. The most used and liked finish.

Polish-rubbed finish. This finish requires a paste filler before the final finish, and is to be used on that type, period, or quality of furniture requiring it.

The most employed *clear* final finishes are varnish, shellac, oil, penetrating wood sealer, and lacquer finish.

Varnish

Varnish is still the most popular furniture finish. It is available in high-gloss, medium-gloss, satin-finish, and completely flat varieties. A good fur-

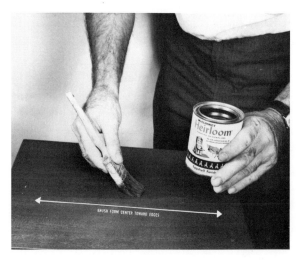

Fig. 8-15. On flat surfaces it is usually best to flow the varnish from the center toward the edges.

niture varnish is resistant to water, alcohol, and other liquids, and should be relatively easy to apply. The number of coats determines the depth and smoothness of the finish.

A good finish requires at least two and preferably three or more coats, with light sanding between each. Avoid working in dusty locations, and never apply varnish when the air is damp or cold. Where possible, lay pieces horizontal to simplify brushing.

Most varnishes today are made of synthetic resins—alkyd, polyurethane or urethane, and vinyl—that dry fairly rapidly to form a hard surface coating that is exceptionally resistant to rough wear. But it is almost impossible for the average home furniture-maker to judge the qualify of the varnish in advance of its use, for it is measured in whiteness, in resistance to yellowing, and thickness of film. Vinyls and urethanes are the clearest, showing very little color change. Some polyurethane and vinyl varnishes are even water-clear and often are sold as such. Phenolic varnishes are usually the most yellow to begin with and tend to turn yellow more readily. Alkyds vary to an extent, and your best assurance of quality is a well-known manufacturer. This, of course, is true of any varnish you purchase. Don't buy a cheap varnish. A small quantity of varnish covers a large area, and a cheap grade will never result in a good or lasting finish.

When applying, be sure to follow the manufacturer's instructions on the container. As a rule spread the varnish on as it comes from the can—evenly and with long strokes, first with the grain, then across the grain, and then with the grain. As varnish is slow-drying, thinned shellac is often used for a sealer coat. The shellac dries quickly and does not soak into the wood, thus speeding up the drying of the varnish.

Although brushing varnish is one of the most difficult of all ordinary brushwork this should not discourage the beginner. Varnish should be flowed onto a surface with a brush in thin, even coats. The process is called laying it on and tipping it off. Most of your varnish work won't require exacting smoothness or freedom from foreign particles. It's important to have a good brush for varnishing.

There are brushes especially made for use with varnish.

A good varnished surface usually requires two or three coats. Let each coat dry for at least forty-eight hours, then rub it down with fine steel wool or extra-fine sandpaper. Remove all dust from the surface, after sanding, by rubbing with a lint-free cloth moistened with turpentine or with a chamois dampened with water. Pumice and oil, followed with rottenstone and oil, will produce a finely polished surface.

Shellac Finishes

For years shellac was a favored finish of home furniture-makers because it was quick-drying and quite easy to apply. In recent times the so-called modern finishes—the synthetic varnishes and penetrating wood sealers—have replaced it to a degree. But for many purposes shellac still is a superior finish. It is perfect for chairs, settees, benches, desks, display racks, picture and mirror frames, clocks, etc. It is not suited to such items as tables, stands, chests, cabinets, bureaus, etc., on which may be placed articles that are hot or contain water or alcoholic beverages, since shellac stains easily and develops white rings.

Shellac is made from the secretion of the lac insect. It is available in three types: orange, bleached (or white), and dewaxed. Orange shellac has a pronounced reddish brown color and is cloudy in appearance. White or bleached shellac is a similar solution, but it is made from bleached resin. Dewaxed shellac is usually light in color; unlike the other two it is wax-free and thus perfectly clear.

Proper thinning of the shellac purchased in commercial mixtures is a vital part of its correct application. The concentration of shellac in alcohol is known as its cut. Most shellac on the market is 4-, 4½-, or 5-pound cut; that is 4, 4½, or 5 pounds of granular shellac are dissolved in 1 gallon of alcohol. The cut is indicated on the label. For almost all purposes commercial shellac will require thinning with alcohol. Table 8-5 shows how to convert one cut to another.

Using this table, you'll be able to convert any

Table 8-5
DILUTION TABLE FOR REDUCING SHELLAC TO DESIRED CUT

Original cut	Desired cut	Mixing Ratio Parts alcohol	Parts shellac
5 lb.	3 lb.	1	2
5 lb.	2 lb.	1	1
5 lb.	1 lb.	2	1
4 lb.	3 lb.	2	1
4 lb.	2 lb.	3	4
4 lb.	1 lb.	2	1
3 lb.	2 lb.	2	5
3 lb.	1 lb.	4	3

quantity, since the proportions are the same even if you are thinning only a pint of shellac. For example if you wish to thin a pint of 4-pound cut (the best cut for general use) to a 2-pound cut, you would use ¾ pint of alcohol to 1 pint of shellac. When thinning the cut, use only pure denatured ethyl or grain alcohol. Never use acetone, gasoline, benzol, or the antifreeze grade of alcohol. Before you use shellac, shake or stir it thoroughly. The first two coats should be thinned to 2-pound-cut consistency, while a 3- or 4-pound cut is best for the final cut.

For a shellac finish (see Fig. 8-16): (A) Prepare your own stains with equal parts turpentine and linseed oil, plus ground-in-oil pigment. (B) Apply prepared stain heavily but evenly along the grain to hide defects such as board joints. (C) Apply three coats of shellac after stain has dried, thinning shellac 50 percent for each application. (D) Prepare a paste of powdered pumice and blooming oil, which is a special acid-free variety of finish oil. (E) Saturate a wad of steel wool in paste and work it over the surface with a light touch to glaze. (F) After removing oil residue, apply a coat of clear paste wax rubbed briskly with a wad of clean cloth.

Since shellac dries very quickly, you must work fast or it will become tacky and hard to handle. Never apply shellac over a damp surface, for the moisture will cause the shellac to become cloudy. Brush with the grain of the wood, and do not brush

Fig. 8-16.   Steps in a shellac finish.

too much. For best results dilute the shellac with alcohol. It is easier to apply thinned shellac, and (unless you are experienced in applying it unthinned) you will generally get a better-finished surface. Several coats of thin shellac are best for a well-finished surface.

Standard shellac ordinarily dries hard in about eight hours; thinned shellac dries in three or four hours, ready for sanding. Go over each coat with fine sandpaper or 2/0 fine steel wool. Sandpaper with the grain of the wood. After each sanding, brush the surface and rub with a cloth dampened with benzine to remove the dust. The final rubbing or polishing should be done with FF pumice stone and rubbing oil, using a felt pad.

French Polishing. This is the most beautiful and lasting of all finishes, used for generations on fine period furniture, grand pianos, etc.

The surface should be painstakingly prepared, stained with water stain only, and allowed to dry thoroughly. Now thin white shellac with alcohol or commercial solvent to a waterlike consistency—approximately a 1-pound cut. Apply this to the wood with a soft, lintless cloth rolled into a ball. Dip the cloth into the shellac, and rub the wood in rapid, straight strokes, with light pressure. After it dries, the wood is sanded, and the process repeated. Continuous coats are applied, each one sanded smooth, until a light glow begins to appear. The surface can be sprinkled lightly with very fine pumice stone before the sanding.

After the first few coats, when a faint sheen develops, add several drops of boiled linseed oil or pure olive oil to the shellac mixture and continue application as before, but with a rotary motion. With subsequent coats add more oil by degrees. The result will be a superb, deeply glowing finish that, with ordinary care, should endure through several lifetimes.

Dip and Rub Finish. Simpler and easier than French polishing, but resulting in a finish almost as satisfactory, is the dip and rub finish.

If the wood is stained, one thin coat of shellac is applied by brush to set the stain. After drying, sand this with No. 00 sandpaper or rub with No. 00 steel wool. Then fill two saucers, one with pure turpen-tine and the other with white shellac (commercial 4-pound). Roll a lintless cloth into a pad and dip it first into the turpentine, then into the shellac. Rub it on the wood with a rotary motion until the entire surface is treated. Apply subsequent coats in the same way. Four or five such coats will give a rich, soft gloss. After this gloss dries for eighteen hours, a still higher polish can be obtained by further rubbing with the cloth dipped only in linseed oil.

Lacquer Finishes

Lacquer is one of the best furniture finishes. It offers a hard, durable, waterproof surface, able to withstand high heat without becoming sticky. It is mirror-smooth and transparent, enhances the colors over which it is laid, and brings out the beauty of wood grain when a natural finish is desired. Some varieties of lacquer are resistant to acids and alcohol, making them ideal for tabletops.

Lacquer is the fastest-drying finish ever developed. The drying time is one and a half to two hours, as compared with at least four hours for the quick-drying paints, varnishes, and enamels. Due to its speed in drying, the best way to apply lacquer is by spraying. This produces an even coat unmarred by brushmarks. When applied with a brush, the lacquer must be "slowed up" to prevent marking and sagging.

Once the wood is ready for the top finish—that is, when it has been sanded, stained, and filled as desired—the lacquer can be applied. At this stage, keep three points in mind:

1. Lacquer is extremely inflammable, and all precautions should be taken to prevent fire and explosion. Keep all lighted cigarettes, pilot lights, etc., out of the room.

2. Dust in the air from sanding, floating lint, etc., will ruin your work. Clean up well before you begin to apply lacquer.

3. The solvent used with the lacquer for thinning or as a cleaner for brushes or a spray gun is lacquer thinner. Thinners suitable for paint and varnish should never be used with lacquer. While paint and varnish can be applied over lacquer, lacquer should never be applied over paint or varnish because the solvent in the lacquer will soften these base coats.

Spraying Technique. Finishing coats of lacquer should be thinned only if instructions on the container call for it. Always check the mix by spraying one or two test patterns—a little wasted here is better than sanding it off the work later. If there is any doubt about dirt or grit, strain the material through a cloth or nylon stocking. Shoot a test pattern by giving the gun trigger a single quick pull. Study the pattern. It should be fairly uniform in shape, wet in the center, and blending out to fine dots around the edges. A heavy-center pattern or a small wet center which fades will give a fine case of orange peel. It can be corrected by thinning the lacquer, by increasing the air pressure, or to a lesser extent by cutting down on the fluid feed. The peanut and heavy-end patterns are caused by a dirty gun. Rotate the air cap a half-turn. If the pattern reverses, the obstruction is in the air cap; if it stays the same, the obstruction is on the fluid tip. Thoroughly clean the parts and replace them to correct the pattern flow. The split-spray pattern usually results from too much air pressure.

Actually the best lacquer-spraying technique requires a pressure of 30 to 40 pounds. With a spray gun of this pressure, a single coat will usually suffice. When the air pressure is lower, the lacquer must be thinned to a point where two or more coats will be necessary.

After obtaining a good pattern, apply the lacquer following the spraying technique described earlier in the chapter.

Brushing Technique

There are a number of slower-drying lacquers prepared especially for application by brushing. However, just remember that you are still using the fastest-drying finish available. The more thinner used, the quicker the drying process becomes. Speed in application is essential, and mistakes are hard to correct. When you buy lacquer, buy twice as much thinner. Some will go to thin the lacquer for application. More will be needed to keep the brush in shape. Still more will be needed for mopping up spots and sticky fingers.

A good brush is a must. A cheap one won't do, for if the bristles drop out they are hard to retrieve

from a lacquered surface without marring the work. Nylon bristles can sometimes be dissolved in lacquer thinners, so avoid them.

To apply lacquer with a brush, prepare the surface and apply stain of the desired color along grain (see Fig. 8-17, A). Wipe off the excess. After the stain has dried apply the first coat of lacquer (B). To apply, fill a container half full of the lacquer. Add thinner. Soak the ends of the brush thoroughly in the mixture, but do not rub off on top of the container as you do with paint, or else the quick-drying lacquer will become sticky and foul the brush on successive trips to the container. Instead, squeeze off any excess against the inner side of the container. Make your brush strokes bold and rapid; a large brush is best. Carry each stroke, applying the lacquer along the grain, as far as you can go without running out the lacquer into separate thin lines. Overlap prior strokes slightly. If the surface is large, work from opposite ends, blending the strokes in the center. When putting lacquer on uneven surfaces, such as beading and carving, take care not to allow the lacquer to accumulate in the hollows. Pick up the excess with the tip of the brush.

Each lacquer coat is rubbed lightly with fine steel wool wadded into a ball and frequently turned inside out (C). Use even pressure. The final coat of lacquer (and there may be from three to five coats) is rubbed with blooming oil and fine-grit water-proof sandpaper (D). Once you've finished the lacquer application, let the work stand for twenty-four to forty-eight hours. Then for the final process: rubbing.

Rubbing with Pumice and Rottenstone

A fine finish for varnish, lacquer, and shellac is obtained by rubbing with pumice or rottenstone. Mix the pumice with either water or oil (paraffin or mineral), and use a felt pad to rub the paste over the finished surface. Rub with the grain. Use pumice with oil, not with water, on shellac finish. Rub until the desired finish is obtained. Rottenstone is much finer than pumice and is used in the same manner, usually following a rubbing with pumice.

Fig. 8-17.   Techniques of applying lacquer with a brush.

If water is used with either pumice or rotten-stone, it makes the mixture cut faster and produces a duller finish. When rubbing edges, corners, and high spots, be very careful not to cut through the finish. After rubbing, clean the surface thoroughly with a soft rag.

Wax Finishes

A wax finish has a pleasing eggshell gloss and is satisfactory for furniture. Fill the wood, give a sealing coat of thinned shellac, lacquer, or varnish, and allow to dry. Sandpaper lightly before applying the wax.

Rub the wax on the surface, spreading only a little at a time, with a soft cloth. Allow to dry for about twenty minutes, and then rub hard with a soft cloth. Several coats are usually required.

Penetrating Resin-Oil Finishes

The resin oils are a fairly new type of finish employed by many homecraft furniture-makers. They actually improve the wood permanently without hours of hand rubbing, yet give that lustrous, hand-rubbed look with a simple application that is longer-lasting, seldom needs replenishing, and never needs resanding.

While you should always follow the manufacturer's specific instructions, here are the basic rules for applying penetrating resin-oil finishes:

1. Apply the first coat of sealer with a cloth to one section at a time. Use a circular motion, working across the wood grain. Immediately remove all surplus sealer, wiping with the grain, before applying sealer on the next section.

2. Rub the sealer in and off with your hands. The warmth of your hands helps the sealer to penetrate into the wood. Rubbing removes the air bubbles and ensures even lapping of the finish.

3. Apply the sealer to any rungs on the piece one at a time, using another piece of nylon hose or fabric. Wipe the surplus away immediately with your hands. Remove the surplus sealer from the edges and carvings with your fingers.

4. Don't let a heavy, glasslike coating of sealer build up on the surface. Wipe off any excess that is not absorbed. Allow the sealer to dry for twenty-four hours.

5. Before applying the next coat, and before every succeeding coat, smooth the surface gently with 3/0 steel wool. This removes the bubbles and makes a "tooth" for the next coat. Wipe the surface with a dry cloth and then with a tack rag.

For the second coat apply the sealer as for the first coat. Rub the sealer on, in, and off. For extreme smoothness on dark woods, use crocus cloth, which is coated with jeweler's rouge (iron oxide) that tints light woods a reddish color that can't be removed. Wrap the crocus cloth around a smoothing block for wide surfaces.

For succeeding coats apply the sealer as for previous coats. Apply several coats to the undersides of table leaves and the insides of drawers. Allow each coat to dry twenty-four hours in good drying weather and thirty-six hours or more if the humidity is high. Then rub the surface lightly with 3/0 steel wool. Wipe with a dry cloth and then with a tack rag.

Continue to apply finish coats until no dull spots appear. For an even, satinlike smoothness and a hard finish, apply three to five coats on chairs or legs of a piece. Apply nine to twenty-one coats of finish on dining and coffee tabletops, depending on the degree of smoothness you desire and the intended use. Let the final coat dry for one week. For extreme smoothness on dining tabletops and similar surfaces rub the surface when thoroughly dry with 8/0 to 10/0 silicon-carbide paper and mild soap (not detergent) solution. Dip the 500A silicon-carbide paper in the warm soap solution and wrap around a smoothing block. Smooth gently with the grain, but not on the edges. When the abrasive begins to drag, dip in the soapy water again, then proceed with the rubbing process.

For a handsome satin finish you can eliminate the rubbing. Simply wait about four hours—preferably overnight—after drying the surface of excess resin oil. Then, using a small amount of resin-oil finish or carnauba (palm oil) stain wax as a lubricant, wet-sand lightly with superfine paper. Wait about 10 minutes before wiping clean and dry. Polish with a soft cloth.

Oil Polish Finish

To obtain a beautiful rich finish on hardwoods:

1. Brush boiled linseed oil on raw, smoothly sanded furniture and let it soak in. Then polish long and vigorously with a soft cloth.

2. Repeat each week until you have reached the desired color and sheen. Let it dry for a few days.

3. Apply a thin coat of shellac and two coats of wax.

ENAMEL AND PAINT FINISHES

In some cases furniture pieces can be turned into possessions of which you can be proud with a coat or two of colorful high-quality enamel and a few hours of pleasant work. Modern enamels are odorless and easy to apply, and they dry in a few hours.

There are three points to remember for a first-class job: (1) buy only high-quality enamel; (2) prepare the surface properly; and (3) apply the enamel correctly. To do the latter, keep the points in mind:

1. Follow the steps outlined for cleaning and preparing the surface described on page 237.

2. Seal the wood with a wash coat of shellac (50 percent shellac—50 percent denatured alcohol). The shellac will help prevent the grain from showing through the enamel.

Fig. 8-18.   (A) All finishing work starts with sanding, first with coarse (2/0) and then with fine (4/0) sandpaper, either by hand or power. (B) Apply both undercoat and enamel from the inside out, starting with hard-to-reach points, then sides, then top, edges last. (C) The wide brush is held at an angle, and enamel is flowed on with even strokes. Always follow along the grain lines of the wood. (D) It is important that the stroke continue out past the end of the surface. Hold brush at near right angle, move in steady strokes. (E) Excess enamel should be picked up by brush to keep it from filling grooves or other recesses. (F) Removable trim, knobs, and hardware are taken off and enameled separately. Provide a place for these to dry.

3. After the shellac is dry, smooth lightly with 3/0 steel wool. Sandpaper does not work well because shellac has a tendency to clog.

4. Tint the enamel undercoat if you plan a single finishing coat of dark enamel. Mix three-quarters of the undercoat with one-quarter of the enamel to be used. Enamel undercoat needs a thorough stirring. Pour off the top liquid, and stir the pigment until it is smooth. Return the liquid slowly as you stir it in.

5. Apply the undercoat and brush it out thoroughly. Avoid a heavy, gummy undercoat. Do not overload your brush. On each part, start painting at the top and work down. Watch carefully for sags and runs, which must be brushed out before they harden.

6. After you have permitted the surface to dry for at least twenty-four hours, smooth the undercoat with 4/0 to 6/0 sandpaper. Use a light touch on the undercoat; this soft surface is easily cut through into the wood. Dust with a turpentine-soaked rag.

7. Do not apply enamel the way you brush out ordinary paint. Fill the brush and apply quickly and freely, flowing the enamel with the grain of the wood. Without refilling the brush, stroke across the grain. This will spread the enamel in an even film, covering any misses. Last, tap the brush fairly dry against the inside of the can and brush lightly once more with the grain, making the strokes as long as possible. This will take up any excess enamel, which might otherwise cause sags.

8. For small pieces or those with intricate surfaces you might find the new self-spraying enamels handy to use. However, these are not meant, for major decorating jobs.

9. If two or more colors are to be used, apply masking tape to stop the finishing coats on a straight line and to prevent running. Brush on the finish, and strip off the tape before the finish hardens. Flow on enamel in small squares, and smooth with a very light cross-brushing. Dip in only half of the brush to avoid overloading it with enamel. Work rapidly and don't overbrush.

10. One coat usually will cover; two will add durability. Before you apply the second coat, roughen the first coat slightly with fine sandpaper after it dries. A good wax can be applied, if desired, for added protection.

Antiquing Furniture

Antiquing is the process of putting a transparent, colored glaze over enameled or varnished furniture to give it an antique look that seems to be the result of natural wear and age. It is often also called glazing.

Glazing adds a note of elegance to otherwise undistinguished pieces and permits them to blend well with more important furniture. The glaze coat plays up and highlights beautiful carvings and molding and at the same time helps to tone down overdecorated surfaces. The oil color you select will determine the final color of the glaze. Raw umber is most often used and will produce the following colors: over yellow, brownish; over red, brick red; over white, old ivory; over blue, blue-green. Burnt umber produces a darker effect than raw umber. Lampblack is used on dark paint to achieve a very old look. Raw sienna and yellow ocher produce a golden tone. If a frost antique finish is desired, use a high-quality white enamel undercoat in place of umber.

Antique glaze is made by combining in a can or cup the following: 3 tablespoons of turpentine and 1½ teaspoons of raw umber oil color. Mix thoroughly, add 1 tablespoon of good varnish, and mix again. Apply the glaze with a brush or spray over either the entire area or section by section,

depending on the size of the piece. After the glaze has been applied to the entire surface, wipe off with a clean, lint-free cloth. Flat surfaces should be wiped with a circular motion, starting at the center and working out toward the edges. Using a small, dry brush, stipple the glaze to soften the edges and bring the color back toward the center again.

A clear coat of high-quality varnish over an antique finish will protect the old look. If extra protection is needed on pieces such as tables, apply several coats of varnish, sanding lightly between coats with fine sandpaper.

One of the greatest advantages in antiquing painted surfaces is that if you don't succeed in achieving the effect you desire with the first coat, you can try again. Wash off the entire glaze with turpentine before it has dried, and then apply another coat, changing the formula slightly.

Distressed Effect. Distressed wood is one of the most popular antiquing effects, and it can be simulated even on a new piece of furniture. Make your own scratches and mars by beating the surface with a heavy tool or a burlap bag filled with chains. Sand the scratches, and apply artist's oil paint, using the color raw umber, straight from the tube. Rub off the excess paint vigorously, and finish in the normal clear-finish procedure.

HARDBOARD FINISHES

When painting hardboard, both surface preparation and the application of a good primer-sealer are essential for a smooth, uniform finish. The hardboard should be clean and dry. All grease and dirt should be removed with a suitable cleaner, and nailheads should be countersunk and the holes filled in.

Good sealing by the primer is required to prevent absorption of the top coat. Good water-thinned and solvent-thinned primer-sealers are available for this purpose. Factory-primed hardboard is ready for painting unless the primer has been damaged. Damaged areas should be spot-primed or given another coat of primer-sealer to ensure proper sealing.

After the hardboard has been properly sealed,

the top coat can be applied. A smoother- and better-appearing finish will be obtained if the sealer is lightly sanded to remove irregularities before the top coat is applied. This is especially true if a gloss enamel is used as the final coat. Usually it is a good idea to apply two coats of paint—semigloss or gloss enamels—with a light sanding between coats.

PARTICLEBOARD FINISHES

In general all particleboard surfaces within habitable spaces that are not covered with finished, adhesive-bonded laminates should be painted. Unpainted, exposed particleboard is easily soiled, difficult to clean, and may sometimes develop an odor when used extensively within confined spaces.

When painting or otherwise finishing particleboard, it is well to know in advance the distinctive characteristics of the material. The basic particleboard surface is somewhat more porous than most finished lumber. Surface characteristics vary from one board to another, with some boards providing a surface that can be painted without using a filler and others requiring a filler to reduce the porosity of the surface. It is a good idea to test scraps to determine the best method for obtaining the desired surface finish.

If a very smooth finish is desired, the particleboard surface should be filled with a paste wood filler or a sanding sealer prior to applying the finish. If the surface is unusually porous, both a filler and sanding sealer should be used. Factory-filled boards, with surfaces ready for painting, are available. Some manufacturers apply a resin-impregnated, fibrous sheet to the faces of their particleboards to provide an excellent base for painting.

Particleboard usually contains a small amount of paraffin wax, which is added during manufacturing to retard the rate of water absorption. If the paint or finish contains materials that are good solvents for wax, some of the wax will be absorbed in the wet paint film and result in areas whose drying rate is slower. The wax can be effectively isolated from painted finishes by applying a thin barrier coat such as shellac, which isn't a solvent for wax.

Appendix A
SAFETY IN THE WORKSHOP

It's a cliché to say that many accidents happen in the home. But trite or not, it's all too true. Most home accidents occur because of sheer carelessness or thoughtlessness on the part of the victim. In the workshop, where powerful sharp-edged tools are constantly in use, the sufferers are usually the users of the tool—and the tragedy of this, as with so many other accidents, is that normal care and routine precautions would prevent them.

Visibility and Ventilation

There should be separate work lights for each permanently installed piece of equipment and adequate overall lighting above the workbench. Continuous-strip lighting with industrial-type fluorescent fixtures is ideal because most shadows are eliminated, but even this should be supplemented by spotlights at points where circular saws, jointers, drill presses, etc., are operated. Reflector hoods with 150-watt frosted bulbs are good for this purpose. If you have a light meter, a 20 foot-candle reading is minimum for general illumination areas. In critical illumination areas readings of 40 to 50 foot-candles should be maintained at all times. Protective wire cages over lights near machines are a good investment.

Adequate ventilation is of prime importance. It allows for faster cooling of overheated tools, dissipates fumes, and lessens the chance of fire through spontaneous combustion of rags, newspaper, wood splinters, and sawdust. If possible, keep at least one window open when you are in the shop.

Housekeeping

A neat and clean work area and workroom pays off in safety as well as appearance. Provide racks and hangers, well out of reach of youngsters, for all hand and portable tools. But the racks won't do their job unless you return the tools to their proper place after use.

Remember that a stray electric power cord can get tangled up with a power tool with disastrous results. To minimize the possibility of tripping over extension cords, use brightly colored cable that is easy to spot.

Keep sawdust on hand to help in mopping up spilled grease or oil, and be sure that all inflammable solvents like benzine or lacquer thinner are in tightly closed metal containers. Always store them in a metal cabinet. Lock it, if possible.

See that all materials not in use are properly stored, not left under foot. In the modern furniture workshop the so-called shop vacuum is almost a must tool. Its use makes shop housekeeping a great deal easier.

Shop Wiring

Don't overload wiring with heavy-duty equipment and expect it to perform properly—or safely. Have your workshop power line installed in metal conduit, making it as permanent as possible. And avoid excessive use of portable extension cords. Permanent wiring adds extra protection by allowing electrically operated equipment to be grounded.

Motors will slow down, overheat, and burn out if they are not kept clean and are not operated at the required voltage. Besides causing damage to expensive equipment and creating a fire hazard, reduced speeds often cause bandsaw blades, for instance, to jam and break, causing injuries to the operator.

If possible, put *all* workshop equipment wiring, lights, and outlets on one main switch near the door. If you have children, a lock on the switch is a wise precaution to prevent them from operating potentially dangerous equipment. If you can't install a master switch for everything, make it a practice to remove fuses when closing up shop.

Tools and Equipment

Keep screwdriver tips properly dressed and use one whose tip makes a snug fit in the screw slot. Keep hammerheads securely fastened to the handle; many an accident has been caused by a flying hammerhead.

Metal chisels and punches should never be allowed to develop mushroomed or split heads. A bevel or radius grinding of the head is recommended practice. Wear safety goggles when using chisels to ship stone, plaster, or concrete.

Don't improvise a grinder by using an old motor, a drive shaft, and an abrasive wheel. Such tools or devices are extremely difficult to operate safely.

In mounting an abrasive wheel to a bench grinder, be sure that the retaining flanges are of equal size and are at least one-third the diameter of the wheel. Never use a cracked wheel or exceed the rotation speed marked on the wheel; it may shatter and cause serious injury. Always wear goggles when grinding. If a power tool develops strange or unusual noises during operation, shut it off at once and examine it carefully for defects. It might need lubrication or a blade—or a part may have cracked or warped. Repair before resuming work.

Always use all built-in safety devices and guards. Always use a stick to push work through when ripping narrow stock or in finishing a cut. Stand out of the direct line of the saw blade to avoid being struck by material that may be kicked back. Never use the rip fence to gauge length of material while crosscutting. This may cause a kickback, jam the saw, or even spring the blade. Don't use a circular saw without a rip fence for ripping operations or a miter gauge for crosscutting. Use jigs and fixtures whenever possible. Freehand sawing without a guide is extremely dangerous. Before operating a jointer-shaper or, for that matter, any machine, thoroughly familiarize yourself with its operation before you turn on the power. Build a jig fixture or stock-holding device designed to prevent your hands from being in the immediate vicinity of the revolving knives. Never start a shaper before testing all fastenings, guards, and holding devices. Be certain that the spindle is running true and that all knives are securely fastened. These machines can throw a loose knife with enough force to kill.

Use a push block on short workpieces and in finishing the cut of the flat side of all work. Don't try to plane the flat surface of veneer or plywood or to join very thin wood unless backed up with a heavier piece. Don't make deep cuts beyond your machine's rated capacity.

Most wood-turning lathes and drill presses are comparatively safe machines, as long as the workpiece is securely fastened in the lathe or clamped to the bed of the drill press and the machine is in good operating condition. But a chisel forced too hard against a workpiece in a lathe may dig in and rip the tool out of your hands. In a drill press a sluggish cutting drill (often an indication that the drill is improperly ground) that is forced may tear the workpiece from the clamp. Never hand-hold work when drilling.

Know Your Limitations

Get to know your equipment; don't try to perform operations beyond your technical skills without first having full instruction. Every manufacturer can supply a list of do's and don't's for safe operations.

Safety starts with knowledge of the proper use of each tool before you flip the switch to put it in motion. Thus safety depends on you; for this reason keep the following in mind:

1. You must really see what you're doing at all times—therefore, assure adequate lighting.

2. Keep a neat and clean work area. Above all, no spillage on the floor, no tangled wires.

3. Dress sensibly. No neckties, no casually turned-back shirt cuffs, no dangling apron ties that could catch on moving parts.

4. Never use a suspect tool—one that is erratic in operation or known to be partially damaged.

5. Don't use power tools when you are tired; reflexes are sluggish and your good habits are impaired.

Appendix B
FURNITURE-MAKING TOOL CHART

The table of hand tools listed below is intended as a guide for the basic furniture-maker tool kit and the additional tools that are an advantage for furniture work.

BASIC HAND TOOLS SUGGESTED FOR PURCHASE

Boring
Bit braces, 8-inch ratchet type
Auger bits, ⅜-, ½-, ¾-inch
Countersink, rose heat, to fit brace
Hand drill, ¼-inch chuck capacity
Twist drills (drill bits), straight shank, ⅛-, 3⁄16-, ¼-inch

Clamping
Woodworker's bench vise
C (screw) clamps, 2 each, 3- and 6- or 8-inch
Clamp clothespins, 6
Pliers, combination step-joint, 6- or 8-inch
Pliers, long-nose, side-cutting, 5- or 6-inch
Screwdrivers, 6- and 8-inch or 10-inch
Screwdriver bit, to fit brace, ⅜- or ½-inch

Cutting
Pocketknife with strong, pointed blade
Old knife, blunt
Razor-blade holder, with blades
Diagonal cutting pliers, 7-inch

Filing
Half-round wood rasp, 10-inch
Smooth mill file, 8-inch
Shoemaker's rasp
Nail file

Gluing
Patching tool

Hammering
Carpenter's nail claw hammer
Tack hammer, claw type, lightweight
Nail-set, 1⁄16-inch
Mallet, rubber- or plastic-headed

Marking
Center punch
Pencil

Measuring
Rule, steel roll-type, 6-foot
Rule, straight, wood, 6- or 12-inch
Try square, 6- or 8-inch

Sawing
Handsaw (panel), crosscut, 26-inch, ten points per inch

Shaving
Plane, "block" (7-inch), or "smooth" (8- to 10-inch)
Chisels, ½-inch plain type (straight edges) and 1-inch beveled edge

Miscellaneous
Icepick, for marking and holding
Oil can, small
Dusting brush and pan
Teaspoon and tablespoon
Clothesline, cotton and strong

ADDITIONAL HAND TOOLS SUGGESTED FOR PURCHASE

Boring
Auger bits, 5⁄8-, 7⁄8-, and 1-inch
Bit-depth gauge, adjustable
Expansive bit, ⅞- to 3-inch capacity

267

Clamping

Woodworker's bench vise, quick-acting type
Hand-screw wood clamps, 2, 5- and 12-inch jaws
Furniture bar clamps, 2, 3 and 5 feet long
Spiral ratchet screwdriver
Monkey wrench, 12-inch
Pipe wrench, 14-inch

Cutting

Scissors or shears, 6- to 8-inch
Tinner's snips, combination type
Cold chisels, ¼- and ⅞-inch

Filing

Rattail file, slim and tapered
File brush

Hammering

Mechanic's ball peen hammer, 13 to 16 oz.
Nail set, ⅛-inch

Marking

Wood-marking gauge
Scratch awl

Measuring

Carpenter's combination square
Slide T bevel square
Steel square (framing), 16x24 inches
Rule, 2-foot, folding
Spirit level, 18 to 24 inches long
Calipers, both inside and outside types
Dividers

Painting

Putty knife, 2 inches wides, flexible blade

Sawing

Ripsaw, 26-inch, eight points per inch
Dovetail saw, 8-inch, seventeen points per inch
Keyhole or compass saw
Coping saw, 6½-inch
Miter box

Backsaw, 12- to 14-inch, thirteen or fourteen points per inch
Hacksaw, type adjustable to length of blades

Shaving

Plane, block (7-inch), or smooth (8- to 10-inch), whichever you do not have already
Plane, junior jack 11½-inch, or jack 14-inch
Plane, fore or joiner, 18-inch
Spokeshave, 2 cutters, blades curved and straight
Drawing knife, medium size
Cabinet scrapers

Miscellaneous

Carpenter's bar, gooseneck 18-inch (commonly called a wrecking bar or pinch bar)
Electric soldering iron
Staple machine and staples, ¼-inch size
Cutter and chisel grinder
Combination oilstone

Other additional items such as bits, chisels, screwdrivers, etc., are not included. These should be added to the basic hand tool list as needed.

POWER TOOLS SUGGESTED FOR PURCHASE

The power tools listed here are listed in the order of suggested purchase. The accessories for such tools should be added as needed.

Hand Power Tools	Stationary Power Tools
Electric drill (⅜-inch)	Table saw or/and radial arm saw
Saber saw	
Recriprocal sander	Jointer
Router	Shop-type vacuum cleaner
Belt sander	Bandsaw
Plane	Lathe
Circular saw	Drill press
	Shaper
	Belt-disk sander
	Jigsaw

Appendix C
VENEER CHARACTERISTICS

As stated in Chapters 1 and 7, there are several methods of cutting the face veneers of plywood. How and where these veneers are cut determine the various visual effects obtained—particularly in the case of the hardwood plywoods.

Two woods of the same species but with their veneers cut differently will have entirely different visual characters even though their color values are similar. Fundamentally there are two reasons for this difference: first, variations in the physical structure of the wood itself, and second, the ingenuity of man in revealing these variations.

We won't discuss here why one tree is straight-grained and another, nearby, is twisted and curly; or why the wood of one is tan, another chocolate-brown, and a third almost black with vivid markings; or why one species frequently produces beautifully figured burls, while burls are unheard of on another species. These questions are for the wood technologist, and we will accept the fact that these peculiarities exist.

The grain pattern and figure on the face of the veneer are of the utmost importance to the craftsman, since the whole character of the completed project may be determined by the choice of veneer. Veneer men, in discussing figure in the wood, usually describe its characteristics as having "a great deal of crossfire" or "a straight or broken stripe," or as being "highly figured." "Figure" refers to the highlights or crossfire running at right angles to the grain direction; the grain character and direction would be described as the "pattern."

The distinctive pattern of stumpwood, crotches and swirls, and burls is caused by the irregular grain of the wood. So, too, irregular grain can produce any number of variations in the appearance of longwood. If the grain of the longwood is wavy, the figures in the veneer may be curly, fiddleback, or roll; if it is interwoven, the stripe and broken stripe (found chiefly in tropical trees), rope, or mottle develops. Other effects caused by variations in the direction of the grain are bird's-eye, blister, quilted figure (a combination of brokenstripe and mottle, or any two or several of the figures above), plum pudding, knots, and various "freak" figures.

Each wood has its distinctive color—blond, red, or brunet—and special personality traits—bland, exotic swirl, or teasingly knotty. But the cutter, like a Svengali, must bring out the beauty of the raw material.

There are at least two-hundred different woods generally used for plywood. The Chart of Veneer Characteristics lists some of the more important.

CHART OF VENEER CHARACTERISTICS

Veneer	Texture	Color	Figure	Origin	Veneer Length Range	Remarks
Ash, American	Medium hard	White to light brown	Growth rings are pronounced in all types of veneer	U.S.A.	Long	Quarter-cut is usually fiddle-back if figured; some burls
Avodire	Medium	Light yellow	Strong, broken rope, plain stripe	Africa	Long	

Veneer	Texture	Color	Figure	Origin	Veneer Length Range	Remarks
Avodire, crotch	Medium	Light yellow	Swirl or feather	Africa	Short	
Avodire, figured	Medium	Light yellow	Strong, with heavy crossfire	Africa	Medium long	Carries heavy figure
Ayous	Soft to medium	Pale straw and yellow	Usually ribbon stripe	Africa	Long	
Birch	Very hard	White to dark brown or reddish brown	Plain, wavy, or curly-grained	U.S.A.	Medium long	Flat-sliced is generally figured; rotary is plain; quartered-dried is generally curly
Bubinga	Hard	Pale to deep flesh with thin purple lines	Straight or broken stripe, mottle or shell	Africa	Long	Rare color, straight lines
Butternut	Soft	Pale brown	Satiny, resembles grain of American walnut	U.S.A.	Medium long	
Cativo	Soft	Pale straw to light brown or tan	Plain to plain stripe	Africa	Long	
Chen Chen	Medium	White to yellowish gray	Stripe similar to mahogany	Africa	Long	Contains a very uniform grain figure
Cherry (black)	Medium	Light to dark reddish brown	Varies from plain to rich mottle	U.S.A.	Rotary cut, short; plain- or quarter-sliced, medium long	A few burls, crotches, and swirls
Duali	Hard	Light brown	Interesting figure and grain	Philippines	Long	
Ebony macassar	Hard	Rich black-brown with tan, orange, or yellow marking	Contrasting stripes	Indonesia	Medium	Heavy, dense wood
Elm, American	Medium	Light brownish red with dark-brown ring marks	Strong	U.S.A.	Long	Most quarter-sliced

Veneer	Texture	Color	Figure	Origin	Veneer Length Range	Remarks
Gum, red	Soft to medium	Pink to reddish brown	Plain; medium to high (wild) figured with chocolate markings	U.S.A.	Short	Ribbon stripe obtained by quartering
Harewood, gray	Medium hard	Silver-gray (dyed) or cream to white (undyed)	Plain, curly fiddleback finger roll with heavy crossfire	England	Medium long	May be successfully dyed
Korina	Medium	Golden blond	Stripe, crossfire, and plain	Africa	Long	Rich, satinlike wood available in good length, width, and uniform color
Lacewood	Soft to medium	Pink to light leather-brown	Small to large flake	Australia	Long	Uniform color
Limba	Medium	Golden blond	Plain, stripe, and crossfire	Africa	Long	Trade-named Korina
Mahogany, figured, & quartered	Medium	Red to red-brown	Striped with some crossfire fire	Africa	Long	Great variety of figure, including crotch
Mahogany, Honduras	Medium	Yellowish white, salmon-pink to rich, golden brown	Straight-grained, moderate crossfire to rich mottle	Central and South America	Long	Flat-sliced; good widths and lengths
Mahogany, mottled	Medium	Salmon-pink to rich golden brown	Broken and crossfire	Africa and Central America	Long	
Mahogany, mottled & figured	Medium	Red to red-brown	Broken stripe and crossfire	Africa	Long	Great variety of figure, including crotch
Mahogany, Philippine	Soft	Pale pinkish yellow to dark reddish brown	Plain	Philippines	Long	Good lengths and widths. (Also called Lauan.)
Mahogany, ribbon-striped	Medium	Red to red-brown	Wide stripe	Africa	Long	Great variety of figure, including crotch
Makore	Fine—smooth surface	Pale pinkish brown to dark reddish or purplish brown	Plain, sometimes mottled	Africa	Long	

Veneer	Texture	Color	Figure	Origin	Veneer Length Range	Remarks
Maple	Very hard	White to light pinkish brown	Plain, curly, bird's-eye, blister, or fiddleback	U.S.A.	Medium long	Obtainable generally in rotary-cut or quartered and flat-sliced; also burls
Nakora	Medium soft	White to light brown or tan	Plain to pronounced grain	Japan	Long	
Narra	Medium hand	Pale yellow to salmon to deep red	Stripe, broken stripe, rolly, mottle, etc.	Philippines	Long	
New Guinea wood	Medium	Brown to light gray with definitive black lines	Plain to highly figured: plain stripe, figured, striped, mottled	Japan, New Britain, Oceania	Long	
Orientalwood	Hard	Brown with lavender-gray or greenish gray to salmon cast	Strong, distinctive figure: stripe, mottle, fiddleback, roll	Australia	Long	Brilliant, clear stripe; sometimes has pronounced crossfire
Paldao	Hard	Variable: tan background with brown to black streaks	Stripe and mottle; figure caused by concentric bands	Philippines	Long	Some crotches
Primavera	Medium	Yellow-white	Broken stripe, mottle, fine feather grain	Central America	Medium	Rich, satinlike wood; some crotches
Rosewood, Brazilian	Hard	Red to brown, streaked with black lines	Wide range of figures caused by pigment coloring; includes "bar" figure	South America	Long	Often cut rotary or half-round, producing beautiful effects
Rosewood	Hard	Variable: purple to straw, striped	Pin and ribbon stripe	Indonesia	Long	Often cut rotary or half-round, producing beautiful effects
Samara	Medium	Light to reddish brown	Swirly grain pattern	Africa	Long	
Sapeli	Medium hard	Medium to dark brown	Pronounced straight, broken, or ribbon stripe: occasionally a slight cross figure	Africa	Long	

Veneer	Texture	Color	Figure	Origin	Veneer Length Range	Remarks
Satinwood	Hard	Light yellow to rich, golden yellow	Nearly all more or less figured; stripe, crossfire, rolly, wavy, mottled	Indonesia	Medium long	The true satinwood
Sycamore	Soft	Tan to pinkish brown	Prominent flake figure; ribbon stripe	U.S.A.	Long	
Teak	Medium hard	Golden brown, darkening with age	Plain, ripple, mottle, sometimes nicely figured	Burma and India	Long	Durable, strong, moderate weight, easy to work
Thuya	Medium	Deep reddish brown	Figure consists of small distinctive "eyes"	Algeria	Short	
Tigerwood	Medium soft	Golden brown	Ribbon stripe, blister, or "snail" figure	Africa	Long	Available in crotch
Walnut, Claro	Medium	Light to rich brown, streaked	Wide black bonding, plain, mottle, wavy	U.S.A.	Medium	Crotches; veneers may carry yellow sapwood
Walnut, French	Soft	Nut brown to dark brown	Various streaked and swirly effects; fine, smooth grain	Europe	Short	Especially beautiful burls and stumpwood
Walnut, figured longwood	Hard	Soft gray-brown, sometimes shaded with darker brown	Mottle, fiddleback, striped, rope figure	U.S.A.	Medium	
Walnut, flat-sliced	Hard	Soft gray-brown, sometimes shaded with darker brown	Plain stripe, pencil stripe without crossfire	U.S.A.	Medium	
Walnut, crotches and swirls	Medium	Soft gray-brown, sometimes shaded with darker brown	Swirl or feather crotch; plain or figured swirls	U.S.A.	Short	Also available in burls
Walnut, plain longwood	Hard	Soft gray-brown, sometimes shaded with darker brown	Plain stripe, pencil stripe	U.S.A.	Medium	

Veneer	Texture	Color	Figure	Origin	Veneer Length Range	Remarks
Walnut stumpwood	Hard	Soft gray-brown, sometimes shaded with darker brown	Plain and figured	U.S.A.	Short	
Zebrawood	Hard	Alternating stripes of tan and dark brown	Narrow stripes from ¼ to ½ inches apart; some shell-cut	Africa	Long	Rich color, straight stripe and delicate markings

FIR PLYWOOD GRADE-USE CHART

Exterior Type for all outdoor and marine uses, as well as application permanently exposed to water or weather (100% waterproof glue)

Grade-Trademark	Typical use	Veneer Quality*			Widths (ft.)	Lengths (ft.)	Thickness (in.)
		Face	Back	Inner ply			
EXT-DFPA A-A	Permanent outdoor uses where appearance of both sides is important. Outdoor furniture, fences, carport enclosures, signs, boats.	A	A	C	4	8	¼, ⅜, ½, ⅝, ¾, 1
EXT-DFPA A-B	Alternate for A-A grade where appearance of one side is less important.	A	B	C	4	8	¼, ⅜, ½, ⅝, ¾, 1
EXT-DFPA PLYSHIELD	Siding of homes and buildings of all types. Also for soffits, breezeways, gable ends. For storefronts, highway stands. The versatile "one-side" grade exterior plywood with waterproof band.	A	C	C	4	8	¼, ⅜, ½, ⅝, ¾, 1
EXT-DFPA UTILITY	As name indicates, a utility outdoor building panel. Farm buildings, etc.	B	C	C	4	8	¼, ⅜, ½, ⅝, ¾
EXT-DFPA UNDERLAYMENT	Base for tile, linoleum, etc. Backing for wall coverings. For application where unusual moisture conditions exist.	C (repaired)	C	C	4	8	¼, ⅜, ½, ⅝, ¾
EXT-DFPA SHEATHING	Unsanded construction panel with waterproof band. Backing or rough construction exposed to weather or excess moisture.	C	C	C	4	8	⁵⁄₁₆, ⅜, ½, ⅝, ¾
EXT-DFPA PLYFORM	Concrete form grade for maximum reuse. Can be reused until wood is literally worn away. Edge-sealed and mill-oiled.	B	B	C	4	8	⅝, ¾
BOAT HULL GRADE	Ideal for boat hulls, cabins, etc.	Exterior-type (Ext-DFPA) panels with special ply construction for marine uses					Standard sizes and king-size panels

*All grades sanded both sides except EXT-DFPA SHEATHING and INTERIOR PLYSCORD.

Interior type for indoor or structural uses (moisture-resistant glue)

Grade-Trademark	Typical use	Face	Back	Inner ply	Widths (ft.)	Lengths (ft.)	Thickness (in.)
INTERIOR A-A DFPA	All interior applications where both sides to be in view. Cabinet doors, built-ins, furniture.	A	A	D	3,4	8	¼, ⅜, ½, ⅝, ¾
INTERIOR A-B DFPA	For all inside uses requiring one surface of highest appearance and opposite side solid and smooth. Alternate for A-A.	A	B	D	3,4	8	¼, ⅜, ½, ⅝, ¾
PLYPANEL	The many-purpose "one-side" material for interior uses. Paneling, built-ins, backing and underlayment, counters, fixtures, displays, cutouts.	A	D	D	3,4	8	¼, ⅜, ½, ⅝, ¾
INTERIOR B-D DFPA	Utility panel for uses requiring one smooth, solid side. Backing, cabinet sides.	B	D	D	4	8	¼, ⅜, ½, ⅝, ¾
PLYBASE	Underlayment grade. Base for tile, linoleum, carpeting.	C (repaired)	D	C‡D	4	8	¼, ⅜, ½, ⅝, ¾
PLYSCORD	Undersanded sheathing or structural grade. Wall and roof sheathing, subflooring. Temporary enclosure, containers, barricades.	C	D	D	4	8	5⁄16, ⅜, ½, ⅝, ¾
PLYSCORD EXTERIOR GLUE	Unsanded structural grade panel with waterproof glue line. For sheathing, subfloor, etc.	C	D	D	4	8	5⁄16, ⅜, ½, ⅝, ¾
INTERIOR PLYFORM	Reusable concrete form plywood. Edge-sealed with distinctive green sealer. Mill-oiled unless otherwise specified.	B	B	C	4	8	⅝, ¾
INTERIOR N-N	Cabinet-grade panels with both sides of select, all-heartwood veneer. For natural or stain finishes.	N	N	D	4	8	¾
INTERIOR N-D	Natural-finish paneling with one side of select, all heartwood veneer. Ideal for wall paneling.	N	D	D	4	8	¼
2·4·1	New combination subfloor and underlayment base for tile, linoleum, carpeting, and wood-strip flooring—on 4-foot span grid system.	C (repaired)	D	D	4	8	1⅛ only

‡ Veneer next to face is C or better.

Index